Using the MBTI® instrument in colleges and universities

Using the MBTI® instrument in colleges and universities

JUDITH A. PROVOST AND SCOTT ANCHORS

Center for Applications of Psychological Type
Gainesville FL

Using the MBTI instrument in colleges and universities / Judith A. Provost, Scott Anchors, editors. — 2nd ed.

p. cm.

Rev. ed. of: Applications of the Myers-Briggs Type Indicator in higher education. c1987.

Includes bibliographical references.

ISBN 0-935652-58-2

1. Counseling in higher education. 2. Myers-Briggs Type Indicator. 3. College students—Psychology. I. Title: Using the Myers-Briggs Type Indicator instrument in colleges and universities. II. Provost, Judith A., 1942- III. Anchors, Scott IV. Applications of the Myers-Briggs Type Indicator in higher education.

LB2343.A65 2003

378'.194—cd21

2003046189

Introduction

JUDITH A. PROVOST AND SCOTT ANCHORS

Fifteen years have passed since *Applications of the Myers-Briggs Type Indicator in Higher Education* was published. At that time Anchors, Robinson, and Wood (1984) had reported on an informal survey of American College Personnel Association members about their use of the MBTI® personality assessment tool. The survey found that the MBTI instrument was one of the few instruments used in higher education that crossed over functional areas. Reported uses were in the areas of career development, academic advising, leadership training, counseling, roommate matching, paraprofessional training, understanding learning and teaching styles, conflict resolution, and development of retention strategies. The survey findings revealed MBTI use in the full range of post-secondary institutions: traditional public and private institutions, two-year vocational colleges, and community or junior colleges. Survey respondents agreed that a major strength of the MBTI instrument was its conceptualization of the *whole person* and its theoretical base from which implications for practice could be derived.

Some changes in patterns of usage of the MBTI instrument in colleges and universities have occurred since then. In putting together this revised edition, we discovered that there is less systematic use across entire educational institutions and more wide use of the MBTI instrument by individual professionals and subdivisions of institutions. The MBTI instrument is a familiar tool on most campuses; many students arrive at college already knowing their types. Thus, readers of this book may be individuals—counselors, teachers, student affairs practitioners, or administrators—looking for specific ways of improving effectiveness by applying their MBTI results in their work.

In the intervening years since the first book, the multicultural movement has greatly heightened our awareness of implications of using the MBTI instrument with culturally different groups. It became crucial, then, to include a new chapter addressing this issue. The other very important addition to this book is a chapter on leadership in higher education, written by a university president. Now that so many educational leaders are aware of type, there are important applications for work with boards of trustees, deans, and all levels of leadership within higher education. These two new chapters greatly enhance the relevance of this book in the 21st century.

Readers also may find this book useful in either expanding current uses of the MBTI tool or in initiating new programs. Both theory and application are offered here. The theories provide a rationale for various approaches described in the twelve chapters. Readers are expected to be already familiar with the MBTI instrument and know "the basics." The basics are thoroughly presented in the *MBTI® Manual* (1998), *Gifts Differing* (Myers 1980), *People Types and Tiger Stripes* (Lawrence, 1993), and in other sources referenced in this book. There is no need to duplicate these excellent sources. If readers are new to psychological type, and especially if they are unclear about Jung's concept of the dominant and the auxiliary, they should read chapter 1 carefully before going on to other chapters. In addition, if readers wish to administer and interpret the MBTI instrument, they need to acquire the knowledge and skill through one of the approved training programs such as ones offered by the Center for Applications of Psychological

Type (CAPT) or the Association for Psychological Type (APT).

Much thought was given to the topics that a book on MBTI uses in higher education should include. These chapters reflect a range of ideas from the traditional uses in career and personal counseling to other uses such as research on college attrition and leadership behaviors. Some applications focus on individual student development, some on patterns of behavior among large groups of students, others on teaching approaches, and yet others on environmental issues. These topics are supplemented by an appendix of type table distributions from various subgroups within higher education.

We have selected contributors who have been innovative in applying the MBTI instrument in a variety of ways and in a variety of institutions. The contributors represent diversity in professional functions, work settings, and disciplines. Brief biographies of these contributors are located on pages 443–451. We have also invited contributors with differing MBTI types, so that different approaches to writing and presenting information will be evident. There has been little attempt to make the writing style uniform, but rather to let the author's type shine through. Each contributor could easily expand his or her chapter into an entire book. We challenged them to provide an overview of their topics, the rationale for their particular uses of the MBTI instrument, and descriptions of their approaches.

In providing a context for this book, it is important to review the origins of the MBTI personality assessment tool. Isabel Myers and her mother, Katharine Briggs, began developing the Indicator in the 1940s through a desire to implement C. G. Jung's theory of psychological type. In 1962, Educational Testing Services (ETS) published Form F of the MBTI instrument to be used for research purposes only. In the 1960s while the Indicator was still a research instrument, several higher education practitioners researched university students' behaviors (Grant, 1965 and Williams, 1980). Auburn and Michigan State

Universities were two early sites of such research. In 1969, Myers began working with Mary McCaulley at the University of Florida to establish a Typology Laboratory for research on type, especially longitudinal studies of students. By 1979, the Laboratory became the Center for Applications of Psychological Type (CAPT), an independent nonprofit corporation. In 1975, Consulting Psychologists Press, Inc. (CPP, Inc.) became the publisher and made the Indicator available to qualified professionals. The Indicator's reliability and validity established it as a stable and effective tool for applications, not just for research. The university research in the '60s and '70s, the availability of the MBTI instrument through CAPT and CPP, Inc., and the leadership of CAPT to promote research and use of the instrument stimulated a rapid expansion of uses within higher education.

In summary, we have reviewed current uses of the MBTI instrument in colleges and universities and added two new chapters on leadership and on multicultural issues. Because of changes in the career-counseling field, we have replaced the previous career chapter with a new chapter. Other chapters have been updated, especially the chapter on research. The chapter, "Theories of Psychological Type Development and College Student Development," has been extensively revised and now also includes a discussion of Robert Kegan's theory of the evolving self. Chapter 1 provides the theoretical foundation for the applications chapters that follow.

References

Anchors, S., D. Robinson, and C. Wood. (1984). *A survey of Myers-Briggs Type Indicator uses in the American College Personnel Association.* Orono, ME: University of Maine.

Grant, W. H. (1963) *Behavior of MBTI types* (research report). Auburn, AL: Student Counseling Service, Auburn University.

Lawrence, G. (1993). *People types and tiger stripes: A practical guide to learning styles,* 3rd ed. Gainesville, FL: Center for Applications of Psychological Type.

Myers, I. B. with P. B. Myers. (1980). *Gifts differing.* Palo Alto, CA: Consulting Psychologists Press.

Myers, I. B., M. H. McCaulley, N. L. Quenk, and A. L. Hammer. (1998). *MBTI® manual: A guide to the development and use of the Myers-Briggs Type Indicator,* 3rd ed. Palo Alto, CA: Consulting Psychologists Press.

Williams, C. (1980). An appreciation of Isabel Briggs Myers. *MBTI News,* 2(4), 8.

CHAPTER 1

Theories of Psychological Type Development and College Student Development

ANN Q. LYNCH

Higher education is based on the premise that individuals with different motivations can be served by different institutions to reach their different goals. Perhaps more so than other parts of our society, colleges and universities are dedicated to ensuring the fulfillment of the human potential through the recognition of individual differences. Psychological type theory is useful in advancing the purposes of higher education to help students understand themselves and others and appreciate their individual differences in addition to promoting learning, career decision making and leadership. Theories of type dynamics and type development deepen our insights about how personality evolves over time.

This chapter addresses individual differences from a psychological type perspective, as applied through the Myers-Briggs Type Indicator® instrument. We are assuming that most readers have a basic knowledge of psychological type. The reader unacquainted with type concepts is encouraged to refer to: *Introduction to Type®* (Myers, 1998), *Gifts Differing* (Myers, 1995) and the *MBTI® Manual: A Guide to the Development and Use of the Myers-Briggs Type Indicator* (Myers, McCaulley, Quenk, and Hammer, 1998). Two other books will also be helpful to the reader: *Introduction to Type in College* (DiTiberio and Hammer, 1993) and *Applications of the Myers-Briggs Type Indicator in Counseling: A Casebook* (Provost, 1993) as well as the booklet, *Strategies for Success: Using Type to Excel in High School and College* (Provost, 1992).

Psychological type theory provides a way of examining some important personality differences. Theories of student development also shed light on how professionals can respond to individual differences. A sound theoretical base is important for us as practitioners to implement our work in higher education. As professionals we need a blend of theory and practice to serve students effectively. Since the focus of this chapter is on various theories, it is helpful to understand the purposes of theory. Goldhaber (2000) delineated the following purposes of human development theories. First, they offer a systematic means to understand the phenomena of our existence; and they provide a means to categorize data, make comparisons, and identify patterns. Second, theories of human development enable us to generalize about specific understandings, and as such, they are economical because from large amounts of data, we can categorize and synthesize as well as extrapolate from them. We can find links between seemingly distinct events as well as the independence of seemly related events. Third, theories provide a basis for decision making, and this allows us to exercise some control over the forces that directly or indirectly affect our lives. Fourth, these theories provide a means of predicting future events to a certain extent, which allows us to make some appropriate preparations and accommodations. Finally, theories help us to know which questions to ask next and are a means of pursing research to validate or refute the theory. Goldhaber offered the criteria of testability, organization, generativity, and precision as defining a theory's integrity and usefulness.

Since much of this chapter will emphasize development, it is helpful to clarify some definitions. Development has been defined as: the organization of increasing complexity or a positive growth process in which the individual becomes increasingly able to integrate and act on many different experiences and influences. Change is an altered condition that may be positive or negative, progressive or regressive. Growth refers to expansion but may be either favorable or unfavorable to overall functioning. Maturation is the process of change that occurs through the biological processes of growth. The study of human development is "the science that seeks to understand how and why people change, and how and why they remain the same, as they grow older" (Berger 2001, p. 4). The life-span perspective, according to Baltes (1987), envisions seven distinct characteristics of development as: *lifelong; multidirectional* (change is not linear gains and losses, compensations and deficits, predictable growth and unexpected transformations); *historically embedded; multicontextual* (each life is embedded in overlapping contexts of cultural and socioeconomic dimensions); *multicultural* (ethnicity, gender, age, sexual orientation, religion, disability status, etc.); *multidisciplinary* (psychology, biology, sociology, economics, education, anthropology, medicine, history, etc.); and *plastic* (almost every individual, every trait is capable of being altered to some extent at any point in the life span).

In this chapter, we first look at diversity and college students today. Then we will examine type development theory and its implications for college students. We will examine a few theories of college student development and how they may inform administrators, faculty, student services professionals, parents, and students. Then we explore student development theory and its implications for psychological type. Finally, we present recommendations for the intentional use of type to contribute to college student development.

Diversity and College Students

As of 1998, there were 14.5 million students enrolled in colleges and universities in the U. S. National Center for Education Statistics (NCES 2000, 193). Despite the large number of smaller institutions, more students attend the larger colleges and universities. While 10 percent of the campuses enrolled 10,000 or more students, which accounted for 49 percent of total enrollments, smaller institutions with 1,000 or fewer students represented 40 percent of institutions of higher education but only 4 percent of total enrollments (NCES 2000, 194). Diversity among the college students in terms of age, gender, and ethnicity has increased dramatically in the past few decades in most institutions. Traditional undergraduate students, ages 18 to 22, with common characteristics of being recent high school graduates, having satisfactory admissions scores, being supported mainly by parents and/or financial aid, and living on or near campus, still comprise a major focus for many colleges and universities. However, adult learners, who are defined more by their roles and responsibilities than by age, have increased substantially over the past two decades. With the rise in community college enrollments and the shift in U. S. age demographics accompanying the baby boomer bulge, more campuses have seen older students and a wider range in age diversity, life experience, commuter status, and part-time enrollment. Many older students are returning to college for second or third careers, to increase their families' income, to improve their skills in technology, and to find more meaning. Still traditional age students comprise the larger proportion of enrollments, in 1998, 59.9 percent of students were under the age of 25 compared with 40.1 percent who were 25 years and older, including both undergraduate and graduate students (NCES 2000, p. 206). Between 1990 and 1999, the number of students under 25 years of age increased by 8 percent while students 25 years and older rose by 7 percent. From 1999 through 2010, NCES projects an increase of 24 percent in enrollments of persons under 25 and only an increase of 9 percent in the number 25 and over (NCES 2000, p. 193).

A change in the ratio of men to women has taken place over the past twenty years. In 1979, for the very first time in this country, women outnumbered men in higher education, and they have continued to be the majority gender. Women in 1997 represented 56.1 percent of enrollments and have increased 16 percent compared with a 6 percent increase for men between 1988 and 1998 (NCES 2000; p. 205, p. 193). During the same time period, part-time enrollment increased by 6 percent while full time enrollment increased by 15 percent. During the '80s and '90s, the greatest change in ethnic composition was evident in predominantly White institutions with the increase of minority students. In 1976, minorities represented 16 percent of enrollments while in 1997, 27 percent of total enrollments in all U. S. colleges and universities were minority students while 3.2 percent were international students (NCES 2000; p. 239, p. 193). Other social changes; legislative and policy changes, such as both financial need and financial aid; greater employment opportunities; affirmative action; academic support services; and greater demand for access have contributed to the varied tapestry that is higher education.

These new students bring with them diversity in academic preparation, socioeconomic status, motivations, goals, and values (Schlossberg, Lynch, and Chickering, 1989). Academic preparation ranges from high school noncompleters and GED graduates to advanced placement graduates and adults experienced in the work world. Entrance test scores, such as the SAT and ACT, attest to the wide range of entering academic backgrounds across institutions, even though there are valid questions about the predictive value of these instruments as entrance criteria. Certainly, various motivations propel students into college, such as, fulfilling parental expectations, following the crowd, improving job capabilities, upgrading skills, earning a credential, gaining a secure future, looking for relationships, improving self esteem, or the pleasure of learning. We might add that psychological type can be viewed as another aspect of diversity.

Type and Type Development Theory

Besides the above visible and invisible differences among college students, there are cognitive and affective differences that influence learning and development. Why do some individuals from apparently advantaged backgrounds succumb or barely survive while others from apparently very disadvantaged backgrounds excel? Knowing about psychological type and type development theory will help the practitioner understand students and give a rationale for predicting some, but certainly not all, important behaviors. Carl Jung can be considered one of the first developmental psychologists. He believed that individual development was a lifelong process and that all humans have an innate psychic energy toward growth. We have everything within us to become healthy, effective people. Myers and Kirby (1994) observed, "Within his (Jung's) model, psychological type is viewed as the compass directing this growth, suggesting the probable course for each type" (p. 21). Isabel Myers (1998) called the types, sixteen paths to excellence.

Type theory begins with recognizing the basis for what appears to be random behavior. Jung (1971) wrote that much seemingly chance variation in human behavior is not due to chance but is the logical result of a few observable differences in mental functioning. Clearly,

Jung believed that type preferences were inborn and Isabel Myers came to the same conclusion (McCaulley, 1999). Myers (1995) wrote, "The hypothesis is that type is inborn, an innate predisposition like right- or left-handedness, but the successful development of type can be greatly helped or hindered by the environment from the beginning" (p. 190). There is growing evidence that type is hard-wired into the brain (Shiflett, 1989; and Wilson and Languis, 1989). In *Psychological Types*, Jung (1971) described extraversion in young children: "The earliest signs of extraversion in a child is his quick adaptation to the environment, and the extraordinary attention he gives to objects and especially to the effect he has on them" (p. 516). He observed introversion as: "One of the earliest signs of introversion in a child is a reflective, thoughtful manner, marked by shyness and even fear of unknown objects . . . . His real world is an inner one" (p. 517). As Myers (1995) proposed, "Within limits, type development can substitute for intelligence, because average intelligence fully utilized through fine type development will give results above expectation" (p. 186).

Psychological type is dynamic, not static. Myers (1998) explained, "Type describes 16 dynamic energy systems, rather than defining static boxes. The four-letter type is much more than simple addition of the four preferences: it is the interaction of the preferences with each other. . . . Everyone uses each of the preferences to some extent. Our type consists of those we prefer" (p. 42). The theory of type development states that everyone has the capability of using all four of the functions: two perception functions and two judgment functions. However, people differ in which functions they naturally prefer to use; that is, they will naturally prefer one of the perception functions, either Sensing (S) or Feeling (F) or one of the judgment functions, either Thinking or Feeling. Many MBTI® experts explain preference by using the metaphor of handedness. Although everyone can use both hands to catch a beach ball, each of us has a natural *preference* for using either the right or left hand for signing our names. Jung (1971) wrote: "The four functions are somewhat like the four points of the compass; they are just as arbitrary and just indispensable" and "I would not for anything dispense with this compass on my psychological journeys of discovery" (p. 415.)

Development of the Dominant and Auxiliary

Young children begin to exercise a preference for one of the ways of perceiving or of judging. As soon as that preference is established, a basic difference in development begins. The child begins to use the favored process more often and to neglect the less favored process. Just as in the handedness metaphor, we develop a natural tendency to use one hand over the other. It becomes easier for us to use that hand; therefore we use it more and become expert at its use. The favorite function is called the *dominant* function and will be a perception process, Sensing or Intuition (N), or a judgment process, Thinking (T) or Feeling. The dominant function is the unifying process in one's life.

If a person is to become fully effective, the dominant must have clear sovereignty, with the opportunity to reach its maximum potential. The dominant is the core or guiding force in one's personality. According to Von Franz and Hillman's (1979) explanation of Jung's theory, the dominant is usually reflected in behavior by kindergarten age. Typically, the mental tool people rely on the most, the dominant function gives overall direction to the personality. "When a final decision needs to be made, it will generally be the one that is congruent with the dominant function" (Myers and Kirby, 1994, p. 5).

Sometimes for environmental reasons the dominant process may not become developed. In such situations, the person often appears confused because there is little or no direction or intensity. Regarding such confusion, Jung (1971) wrote: "As a rule, whenever such a falsification of type takes place as a result of external influence, the individual becomes neurotic later, and can be cured only by developing the attitude consonant with his nature" (p. 415).

Having a well-developed dominant function is not enough; so one of the remaining functions of the other pair becomes the *auxiliary* or supplemental process. If the person prefers a perception Sensing or Intuition function for the dominant, the judgment Thinking or Feeling function becomes the auxiliary or vice versa. To be well balanced, the individual needs an adequate but not equal development of the auxiliary or second process. If the right hand is preferred, the left hand is used for support or balance, or vice versa. If Intuition is the dominant perception function, then Thinking or Feeling will be the auxiliary judgment function, or if Feeling is the dominant judgment function, then Sensing or Intuition will be the auxiliary perception function. The development of the auxiliary usually begins in late adolescence or young adulthood, although there is no specific timetable for this. Its development is very important to effective functioning.

For example, a perceptive type with an underdeveloped auxiliary judgment process would gather information and not be able to use it to make a decision. In college students, such underdevelopment of a judgment auxiliary is often illustrated in the aimless wanderings in search of a major over a period of years. It is also evident in students who gather information for a paper but cannot decide on a topic or cannot begin the writing because they do not know when to stop gathering material. On the other hand, a judging type without a well-developed perception auxiliary, tends to make decisions without information. This lack of development is often seen in freshman or sophomore students who choose majors or careers with only the slightest bit of knowledge of the educational requirements, working conditions, or job possibilities. In writing term papers, students who have not developed a perception auxiliary will decide on the topic and write the paper with little, if any, supporting evidence.

We have discussed two of the four MBTI personality dichotomies, which have to do with basic functions of perception Sensing or Intuition and judgment Thinking or Feeling. The other two dichotomies are called *attitudes*, or sometimes *orientations*, as opposed to functions. The attitudes indicate a person's dominant and auxiliary and which function is used in the outer world. The first variable is the attitude toward life, Extraversion (E) or Introversion (I). This attitude represents the world in which the person becomes energized; that is, the direction of the flow of attention—either outward for Extraverts or inward for Introverts. The other variable or attitude indicates whether a Judging (J) or a Perceiving (P) function is used in the outer world. This orientation to the outer world also indicates how people structure or organize their lives and the degree of closure they prefer, and is sometimes referred to as "lifestyle."

According to Jung (1971), individuals use their dominant in their preferred world, that is: the outer world for Extraverts and the inner world for Introverts. Therefore, the dominant function can be expressed in eight different ways. These are the eight distinct types described by Jung or the eight mental tools: ES, IS, EN, and IN for perceiving and: ET, IT, EF, and IF for judging. The dominant function is used in the attitude, either Extraversion or Introversion, which interests the person the most, where the person becomes energized, and where the person's best work is done. For example, the Extraverted Intuitive (EN) student is likely to show creativity for all the world to see through innovation. This student uses the dominant Intuition in the extraverted attitude. Conversely, the Introverted Intuitive (IN) student can be just as creative, but in a more private way because the dominant intuitive process remains unseen in the inner world. Extraverted Sensing (ES) students will show themselves as action-oriented realists using the dominant Sensing in the outer world, while

Introverted Sensing (IS) types will apply their realistic and fact-oriented perception within their inner world.

The auxiliary then takes care of the less vital matters in the attitude that holds less importance for the person. The auxiliary handles the extraverted process for the Introvert and the introverted process for the Extravert. For example, the Extraverted Intuitive with Feeling as auxiliary (ENFP) uses the dominant Intuition in the external world (extraverted) and the auxiliary Feeling in the internal world (introverted); i.e., the imagination is shown to the world while the subjective values are kept inside. To summarize, well-balanced type development occurs under the following conditions:

1. A dominant process (a perception process, S or N; or judgment process, T or F) is clearly preferred and used.
2. An auxiliary process (the remaining perception or judgment process) is used to supplement the dominant.
3. The dominant is used in the preferred attitude or world (E or I) while the auxiliary is used in the opposite attitude or world (I or E).

As Myers (1995) so eloquently put it:

> Balance does not refer to equality of two processes or attitudes; instead, it means superior skill in one, supplemented by a helpful but not competitive skill in then other. The need for such supplementing is obvious. Perception without judgment is spineless; judgment with no perception is blind. Introversion lacking any extraversion is impractical; extraversion with no introversion is superficial. (p. 182)

Balance or Complementarity

Quenk (1984) described the balance between preferences and attitudes as "complementarity." She further explained that when such complementarity does not occur, one or more of the following conditions might prevail:

1. Failure to develop one of each pair of opposites more than the other.

If a pair of opposites is developed relatively equally, a situation of potential conflict exists, such as a competition between Sensing and Intuition or a competition between Thinking and Feeling. As Myers (1995) wrote, "Expert perception and judgment result from specialization, from using one of a pair of opposites rather than the other. One of the opposites must be tuned out in order to have a chance to develop either of them" (p. 182).

EXAMPLE: If Mary (ENFP) were well developed, she would have extraverted Intuition as dominant with introverted Feeling as auxiliary. She does not seem to be able to make a choice between her objective and subjective reasons in choosing a major or deciding whether to be in college or not. She entered college because she had been working as a secretary and did not find the work challenging. Mary has difficulty deciding on courses, her major, and whether she can hold a job while going to school. She thinks she wants to do something with people, but she also likes reading and thinking about ideas. She has considered a nursing program so that she will have a definite job when she graduates. She seems to have some confusion in the Perception function—moving between Sensing by considering practical occupations such as nursing, and Intuition debating about a liberal arts major, such as history or philosophy. She also has some confusion in the Judgment function—bouncing between logical, objective

Thinking because she thinks she would eventually like to go to law school and value-oriented, subjective Feeling since she wants to work with people.

2. Lack of clear development of the dominant function.

In this case, the preferred perceiving (S or N) and judging (T or F) functions compete for energy and attention. Neither is clearly dominant and neither is clearly auxiliary. Such individuals may appear inconsistent and unpredictable.

EXAMPLE: Charlie (ESFP), if well developed, would have extraverted Sensing as dominant with introverted Feeling as auxiliary. He changed majors many times from business to health sciences and then to physical education. His father wanted him to take accounting courses to get ahead. Even though he had difficulty in biology, Charlie had an interest in health from a high school summer job he had in a medical lab. He enjoyed playing team sports but would often be late for practice. Toward the end of his sophomore year, his lack of responsibility on the baseball team made the coach remove him from the team. Charlie shrugged off his desire for a sports career, dropped out of college, and got married. Now he is selling appliances in a local department store, much to his parents' and his own disappointment. Charlie did not have a clear preference between a dominant Sensing and an auxiliary Feeling. He did not have well-developed "complementarity." He vacillated when gathering practical information and allowed his decisions to be heavily influenced by others' feelings.

3. Failure to use the auxiliary in the attitude opposite to that associated with the dominant.

Some students may be seen as shy, socially inept, or even antisocial. They avoid all social situations and appear unable to express themselves interpersonally. They often become anxious and embarrassed when required to deal with people or the external world. Such students may be using both the perceiving and judging functions in an introverted mode. They may not have developed a comfortable way of dealing with the outside world. Such college students may often be isolates, having no successful way of dealing with people or things around them. They may be particularly disadvantaged since many college activities require interacting with others, working in groups, and making oral presentations.

EXAMPLE: Roger (INTP), if well developed, would have introverted Thinking as dominant and extraverted Intuition as auxiliary. He is seen by the other students as reclusive and stand-offish. At times they refer to him as the "ghost." He is hardly ever visible, preferring to remain in his room reading, studying, and using the computer. When he does venture forth, he seldom has a conversation with another person; yet he takes tests well and maintains a respectable grade point average. He is the kind of student whom the sensitive advisor or resident assistant may try to involve in activities without much success. Roger seems to be introverting both his dominant Thinking (T) and his auxiliary Intuition .

Individuals who extravert *both* their dominant and auxiliary have fewer apparent difficulties than Introverts who introvert both functions, especially if this occurs early in life. When Extraverts use both their dominant and auxiliary in an extraverted fashion, this results in a lack of trust in the inner life.

EXAMPLE: Joan (ESFJ), if well developed, would have extraverted Feeling as dominant with introverted Sensing as auxiliary. She has become over-involved in student activities to such an extent that she seldom goes to class. She rationalizes her activities as being practical when applied to her public relations major. She appears to enjoy the attention and expends much energy on being with others. At night she roams the residence hall looking for someone—anyone—with whom she can talk in detail about her day's activities. It is almost as if she is afraid to be alone. Joan seems to be extraverting both her dominant Feeling and her auxiliary Sensing.

When Extraverts reach middle age and still have not developed their auxiliary in the introverted mode, they may experience feelings of emptiness and meaninglessness and be perceived by friends and family as shallow. They are seen as lacking conviction and flitting from absorption to total disinterest in projects. They are often described by others as "gushing," "inappropriately friendly" or "overwhelming." Quenk (1985b) delineated the lack of empathy of such Extraverts: "They seek out other's advice and sympathy but are unavailable to reciprocate for a friend in need" (p. 29).

EXAMPLE: George (ESTP) is an Extravert. If well developed, he would have extraverted Sensing as dominant balanced with introverted Thinking as auxiliary. However, George seems shallow and undisciplined, touching on many different interests and people. He entered college at age 29 after his second divorce, intending to make up for all that he missed. He went to every football game and appeared to delve into his studies, but by midterm he had lost interest. He talked to the other students about his divorce, but when a friend needed help moving, he was unavailable. He had no real friends because he was hypercritical of their behavior. George dropped out of college for the third time. He appears to be extraverting both his dominant Sensing and his auxiliary Thinking.

Effective Type Development and the Inferior Function

For effective type development it is essential to develop trust in the dominant process, with the auxiliary focused in the opposite attitude. This frees one later in life to explore less-preferred patterns. Quenk (1984) explained, "A person who is clear about the dominant versus the auxiliary has specialized in one of each pair of opposites and uses the auxiliary in the less-preferred attitude may be seen as well developed in terms of type." (p. 17).

Quenk (1985) reported that clinically the most frequent evidence for inadequate type development occurs in the judging function, Thinking or Feeling, with much reported distress in decision making. If the Thinking–Feeling function is poorly differentiated and is the dominant process, the conflict is particularly disruptive. There appears to be a shifting back and forth between Thinking and Feeling. The final decision emerges in fatigue and confusion and later proves to be a poor one, based on reports by that person as well as by significant others.

EXAMPLE: Sharon (INFP), if well developed, would have introverted Feeling as dominant with extraverted Intuition as auxiliary. She seems to be confused in making decisions, not knowing whether to attend to objective or subjective values. Last semester, Sharon found that one of her best friends cheated on the midterm exam. Her sense of justice said that she should report the situation to the teacher, but her sense of loyalty to her friend put her in a quandary. To make matters worse, Sharon was put on the awards committee and found that her friend was eligible for honors, and she knew that anyone found cheating would be eliminated automatically. Sharon felt caught between her two loyalties. After many hours of worry, she resigned from the committee, did not report the cheating incident, withdrew from other activities, and avoided her friend. By default, she let her subjective values prevail but continued to feel that she had betrayed her objective values. She has some confusion between her Feeling and Thinking judgment as her dominant process.

A poor differentiation in perception between Sensing and Intuition is more difficult to identify. The individual sometimes uses Sensing to gather information and sometimes Intuition, but trusts neither function completely. The result is a lack of self-confidence and erratic performance.

EXAMPLE: Bill (ISTP), if well developed, would have introverted Thinking as dominant with extraverted Sensing as auxiliary. He sometimes takes specific information and uses his imagination to jump to erroneous conclusions. As a biology major, he once conducted an experiment on a frog. He extracted tissue that had a dark appearance and immediately speculated that the frog had cancer. The lab instructor told him that it was an area of tissue that was generally light in color, but these particular frogs came from a different locale causing that tissue to be dark. Bill felt embarrassed about jumping to such a conclusion about the cancer without much evidence. He does not use his Sensing well and often drifts into his less-preferred Intuition function.

Stages of Type Development

Jung (1971) maintained that the goal of the first half of life is to make one's place in the world and establish an identity through the successful achievement of a career and personal relationships. The second half of life he proposed was for balancing and completing the individuation process. He explained that the growth of a healthy personality goes through two important stages. In the first stage of life, we specialize; we develop clear preferences and use them freely. In the second stage of life, we strive to become more complete and less specialized. In a favorite quote of this writer, Jung (1933) wrote, "We cannot live the afternoon of life according to the morning of life's program" (p. 116). At this stage, which is generally midlife, many adults become more interested in developing their third and fourth functions. They are ready for a change! Perhaps this is one motivation propelling so many adult learners to return to college. Later in life some individuals do learn to use their third and fourth functions more freely, though never as expertly as their first and second functions.

People also differ in the order in which they develop their functions and the degree of use of the four functions. The natural order to type development is: the dominant one, to the auxiliary two, to three (the function opposite two); and finally to four (the function opposite the dominant, one). For example, if Intuition is dominant and Feeling is auxiliary, then Thinking becomes three and Sensing becomes four. In type circles, there has been some confusion about the attitude of the third function. McCaulley (1998) asked Myers where her model of "the dominant one way and the other three the other way" came from. Myers gave this quotation from Jung (1971):

> The thinking of the introverted type is positive and synthetic in developing ideas which approximate more and more to the internal validity of primordial images. The counterbalancing functions of feeling, intuition and sensation are comparatively unconscious and inferior, and therefore have a primitive extroverted character that accounts for all the troublesome influences from outside to which the introverted thinker is prone" (pp. 386–387).

McCaulley (1998) concurred with Jung's and Myers' belief that clearly the other three functions are in the opposite attitude from the dominant function.

The fourth function is the least developed, the least preferred, and the most difficult to access. It is sometimes referred to as the inferior or "the shadow," but the latter term causes confusion with Jung's meaning of the personal unconscious and non-accepted aspects of the self. In MBTI circles the fourth function is simply referred to as the least preferred or inferior without any negative connotation. Quenk (1993 and 1996) devoted much effort to help us understand the dynamics of the inferior function when we are "beside ourselves" or "in the grip." As Provost (1993) described, "If and when No. 4 and No. 3 can be utilized in mature adulthood, the outcome is often positive, even exhilarating" (p. 4).

The least preferred inferior function is the process that causes the person the most difficulty. It is slow and loaded with emotionality. This inferior function lies opposite to the dominant function. Von Franz and Hillman (1979) described the problems that the inferior function presents to individuals who are often unaware of its magnitude. They especially emphasized the slowness of the inferior function when compared with the dominant function and recognized that "in this realm, one has to waste time which gives the unconscious a chance to come in" (p. 8). Jung (1971) called the inferior function "infantile" and "tyrannical." In developing the inferior function, the person should give it a lot of time and recognize that it develops in the attitude that is opposite the preferred attitude. For example, the dominant Extraverted Intuitive would explore the inferior Sensing through the introverted attitude. However, it should be remembered that the inferior function cannot be relied upon to act according to needs or dictates. A person cannot cross directly to the opposite function; the functions S or N and T or F exclude each other; they are dichotomous and incompatible. Therefore, it is a serious mistake to try to help someone to "work directly on his or her inferior function" with the expectation that the fourth function will ever reach the capacity of the first.

The development of the third and fourth functions probably best applies to mature adult learners who are in midlife and beyond. Therefore, much of the student development literature does not address their concerns. However, it behooves those of us in higher education to understand how these type dynamics might impact those returning to college for second careers or just for the joy of learning.

Environmental Effects on Type Development

Jung proposed first that people have a natural bent or preference and will become happier and more effective if they follow their natural pathways. The second assumption is that following a natural pathway leads to lifelong development. However, environment affects development and expression of type. Students can be affirmed for who they are in their families, or they can have their true type discouraged. Falsification of type occurs because it is not safe to be "the person one truly is," as conceptualized by Carl Rogers (1961). Jung (1971) explained: ". . . a reversal of type often proves exceedingly harmful to the physiological well-being of an organism, usually causing complete exhaustion" (p. 333). Crises and stress can also contribute to inconsistencies in the expression of type. Stress may push individuals into their inferior function rather than toward type development.

According to McCaulley (1985) "true type" is shorthand for the concept that "Jung's theory appears to assume that each person has a constitutional predisposition to develop certain preferences over others, if this development is not falsified by the environment" (p. 30). She also posited some of the reasons why we cannot expect the MBTI instrument or any other instrument to report "true types" one hundred percent of the time.

Effective type development cannot be determined by scores McCaulley, (1981). It is important for practitioners to keep this in mind when giving feedback to students. Neither slight nor very clear scores on the MBTI assessment tool should be taken as absolutes regarding type development, rather scores farther from the center indicate the clarity of type preferences. In light of these limitations, it is truly amazing how often students report that the MBTI descriptions fit their "true type." Perhaps it would be better to expect the MBTI instrument to be wrong and to be pleasantly surprised when the student reports that the description is accurate. McCaulley (1985) proposed that a better term than "true type" which indicates more certainty than is possible would be "currently best-fit type," to allow for growth and development.

Provost (1993) described different developmental issues that arise in counseling, which seem applicable for college students generally as well. She proposed the following questions, which can serve as a guide for those of us who are concerned with type development in college students:

1. How well does the student use the functions? Which are preferred? In which does the student have confidence? Which are avoided? Are the consequences problematic?
2. What has been the pattern of function development? What are the implications for the student?
3. Has the normal developmental order of the functions been interfered with? By what environmental or circumstantial factors? With what consequences?
4. What can facilitate development of all four functions, but particularly of the natural functions? What can be done to develop a balanced personality, the ability to use the function appropriate to the situation and not to overuse or rely solely on one function? (p. 3)

Both Carskadon (1994) and Provost (1998) encourage students to be aware of their type and to recognize that procrastination can cause the most problems in academic life.

Student Development Theory and Type Implications

Fostering student development is a central task of higher education when learning is broadly construed in terms of the potential for lifelong growth and effective citizenship as Arnold and King (1997) proposed. A developmental perspective encompasses a somewhat predictable sequence of growth, adaptation, and transformation. A general definition of development refers to orderly and sequential changes in characteristics and attitudes over time. Earlier characteristics help shape later characteristics and an understanding of antecedent-consequent patterns is useful to students and to those helping them. It is important to remember that not all change is synonymous with growth or development. Changes can be purely external and do not necessarily imply improvement, maturation, or predictable sequentiality. While developmental change does occur over time, few changes occur simply as a result of time. Two decades ago, Weathersby and Tarule (1980) so articulately wrote:

> The dynamics of development involve learning that is irreversible and sometimes at the core of our lives. Further, the process of developmental change implies both choice and necessity in interaction with life circumstances. Development is not merely additive; it involves a process of qualitative change. (p. 2)

Many developmental theories had their base in the psychosexual stages of Freud, the psychosocial stages of Erikson, and the cognitive stages of Piaget. During the past twenty years, theories of adult development have gained credence based in part on research with selected groups of adults, some in college and some outside.

Pascarella and Terenzini (1991) reviewed all major research reports from 1967 through 1990 on the impact of higher education on student development. Arnold and King (1997) categorized the major college student development theories. Love and Guthrie (1999) focused on understanding cognitive development theories applied to college students while Evans, Forney, and Guido-DiBrito (1998) systematically presented the major theories of student development, their research and applications. Synthesizing these overviews suggests the following broad categories for organizing the theories with a few examples of their major proponents:

1. **Psychosocial theories** that view development as a series of tasks or stages: Erikson's eight developmental crises; Sanford's stages of freshman development; Chickering's seven vectors of student development; Marcia's model of ego identity status; W. Cross's model of Black identity formation; Sue's minority identity model; Helms's nonracist White identity model, Heath's maturity model; Josselson's pathways of identity development in women; Cass's homosexual identity and D'Augelli's gay, lesbian and bisexual identity model; and various life-span theories of adult development, such as Levinson's, Gould's, Valliant's, and Schlossberg's transition theory.
2. **Cognitive development theories** that describe changes in thinking and the evolving frames of reference that structure assumptions, values and beliefs: Perry's scheme of intellectual and ethical development; Loevinger's theory of ego development; Belenky, Clinchy, Goldberger, and Tarule's women's ways of knowing, Baxter Magolda's epistemological reflection model; Kitchener and King's reflective judgment model; Kohlberg's theory of moral development; Gilligan's different voices model; Fowler's stages of faith development; and Kegan's evolving self theory.
3. **Typology theories** that describe distinctive but stable: Myers-Briggs's typology; Keisey and Bates' temperament differences; Kolb's learning styles; and K. P. Cross's work on socioeconomic characteristics.

4. **Contextual theories** that focus on how the environment influences behavior through its interactions with characteristics of the individual: ecological theories such as Brofenbrenner's; and Banning and Kaiser's; Holland's theory of vocational personalities and work environments; perceptual models such as Moos', Stern's, Pace's and Pervin's; and Astin's student involvement theory.

This chapter cannot address all of these theories or models; however, one major theory, Chickering's psychosocial model of student development is explored with implications for psychological type. And some reflections on Kegan's orders of consciousness constructivist-developmental model are presented. Perhaps this examination of these models with type implications can serve as a template for exploring type and other student development theories.

Human development theories have not been systematically related to psychological type. There has been little research to indicate the connection between student development theory and type. What follows, therefore, are some *reasoned speculations* based on our knowledge of type theory and student development theories. The reader should be aware that these are *speculations* and not use them for fact, but be spurred on to conduct research to validate, refine, or disprove these speculations.

Type theory gives the foundation for hypothesizing about the connections between life cycle theory and theories of student development. If we can consider type "the given" for the student, we have enough evidence to know that different types deal with life cycle developmental tasks differently. We also know that different types experience college in different ways. As a foundation for most theories of human development, concepts from life cycle stage theory can also enlighten our understanding of student development.

Life Cycle Stage Theory

Life cycle stage theory helps us be aware that students have certain milestones and marker events in which those who are within relatively the same age group may have many commonalities. Life cycle stages form the foundation for much of the adult development literature and provide important concepts for understanding students. Adulthood is not a stable state, but is divided into successive life periods, each with its own learning tasks. Some of the research indicates that most American adults' lives are patterned in predictable sequences with certain key issues and tasks associated with each life stage. Some of the life cycle concepts and their relation to students follow:

1. ***Life stage: an age-linked period in which certain issues and adaptive tasks or marker events are paramount.*** Developmental tasks have been associated with different life stages. The life phase of "leaving the family" ages 18 to 24 means coping with the major psychic tasks of separating from family, reducing dependence on family support and authority, and regarding one's self as an adult. Marker events for this time involve leaving home, developing new roles, and making autonomous living arrangements. Such markers for the young adult might include college, travel, military service, job, education, career plans, and love relationships. The characteristic stance for this life stage is a balance between "being in" and "moving out" of the family.
2. ***Developmental task: external and internal components required in adjusting to life events.*** Regarding the tasks of adulthood, Freud said that the normal person should be able to do these two things well: to work and to love. Erikson (1959) created a formulation of critical issues to be resolved in eight

> stages of the life cycle. The stages for early childhood and adolescence involve trust vs. mistrust, autonomy vs. shame and doubt, initiative vs. guilt, and industry versus inferiority. The stages generally confronting late adolescents and young adults are identity versus role confusion and intimacy versus isolation. However, if students reach college and have not coped with the first four stages, they will have difficulty forming an identity and handling subsequent stages. Middle age adults address the crisis of generativity versus stagnation and older adults confront integrity versus despair.

If the major developmental task for most 18 to 24 year olds is "leaving the family," we can predict that different types will experience this phase in different ways. As an example, take John (ISTJ), 18, who may be very practical in moving from home to college. He knows that college is his place to learn and to select his career. He is very planful about selecting specific courses and wants to be sure that he is taking only what is needed to major in his chosen field. When it comes to personal relationships, he has more difficulty in making friends and has dated very little.

Contrast John with Bill (ESFP), 18, who is also leaving home for the first time and sees college as the opportunity to "live it up." He makes lots of friends and becomes involved in sports and student activities. He figures that courses and majors will take care of themselves and that he has plenty of time to make those lifelong decisions.

The major developmental task for persons aged 35 to 45 is coping with the midlife transition. They are adapting to a changing time perspective, revising career plans, and redefining family relationships. Students returning to college at this age have very different purposes and motivations from traditional-aged students.

Consider John and Bill, neither of whom finished college, now at a later period in their lives. John (ISTJ), now 36, has reexamined his career as a supermarket manager. He knows that he worked hard to get where he is, but that there is not much of a future for him unless he finishes college. Although it is a sacrifice for his wife and family, they have decided that it is best for him to return to college and to get his degree in accounting. This decision will provide greater opportunities for their future.

Bill (ESFP), also now 36, has gone through a difficult time trying to decide on a career. He has moved from one job to another, primarily in sales. He still has lots of friends and fond memories of the "good times" in college but has some regrets that he did not settle down and major in something that would lead to a more substantial future. Upon reexamining his current traveling job in sales, he decided to apply for admission to an external degree program that would give him a credential. His wife gave him encouragement, since it could mean a more secure future for the family. After a few months of studying at night following a full day of sales, Bill recognized that he could not devote as much time to his family and friends as he had in the past. He lost his incentive and dropped out of college again.

We need to examine these hypothetical situations and recognize, first, that John and Bill are stereotypes of their types. Nevertheless, we can learn from them. There are consistent themes that prevail, such as both men being practical, with Sensing as their dominant function. There are also several important differences. John tends to be more serious from his Introversion, and more planful from his Judging function. Bill expresses himself in an open way from his Extraversion and in a spontaneous manner from his Perceiving function. However, a major difference in their types comes from the auxiliary, with John being more logical and objective from his Thinking function, and Bill being more oriented toward personal values from his Feeling function.

These type and life cycle differences combined with life circumstances help us better understand students like John and Bill. Recognition that motivations for college are different at age 36 than at age 18 also helps us acknowledge and affirm students, no matter what phase they are negotiating in the life cycle. Academic advising, career counseling, and instruction, all need to take these developmental task differences into account.

Chickering's Vectors of Student Development

Perhaps the best known and most widely used theory of student development is that first conceived by Arthur W. Chickering (1969) in *Education and Identity.* His early formulation, based on his own research and on earlier studies of college students, consisted of seven conceptual clusters which he called: "vectors of development" because they seem to have both direction and magnitude. Chickering's and Reisser's (1993) renamed and repositioned seven vectors will be used here. These seven vectors of student development apply to late adolescents and young adults, and also to most older adults returning to college who find themselves confronted with important existential issues at a different level.

Developing Competence. This first vector includes three major elements: intellectual competence, physical and manual competence, and social and interpersonal competence. The major focus of most higher education institutions is on intellectual competence, which is skill in using one's mind. Intellectual competence involves mastering content, gaining intellectual strength and sophistication; and building a repertoire of skills to comprehend, analyze, and synthesize as well as developing new frames of reference. The attainment of intellectual competence, or lack of such, generally influences professional and vocational alternatives chosen later.

Physical and manual competence, important in terms of sports, athletics, dexterity, and strength to pursue life's tasks, takes on high visibility and status in most college environments. Interpersonal competence entails skills in listening, cooperating, and communicating effectively. Interpersonal competence is necessary because most life tasks require cooperative efforts and effectiveness generally depends upon the ability to work with others. More important is a "sense of competence," which is the confidence one has in one's ability to cope with whatever comes and to achieve successfully what one sets out to do.

Managing Emotions. The managing emotions vector addresses the area of self-control and involves the ability to recognize and to manage sexual and aggressive impulses as well as anxiety, fear, hurt, depression, boredom, and other emotions. Through increased self-awareness and through opportunities for self-expression and feedback, the student can achieve forms of expression more appropriate to the circumstances.

Moving through Autonomy toward Interdependence. This vector means learning to function with relative self-sufficiency, take responsibility for pursing self-chosen goals, and be less tied to the opinions of others. Renaming this vector places an emphasis on interdependence rather than autonomy that indicates a maturing of perspective. Emotional and instrumental independence and recognition of one's interdependence are a part of becoming autonomous. Emotional independence happens when the student is free from the continual and pressing need for reassurance, affection, or approval from parents, peers, and others. Instrumental independence is when students have the ability to initiate activities on their own and to cope with problems without always seeking help. Being autonomous means having the ability to be mobile in relation to one's needs or desires. Recognition and acceptance of interdependence is the capstone of autonomy. "Developing autonomy culminates in the recognition that one does not operate in a vacuum and that greater autonomy enables healthier forms of interdependence" (Chickering and Reisser, 1993, p. 47).

Developing Mature Interpersonal Relationships. This vector involves increasing tolerance and appreciating differences and developing the capacity for intimacy. Tolerance is first the increasing capacity to respond to persons for themselves rather than as stereotypes. Through respecting their friends, students learn to generalize to others from different cultures and different continents. In this vector the capacity for healthy intimacy increases and shifts from the narcissism of teen romances to choosing healthy, loving relationships to making lasting commitments based on honesty and unconditional positive regard. Chickering and Reisser (1993) repositioned this vector before identity because more research indicated that for many students, especially for women, maturity in relationships preceded the formation of a complete identity.

Establishing Identity. For the young adult, establishing identity is more than the aggregate of change in competence, emotional maturity, autonomy and positive relationships. As Erikson (1959) defined it, identity is "the accrued confidence that one's ability to maintain inner sameness and continuity is matched by the sameness and continuity of one's meaning for others" (p. 135). Identity involves comfort with body and appearance and with gender and sexual orientation; a sense of self in a social, historical and cultural context and in response to feedback from valued others; clarification of one's self-concept through roles and lifestyle; self acceptance and self-esteem; and personal stability and integration. Establishing identity includes reflecting on one's family of origin and ethnic heritage, defining one's self as a part of a religious or cultural tradition and seeing one's self within a social and historical context. It means finding roles and styles at school, at work, at play, and at home that are genuine expressions of self. Adult learners must often renegotiate their identities to include being students as well as being partners, parents, and supporters of aging parents as well as workers and seekers of new careers and roles. A solid sense of identity fosters change in the last two vectors of purpose and integrity.

Purpose. Questions such as "where am I going?" and "who do I want to be?" are answered with increased clarity and conviction as purpose evolves. Formulating plans and setting priorities that integrate vocational plans and aspirations, personal interests, and interpersonal and family commitments are a part of developing purpose. "It involves a growing ability to unify one's many different goals within the scope of a larger, more meaningful purpose, and to exercise intentionality on a daily basis" (Chickering and Reisser, 1993, p. 50).

Developing Integrity. This vector is closely associated with integrity and purpose and involves three sequential but overlapping stages: 1) Humanizing values, 2) Personalizing values, and 3) Developing congruence. Humanizing values includes the shift from a literal belief in the absoluteness of rules and the purposes they are meant to serve to a more relative view, where connections are made between rules and the purposes they are meant to serve. Thus students move from internalizing their parents' values to forming their own. Personalizing of values leads to the achievement of behavior consistent with the values held in which students select guidelines to suit themselves and to suit the conditions of their lives. Congruence is achieved in the integration of values and the development of one's own standards for living. As Chickening (1969) concluded, "With such integration, life flows with direction and meaning" (p. 17).

Chickering and Reisser's Vectors and Some Implications for Type

Now let us speculate about the ease or discomfort with which different types develop in Chickering and Reisser's vectors of student development. These speculations and comparisons have important implications for education.

Developing competence, especially intellectual competence, is the realm of all types in the college environment. Effective type development can significantly enhance the use of one's intelligence. Myers (1998) indicated that it could almost be a substitute. Academic achievement requires the capacity to deal with concepts and ideas, the main province of Introversion as well as the capacity to work with abstraction, symbols, and theory, the province of Intuition. The research in Myers, McCaulley, Quenk and Hammer (1998) found that persons who prefer Introversion and Intuition (IN) tend to show greater aptitude for education than persons who favor Extraversion and Sensing (ES). The latter's gifts lie in the practical world of action. Thus, type theory predicts that Introverted Intuitives (INs) will have a relative advantage, since their preferences more closely match the majority of academic tasks. Anchors and Robinson (1992) found several correlations between MBTI preferences and scales on the Student Development Task Inventory-2, a measure of Chickering's vectors, indicating that personality type plays a role in the accomplishment of developmental tasks.

Most aptitude tests are designed to measure knowledge and aptitude in the Introverted Intuitive (IN) domain, although there are many interests and capabilities that aptitude tests do not measure. Data from many studies indicate that Introverts consistently score higher than Extraverts on the SAT Verbal and that Intuitive types consistently score higher than Sensing types, with Sensing–Intuition differences being greater than Extraversion–Introversion differences Myers, McCaulley, Quenk, and Hammer (1998).

In general, the Thinking–Feeling (T–F) function seems to have much less importance than the Sensing–Intuition (S–N) function in understanding academic aptitude. However, academic tasks requiring understanding of human motivations favor Feeling types. Perhaps that is why so many students in psychology classes are Feeling types and are often Intuitive Feeling types. With so much college research being conducted in sophomore psychology classes, type theory would have us question the generalization of the findings to the entire population. In regards to the J–P preference, the Perceiving attitude favors a wide acquaintance with many subjects, which can lead to higher scores on aptitude measures. However, the Judging attitude is related to application and may be more often associated with higher grades. Since grades are the end product of the interaction among aptitude, application, and interest, they are a relevant measure to be considered and a major concern of most students.

More college professors are Intuitive types than Sensing types. They also write exams that more frequently fit their own type. Since many college instructors require students in introductory courses to memorize facts and to recall them for tests, students who are Sensing and Judging may have more opportunity to excel in initial courses rather than in later courses. Depending on the discipline, as professors require more hypothesizing and give more essay tests, students who are Intuitive types will have more of an advantage. It is well to remember that every type can learn to survive in the academic world if he or she can learn good study skills and apply them appropriately. Different majors attract types who predominately appear to excel in those majors. It is important to be reminded that even non-predominate types may excel and make a contribution in a given major and career.

Competence in physical and manual skills also can be the domain of every type. However, interest in physical education as a major might generally indicate interest in physical and manual skills. Sensing types who chose this major have been over-represented in many studies as well as women Sensing types who chose business practices as measured by the Strong Interest Inventory (Myers, McCaulley, Quenk, and Hammer, 1998). It is important to ask whether there are cultural expectations and gender role conditioning involved in these type data. Research is needed to explore relationships between successes, or those who persist in different majors, versus dropouts, and type preferences. We need to understand type in relation to *excellence*, beyond *interest* in majors and careers.

Interpersonal competence can be predicted from type theory to be related to Extraversion and to Feeling. Extraverts focus their attention on the external world of people and action. Feeling types are concerned about the impact of their decisions on themselves and others. Significantly more students with Intuitive Feeling (NF) preferences were enrolled in programs of clinical psychology, counseling psychology, counseling, and social work than were those with other combinations (Myers, McCaulley, Quenk, and Hammer, 1998). Since awareness is the first step in developing interpersonal relationships, there appears to be an advantage for Feeling types in relying on subjective values. Their strong need for harmony means they generally take into consideration the impact of their actions on others and themselves. For Thinking types, their competence lies more in analyzing objective information and events than in evaluating their own and others' subjective responses.

Managing emotions may be easier for all types who are well developed. Adolescence, late adolescence, and early adulthood are times for learning to express emotions appropriately. When students become overly aggressive or act on their sexual impulses, one might look for inadequate type development. Clinically, I have observed that this behavior tends to happen more often in the case of Extraverts than for Introverts. Since Thinking types do not frequently express their feelings, but rather attend more to logic and objectivity, their emotions may emerge or even explode unexpectedly. Because their focus is not on the Feeling dimension, they may be surprised by a sudden emergence of emotions. With dominant Thinking, emergence of emotions may signal expression of the inferior Feeling function in a primitive, unpredictable way. A dominant Feeling type, on the other hand, under acute emotional stress, may express a primitive inferior Thinking function through inappropriate and cutting criticism. Again, one should not assume that Thinking types do not have emotions; it just may be more difficult for them to process and express their emotions than it is for Feeling types.

Moving through autonomy toward interdependence is taken as a sign of maturity in this culture. Emotional independence may be easier for Thinking types than for Feeling types because their first loyalty is to ideas rather than to people, since Thinking types tend to use objective values in their decision making. However, as Feeling types mature, they can become freer of the need for constant reassurance and approval from significant others. Their need for harmony will probably always demand that they consider other people in their decision making. Recognizing and acting on one's interdependence with others takes significant type development.

Developing mature interpersonal relationships calls for increased tolerance of differences and expanded capacity for intimacy. Helping students to understand their own and others' type can promote an appreciation for individual differences. Teaching the ability to tolerate and appreciate differences is one of the major goals of professionals using type in working with college students. Since Perceptive types tend to be more open and spontaneous, they probably are able to have freer relationships, but not necessarily more mature relationships. Some students who have a Judging orientation to the external world may need more help in learning to respond to others for themselves rather than as stereotypes. Because of their need for closure, they often draw conclusions (Judging) without enough information (Perceiving). All types need to work toward having greater intimacy in their relationships and toward making lasting commitments that will be satisfying and fulfilling.

Establishing identity seems to be related to Jung's concept of wholeness. As we mature, we move toward an identity that is consistent, yet expresses the totality of our personhood. Men and women in college are expected to form an identity that expresses themselves in terms of appearance, gender roles, and sexual preference. Extraverts with their focus on the external world may be more conscious of their appearances and spend more time deciding about clothes and hairstyles than Introverts. Yet a truly sensitive ISFJ can be just as immobilized about issues of appearance as an ENFJ. It may be somewhat more problematic for female Thinking types and male Feeling types to explain themselves because of our cultural stereotypes that identify logic for males and expressiveness for females. This congruence or incongruence may have more to do with the match between the person and the specific institution or specific community environment than the person's type. For example, our society may make it harder for a gay ISTJ male student than for a gay ENFP male student, who may be more comfortable with an experimental lifestyle.

An appreciation of differences can be enriched through recognition of the mutual usefulness of opposites. Sensing types can discover what they can use from Intuitive types and vice versa, and Thinking types can discover the contribution of Feeling types and vice versa.

Myers (1998) reminded us that the clearest vision of the future comes from an Intuitive type, the most practical realism from a Sensing type, the most incisive analysis from a Thinking type, and the most skillful handling of people from a Feeling type. Success for any endeavor demands a variety of types, each in the place best suited for him or her.

Developing purpose requires students to form plans and to set priorities about educational and career goals as well as about vocational and general lifestyle strategies. Purpose calls for the development of both perception and judgment and the appropriate use of the external and internal modes. Setting priorities may pose difficulties for Perceiving types, while premature closure on career plans often causes problems for Judging types. Providing information about work settings in type terms can help students make more informed choices. With an ethical and informed counselor, a student can explore his or her type in interaction with the distribution of types among various careers. We must remember that predominance of certain types in specific careers still does not tell us who is successful or happy in those careers, but only who is *attracted* to certain fields. Therefore, precautions need to be taken when sharing these data.

Developing integrity occurs when students form their own personally valid and internally consistent set of beliefs that they use to guide their behavior. In shifting from a literal belief in the absoluteness of rules to a more relative view, students begin to humanize their values. Intuitive types enjoy seeing patterns and possibilities, so they may challenge their parents' beliefs and compare them with their own. Sensing types may tend to accept the rules literally until they reach a point where their parents' rules conflict with their own needs. When students arrive at behavior that is consistent with their own values, they have come to personalize their values.

We should keep in mind that development of the Judging function serves as a yardstick for choice. With development comes consistency in the intentional and appropriate use of type to the specific need or situation. Then congruence can truly mean achieving an integration of one's values with one's standards for living. Perhaps congruence and integrity are what Jung meant by the individual's striving toward wholeness or individuation. As Jung saw individuation as the discovering and refining of one's unique way of being, we need to remind students that it is the journey not the end that is important.

Kegan's Meaning-Making Theory

Robert Kegan in *The Evolving Self: Problem and Process in Human Development* (1982) acknowledged the contributions of Erikson and especially Piaget and both Kohlberg and Perry at Harvard in creating his constructivist-developmental theory of the person as an "ever progressive motion engaged in giving itself a new form" (p. 8). He described himself as a teacher, therapist, and researcher who seeks to engage others in an exploration of just how much can be understood about a person by understanding his or her meaning-making system. Meaning making is a physical activity (grasping, seeing), a social activity (requires another), and a survival activity (through doing it, we live). Although it is intrinsically cognitive, it is also affective. He described the individual's personal evolution of meaning as a balancing and rebalancing of subject and object, of self and other.

Kegan (1982) proposed a helix of evolutionary truces between the yearning to be included and the yearning to be independent. He defined the psychologies of inclusion as "the yearning to be included, to be a part of, close to, joined with, to be held, admitted, accompanied" and the psychologies favoring independence as "the yearning to be independent or autonomous, to experience one's distinctness, the self-chosen-ness of one's directions, one's individual integrity" (Kegan,

1982, p. 107). As we develop, we become temporarily embedded in one pattern until its inherent imbalance impels us to break away from it and move toward the other polarity. Each time we shift, we change how we construct meaning. In order to develop a new way to interpret our experience, we must first be able to observe the old one with greater detachment and to see a new boundary between what is "me" subject and what is "not me" object. *The Evolving Self* describes five levels of sense-making that occur throughout the life span as a helix of evolutionary structures, starting with the incorporative self, and moving to the impulsive self, to the imperial self, to the interpersonal self, to the institutional self, and lastly, to the inter-individual self. The evolution involves the growth and the loss of each successive self, although a majority of adults do not reach the institutional self or inter-individual self. In his subsequent book, *In Over Our Heads: The Mental Demands of Modern Life*, complementarity (Kegan, 1994) described five orders of consciousness. The premise is that there is a "mismatch" between the culture's complex curriculum and our mental capacity to deal with the demands of adult life. If we as educators are preparing students for life after college, then we must address this "mismatch" and shape the educational agenda for students. Kegan's (1994) extension of his 1982 "empirically grounded speculation" was reinforced through cross-sectional studies and longitudinal research using the Subject-Object Interview. It is important to understand the subject-object distinction. In essence, we *are* subject and we *have* object. Kegan (1994) offers the following definitions:

> "'Subject' refers to those elements of our knowing or organizing that we are identified with, tied to, fused with or embedded in"
>
> "'Object' refers to those elements of our knowing or organizing that we can reflect on, handle, look at, be

> responsible for, relate to each other, take control of, internalize, assimilate or otherwise set apart" (p. 32)

Kegan's (1994) five orders of consciousness are principles of organization that affect thinking, feeling, and relating to self and others. He uses the term order to indicate a dimensional quality or level rather than a strict sequence or stage: "Each successive principle transcends the last in that the new way of knowing incorporates the meaning-making abilities of the last and the individual becomes able to reflect on these abilities" (Love and Guthrie, 1999, p. 67). Each order has both intrapersonal (self-concept) and interpersonal (relationship) dimensions. Five important assumptions are involved in Kegan's theory:

1. The orders of consciousness not only refer to how one thinks, but more generally to how one constructs experience, which includes thinking, feeling, and relating to others.
2. The orders concern the organization of one's thinking, feeling, and relating rather than the content.
3. Each order of consciousness is constituted by a different subject-object relationship.
4. The orders of consciousness are related to each other, i.e., each successive principle subsumes the prior principle. The new order is higher, more complex, and more inclusive.
5. What is taken as subject and object are not fixed. What was subject at one order becomes object at the next order. Therefore, there is a developing ability to relate to and to see that in which we were formerly enmeshed.

Kegan's Orders of Consciousness

At the first order of consciousness, young children birth to age eight do not have the capacity for abstract thought, rather thinking is concrete. Meaning is made from a very egocentric, fantasy filled position. There is no realization that others have separate minds, intentions or points of view. Impulse control is not possible because children are subject to their impulses. In the second order of consciousness, individuals from late childhood to late adolescence or early adulthood make meaning by constructing "durable categories," which are lasting classifications that have properties of their own distinct from "me." In the transition from first to second order of consciousness, momentary impulses and immediate perceptions move from being the subject to being the object and the new subject becomes the durable category. Thinking becomes the relating of concrete concepts and is not yet abstract. Children and adolescents now recognize that they are individuals with their own characteristics, and this creates a self-concept. Other people become "property-bearing selves distinct from me" (Kegan, 1994, p. 23). Desires change from being primarily about impulses and wishes to being about ongoing needs and preferences. A shift from a fantasy to a reality orientation occurs and the individual begins to develop self-sufficiency and takes on a social role. The capacity to "take the role" of another and to see that others have a perspective of their own develops. Individuals at the second order are still concerned with the pursuit and satisfaction of their own interests and are not yet able to own membership in the wider community. Actions are determined in the context of one's own needs; however, how others will react to their actions is of critical importance to them. This second stage is of imperial balance because others are judged according to whether or not they "meet my needs, fulfill my wishes, pursue my interests" (Kegan, 1982, p. 91). A sense of shared reality does not exist and others have to be controlled, manipulated, or at least predicted in terms of their behavior.

The transition from second order to third order of consciousness takes place between ages twelve and twenty. Since Kegan notes that many adolescents are unable to meet the expectations the adult culture has for them, Love and Guthrie (1999) suggest that it behooves student affairs professionals to reconsider the expectations that we have for beginning college students. If thinking abstractly and being a part of a community are required, perhaps many freshmen need greater support in making this transition. Kegan hypothesized that they need to learn the "rules of the game" to meet the expectations of society and college life. Recognition of conflicts between roommates and infringements on the rights of others are often indicative of the need to move from the second to the third order of consciousness.

In the third order of consciousness, one is able to "think abstractly, identify a complex internal psychological life, orient to the welfare of a human relationship, construct values and ideals self-consciously . . . and subordinate one's own interests" (Kegan, 1994, p. 75). The major capacity of this order is the ability to experience the self in relation to a given category rather than as the category itself. Individuals start to reflect on what type of friends they are, consider what will happen to the bonds of the relationships in their lives and are able to subordinate some of their interests to shared interests. Besides being able to construct their own point of view, they come to realize that others are constructing their own view points. They move from "I am my point of view" to "I have a point of view." This cross-categorical thinking is involved in pro-social expectations, such as being a good citizen and considering how my actions will affect my relationships. Cross-categorical thinking makes it possible to experience emotions as inner psychological states; for example, instead of emotion as subject as in "I am depressed" one discovers emotion as object as in "I am experiencing depression." In this third order of consciousness, values, ideals, and broad beliefs are constructed. Instead of considering themselves concretely as honest or dishonest persons, individuals at the third order can consider themselves as persons who value honesty and strive to live up to that ideal. This interpersonal level is not intimate although a significant other is usually needed to feel complete, to define one's self, to make life meaningful. "There is no self to share with another, instead the other is required to bring the self into being. Fusion is not intimacy. If one can feel manipulated by the imperial balance, one can feel devoured by the interpersonal one" (Kegan, 1982, pp. 96–97).

Kegan asserts that the transition from the third to the fourth order of consciousness is the major transformation of adulthood. "It basically involves attaining self-authorship: the ability to 'write' one's own life" (Love and Guthrie, 1999, p. 71). At the third order, individuals make meaning through a system that occurs outside of self, in realities shared with others, which Kegan (1994) refers to as "the triumph and limit of the third order" (p. 126). They triumph by being a part of a community, but they are limited by being unable to stand apart from it and reflect and act on it. This transition from the third to fourth order is sometimes signaled by a loss of energy or even anger at being expected to live up to others' expectations and may come as a result of the loss of an important relationship. At the third order, students are their relationships (subject) rather than they have relationships (object). Before students can get to level four, the institutional balance, there must be a relatively autonomous self who can accomplish this *having*, who can take command of the personality, administering it like a kind of *psychic institution* with which it then identifies. In this transition, students begin to develop an independent selfhood with their own ideology. Going away to college "can provide a new evolutionary medium that recognizes and cultures the moves toward self-authorship and psychological autonomy which characterize the new balance" (Kegan, 1982, p. 186). Student affairs professionals and faculty can offer students support during this sometimes painful transition by recognizing them as independent individuals, by publicly acknowledging their personal achievements, by providing the opportunity to participate in a group associated with their self-authored identity, or by providing guidance regarding their entry into the work world (Love and Guthrie, 1999).

The fourth order of consciousness is labeled "cross-categorical constructing" which highlights the person's new ability to construct generalizations across abstractions (as opposed to "cross-categorical thinking" of the third order). This order involves an internally consistent organization (identity) that uses a formal system to related concrete and context-bound particulars as well as abstractions. (Kegan, 1994) states that "one-half to two-thirds of the adult population appear not to have reached the fourth order of consciousness" (p. 191). Individuals who reach the fourth order develop the capacity to stand outside of their values and form a deeper set of convictions that form a context for and regulate behavior. These values *about* values provide a way of *choosing* among values when they conflict. A person at the fourth order would be able to "subordinate a perfectly respectable ideal like 'openness and honesty' to a bigger theory or ideology that can regulate the ideal" (Kegan, 1994, pp. 89–90). The making of an ideology involves the ability "to subordinate, regulate, or indeed create (rather than be created by) our values and ideals—the ability to take values and ideals as the object rather than the subject of our knowing" (Kegan, 1994, p. 91). "This capacity is referred to as *self-authorship* and incorporates the ideas of self-regulation, identity, autonomy, and individuation, as opposed to relying on others to frame the problems or determine whether things are going acceptably well" (Love and Guthrie, 1999, p. 72). In moving beyond another person's expectations, an individual using this fourth order can create a context that involves "a relationship to the relationship" (Kegan, 1994, p. 92). Using fourth order consciousness, higher education professionals can foster a student's development as a self-directed learner, a person who acts on the world for the betterment of society rather than is acted upon, an engaged citizen with a strong sense of values and a clear identity that is internally defined. Kegan (1994) makes the point that to be effective as partners, parents, workers, and leaders, individuals must be capable of self-authorship.

The fifth order of consciousness involves an individual's identity system moving from subject to object and brings into being a new inter-individual way of organizing reality that emphasizes a refusal to see oneself or the other as a single system. Kegan (1994) indicated that "it was rare to see people moving beyond the fourth order, but when they do, it is never before their forties" (p. 352). Since "I" exist apart from my role or my performance, I can be less defensive about how others evaluate me. I can seek out information that helps me operate more smoothly, even if it is criticism. "The ability to take in feedback must parallel increased access to feelings that were formerly held hostage by an internal censor guarding a somewhat fragile ego from threatening emotions" (Chickering and Reisser, 1993, p. 30). One can observe conflicts within the self and not be so quick to suppress them: "When the self is located not in the institutional but in the coordinating of the institutional, one's own and others, the interior life gets 'freed up' (or 'broken open') within oneself and with others; this new dynamism, flow, or play results from the capacity of the new self to move back and forth between psychic systems within itself" (Kegan, 1982, p. 105). This concept goes beyond the claim of usual maturity that puts the autonomy of establishing one's identity at the peak and points to the individual being able to experience a sharing and intimacy with others. The self-as-system is seen as incomplete, as only a partial construction of all that the self is. "It is only in relationship that we are who we are . . . It is the process of creating self through relationships that is imperative" (Love and Guthrie, 1999, p. 73). "There is now a self who *directs* the organization rather than a self who was the organization. Stage five is called inter-individual because here people can truly experience interdependence as the capstone of autonomy and the foundation of community" (Chickering and Reisser, 1993, p. 28). One of the central components of this order is an orientation toward contradiction and paradox. Instead of choosing between two poles, the person orients toward the relationship between the two poles. Thus contradictions do not threaten the system or necessarily need to be reconciled. Perhaps the ability to tolerate an internal plurality of inner voices enables increasing tolerance of external conflicts.

Kegan (1982) disputed the idea that development is a linear, sequential series of accomplishments, with independence as the pinnacle.

> "The model also recognizes the equal dignity of each yearning and in this respect offers a corrective to all present developmental frameworks which unequivocally define growth in terms of differentiation, separation, increasing autonomy and lose sight of the fact that adaptation is equally about integration, attachment, inclusion. The net effect of this myopia, as femininist psychologists are now pointing out . . . has been that differentiation (the stereotypically male overemphasis in this most human ambivalence) is favored with the language of growth and development, while integration (the stereotypically female overemphasis) gets spoken of in terms of dependency and immaturity." (pp. 108–109)

Kegan observed that men have more difficulty moving from orders that favor autonomy (the imperial and institutional levels) and women have more difficulty moving from levels that favor inclusion (the interpersonal and the inter-individual levels). If there is some intrinsic bias toward separation in males and inclusion in females, then men may move through all the levels in a more differentiated way and women may move through all orders in a more integrated way.

Regardless of gender, human beings must find a balance between too much dependence and too much independence. Men and women must blend care of the self with care for others and to speak and act authentically without confusing genuine caring with placating (Chickering and Reisser, 1993). Gilligan's (1982) research indicated that this redefinition of care marks the shift from childhood to adulthood. "When the distinction between helping and pleasing frees the activity of care from the wish for approval by others, the ethic of responsibility can become a self-chosen anchor of personal integrity and strength" (Gilligan, 1982, p. 171).

Love and Guthrie (1999) translated Kegan's (1994) work from the mental demands of adult life to working with college students. They suggest student affairs practitioners can be effective in creating environments where challenge and support foster students' growth. Most of society provides multiple applications of challenge but often support is the missing ingredient. Kegan maintains that it is not necessarily a bad thing to be "in over our heads" provided that effective support is available and suggests that "sympathetic coaching" can provide the support that students need to make the transitions from lower to higher orders of consciousness. Sympathetic coaches can acknowledge students as the persons they are while they gradually outgrow an old way of knowing the world. Through coaching, student affairs professionals can nurture the seeds of the productive "undoing" of the prior order of consciousness and provide contradiction that supports the transformation of knowing the subsequent order. For example, engaging students at the second order of consciousness to become involved in service activities by appealing to their personal gains might facilitate their change in meaning-making to subordinate their own needs to the needs of others and help move them toward the third order of consciousness. Kegan identified two ways that educators fail to provide support: by neglecting to build a bridge out of and beyond the old way of thinking and by expecting students to take up immediate residence in the new world or order of consciousness. Kegan uses the term *holding environment* to indicate that environments need to hold and support rather than keep and confine. Peers provide opportunities for students in the second order of consciousness to "get inside" a view separate from their own. Peer relationships also can be the medium for the transition from third to fourth order of consciousness as individuals consider their relationship to their relationships.

Kegan's theory emphasizes the importance of creating programs that are acknowledging of students' current ways of meaning making while at the same time promoting the development of higher orders of consciousness. As educators, we must hold ourselves "to the rigors of addressing the *person* added in the experience of meaning-making, rather than the meaning that the person has made" (Kegan, 1994, p. 293). Kegan's theory provides a powerful lens through which to learn about college students and to promote them in their developmental evolution of self.

Kegan's Theory Regarding Psychological Type

Kegan (1994) addresses psychological type and the Myers-Briggs Type Indicator personality assessment tool, primarily from a work and management training perspective. He views the "type" approach to "ways of knowing" as sharing with subject-object structures two central constructivist features. First, according to Kegan, "type" posits a way in which people actively design rather than "happen upon" their realities. He gave the example that the information that Sensing types take in deals more with the specifics of what has been said or has taken place, and for Intuitive types, implications and meanings about what has transpired are far more important. Secondly, he explained that the "type" approach claims a holism and consistency across different life contexts. He gave the example of an Introverted Sensing type with Thinking (ISTJ) as presuming to approach a variety of work issues the same way as well as family life.

Kegan proposed that there are important differences between MBTI *types* and subject-object *principles* as ways of knowing. The first difference, he stated as "one's type is not presumed to change, while one's subject-object principle gradually may" (Kegan, 1994, p. 201). The second difference he cited was "that Myers-Briggs types are simply *preferences about* the way we know, rather than competencies or capacities in our knowing, as is the case with subject-object principles. The difference between types are non-normative differences of epistemological *style* not hierarchical differences of epistemological capacity" (Kegan, 1994, p. 201). He further delineated the benefit of such non-normative distinctions in the construct of types of removing inappropriate judgmental attitude, such as a "thinking" preference is not inherently better than a "feeling" preference. However, he cited the limitation of distinctions between ways of knowing that do not address lesser or greater capacity in that they may have little to do with competence. He suggested that the only curricular purpose of such stylistic distinctions is an enhanced ability to understand one's own and others' preferences and self-consciously learning to use a style other than one's own. Although knowledge of one's type may improve communication, it may have little to do with the right decisions being made.

Kegan (1994) posited that the difference between a "types" approach and a "subject-object" approach to ways of knowing may be clear theoretically but less clear when focused on real phenomenon as to whether it is better understood in terms of epistemological style or epistemological capacity. He explained that the difference between "cross-categorical" (third order of consciousness) and "systemic" (fourth order) principles and between "extraversion" and "introversion" is unlikely to be confused, however, the difference between "thinking" and "feeling" and third and fourth orders of consciousness may be less clear. He made the valid point that even though type is durable throughout one's lifetime, if the order of one's consciousness changes as it does between the twenties and the fifties for many people, then the form or complexity of that style should alter throughout one's life span. He suggested that perhaps some of the stylistic descriptions of the MBTI instrument may be constructed from a particular order of consciousness, so that style and capacity may be being confused.

Kegan (1994) implied that perhaps a jointly stylistic and structural approach might be most helpful in understanding gender differences in our ways of knowing. Some have hypothesized that cross-categorical knowing may be more akin to women's relational organizing according to Gilligan's (1982) theory while a self-authorizing, systemic knowing may appear to be more related to men's separated approach. Kegan (1994) cites as the most promising feature of the gender styles approach as "its capacity to enhance communication across non-normative differences by helping us to resist our tendencies to privilege what is familiar and judge critically what is different" (p. 204). He further explained that gender differences might be better understood if we consider them from a cultural perspective. Just as our immersion in American culture can lead to ethnocentrism from a constructivist influence, our immersion in our own gender can lead to "gender-centrism." We make attributions to the other gender that sometimes are similar to attributions that are made to persons from other cultures. In workplace settings, for example, this is like the implicit thought: "Hispanics or African-Americans, you can come into our establishment as long as you act like Whites, or women, you can come too if you act like men." If women speak from a personal, narrative style and men from a "objective," de-contextual style which is used in "winning", then women can feel disenfranchised and lose their "voice," or they can adopt male language and be perceived as inauthentic. Other stylistic differences may be attributed to gender, such as differences between process and product mentalities, or differences between inductive and deductive reasoning or even in the perception of different purposes of a business meeting. A work environment refashioned as a truly respectful, multicultural environment would be one in which neither gender feels like a "visitor" and that no one has a "home court" advantage.

Kegan (1994) sees these non-normative differences to which Gilligan (1982) referred to voices as "separate" or "connected," not as polarities or dichotomies but rather as "figure" and "ground," that is, not favoring one over the other. Although in *The Evolving Self*, Kegan (1982) explained the yearning to be included and the yearning to be autonomous, in *Over Our Heads* (1994), he unravels the confusion between style and orders of consciousness by emphasizing the difference between "deciding for oneself" (structure) with "deciding by oneself" (voice). In *Women's Ways of Knowing*, (Belenky, Clinchy, Goldberger, and Tarule, 1986) differentiated between "received knowing" and "procedural knowing." Kegan sees their approach as using both style and structure, and he calls them constructivist-developmentalists. "Subject-object theory clarifies the distinction between cross-categorical embeddedness in the values, beliefs and definition of the psychological surround, and the psychological authority to reflect upon values and beliefs (one's own and others')"

(Kegan, 1994, p. 231). We can do something about or with our reactions only if we "have" them, not if we "are" them. One of the mental demands of adult life is also on the capacity "to respect diversity" which can be met by recognizing that the actual differences we experience are differences in attributions—differences we create by viewing the other according to the rightness of our own preferences. However, the major contribution of diversity is that it assures the greatest source of growth and development that comes from the experience of difference, discrepancy and anomaly. Thus, developmental educators can help others move toward higher orders of consciousness and respond to the mental demands on them in more effective and compassionate ways.

Some Reflections on Kegan's Theory and Psychological Type

Much of what has been said in the type community seems to be echoed in Kegan's theory. We celebrate diversity and are dedicated to appreciating differences. We know that there are biases, and yet we try to overcome them both in training and in research. More has been written about gender differences perhaps being more akin to type differences, especially Thinking and Feeling differences. It might be well to think of the pull for inclusion being strongest in dominant Extraverted Feeling types while the pull for separation as being strongest in dominant Introverted Thinking types. Since more women are Feeling types and more men are Thinking types, some confusion about gender differences and type seems to arise from this perspective.

Regarding Kegan's orders of consciousness, it might be true that second order SJs may tend to remain in that order longer than NPs because Sensing types tend to stick with the facts and Intuitive types tend to look for possibilities and meaning. Brown and DeCoster

(1991) found that higher scores on Intuition predicted higher conceptual levels of increased complexity and demonstrated movement from concrete to abstract thinking. Carter (1990) explored the relationship of MBTI results and learning style as defined by Belenky et al. (1986) used by nontraditional women students. Separate Knowers more often preferred Intuition over Sensing and Perceiving over Judging, whereas Connected Knowers preferred Extraversion over Introversion and Feeling over Thinking. However, since the type community tends to be predominantly Intuitive types, we must be careful not to privilege what is known and to criticize what is unfamiliar.

It seems to this writer that Kegan has not been exposed to the literature on type development, and so he seems to be seeing type as static rather than dynamic. It appears plausible that to shift from a second order to a third order of consciousness, that both the dominant and the auxiliary must be developed. It also seems that to shift from third order to fourth order of consciousness requires some development and awareness of the tertiary and even the inferior functions. Even Jung acknowledged that midlife seems to be the time that major transitions take place, and Kegan stated that development beyond fourth order consciousness does not occur before the forties. Fitzgerald (1997) explained that for Thinking types, midlife Feeling involves discovering their "softer side" and in the process, Thinking types experience a new desire for intimacy with others and a new tendency to be emotionally touched by certain expressions of feeling. For Feeling types, she found that midlife Thinking involves discovering their tough-minded side, a sharpness of mind according to Jung, an inner push to be more objective and more separate from others and to focus on "What do I want for myself" as opposed to feeling obliged to respond to others' needs. It seems possible that fourth (self-authoring) order and the rarer fifth (inter-individual) order of consciousness might be easier for NPs because they seem to tolerate contradiction and paradox more easily than SJs. Quenk (1993) referred to being "in the grip" of the inferior and perhaps that is what Kegan means by "being" our reactions rather than "having" our reactions, the difference between subject and object or the movement from third order to fourth order. The ability "to hold the tension of the opposites," which Jung (1971) saw as a sign of individuation, may be what Kegan means when describing the fifth order of consciousness as having a relationship to our relationships.

Kegan has given us much to consider, especially about style and structural differences and how they may compliment each other. It would behoove us to learn from his theory and examine type descriptions of mature, clear, verified types rather than the earlier descriptions that Myers developed of young people's types. For example, we in the type community know that a team made of all INTJs would be a disaster because the best team is made of different types, each making his or her unique contribution. Moreover, we must acknowledge that little research has been conducted on the quality and longevity of decisions made by teams composed of different types. Kegan makes the point in discussing cultural and gender differences that a true appreciation of differences can best be understood through the contrast of differences and at the level of relationship to relationship (fifth order of consciousness). Carskadon (1994) delineated ways that faculty could enhance class discussions through assignment of students within a classroom according to their types. This approach tends to discourage students sitting with those they already know, such as Whites with Whites, thus promoting better assimilation with others from different backgrounds as Kegan has proposed.

Perhaps we need to be more open to understanding what makes for the best of each type at more advanced stages of life. A fertile area for research could employ Kegan's Subject-Object Interview with persons of recognized type and maturity. Since in higher education, adult learners constitute a larger proportion of the student body, it is possible that the complexity of knowing among adults who have led varied lives and have had experiences with other cultures may make an even greater contribution. Student affairs professionals and faculty have even more reason to encourage students and each other to seek opportunities to form relationships with others from diverse backgrounds and to reflect on those experiences. In addition, the richness of faculty-student and staff-student relationships can enhance the college experience for all concerned. Colleges and universities can provide the opportunity for students to become involved in volunteer activities and to make an impact on their environment—to employ agency and become self-authoring. In the global society that we are becoming and especially with the advent and the immediacy of the Internet for all kinds of information and relationships, we recognize that there is an even greater opportunity for individuals to raise their levels of consciousness and to improve their capacity for new ways of knowing while recognizing the contribution of knowledge about psychological type.

Ideas for the Intentional Use of Type to Promote Student Development

The following recommendations are based on knowledge of type, student development theory, and current higher education literature.

For administrators:

1. Implement studies of type within the institution. Provide feedback to faculty and student services professionals regarding student profiles according to major, career choice, instructional preferences, and other needs.
2. Provide professional development for interested faculty and

staff about psychological type and student development.

3. Provide, within the curriculum, opportunities for students to learn about type; life cycle; other cultures and student development; and the implications for learning, educational planning, and career and life choices.

For faculty:

4. Develop awareness of psychological type and how it affects learning.
5. Examine course syllabi and instructional strategies for opportunities to teach in different ways to appeal to different types as well as students from different backgrounds. Recognize that different types can learn better if they have a chance to exercise their favorite functions. They can also be challenged to grow when they are supported and coached to have opportunities to expand their repertoire of skills and experiences with others different from themselves.
6. Examine the methods of evaluation currently used, to determine if they favor certain types. Vary tests and other measures of evaluation so that different types are given a fair chance.
7. In advising students, keep in mind that each one is an individual and has unique needs. Type knowledge can help in identifying some consistent patterns of behaviors and needs.

For student services professionals:

8. Be aware of the implications of type in each of the specialty areas.
   - Career counselors can learn about type patterns in different occupations, not to steer students

whose type matches the predominant type into an occupation, but to provide full information regarding work settings and implications for type.

- Personal counselors can be most effective in helping students understand their own type, especially when they are having some difficulties in type development and in relationships with peers and others.
- Student activities staff can use type knowledge in varying programming and in helping students to use their co-curricular and volunteer activities for full development.
- Residential life staff members can use type in roommate conflict resolution, environmental planning, programming, and staff training.

9. Begin a developmental transcript approach to accompany an academic transcript that will help students recognize that they can use student activities, work, and volunteer experiences in gaining skills and knowledge for future careers and for living a more complex and fuller life.

For students:

10. Learn about psychological type, life cycle, and student development theories to understand what current and future developmental tasks you will be facing. Make intentional use of type in selecting courses, majors, and instructors and for understanding career and life choices. Do not use type as an excuse for not accomplishing your goals. Remember that you need both challenge and support to grow and develop fully.

References

Anchors, W. S. and D. C. Robinson (1992). Psychological type and the accomplishment of student development tasks. *NASPA Journal,* 29(2), 131–135.

Arnold, K. and I. C. King, (Eds.). (1997). *College student development and academic life: Psychological, intellectual, social and moral issues.* New York: Garland Publishing.

Baltes, P. B. (1987). Theoretical propositions of life span developmental psychology: On the dynamics between growth and decline. *Developmental Psychology,* 23, 611–626.

Belenky, M. F., B. M. Clinchy, N. R. Golberger, and J. M. Tarule. (1986). *Women's ways of knowing: The development of self, voice and mind.* New York: Basic Books, Inc., Publishers.

Berger, K. S. (2001). *The developing person through the life span,* 5th ed. New York: Worth Publishers.

Brown, V. L. and D. A. DeCoster, (1991). The Myers-Briggs Type Indicator as a developmental measure: Implications for student learners. *Journal of College Student Development,* 32, 378–379.

Carskadon, T. G. (1994). Student personality factors: Psychological type and the Myers-Briggs Type Indicator. In *Handbook of college teaching: Theory and applications.* K. W. Pritchard and R. M. Sawyer, (Eds.). Westport. CT: Greenwood Press.

Chickering, A. W. (1969). *Education and identity.* San Francisco: Jossey-Bass.

Chickering, A. W. and L. Reisser. (1993). *Education and identity,* 2nd ed. San Francisco, CA: Jossey-Bass.

DiTiberio, J. K. and A. L. Hammer. (1993). *Introduction to type in college.* Palo Alto, CA: Consulting Psychologists Press.

Erikson, E. H. (1959). *Identity and the life cycle.* Psychological Issues Monograph I. New York: International Universities Press.

Evans, N. J., D. S. Forney, and F. Guido-DiBrito. (1998). *Student development in college: Theory, research and practice.* San Francisco, CA: Jossey-Bass.

Fitzgerald, C. (1997). Type development and leadership development: Integrating reality and vision, mind and heart. In C. Fitzgerald and L. K. Kirby (Eds.), D*eveloping leaders: Research and applications of psychological type and leadership development* (pp. 311–335). Palo Alto, CA: Davies-Black.

Goldhaber, D. E. (2000). *Theories of human development: Integrative perspectives.* Mountain View, CA: Mayfield Publishing Company.

Jung. C. G. (1923/1971). *Psychological types.* Princeton, NJ: Princeton University Press.

———. 1933. *Modern man in search of a soul.* New York: Harcourt, Brace, Jovanovich.

Kegan, R. (1982). *The evolving self: Problems and process in human development.* Cambridge, MA: Harvard University Press.

———. (1994). *In over our heads: The mental demands of modern life.* Cambridge, MA: Harvard University Press.

Love, P. G. and V. L. Guthrie. (1999). *Understanding and applying cognitive development theory.* New Directions in Student Services, no 88. San Francisco: Jossey-Bass.

McCaulley, M. H. (1999). Lifelong type development: Insights from the letters of Isabel Briggs Myers. In *Proceedings of Mind, Body and Personality Conference* (pp. 3–17). Gainesville, FL: Center for the Applications of Psychological Type.

———. (1985). True types. *Bulletin of Psychological Type,* 8(1), 30.

McCaulley, M. H. 1981. Jung's theory of psychological types and the Myers-Briggs Type Indicator. In *Advances in personality assessment,* edited by P. McReynolds. San Francisco: Jossey-Bass.

Myers, I. B. (1998). *Introduction to type*, 8th ed. Palo Alto, CA: Consulting Psychologists Press.

Myers, I. B. with P. B. Myers. (1995). *Gifts differing: Understanding personality type*. Palo Alto, CA: Davies-Black.

Myers, I. B., M. H. McCaulley, N. L. Quenk, and A. L. Hammer (1998). *MBTI® Manual: A guide to the development and use of the Myers-Briggs Type Indicator*, 3rd ed. Palo Alto, CA: Consulting Psychologists Press.

Myers, K. D. and L. K. Kirby (1994). *Introduction to type dynamics and development: Exploring the next level of type*. Palo Alto, CA: Consulting Psychologists Press.

National Center for Educational Statistics NCES 2000. The condition of education. Retrieved from nces.ed.gov, November 20, 2000.

Pascarella, E. T. and P. T. Terrazini (1991). *How college affects students: Findings and insights from twenty years of research*. San Francisco: Jossey-Bass.

Provost, J. A. (1992). *Strategies for success: Using type to excel in high school and college*. Gainesville, FL: Center for the Applications of Psychological Type.

———. 1993. *Applications of the Myers-Briggs Type Indicator in counseling: A casebook*. Gainesville, FL: Center for the Applications of Psychological Type.

———. 1998. *Procrastination: Using psychological type concepts to help students*. Gainesville, FL: Center for the Applications of Psychological Type.

Quenk, N. L. (1993). *Beside ourselves: Our hidden personality in everyday life*. Palo Alto, CA: Davies-Black.

———. (1996). *In the grip: Our hidden personality*. Palo Alto, CA: Consulting Psychologist Press.

———. (1984). The dynamics of type development. *MBTI News* 7(1), 1, 17.

———. (1985a). Conflicts in function development. *MBTI News* 7(2), 6–7.

———. (1985b). Directionality of the auxiliary function. *Bulletin of Psychological Type,* 8(1), 27–29.

Rogers, C. R. (1961). *On becoming a person.* Boston: Houghton Mifflin.

Schlossberg, N. K., A. Q. Lynch, and A. W. Chickering (1989). *Improving higher education environments for adults: Responsive programs and services from entry to departure.* San Francisco: Jossey-Bass.

Shiflett, S. C. (1989). Validity evidence for the Myers-Briggs Type Indicator as a measure of hemispheric dominance. *Educational and Psychological Measurement,* 493, 741–745.

Von Franz, M. L. and J. Hillman. (1979). *Jung's typology.* Irving, TX: Spring Publishers.

Weathersby, R. P. and J. M. Tarule (1980) *Adult development: Implications for higher education.* AAHE-ERIC Higher Education Research Report, no 4. Washington, DC: American Association for Higher Education.

Wilson, M. A. and M. L. Languis (1989). Differences in brain activity patterns between introverted and extraverted adults. *Journal of Psychological Type* 18: 14–23.

CHAPTER 2

Leadership Styles and Educational Challenges

FAITH GABELNICK

During the latter part of the twentieth century, books on leadership have proliferated. We realize that the skills and competencies and psychological maturity needed to be effective leaders are increasing, as is the complexity of issues a leader must face. Educational institutions that operate in one of the most competitive industries of our society are particularly challenged. Presidents or chancellors of public institutions have relatively short terms of office (three to five years), while private college leadership extends to an average of seven years. Yet if one talks with presidents, many say that it takes them several years to begin to understand and grapple with the issues. One president who is in his second presidency at a prominent university once said to me, "In my first presidency, it took me five years even to know what questions to ask."

Inevitably, the questions that presidents and other academic leaders must ask concern the management of the organization and the management of the people in the organization. In *Leading People* (1996), Robert Rosen writes:

> But above all, leaders must cultivate healthy adult-adult relationships. Why is this so critical? Because in our fast-

> paced, complex, highly technical world, people need to work together and share a common vision to produce high quality work. Their relationships, therefore, are crucial. Indeed, these relationships are the glue that holds the enterprise together, connecting its strategy, structure, systems and technology. The new glue is shared values, a common purpose, clear responsibilities, and the relationships between the adults who make up (indeed, who *are*) the organization. (pp. 17–18)

The Myers Briggs Type Indicator® personality assessment instrument is extraordinarily useful in assisting leaders because it allows members of an organization to encounter and create a work culture that is respectful, compassionate, and productive. Too often leaders are judged only by outcomes, data that seem to measure the competence of both the organization and the leadership of that organization—how big is the endowment; what are the national rankings of the institution; how many books are there in the library; what is the admission rate, the retention rate, the graduation rate? The nineteenth century assumption that growth and progress have an intrinsic positive value again drives institutions and the leadership of those institutions to strive constantly to improve, to better one's market share, to launch increasingly bigger fund-raising campaigns. And what may be forgotten is why the educational enterprise exists: to educate students to be thoughtful, engaged citizens and leaders for the next generation.

This chapter focuses on three issues that confront leaders: strategic planning, crisis management, and team building. Each of these areas involves the entire community and poses a challenge for any leader or team of leaders. And depending on the type characteristics, these issues look quite different. The comments and observations in this chapter are based on a number of conversations with academic leaders who chose to remain anonymous but who have used the MBTI® instrument in a variety of ways on their campuses. These observations are offered in a spirit of collaborative inquiry, exploration, and adaptation. Ronald Heifetz's recent book, *Leadership without Easy Answers* (1994), notes that effective leaders must be adaptive.

> If we define problems by the disparity between values and circumstances, then an adaptive challenge is a particular kind of problem where the gap cannot be closed by the application of current technical know-how or routine behavior. To make progress, not only must invention and action change circumstances to align reality with values, but the values themselves may also have to change. Leadership will consist not only of answers or assured visions but also of taking action to clarify values. It asks questions like: What are we missing here? Are there values of competing groups that we suppress rather than apply to our understanding of the problem at hand? Are there shared values that might enable us to engage competing views? Ongoing adaptive capacity requires a rich and evolving mix of values to inform a society's process of reality testing. It requires leadership to fire and contain the forces of invention and change, and to extract the next step. (p. 35)

Using the MBTI® instrument, one can be supportive as an adaptive leader, challenging the organization to reflect on its practices, to understand the messages it sends out to a diverse community and to clarify continuously the assumptions upon which the organization operates. But as Heifetz reminds us, "answers" are not the goal nor are solutions "easy" to achieve.

Strategic Planning. Ask academic leaders how they orchestrate strategic planning, and you will have a pretty clear indicator of their MBTI types. ESTJ/ENTJ leaders set up numerous task forces, intensely shape objectives, create benchmark charts and accountability streams. A newsletter updating the campus about the process and progress of the dozen or more task forces that are established to accomplish this task often accompanies the process. The strategic planning process becomes the work of the campus for at least a year, and the document that results becomes a specific guideline for annual planning. One ENTJ president carried his strategic plan and the annual initiatives and objectives with him wherever he went. He has said that the plan was his "Bible," and indeed the documents were bound in book form and had a textual as well as strategic presence on campus. Each year he reported to the campus on the progress of the plan. The plan was redone each five years. This president is so committed to strategic planning almost as a work of art that he is currently writing a book on how strategic plans help to tell the story of an institution. Being an ENTJ, he broadened the strategic exercise to encompass the symbolic and practical leadership challenges of his presidency. He used the occasion of strategic planning as the way to address the theory and practice of university leadership.

When NF leaders conduct strategic planning, the campus is invited to reflect at length on its core values, its relations with the various departments, and the broad goals the institution hopes to achieve. These NF leaders will spend more time at the beginning of this process shaping the general ambience or work culture under which the planning will take place and will place great emphasis on who leads what task forces and how well the task forces are working. The goals and even the structure of the document may not vary too much from the NT document except in one important dimension: length. The NF leadership, mindful of being highly collaborative, will probably produce a lengthy document in which most of the voices of the academic community will find representation. The document may have a longer narrative style and paradoxically may have more details than a document produced by an STJ or NTJ. Informal conversations with NF leaders who produce strategic documents reveal a high concern with "inclusiveness." That inclusiveness is focused not only on the people who are to be involved in the planning but also on the issues brought to the table to be addressed. As an NT leader who has worked with NF administrators, I have observed that one of the most challenging aspects of strategic planning is being able to prioritize and therefore to select from a full universe of options and craft several important initiatives. The NF leader is importantly and appropriately concerned with how the strategic plan will reflect the values of the organization. From the NF perspective, the goal of the plan is to deliver services and programs that benefit students and that are supportive to the members of the community. While the NTJ or STJ planner is concerned with institutional integrity from the perspective of efficiency, standards and accountability, and structural coherence, the NF planner is more concerned with institutional integrity from the perspective of alignment with core values and with including all community perspectives on any one issue.

Thus, the concept of inclusiveness drives the discussions in many different directions and often uncovers important yet hidden dynamics that may affect the culture of the institution. The issue of diversity is such an example. STJs and NTJs tend to prefer to address the issue of diversity through demographic or enrollment data and through programs targeted at certain populations; in contrast, the NF leader will ask how we are creating a learning environment that will be inviting to people from different cultures and races; how we will create supportive programs to sustain and deepen their engagement with the university; and how we will, with integrity, be able to say that we provide a safe learning environment for students of different backgrounds. As these discussions occur, the STJ and NTJ may drive towards "solutions" that the NF feels are not addressing the underlying issues. This is when conflicts occur during the planning process. The value of the MBTI instrument in this, and similar planning exercises, is that people can address a complex issue such as diversity in a multidimensional way. Engaging different types in discussing vital institutional challenges provides a way of working more sensitively and ultimately more intimately with one another. The role of the leader, regardless of type preference, is to enable these apparently conflicting modalities to surface and to act as a kind of type ambassador to the different "camps" on a university campus.

The scrutiny about the document and the strategic planning process thus mirror the type preferences of the leadership. STJ/NTJ scrutiny will focus on the structure and shape of the document; the connective logic of the strategic goals and; especially with STJs, the financial reality of the plan. NF scrutiny will focus on the values issues of the campus and how the goals drive the institution to a deeper commitment to and enacting of those values. Involvement of college boards, which usually have large numbers of STJs as trustees, can be a challenge to an NF/NT dominated campus. Trustees tend to scrutinize the financial modeling of a strategic plan more fully than any other aspect, and they want to hear reports about the progress of the plan in terms of numerical benchmarks. An NF leader reporting to an STJ-dominated board of trustees must prepare materials that are succinct, data-driven or derived, and directly stated. On our campus, an INFJ chief financial officer involved in preparing such a financial document for the board of trustees was greatly motivated by a desire to communicate and to reassure the board that the plan was viable financially. He discovered that the STJ board finance committee was less concerned with being reassured about the document and was much more attentive to the style and brevity of presentation and the worst case and best case scenarios that the planners could devise. The discussions at the finance committee continued for several months while the trustees worked with the CFO to prepare these several scenarios and to design a document that looked like the documents they reviewed in their work places. While the campus may put more stock in the language of a planning document, trustees will pay more attention to the bottom line of all that planning. Their tolerance for prolonged discussion on any issue is low, and from their perspective, the shorter the document the more easily they will be able to monitor its progress. This is not to say that trustees are overwhelmingly dispassionate or cynical about the planning process, but it is clear that trustees, like any other college constituency, also bring their type preferences to bear on strategic planning. Campus leaders need to understand the importance of strategic communications that are delivered in the style of the majority of listeners, in this case, trustees.

Crisis Management. Defining what constitutes a crisis and therefore what is necessary to manage a crisis is shaped by type preference. Many people enjoy crisis management: witness those who work in crisis-oriented occupations like firefighters, police officers, or emergency room nurses and doctors. Individuals who enjoy spontaneity, who learn as they are encountering a situation such as SPs or NPs will probably function well in a situation that requires quick reaction and the assimilation of a variety of stimuli and information. On the other hand, people whose roles are to manage crises or prevent crises on college campuses are apt to be ISTJs or ISTPs and work in the campus security office. Student affairs personnel, who tend to be NFs, also encounter and manage crises and teach students how to mediate conflict and how to deal with potential crises such as drug and alcohol abuse, eating disorders, or academic failure. NTs and STJs tend to manage crises by analysis and policy-making and sometimes forget that people create and resolve crises.

My own observation of crisis-oriented activity is that under these circumstances, the shadow preference becomes mobilized. Thus while individuals are trying to manage stressful circumstances, they regress to a less-developed function and handicap their decision making to some degree. For example, a common situation on college campuses is alcohol abuse. Depending on the type preferences of the leadership, the institution may define the situation as severe and may respond with a more stringent enforcement of a policy. On the other hand, an institution may see alcohol abuse or the potential of alcohol abuse as a teaching moment and set up ways to work with the students, the residence life staff and local enforcement officers to provide educational, legal, and emotional support to students. Or the institution may use both kinds (or other kinds) of approaches. However, if a true crisis develops where students are arrested for alcohol abuse or a student dies through the results of alcohol, a full, public crisis may ensue, which will require the collaborative efforts of public relations, student life, and the president's office. This is when shadow preferences tend to become mobilized, and effective leadership is necessary to sort out recommendations for action that will help to address the issue and not to exacerbate it. For example, an NF whose shadow is Thinking may find him or herself being too legalistic, even too rigid while in the midst of a crisis. Suddenly, an otherwise affable and collaborative NF will seem punishing and uncompromising while a normally calm NT will become visibly emotional and even immobilized.

Further challenges for leaders occur during everyday experiences on university campuses because certain type preferences tend to be more alert to impending disaster. SJs, whose shadow is Intuition, tend to see a potential crisis in most social or political events, and they are wary of "things that may go wrong." This watchfulness makes them excellent security officers but also can create the climate of a crisis before it actually happens. One ISTJ security officer would send reports to a president about any theft, however minor, with the warning that more might occur and that the university might lose great amounts of money as the thefts increased; he saw any skate-boarders as posing potential liability law suits against the university if they were to fall or skate into a student or employee of the university; he watched the trees swaying in a storm as potentially lethal occurrences if they were to fall on innocent passers-by. The officer was sincere in his attention to potential liability for the university but overzealous and catastrophic in his observations. Faculty, who are predominantly NTs, also find themselves in a crisis or catastrophic mode when they default to their shadow of Sensing or Feeling. Many faculty develop a "watch-dog" mentality with the administration, looking for possible budget crises or other indicators of doom and gloom. They become detailed inquirers, asking for more specifics than can be useful to address a certain issue, or they become angry and highly distressed because of an administration policy or lack of perceived administrative support. Similarly, administrators default to shadow politics by becoming hypervigilant and defensive when they perceive that they are being attacked by students, faculty, or the public. These "worst practices" paradoxically occur when people's "best practices" are being called on, and crises are often created or deepened through the misunderstandings and miscommunications that arise when shadow preferences hold sway.

Crises are also a time when organizations can come together. During the first semester of my first year at Pacific University, the campus was hit by a storm with very high winds. The storm was predicted to reach its most powerful on the last day of final examinations. I, as an INTJ in crisis, wanted to send the students home and let them return in January to finish their examinations. The dean of students, an INFP, wanted to make sure that the students were not outside where trees could fall on them. The dean of arts and sciences, an ENTJ, wanted the examinations to be completed and the semester's end to be achieved on schedule; and the public information director, an INTP, wanted to make sure that information would be available on the radio and elsewhere so that parents could be informed about what was happening. When I asked about our crisis management policy, I discovered that we did not have one; and when I asked about emergency lighting, I discovered that the lighting would last only one hour in the main administration building. This chaotic day resulted in many benefits and insights. We met as a crisis management team and made decisions every three hours. These were communicated to the faculty and students, on campus and on the radio. We learned where we were weak in our communications links and in our general emergency plans and we developed an emergency manual with a series of procedures and a system for personnel to be mobilized quickly. We supported the faculty and students who wanted to remain to complete their exams, and we provided instructions about departures from campus that would help to safeguard the travelers. And we were lucky: as the electricity went off in one academic building, students were moved to the library. Suddenly a very large tree blew over toward the library. Its fall was broken by a 200 year old oak, and neither students nor library and its personnel were injured. After the storm, the SPs and SJs methodically cut down the trees for firewood; the NFs suggested that some of the wood be given to the needy; and the NT's analyzed the ages of the trees and began to think about better root management for the other older trees. The Extraverts told the story of the storm again and again, and the Introverts pulled back to reflect on all that had transpired in less than twenty-four hours.

When crises do occur, the MBTI instrument can be invaluable to leaders who understand how people perceive events and can begin to sort out the complex bases for the recommendations and actions that come forth. Like any other important occurrence in an organization, a crisis can become the basis for more effective communication, for better procedures, and for learning about what matters most for the institution. And leaders who know their types and are familiar with the MBTI instrument can be engaged in crisis management discussions through type so that problems and possible solutions can and do emerge in unexpected ways.

Team Building. When we think about the MBTI instrument and leadership challenges, we usually think about team building. The Indicator has been used for decades in almost any organizational setting to increase individuals' awareness of and empathy for differences. When we think about team building on college campuses, we can look at several ways in which type is useful: in classes, with faculty, with administration, with boards of trustees. Allowing these groups to use and discover the possibilities for enhanced work together supports more collaborative leadership and develops a more vigorous community.

Many years ago a faculty member at a large research institution (Gabelnick and Pearson, 1985) complained that students were dropping out of her lecture class. As an INFP, she had carefully organized her large class of 180 students into small study groups that were facilitated by teaching assistants, but she received complaints from the small group environment also. As an INFP, she saw herself as a collegial and engaged teacher and was at a loss as to why her students seemed disaffected. We administered the MBTI instrument to the class and to the teaching assistants and discovered that of the 180 students less than 10 were INFPs and that most of the teaching assistants were NFPs. The syllabus used phrases such as "describe your journey," "write about your feelings," or "generate a narrative about;" and the process in the small study groups supported this NF approach. Team building here resulted in creating a more diversified teaching assistant team and a different way for the instructor to "team" with her class. She changed the language of her syllabus, reviewed the readings she offered and the types of questions she asked them to write about. She also realized that she was teaching from her type and, while that was certainly a natural approach, she needed to be mindful of her students' diverse learning preferences and challenge herself to construct a more diversified approach.

Team building among departmental faculties can also enhance ways of working with each other and therefore develop a better faculty "team." One of the most crucial elements of an educational institution is the academic department, and one of the most difficult roles is that of department chair. We know from extensive use of the MBTI instrument on college campuses that the majority of faculty, especially in arts and sciences, are NTs—and predominantly among that group, INTPs and INTJs. While these types are excellent analysts and critics, they are not particularly skilled at building and sustaining communities unless there are demonstrated logical reasons for the process. Department chairs that are faculty members themselves enter this administrative role and discover that their otherwise rational colleagues become demanding, unreasonable members of a group that may have a variety of feelings about its power and position in its college. The department chair discovers that he or she may be responsible for certain resource allocations, tenure letters, sexual harassment issues, as well as course allocations and work load assignments. These issues, unlike academic discussions about how well a course is going, or what texts to use, raise competition and envy. A fatherly colleague may transform into a stern and critically presumptuous departmental member who expects that certain courses will be offered on his schedule. A peer colleague with whom you have had lunch for the past several years now expects that friendship to yield results in terms of excellent teaching recommendations. Department chairs report through the American Council on Education's Workshop for Department Chairs that stress is highest among this group of faculty who receive very little preparation for the role and who may suffer through it for the appointed period and never again seek another administrative role.

If university administrators provide consultation and training for department chairs, then the MBTI instrument can be extraordinarily helpful in reducing stress and anxiety and even burnout. Successful chairs intuitively and then more explicitly identify issues through departmental dialogue, hold regular meetings of their faculty, and communicate larger institutional issues to the department in such a way as to connect the department with these issues. The dean of the college or school can bring together these department chairs to share common concerns, provide technical information about potential legal issues, and facilitate open expression of how it feels to be in this role. Since many of the players in this drama are Introverts and Intuitive Thinking types, these kinds of group discussions are not greeted enthusiastically. However, as a culture of dialogue is established and some of the chairs, which will inevitably be NFs, begin to model a different way of expressing the work role, more effective department leadership can occur.

When faculty are knowledgeable about the Indicator, one of the first observations they make is that their students are very different from them and seem to want to learn in different ways. As was noted above, this is a common occurrence. However, what faculty do not readily admit is that their colleagues also learn in different ways. When faculty learn about the MBTI instrument, one of the first exclamations is directed toward a certain faculty colleague who sits on a committee with others and has always seemed like the "odd one out." Faculty will say, "Well, that explains Joe's behavior! I always thought he was weird." When everyone has had a good chuckle about Joe and his quirks, Joe usually says something such as, "I always knew I was special!" Repeatedly, I have observed this process. People begin to look at each other (literally and figuratively) in modified ways. The discovery of difference without judgment lightens what may have been a long history of grumpiness and even social ostracism. Discovering the different types paradoxically serves as a way to include those who have been excluded and to use the special perspective of the "different" one. In one group, for example, a person discovered that he was the only Extrovert. The group had used this person to be the spokesperson and yet had accumulated a great deal of resentment towards what they perceived as the dominance. When the Indicator was administered and people talked about their types, an opportunity arose for each person to speak about being crowded out and not being afforded enough time to reflect and then to speak. The Extravert learned the value of holding back and allowing colleagues to share the verbal space and thereafter felt less tired and burdened.

When using the MBTI instrument for team building, it is important for the team leader to remember that she, too, leads from her type. She may set up and conduct meetings in a way that is acceptable to some and possibly infuriating to others. Discussions that seem to analyze an issue and set deadlines for the task completion can be experienced by others as cold and too focused on results rather than process. On the other hand, process-oriented leaders often annoy results-oriented members who may experience them as wasting a lot of time discussing endlessly an issue and never making a decision. The leader's role is to recognize recommendations for action or reflection in terms of type and to design meetings that allow different types to be and feel successful. Using type explicitly when meetings are arranged and then commenting or encouraging other team members to comment on their ideas and recommendations from the perspective of type also encourages the team to examine an issue from a variety of perspectives. As an INTJ surrounded by other NTs, I rely a great deal on the NF administrators to balance all of the intense analysis of an issue with some perspective on how the decision would be experienced by members of the community. When rehearsing for a presentation to the community, I am often advised on how to incorporate and verbalize perspectives that will be received and understood by a variety of constituents. This use of type creates a more inclusive stance and supports the leader's listening to and valuing different perspectives.

An area of team building that is crucial in academic leadership is building an effective board of trustees. The chair of the board and the president usually represent two different economic industries, business and education. In industry, quantitative results are indicators of success, and the pace of decision making is light years ahead of academia. Trustees usually work in an STJ environment, and, when they serve on boards, they bring this style to bear on issues at hand. From this perspective, academia is more process oriented and business more outcomes oriented. Still, there are many differences in type among trustees. One group of trustees held a retreat and allowed the Thinking types to carry the day on an issue. When the group as a whole examined it, several said, "This is not what we believe in. We want to discuss the issue further." What they had discovered was that their recommendations were too one-sided and did not include the Feeling aspects of the project. They remembered that they were there to encourage and support the education of students not to run a for-profit company.

Like campus committees, board committees often attract certain types: a finance committee attracts STJs and some NTJs, most of whom are Introverts; while a student life committee tends to attract

NFs and SFs. A campus property committee also attracts those who prefer the concrete to the abstract, while an educational policy committee is usually dominated by NTs. When the full board comes together, the reports that follow mirror these types. The challenge for the board chair and the president is to assist in the presentation of information and to act as a translator. Trustees may discount the information because of the style of the presentation of the information. This is a difficult situation for campus officials who may be encouraged to shorten and focus their presentation to a few phrases and sentences when they are intent on describing the full extent of the issue and engaging the board in a thorough discussion. On the other hand, trustees need to be encouraged not to take a bottom-line only view of the university and to appreciate and investigate some issues more thoroughly. This investigation can encourage a more engaged perspective and actually develop better connections among the trustees and with the campus.

The president's role at trustee meetings or campus events can be strengthened through a knowledge and application of type. Presidents who are knowledgeable about the MBTI instrument have an additional tool to use in negotiation, decision making, fund-raising, and strategic planning. In a group of presidents, it is easy to identify the Extraverted Feeling types, the Introverted Thinking types or those with a dominant preference for Intuition. One president, an ENFP, focuses his presidency on community building and diversity. He is everywhere on campus, sometimes creating trouble for himself but intent on building a multicultural environment and convincing others that this is the "right thing to do." Another president, an ENTJ, wants to raise the status of her institution: she raises money, is focused on the endowment, and builds business connections. In a room full of presidents, conversation flows from endowments, to student enrollments, to retention, to community initiatives, corporate partnerships, and fund-raising. One NF president says that he always takes students with him on major fund-raising trips so that they can meet with donors. Another simply talks about the big gift the institution has just received. Every president is bragging and trying to demonstrate how effective she or he is, and not surprisingly the benchmarks for that success vary widely and reflect to some degree the type of the president.

Concluding Reflections

Leadership in the twenty-first century demands an extraordinary level of flexibility, insight, and adaptiveness. Organizations move quickly and have enormous expectations of those who step forward in leadership positions. Academic institutions mirror most other organizations in their desire to succeed, to prosper and to work collaboratively. The MBTI instrument assists leaders in a variety of ways by building a diverse perspective on everyday problems.

As it enables an increase in empathy, in cooperation and tolerance for difference, the Indicator also facilitates communication about difficult issues. As Rosen notes in his book, *Leading People*, the most valuable aspect of any organization is its workforce and its customers. For educational institutions, that translates to faculty, staff, and students. Teachers who are sensitive to their students' different ways of perceiving the world and making decisions about that world can shape assignments that offer a variety of challenges and open paths of inquiry that students may not immediately select. This type of complex pedagogy will truly prepare students for the world beyond the classroom.

Administrators who understand and apply the MBTI instrument in their work arenas will be more adept and sensitive to their colleagues and will be able to enlist others in solving problems and creating better work environments. Presidents and board chairs will find ways to convey the issues of the campus to trustees who may not have the experience and predisposition to become overly familiar with each issue of the school. In each of these areas, the possibilities for better communication and a more effective institution abound.

In all, the MBTI instrument is a vehicle for hope and connection. Educational institutions are extremely difficult to lead and to change, but leaders who believe that institutional transformation must occur in order for the enterprise to survive need effective ways to examine, discuss and decide about issues. They need to have a perspective that is inclusive and respectful of difference. They need to know themselves and their vulnerabilities. The Indicator is an exceptional tool to make an impossible job a little more manageable.

References

Gabelnick, F. and C. Pearson (1985). Finding their voices. *Feminist Teacher*, 1 (3).

Heifetz, R. (1994). *Leadership without easy answers.* Cambridge, MA: Harvard University Press.

Rosen, R. (1996). *Leading people.* NY: Viking.

CHAPTER 3

Campus Retention: The MBTI® Instrument in Institutional Self-Studies

DAVID H. KALSBEEK

There is a clear and valuable role for the Myers-Briggs Type Indicator® personality assessment tool in campus retention efforts. This chapter illustrates one process for laying the foundation for effective retention strategies, a process that uses the MBTI® instrument as a central construct. First, one conceptual model of student attrition is presented and some implications of that model are discussed. Second, the manner in which the MBTI instrument can be integrated in this model through institutional research and analysis is discussed. Effective management of campus MBTI information is presented as a key first step in campus retention awareness and one successful approach to this task is used to illustrate the process.

A Conceptual Model for Understanding Student Attrition

Though retention and attrition are very complex issues with many intervening variables and factors, a theoretical framework or model offers a common ground for discussions, research, and action. In a summary of existing retention models, Bean (1982) explains:

> A model of student attrition is a representation of the factors presumed to influence decisions to drop out of an institution. The model identifies the interrelationships among the various factors and the relationships between these factors and the dropout decision. The use of any model is based on certain assumptions about what is important in a dropout decision at a particular institution. (p. 18)

As Pascarella suggests in the introduction to the same volume (Pascarella, 1982, p. 8), "Such models can be particularly useful to institutional researchers and others studying the attrition phenomenon, in that the models provide a parsimonious guide to the selection of variables and to their relationships in student persistence/withdrawal behavior."

One such model of student attrition that has been widely cited and tested is that of Tinto (1975). Tinto suggests that when educators begin the task of making sense of retention or attrition patterns at their institution, they focus on meaningful background characteristics of the students matriculating at the institution. Tinto goes on to suggest that the rich diversity of student background characteristics shapes specific commitments students bring to campus; their commitments to educational objectives and to their chosen college or university play a prominent role in the Tinto model.

From their first contact with the institution, students experience the complexity of the college or university environment. Throughout their ongoing encounters with that environment, students continually gauge the degree to which the institution fits with their preconceptions, expectations, preferences, needs, values, or their abilities to cope. Tinto suggests that the critical factor in campus retention is the degree of congruence between the needs, interests, abilities, expectations, and commitments of the students and the academic and social systems of the institution with all of the demands, rewards, constraints, and challenges therein. Every student inevitably experiences some degree of integration or "fit" with the environment, both academically and socially. The model suggests that it is this degree of integration experienced by each individual student that leads to a reappraisal of their initial commitment to an educational degree and to a specific institution, which, in turn, is manifested in the student persisting or withdrawing from the institution.

Implications

The Tinto model has several clear implications for those interested in mobilizing campus retention efforts, and particularly retention research. First, if dropout is viewed as a process as the Tinto model suggests, then retention must be viewed as an outcome and not a goal in and of itself. The appropriate focus of retention efforts is the nature of the interaction of the individual student with the total campus environment. The greater the degree of academic and social integration experienced by the student, the greater the likelihood of his/her continued enrollment. By targeting efforts to maximize the fit students experience with the campus climate, the Tinto model suggests that retention may take care of itself. To view retention statistics (such as freshman dropout rates or five-year graduation rates) as the goal rather than a proxy measure of the quality of students' experiences may launch enrollment management strategies on the wrong foot.

A second clear implication of viewing dropout as a process is that retention is a total campus responsibility. Since the focus of retention efforts is the quality of each student's academic and social experience and the fit students experience with the institution, then everyone who works, teaches, and studies at an institution has a role in that retention effort. The campus security officer, the financial aid secretary, the server in the cafeteria, the chemistry department chairperson, and the dean of students all have the opportunity (and the responsibility) to affect the student's experience at the institution. The responsibility for retention cannot and does not rest with the student affairs staff or with some retention committee. It is a collective challenge to the total college or university community.

A third implication of viewing dropout as the process Tinto suggests is that any attempt to gather useful information about students' enrollment patterns must consider a broad array of student characteristics, not the least of which are their commitments as discussed above. Attrition researchers often investigate the relationship between very traditional but limited student factors such as aptitude measures, race, hometown, or type of high school and persistence patterns. Such research uses rather static student characteristics without attending to those characteristics that may have a dynamic role in the student's interactions and experiences with the campus climate. Retention research must involve much more complex and encompassing student characteristics.

A final implication closely follows the previous one: accepting dropout as a process suggests that meaningful retention research must be longitudinal in nature. Information must be gathered over time about the ongoing nature of the student experience, attempting to monitor the types of integration certain types of students achieve in certain types of academic and social endeavors. To assume that a one-time snapshot of a student population serves to enlighten an institution as to its retention phenomenon may reflect more of an "event perspective" than a "process perspective." The "event perspective" is exemplified in so-called autopsy studies which survey withdrawing students at the moment of their withdrawal from the institution. The Tinto model would suggest that such research is minimally useful and Terenzini (1982) also suggests that such studies do little to explain enrollment phenomena.

The MBTI and the Tinto Model

There is a clear and valuable role for the MBTI instrument in a retention effort based on the Tinto conceptual model. To understand the retention phenomenon at any one institution, it is necessary to understand the way students experience the campus climate in all of its many facets and the way students interact with the many social and academic challenges they inevitably face in their collegiate experience. If, as Tinto suggests, the critical factor in retention is the degree of congruence experienced by individual students with the academic and social dimensions of the campus climate, then it seems imperative to understand the personal processes at work as students negotiate the academic and social system.

All that we know about personality type from both the theory and the existing research suggests that the MBTI instrument can be one effective tool in making sense of that interaction. We know that the MBTI instrument presents us with important information about students' natural interests, learning styles, commitments and values, and work habits. Therefore, it seems that the MBTI tool, in one single profile, may offer a wealth of useful insights regarding students' academic and social integration with specific campus climates. Type theory suggests that student preferences will determine to a large extent the degree of integration they will experience. Such preferences may be directly related to the processes students use as they appraise and reappraise their commitments to educational objectives and the institution.

Not only is the MBTI instrument useful in describing individual students and understanding the nature of their experience, but it also allows educators to describe the prevailing climates of certain social and academic environments. A number of person-environment theorists (Walsh ,1973) suggest that it is the prevailing or dominant characteristics of a group that, in effect, determine the essential nature of the environment. If we can describe a group of students (nursing majors, floor residents, members of some campus organization, etc.) using type dimensions, we can go a long way toward understanding the experience of students interacting with that group. Understanding the type profile of the faculty in a department may describe in part the academic challenges students in that department may face and the degree of integration or fit they may experience in that department. In short, type profiles offer added insight to both sides of the interaction equation; the MBTI instrument can effectively describe both the individual student and dimensions of the environment encountered by that student.

The remainder of this chapter presents information related to the role of the MBTI tool in institutional retention research and actual retention efforts. Much of this chapter describes one particular research project that had as its specific objective the use of the MBTI instrument in understanding the enrollment patterns at one university. The research endeavor entitled TRAILS (Tracking Retention and Academic Integration by Learning Style) was guided by the Tinto model and provided information that fit with the assumptions and premises of the model (Kalsbeek, 1986).

The TRAILS Project

The major goals and objectives of the TRAILS project were:

- to streamline the use of the MBTI instrument

by the university community by effectively managing MBTI data with appropriate information technologies;

- to provide educators necessary institutional data on how student characteristics are related to choice of major, academic "aptitude," academic performance in specific curricular areas, and attrition;
- to provide the information infrastructure for specific programs using type concepts in improving the quality of the academic and social experience of students at the university;
- to provide the research base needed to mobilize the university community in retention strategies;
- to allow student development professionals a mechanism for building bridges with academic colleagues in the service of students; and
- to add to the existing knowledge in the field of how type is related to student performance and persistence in higher education.

Each fall semester through the 1980s, a large proportion of the entering freshman class at Saint Louis University completed the Myers-Briggs Type Indicator instrument. The MBTI data for each student were then merged with other institutional information such as ACT/SAT scores, high school grade point average, demographic factors like sex and race, etc. Each subsequent academic term, academic data such as major and GPA were entered in the database for each student. By maintaining such records in a computerized database, researchers can readily answer questions such as: What types of students tend to gravitate to certain majors? How well do different types of students do in certain schools? Do some types of learners do better early in their academic work than in subsequent studies? What types drop out at a greater rate than others?

Some preliminary findings of the TRAILS research will next be discussed to illustrate one process for using the Myers-Briggs Type Indicator instrument in retention research.

Population Descriptions

When using the Tinto model in addressing institutional retention, one must be able to describe both the students and the environments students encounter at an institution. If we use the MBTI instrument to do that, we need to investigate the type distributions of distinct groups of students, recognizing that this distribution tells us much about that climate or environment. Population description becomes the necessary first step.

Fortunately, there is an ever-increasing accumulation of research with the MBTI tool that describes specific populations. Generally such research is designed to investigate hypotheses about the role of MBTI preferences in choice of academic major, occupation or career, and so on. For example, Myers (1980) presents some research findings using type tables to describe various academic populations. She presents MBTI profiles for engineering students, liberal arts students, finance and commerce students, counselor education students, etc. Likewise, in a major study of type and medical professions, McCaulley (1978) presents numerous type tables for students in a wide variety of medical-related academic pursuits. The point of such research is that different types of students are disproportionately represented in certain academic disciplines. When one considers any academic major at an institution as an academic and social environment with its own unique interpersonal dimensions, rewards, constraints, challenges, and supports, then the type profile of the students (as well as the faculty) is vitally important environmental information.

Type and Academic Majors

At the institutional level, one needs to identify the type variables that distinguish specific schools or majors in order to make sense of the student-environment interaction that is so basic to Tinto's model. Three type tables from the TRAILS data at Saint Louis University are presented here (Tables 3.1–3.3); these tables illustrate the predominant characteristics of several individual colleges and majors at the university. It is important to note that though all sixteen types are represented in each college, the self-selection ratio (SSR) shows clearly that certain types are disproportionately represented in certain academic environments. For those unfamiliar with interpreting the type table and the SSR, see the *MBTI® Manual* (Myers, McCaulley, Quenk, and Hammer, 1998).

What the TRAILS data clearly illustrate is that at Saint Louis University the ST types were most overrepresented in business majors, the Sensing types were most overrepresented in the nursing school, and the NT types were most overrepresented in the College of Arts and Sciences. These differences are significant and serve to make one key point: while it is widely acknowledged that differences in certain student characteristics are often manifested in academic and career interests, the MBTI instrument is an effective tool for portraying and understanding those differences. As indicated previously, this is the necessary first step in making sense of retention phenomena. Using the MBTI tool to describe student populations offers educators insight to the peculiar and unique characteristics of key student groups. Knowing that what distinguishes the business program from others is the predominance of STs may tell us something important about the flavor of that environment for students.

All SLU Business Majors, 1982–85

N = 370

SENSING: THINKING	SENSING: FEELING	INTUITION: FEELING	INTUITION: THINKING	
ISTJ N = 35 % = 9.46 I = 1.29 ■■■■■■■■■■	**ISFJ** N = 28 % = 7.57 I = 1.15 ■■■■■■■	**INFJ** N = 9 % = 2.43 I = 0.64 ■■	**INTJ** N = 6 % = 1.62 I = 0.56 ■	INTROVERSION JUDGMENT
ISTP N = 19 % = 5.14 I = 1.57 ■■■■■	**ISFP** N = 19 % = 5.14 I = 1.10 ■■■■■	**INFP** N = 23 % = 6.22 I = 0.84 ■■■■■■	**INTP** N = 6 % = 1.62 I = 0.43* ■	INTROVERSION PERCEPTION
ESTP N = 17 % = 4.59 I = 1.11 ■■■■	**ESFP** N = 25 % = 6.76 I = 0.91 ■■■■■■	**ENFP** N = 55 % = 14.86 I = 0.99 ■■■■■■■■■■■■■■	**ENTP** N = 29 % = 7.84 I = 1.50* ■■■■■■■	EXTRAVERSION PERCEPTION
ESTJ N = 36 % = 9.73 I = 1.30 ■■■■■■■■■■	**ESFJ** N = 35 % = 9.46 I = 0.89 ■■■■■■■■■■	**ENFJ** N = 16 % = 4.32 I = 0.69 ■■■■	**ENTJ** N = 12 % = 3.24 I = 0.80 ■■■	EXTRAVERSION JUDGMENT

Notes: ■ = One Percent; Base Population = All SLU Students; N = 1951.

	N	%	I
E	225	60.81	1.01
I	145	39.19	0.99
S	214	57.84	1.12
N	156	42.16	0.87
T	160	43.24	1.13
F	210	56.76	0.92
J	177	47.84	0.98
P	193	52.16	1.02
IJ	78	21.08	1.02
IP	67	18.11	0.95
EP	126	34.05	1.07
EJ	99	26.76	0.94
ST	107	28.92	1.30
SF	107	28.92	0.99
NF	103	27.84	0.86
NT	53	14.32	0.90
SJ	134	36.22	1.13
SP	80	21.62	1.11
NP	113	30.54	0.97
NJ	43	11.62	0.68
TJ	89	24.05	1.10
TP	71	19.19	1.17
FP	122	32.97	0.95
FJ	88	23.78	0.87
IN	44	11.89	0.66
EN	112	30.27	0.99
IS	101	27.30	1.25
ES	113	30.54	1.03
ET	94	25.41	1.21
EF	131	35.41	0.90
IF	79	21.35	0.95
IT	66	17.84	1.03
Sdom	105	28.38	1.11
Ndom	99	26.76	0.99
Tdom	73	19.73	1.06
Fdom	93	25.14	0.87

I = self selection index
* = p > .05
** = p > .01
*** = p > .001

Table 3.1

All SLU Nursing Majors, 1982–85

N = 164

	SENSING: THINKING	SENSING: FEELING	INTUITION: FEELING	INTUITION: THINKING	
	ISTJ N = 7 % = 4.27 I = 0.58	**ISFJ** N = 11 % = 6.71 I = 1.02	**INFJ** N = 6 % = 3.66 I = 0.96	**INTJ** N = 1 % = 0.61 I = 0.21	JUDGMENT / INTROVERSION
	ISTP N = 3 % = 1.83 I = 0.56	**ISFP** N = 10 % = 6.10 I = 1.31	**INFP** N = 6 % = 3.66 I = 0.49	**INTP** N = 1 % = 0.61 I = 0.16	PERCEPTION / INTROVERSION
	ESTP N = 4 % = 2.44 I = 0.59	**ESFP** N = 22 % = 13.41 I = 1.80**	**ENFP** N = 32 % = 19.51 I = 1.30	**ENTP** N = 4 % = 2.44 I = 0.47	PERCEPTION / EXTRAVERSION
	ESTJ N = 17 % = 10.37 I = 1.39	**ESFJ** N = 22 % = 13.41 I = 1.26	**ENFJ** N = 15 % = 9.15 I = 1.45	**ENTJ** N = 3 % = 1.83 I = 0.45	JUDGMENT / EXTRAVERSION

Notes: ■ = One Percent; Base Population = All SLU Students; N = 1951.

	N	%	I
E	119	72.56	1.20
I	45	27.44	0.69
S	96	58.54	1.14
N	68	41.46	0.86
T	40	24.39	0.64
F	124	75.61	1.22
J	82	50.00	1.02
P	82	50.00	0.98
IJ	25	15.24	0.74
IP	20	12.20	0.64
EP	62	37.80	1.19
EJ	57	34.76	1.22
ST	31	18.90	0.85
SF	65	39.63	1.35
NF	59	35.98	1.11
NT	9	5.49	0.34
SJ	57	34.76	1.09
SP	39	23.78	1.22
NP	43	26.22	0.83
NJ	25	15.24	0.89
TJ	28	17.07	0.78
TP	12	7.32	0.45
FP	70	42.68	1.24
FJ	54	32.93	1.21
IN	14	8.54	0.48
EN	54	32.93	1.08
IS	31	18.90	0.87
ES	65	39.63	1.34
ET	28	17.07	0.82
EF	91	55.49	1.41
IF	33	20.12	0.90
IT	12	7.32	0.42
Sdom	44	26.83	1.05
Ndom	43	26.22	0.97
Tdom	24	14.63	0.79
Fdom	53	32.32	1.11

I = self selection index
* = p > .05
** = p > .01
*** = p > .001

Table 3.2

All SLU Arts and Science Majors, 1982–85

N = 1053

	SENSING — THINKING	SENSING — FEELING	INTUITION — FEELING	INTUITION — THINKING
	ISTJ N = 85, % = 8.07, I = 1.10	**ISFJ** N = 63, % = 5.98, I = 0.91	**INFJ** N = 28, % = 2.66, I = 0.70	**INTJ** N = 44, % = 4.18, I = 1.43
	ISTP N = 40, % = 3.80, I = 1.16	**ISFP** N = 37, % = 3.51, I = 0.75	**INFP** N = 95, % = 9.02, I = 1.21	**INTP** N = 50, % = 4.75, I = 1.27
	ESTP N = 46, % = 4.37, I = 1.05	**ESFP** N = 67, % = 6.36, I = 0.86	**ENFP** N = 144, % = 13.68, I = 0.91	**ENTP** N = 59, % = 5.60, I = 1.07
	ESTJ N = 76, % = 7.22, I = 0.96	**ESFJ** N = 100, % = 9.50, I = 0.90	**ENFJ** N = 65, % = 6.17, I = 0.98	**ENTJ** N = 54, % = 5.13, I = 1.27

JUDGMENT / INTROVERSION / PERCEPTION / PERCEPTION / EXTRAVERSION / JUDGMENT

	N	%	I
E	611	58.02	0.9
I	442	41.98	1.0
S	514	48.81	0.9
N	539	51.19	1.0
T	454	43.11	1.1
F	599	56.89	0.9
J	515	48.91	1.0
P	538	51.09	1.0
IJ	220	20.89	1.0
IP	222	21.08	1.1
EP	316	30.01	0.9
EJ	295	28.02	0.9
ST	247	23.46	1.0
SF	267	25.36	0.8
NF	332	31.53	0.9
NT	207	19.66	1.2
SJ	324	30.77	0.9
SP	190	18.04	0.9
NP	348	33.05	1.0
NJ	191	18.14	1.0
TJ	259	24.60	1.1
TP	195	18.52	1.1
FP	343	32.57	0.9
FJ	256	24.31	0.8
IN	217	20.61	1.1
EN	322	30.58	1.0
IS	225	21.37	0.9
ES	289	27.45	0.9
ET	235	22.32	1.0
EF	376	35.71	0.9
IF	223	21.18	0.9
IT	219	20.80	1.2
Sdom	261	24.79	0.9
Ndom	275	26.12	0.9
Tdom	220	20.89	1.1
Fdom	297	28.21	0.9

Notes: ■ = One Percent; Base Population = All SLU Students; N = 1951.

I = self selection index
* = p > .05
** = p > .01
*** = p > .001

Table 3.3

Another population of great importance in any retention effort are those undecided about majors. According to the Tinto model, being uncommitted to a specific major or career may put students at risk. Many institutions find that these undecided students are indeed extremely likely to drop out. The TRAILS data (Table 3.4) suggest that the STP combination was overrepresented as "Undecided" compared to the undergraduate population at large.

Type and Faculty Profiles

Student populations are not the only type profiles worth ascertaining in efforts to map out the type characteristics of an academic environment. Understanding the predominant characteristics of the faculty is equally important. Table 3.5 illustrates type distributions for one department faculty at Saint Louis University. Though the number of faculty is small, some patterns are important to note. The ratios reflect the difference between the faculty and the student percentage distribution in this specific department. Such information is useful in efforts to explore student-faculty interaction and the quality of the educational experience both in and out of the classroom. For example, the fact that the faculty were predominantly Judging types and the students majoring in that department were predominantly Extraverted Perceiving types may suggest a lot about the challenges and frustrations experienced by both students and faculty in that department.

Using the MBTI with Other Enrollment Data Sources

Type distributions are not the only means of describing student groups in such a way as to aid the retention effort. The TRAILS project (or any such institutional database of student type scores) can be effectively related to other institutional data sources so as to provide added insight about the student population. For example, many institutions

Ratios of Undecided Students Compared with All Undergraduates

N = 248

SENSING: THINKING	SENSING: FEELING	INTUITION: FEELING	INTUITION: THINKING	
ISTJ N = 17 % = 6.85 I = 0.94 ■■■■■■■	**ISFJ** N = 14 % = 5.65 I = 0.86 ■■■■■■	**INFJ** N = 12 % = 4.84 I = 1.28 ■■■■■	**INTJ** N = 7 % = 2.82 I = 0.97 ■■■	INTROVERSION / JUDGMENT
ISTP N = 11 % = 4.44 I = 1.35 ■■■■	**ISFP** N = 12 % = 4.84 I = 1.04 ■■■■■	**INFP** N = 19 % = 7.66 I = 1.03 ■■■■■■■■	**INTP** N = 10 % = 4.03 I = 1.08 ■■■■	INTROVERSION / PERCEPTION
ESTP N = 15 % = 6.05 I = 1.46 ■■■■■■	**ESFP** N = 21 % = 8.47 I = 1.14 ■■■■■■■■	**ENFP** N = 27 % = 10.89 I = 0.72 ■■■■■■■■■■■	**ENTP** N = 14 % = 5.65 I = 1.08 ■■■■■■	EXTRAVERSION / PERCEPTION
ESTJ N = 18 % = 7.26 I = 0.97 ■■■■■■■	**ESFJ** N = 25 % = 10.08 I = 0.95 ■■■■■■■■■■	**ENFJ** N = 17 % = 6.85 I = 1.09 ■■■■■■■	**ENTJ** N = 9 % = 3.63 I = 0.90 ■■■■	EXTRAVERSION / JUDGMENT

Notes: ■ = One Percent; Base Population = All SLU Students; N = 1951.

	N	%	I
E	146	58.87	0.98
I	102	41.13	1.04
S	133	53.63	1.04
N	115	46.37	0.96
T	101	40.73	1.07
F	147	59.27	0.96
J	119	47.98	0.98
P	129	52.02	1.02
IJ	50	20.16	0.98
IP	52	20.97	1.10
EP	77	31.05	0.98
EJ	69	27.82	0.98
ST	61	24.60	1.11
SF	72	29.03	0.99
NF	75	30.24	0.93
NT	40	16.13	1.01
SJ	74	29.84	0.93
SP	59	23.79	1.22
NP	70	28.23	0.90
NJ	45	18.15	1.06
TJ	51	20.56	0.94
TP	50	20.16	1.23
FP	79	31.85	0.92
FJ	68	27.42	1.01
IN	48	19.35	1.08
EN	67	27.02	0.88
IS	54	21.77	1.00
ES	79	31.85	1.07
ET	56	22.58	1.08
EF	90	36.29	0.92
IF	57	22.98	1.02
IT	45	18.15	1.05
Sdom	67	27.02	1.06
Ndom	60	24.19	0.90
Tdom	48	19.35	1.04
Fdom	73	29.44	1.01

I = self selection index
* = p > .05
** = p > .01
*** = p > .001

Table 3.4

Faculty in Department X, 1985

N = 11

	SENSING THINKING	SENSING FEELING	INTUITION FEELING	INTUITION THINKING	
INTROVERSION JUDGMENT	ISTJ N = 0 % = 0.00	ISFJ N = 1 % = 9.09 ■■■■■■■■■	INFJ N = 0 % = 0.00	INTJ N = 4 % = 36.36 ■■■■■■■■■■■■■■■■■■■■■■■■■■■■■■■■■■■■	
INTROVERSION PERCEPTION	ISTP N = 0 % = 0.00	ISFP N = 0 % = 0.00	INFP N = 2 % = 18.18 ■■■■■■■■■■■■■■■■■■	INTP N = 0 % = 0.00	
EXTRAVERSION PERCEPTION	ESTP N = 0 % = 0.00	ESFP N = 0 % = 0.00	ENFP N = 0 % = 0.00	ENTP N = 0 % = 0.00	
EXTRAVERSION JUDGMENT	ESTJ N = 0 % = 0.00	ESFJ N = 1 % = 9.09 ■■■■■■■■■	ENFJ N = 2 % = 18.18 ■■■■■■■■■■■■■■■■■■	ENTJ N = 1 % = 9.09 ■■■■■■■■■	

Notes: ■ = One Percent
Base Population = Undergraduate students in department X (N = 171)

	N	%	I
E	4	36.36	.49
I	7	63.64	2.53
S	2	18.18	.33
N	9	81.82	1.84
T	5	45.45	2.10
F	6	54.55	.70
J	9	81.82	1.77
P	2	18.18	.34
IJ	5	45.45	4.09
IP	2	18.18	1.30
EP	0	0.00	.00
EJ	4	36.36	1.04
ST	0	0.00	.00
SF	2	18.18	.45
NF	4	36.36	.96
NT	5	45.45	7.07
SJ	2	18.18	.60
SP	0	0.00	.00
NP	2	18.18	.63
NJ	7	63.64	4.03
TJ	5	45.45	3.24
TP	0	0.00	.00
FP	2	18.18	.39
FJ	4	36.36	1.13
IN	6	54.55	6.66
EN	3	27.27	.75
IS	1	9.09	.54
ES	1	9.09	.24

I = self selection index
* = p > .05
** = p > .01
*** = p > .001

Table 3.5

participate in the Cooperative Institutional Research Project (CIRP), the national freshman survey conducted by Alexander Astin at UCLA and cosponsored by the American Council on Education. This national survey provides a rich and useful profile of entering freshmen and allows educators to monitor changes in students over time and to compare their freshmen with students entering comparable institutions nationwide. For some institutions, the CIRP is the only concerted and comprehensive effort to ascertain a profile of the student population.

When TRAILS data were used to investigate relationships between type and student responses on the CIRP, clear patterns were apparent. For example, on one portion of the CIRP survey, students indicate the importance of certain factors as reasons for going to college. The TRAILS project found that some factors were significantly more important to some types of students than to others. Such patterns are important since the Tinto retention model suggests that these initial objectives, commitments, and intentions of students matriculating at an institution are important factors in understanding attrition. By merging type data with other institutional information such as the CIRP, one can embellish an institution's understanding of the freshman population, and thereby glean important insights related to the retention model.

Type and Academic Aptitude

While it is important to recognize that type distributions provide useful information for the retention model, it is equally important to investigate the degree to which type is related to traditional measures of student academic preparedness, as measured through college entrance exams. This is important for retention purposes for two reasons:

1. Entrance exams are often determining factors in students' sense of competence, and thereby may influence the degree of commitment they have to an institution and to an educational objective. The literature is replete with insights about the power of expectations and the so-called self-fulfilling prophecy; ACT/SAT measures, when used as indicators of the likelihood of students performing successfully, are powerful sources of expectations.
2. Entrance exams are often used to place students in special academic programs. High scorers are referred to honors programs; low scorers are often conditionally admitted through special "academic support" offices. As such, these scores determine a whole range of academic and social experiences students have upon matriculating at an institution.

It is generally acknowledged that there is some relationship between type preferences and performance on standardized aptitude measures. The argument is often made that Sensing intelligence cannot be measured by paper-and-pencil instruments, and that Sensing students (especially Extraverted Sensors) are at a disadvantage on any timed examination that focuses on the ability to quickly manipulate symbols, see patterns and relationships between words and concepts, and so on. The TRAILS data clearly supported these patterns; on both the ACT and the SAT, the IN types scored the highest, followed by the EN, IS, and ES types (see Table 3.6). These differences are both statistically and practically significant and such patterns have been remarkably consistent across several institutions.

Correlations Using Continuous Scores

The TRAILS data included strength of preference scores in addition to

One-Way Analysis of Variance of Aptitude Score (SAT) by Learning Style

Group	N	Mean SAT	SD	Scheffe Post Hoc Comparisons	IN	EN	IS	ES
IN	148	1110	184.7	**IN**				
EN	312	1052	177.1	**EN**	*			
IS	188	1008	224.1	**IS**	*	*		
ES	250	932	196.1	**ES**	*	*	*	
TOTAL	989	1019	203.6					

F (3,984) = 30.5
p<.001

Note: *denotes p < .05

Table 3.6

Myers-Briggs Type Indicator and Academic Aptitude (ACT and SAT) Results of a Stepwise Multiple Regression

Variable	Greek beta	R^2	F
Sensing–Intuition	.30	.08	22.96**
Extraversion–Introversion	.10	.09	2.86
Thinking–Feeling	– .06	.09	.95
Judgment–Perception	.02	.09	.07

Note: **denotes p < .05

Table 3.7

the simple four-letter type scores of individuals. This allows the proper investigation of the linear relationship between variables, to see, for example, if the strength of preference for intuition is related to ACT/SAT performance. Such an approach may provide more insight regarding the relationship between these variables than if one simply compared the ACT/SAT scores of all Intuitive types with all Sensing types. Table 3.7 illustrates these relationships.

The first step was to convert each preference score to a continuous score, with 100 being the midpoint on the scale. An extreme Sensing preference then has a score around 59 while an extreme Intuition preference would score around 139. Therefore, the Sensing–Intuition dimension has a single score that reflects both the strength and the direction of the preference. The researcher, using a multiple regression approach, can then answer the question: Is it true that the stronger the preference for Intuition, the higher the ACT/SAT score? What about preferences for Extraversion vs. Introversion? Preferences for Thinking–Feeling or Judging–Perceiving? The results of such a regression are shown in Table 3.7. In other words, the table shows the degree of the relationship between each MBTI scale and the entrance exam performance (which in this case is the ACT composite score and the SAT combined score) when all MBTI scales are considered simultaneously in the regression equation.

The Sensing–Intuition scale has the strongest relationship with ACT/SAT test performance and the analysis suggests that the stronger the preference for Intuition, the higher the ACT/SAT score. The preferences for the Extraversion–Introversion, Thinking–Feeling, and Judging–Perceiving dimensions are not related to test scores to a statistically significant degree.

Implications

These findings are important in the overall attempt to make sense of retention and to use the MBTI instrument in retention efforts. First, it seems that the Intuition preference may be advantaged in traditional measures of academic preparedness; students with this preference may therefore be less likely to be found in "remedial" or "'special support" programs prescribed for students with low ACT/SAT scores. Table 3.8 shows the type distribution for one such program. The ratios show that ES learners are more than 1.5 times more likely to be found in this group than one would expect from the overall type distribution of the student body.

Given that certain types of learners tend to score lower on ACT/SAT tests than other learners, the trend of declining entrance scores faced by some institutions takes on new meaning. Available data suggest that an ever-increasing number of Sensing students are entering American colleges and universities and that, contrary to ten or twenty years prior, the majority of college students today have a Sensing preference (Myers, 1980; Davis and Schroeder, 1980). Academic programs that have witnessed a decline in ACT/SAT scores might benefit from investigating shifts in the prevailing learning style of their students via the MBTI instrument.

Finally, knowing this relationship between type preferences and academic preparedness and aptitude (as measured by standardized tests) enables us to make better sense of the academic performance of certain types of students in certain curricular areas. As will be shown in the following section, there is evidence that Sensing learners may be the most successful students in certain academic pursuits, in spite of a poor performance on the ACT or SAT. Using such entrance exams to screen students for admission may be a disservice to some students and also perhaps to the vitality and success of specific academic programs. In a broader perspective, the trend in public policy to monitor the quality of undergraduate programs through comprehensive assessment of student learning outcomes tends to focus on the use

Selection of Students in "High Risk Program"

N = 155

SENSING: THINKING	SENSING: FEELING	INTUITION: FEELING	INTUITION: THINKING	
ISTJ N = 22 % = 14.19 I = 1.94** ■■■■■■■■■■■■■■	**ISFJ** N = 7 % = 4.52 I = 0.69 ■■■■	**INFJ** N = 4 % = 2.58 I = 0.68 ■■	**INTJ** N = 3 % = 1.94 I = 0.66 ■	JUDGMENT / INTROVERSION
ISTP N = 10 % = 6.45 I = 1.97* ■■■■■■	**ISFP** N = 8 % = 5.16 I = 1.11 ■■■■■	**INFP** N = 3 % = 1.94 I = 0.26 ■	**INTP** N = 3 % = 1.94 I = 0.52 ■	PERCEPTION
ESTP N = 20 % = 12.90 I = 3.11*** ■■■■■■■■■■■■	**ESFP** N = 8 % = 5.16 I = 0.69 ■■■■■	**ENFP** N = 7 % = 4.52 I = 0.30*** ■■■■	**ENTP** N = 4 % = 2.58 I = 0.49 ■■	PERCEPTION / EXTRAVERSION
ESTJ N = 23 % = 14.84 I = 1.98** ■■■■■■■■■■■■■■	**ESFJ** N = 20 % = 12.90 I = 1.22 ■■■■■■■■■■■■	**ENFJ** N = 6 % = 3.87 I = 0.61 ■■■	**ENTJ** N = 7 % = 4.52 I = 1.12 ■■■■	JUDGMENT

Notes: ■ = One Percent; Base Population = All SLU Students; N = 1951.

	N	%	I
E	95	61.29	1.02
I	60	38.71	0.97
S	118	76.13	1.48**
N	37	23.87	0.49**
T	92	59.35	1.55**
F	63	40.65	0.66**
J	92	59.35	1.21*
P	63	40.65	0.80*
IJ	36	23.23	1.13
IP	24	15.48	0.81
EP	39	25.16	0.79
EJ	56	36.13	1.27*
ST	75	48.39	2.18**
SF	43	27.74	0.95
NF	20	12.90	0.40**
NT	17	10.97	0.69
SJ	72	46.45	1.45**
SP	46	29.68	1.52**
NP	17	10.97	0.35**
NJ	20	12.90	0.76
TJ	55	35.48	1.63**
TP	37	23.87	1.46*
FP	26	16.77	0.49**
FJ	37	23.87	0.88
IN	13	8.39	0.47**
EN	24	15.48	0.51**
IS	47	30.32	1.39*
ES	71	45.81	1.54**
ET	54	34.84	1.67**
EF	41	26.45	0.67**
IF	22	14.19	0.63*
IT	38	24.52	1.42*
Sdom	57	36.77	1.44**
Ndom	18	11.61	0.43**
Tdom	43	27.74	1.50**
Fdom	37	23.87	0.82

I = self selection index
* = p > .05
** = p > .01
*** = p > .001

Table 3.8

of standardized assessment measures. Data on the relationship of type to test performance have implications for such policies at both the state and federal levels.

The ultimate utility of these data at any one institution may be their potential for getting the attention of faculty and academic administrators. Because entrance exam scores are accepted at many institutions as important indices of quality, any information that can be directly related to these scores and that may help explain shifting patterns in such scores is likely to at least get the attention of key campus personnel. This information thereby becomes a valuable political resource for mobilizing campus retention efforts. Research on the relationship of type data to aptitude test scores may be an effective entree to the campus decision-making structure and in turn may be an effective means of improving the quality of the learning environment for students, and hence improve retention.

Type and Academic Achievement

Academic achievement has a prominent role in any investigation of retention patterns. At many institutions, the inability of students to perform academically is the single most important factor contributing to attrition. In the Tinto model, academic performance is one measure of academic integration and is an important consideration as students reassess their commitments both to the institution and to their educational objectives. It is necessary to investigate the relationship of type to academic achievement in order to fully integrate the MBTI with the retention model.

One of the more popular institutional efforts to improve retention is the creation of support programs to assist students having academic difficulty. Such programs often intend to provide the kinds of support and structure some students need but which are not available in the traditional classroom. Ideally, such programs would be able to identify early in a semester those students likely to experience academic difficulty. However, it is usually difficult if not impossible to predict which students will encounter difficulty in any one course or any one curricular area. The use of aptitude measures is not always the most effective approach and as we have seen, such measures may be related to personality type. The MBTI instrument may be useful in identifying students who are likely to experience difficulty or special challenges in a given academic area and in facilitating a good educational fit between the learner and the instructor.

Correlations with First-Term GPA

It is not uncommon to find MBTI researchers ranking the GPA of the sixteen types from high to low in order to understand the relationship between type and academic performance. At other times, researcher may compare the grades of Intuitive types to those of Sensing types, Extraverts to Introverts and so on. As indicated earlier, it may be appropriate to investigate the strength of preference to see whether or not the preference on any MBTI dimension leads to better grades. Table 3.9 illustrates this relationship of strength of preference to first-term GPA at Saint Louis University.

First we see in section I of Table 3.9 that there is a relationship between strength of preference on three of the four MBTI dimensions and academic achievement in the first semester. The greater the preference for Intuition, the greater the preference for Introversion, and the greater the preference for Judging, the better the GPA. There is a slight, though statistically insignificant, relationship between Thinking–Feeling and academic achievement in the first term.

Institutional researchers usually investigate the relationship between grades and entrance exams in order to verify that the use of

Four Myers-Briggs® Indices and First-Term GPA Academic Achievement

I. Results of a Stepwise Multiple Regression—without aptitude SAT

Variable	B	R^2	F
Extraversion–Introversion	.24	.05	16.71**
Judgment–Perception	–.13	.06	4.47*
Sensing–Intuition	.13	.08	4.15*
Thinking–Feeling	.10	.08	3.00

II. Results of a Stepwise Multiple Regression—with aptitude SAT

Variable	B	R^2	F
Aptitude Score (SAT)	.43	.18	67.35**
Extraversion–Introversion	.20	.22	13.85*
Judgment–Perception	–.14	.23	6.68*
Sensing–Intuition	.13	.24	5.73
Thinking–Feeling	.00	.24	.00

Note: *denotes $p < .05$ ** denotes $p < .01$

Table 3.9

aptitude measures to screen students in the admissions process and to place students in appropriate course sections is a worthwhile and effective endeavor. ACT/SAT measures have been found to be somewhat predictive of first-semester academic achievement. But what would happen if we rolled all of this information together? Table 3.9, section II illustrates that inquiry as part of the TRAILS project.

First we see that ACT/SAT scores are the best predictors of academic performance. We also see that the impact of the Sensing–Intuition preference on grades is lessened once we consider ACT/SAT scores in addition to MBTI preference scores in predicting

GPA. As indicated in Table 3.7 (page 104), the preference for Intuition is positively related to ACT/SAT scores. Therefore, once we have rolled these scores together with type scores in the equation for predicting GPA, much of the impact of Intuition is already accounted for in the entrance exam measure. Since it seems that these measures and the MBTI dimension of Sensing–Intuition may in part be measuring the same thing (given the positive correlation), the impact on grades of this one MBTI preference is diminished once we consider ACT/SAT scores.

Such is not the case in the TRAILS findings with the other type dimensions. First of all, Table 3.7 (page 104) showed no relationship between the Judging–Perceiving dimension and ACT/SAT scores. However, in Table 3.9 we see that even after considering these scores, the greater the preference for Judging, the better the first-term GPA. Therefore, even when considering ACT/SAT, the Judging–Perceiving preference adds more insight regarding first-tern academic achievement. Also, we found in Table 3.7 (page 104) no relationship between the Thinking–Feeling dimension and the ACT/SAT score, while in Table 3.9 we see that the stronger the preference for Feeling, the higher the grades. Hence, even after considering entrance exam scores, the stronger the preference for Feeling the better the first-term grades at Saint Louis University. Finally, though there was no significant relationship between Extraversion and Introversion and ACT/SAT scores, the preference for Introversion is related to higher first-term grades even after considering entrance exam scores in the regression.

In summary, the preliminary evidence from the TRAILS studies suggest that MBTI preferences are related to first-term academic achievement. Preferences for Intuition may be predictive of academic performance in ways similar to the predictive nature of ACT/SAT scores. The data suggest that the stronger the preference for Feeling judgment, the better the first-term grade (though ACT/SAT scores do not correlate significantly with preferences for Thinking–Feeling). We also find that though entrance exams may favor neither the Judging nor the Perceiving preference, the Judging attitude seems advantageous for academic achievement. Therefore, in predicting first-term academic performance, the Judging–Perceiving dimension adds a great deal to an entrance exam.

None of this is particularly surprising. The Judging–Perceiving dimension tells us much about students' work habits which surely are manifested in academic performance. Many academic expectations and requirements favor the Judging bias towards closure, structure, and order. In addition, many academic measures are structured similarly to the ACT and the SAT, requiring the quick grasp of patterns and relationships of symbols—which is the gift of Introversion and Intuition. This may explain in part why the ACT and SAT have been moderately useful through the years in predicting students' first-term academic performance, since performance is so often measured in such a way that it taps into those same Intuitive gifts.

It must be emphasized that these findings are for aggregate data. Such group trends cannot and should not be used to predict any individual student's performance on aptitude tests or in academic achievement. Other chapters in this volume discuss the appropriate use of MBTI scores in counseling or advising students; the same concerns are present in using the results of studies such as these in predicting individual behavior or performance. These group data best serve to enlighten educators about the environmental challenges students face at an institution or in a specific curriculum.

The Relationship of Type to Advanced Academic Performance

The TRAILS data presented in the last section reflect the grades achieved by students in the *first semester* of a liberal arts curriculum.

Students are engaged in philosophy and theology, history, English, and mathematics courses, all of which may indeed favor the Intuitive and Introverted preferences. Once students engage more directly in studies related to their chosen major, other preferences may be more advantageous. For example, a student with a strong preference for Intuition may find the challenges of pursuing an accounting major uncomfortable while a student preferring Sensing may excel, contrary to what would be predicted by ACT/SAT measures alone or by their first-term performance in the core liberal arts curriculum. The nursing curriculum, especially in clinical studies, may favor the Extraverted Sensing students whose natural gifts may give them an advantage in the specifics of patient care.

Table 3.10 presents preliminary TRAILS findings on the relationship of the MBTI instrument to academic achievement in the sixth semester for students in four colleges: business, arts and sciences, nursing, and allied health. Using the fall semester GPA for juniors and seniors as the dependent variable and the four "learning style" groups as independent variables, one-way analyses of variance for each school show no significant differences by learning style.

It is important to look back to Tables 3.7 (page 104) and 3.9 (page 110) and compare these findings with those for first-semester performance. While first-semester performance apparently strongly favors Introversion and Intuition, more advanced study in any of the schools does not demonstrate significant differences between the learning styles defined by these two MBTI dimensions. The implications of these preliminary TRAILS analyses are that personality dimensions which are strongly related to entrance exam scores and to first-semester performance may in no way be related to academic achievement in the upper-class curricula.

In summary, the longitudinal, multivariate approach required by the Tinto model is the approach that is maximally useful for

Results on Four One-Way Analysis of Variance for Each College: Mean Upperclass GPA by Learning Style

Learning Styles	Arts/Sciences *n*	mean	Business *n*	mean	Nursing *n*	mean	Allied Health *n*	mean
IN	64	3.32	15	2.91	5	3.20	17	3.31
EN	82	3.26	42	2.93	23	3.37	30	3.64
IS	68	3.17	35	3.15	12	3.51	12	3.51
ES	75	3.22	42	3.04	25	3.26	37	3.48
TOTAL	289	3.24	134	3.02	65	3.34	96	3.50
F ratio		.53		1.03		.61		1.29
F probability		.66		.38		.61		.28

Table 3.10

understanding how some preferences may place certain learners at an advantage or disadvantage in certain academic pursuits. As we have seen, type concepts richly embellish the Tinto model and tell us more than we could glean from ACT/SAT measures alone about the academic performance students. Type data also help us understand the differing challenges in the first semester and subsequent semesters. However, though such group data enlighten educators about general trends in students' performance within a given curriculum, educators cannot take such aggregate findings and apply them to each and every individual student experience. To do so violates the ethical principles of educational research in general and type theory in particular.

Type and Attrition

Comparing persisting populations to those who drop out, while also considering the aptitude and achievement findings discussed previously, is the final objective of this approach to retention research. This chapter has hopefully made the point that any worthwhile investigation of attrition must be longitudinal (following some distinct cohort of students over time through their enrollment experience) and must focus on carefully selected variables pertaining to the interaction of certain learners with certain social and academic environments. The TRAILS project illustrates one step toward this kind of retention research model.

For example, Tables 3.11, 3.12, and 3.13 compare the dropout population with persisting populations in the nursing, arts and sciences, and business programs, respectively. One can see some patterns that may fit well with some common preconceptions about the interaction of types of learners with these academic programs.

The nursing dropout table (Table 3.11) suggests a relationship between the Thinking–Feeling dimension and attrition. While students with a preference for Thinking comprise about 26 percent of the Nursing student group as a whole, they comprise 40 percent of the nursing dropouts. The TJ group is more than twice as likely to drop out as one would expect from the overall type distribution. On the whole, it is the Thinking–Feeling dimension that accounts for most of the dropout phenomenon in nursing, with Thinking types being most at risk.

Of course, not all attrition is problematic or symptomatic of institutional problems. For example, there are multiple explanations for why Thinking types may leave a nursing program at a higher rate than Feeling types. An argument could be made that students with strong preferences for Thinking may not find adequate rewards or support in a nursing career and that it is in their best interest to

Dropout Ratios of Nursing Students

N = 30

SENSING THINKING	SENSING FEELING	INTUITION FEELING	INTUITION THINKING	
ISTJ N = 2 % = 6.67 I = 1.56 ■■■■■■	**ISFJ** N = 1 % = 3.33 I = 0.50 ■■■	**INFJ** N = 0 % = 0.00 I = 0.00	**INTJ** N = 1 % = 3.33 I = 5.47 ■■■	JUDGMENT INTROVERSION
ISTP N = 1 % = 3.33 I = 1.82 ■■■	**ISFP** N = 1 % = 3.33 I = 0.55 ■■■	**INFP** N = 1 % = 3.33 I = 0.91 ■■■	**INTP** N = 0 % = 0.00 I = 0.00	PERCEPTION INTROVERSION
ESTP N = 0 % = 0.00 I = 0.00	**ESFP** N = 4 % = 13.33 I = 0.99 ■■■■■■■■■■■■■	**ENFP** N = 5 % = 16.67 I = 0.85 ■■■■■■■■■■■■■■■■■	**ENTP** N = 1 % = 3.33 I = 1.37 ■■■	PERCEPTION EXTRAVERSION
ESTJ N = 6 % = 20.00 I = 1.93 ■■■■■■■■■■■■■■■■■■■■	**ESFJ** N = 5 % = 16.67 I = 1.24 ■■■■■■■■■■■■■■■■■	**ENFJ** N = 1 % = 3.33 I = 0.36 ■■■	**ENTJ** N = 1 % = 3.33 I = 1.82 ■■■	JUDGMENT EXTRAVERSION

Notes: ■ = One Percent; Base Population = All Nursing undergraduates; N = 164.

	N	%	I
E	23	76.67	1.06
I	7	23.33	0.85
S	20	66.67	1.14
N	10	33.33	0.80
T	12	40.00	1.64
F	18	60.00	0.79
J	17	56.67	1.13
P	13	43.33	0.87
IJ	4	13.33	0.87
IP	3	10.00	0.82
EP	10	33.33	0.88
EJ	13	43.33	1.25
ST	9	30.00	1.59
SF	11	36.67	0.93
NF	7	23.33	0.65
NT	3	10.00	1.82
SJ	14	46.67	1.34
SP	6	20.00	0.84
NP	7	23.33	0.89
NJ	3	10.00	0.66
TJ	10	33.33	1.95
TP	2	6.67	0.91
FP	11	36.67	0.86
FJ	7	23.33	0.71
IN	2	6.67	0.78
EN	8	26.67	0.81
IS	5	16.67	0.88
ES	15	50.00	1.26
ET	8	26.67	1.56
EF	15	50.00	0.90
IF	3	10.00	0.50
IT	4	13.33	1.82
Sdom	7	23.33	0.87
Ndom	7	23.33	0.89
Tdom	8	26.67	1.82
Fdom	8	26.67	0.83

I = self selection index
* = p > .05
** = p > .01
*** = p > .001

Table 3.11

Dropout Ratios of Business School Students

N = 75

	SENSING THINKING	SENSING FEELING	INTUITION FEELING	INTUITION THINKING
INTROVERSION JUDGMENT	**ISTJ** N = 9 % = 12.00 I = 1.27	**ISFJ** N = 3 % = 4.00 I = 0.53	**INFJ** N = 2 % = 2.67 I = 1.10	**INTJ** N = 1 % = 1.33 I = 0.82
INTROVERSION PERCEPTION	**ISTP** N = 4 % = 5.33 I = 1.04	**ISFP** N = 7 % = 9.33 I = 1.82	**INFP** N = 5 % = 6.67 I = 1.07	**INTP** N = 1 % = 1.33 I = 0.82
EXTRAVERSION PERCEPTION	**ESTP** N = 2 % = 2.67 I = 0.58	**ESFP** N = 4 % = 5.33 I = 0.79	**ENFP** N = 13 % = 17.33 I = 1.17	**ENTP** N = 5 % = 6.67 I = 0.85
EXTRAVERSION JUDGMENT	**ESTJ** N = 5 % = 6.67 I = 0.69	**ESFJ** N = 7 % = 9.33 I = 0.99	**ENFJ** N = 4 % = 5.33 I = 1.23	**ENTJ** N = 3 % = 4.00 I = 1.23

Notes: ■ = One Percent; Base Population = All Business undergraduates; N = 370.

	N	%	I
E	43	57.33	0.94
I	32	42.67	1.09
S	41	54.67	0.95
N	34	45.33	1.08
T	30	40.00	0.93
F	45	60.00	1.06
J	34	45.33	0.95
P	41	54.67	1.05
IJ	15	20.00	0.95
IP	17	22.67	1.25
EP	24	32.00	0.94
EJ	19	25.33	0.95
ST	20	26.67	0.92
SF	21	28.00	0.97
NF	24	32.00	1.15
NT	10	13.33	0.93
SJ	24	32.00	0.88
SP	17	22.67	1.05
NP	24	32.00	1.05
NJ	10	13.33	1.15
TJ	18	24.00	1.00
TP	12	16.00	0.83
FP	29	38.67	1.17
FJ	16	21.33	0.90
IN	9	12.00	1.01
EN	25	33.33	1.10
IS	23	30.67	1.12
ES	18	24.00	0.79
ET	15	20.00	0.79
EF	28	37.33	1.05
IF	17	22.67	1.06
IT	15	20.00	1.12
Sdom	18	24.00	0.85
Ndom	21	28.00	1.05
Tdom	13	17.33	0.88
Fdom	23	30.67	1.22

I = self selection index
* = p > .05
** = p > .01
*** = p > .001

Table 3.12

Dropout Ratios of Arts and Science Students

N = 225

	SENSING THINKING	SENSING FEELING	INTUITION FEELING	INTUITION THINKING
INTROVERSION JUDGMENT	**ISTJ** N = 21 % = 9.33 I = 1.16	**ISFJ** N = 8 % = 3.56 I = 0.59	**INFJ** N = 13 % = 5.78 I = 2.17*	**INTJ** N = 8 % = 3.56 I = 0.85
INTROVERSION PERCEPTION	**ISTP** N = 6 % = 2.67 I = 0.70	**ISFP** N = 9 % = 4.00 I = 1.14	**INFP** N = 27 % = 12.00 I = 1.33	**INTP** N = 16 % = 7.11 I = 1.50
EXTRAVERSION PERCEPTION	**ESTP** N = 6 % = 2.67 I = 0.61	**ESFP** N = 14 % = 6.22 I = 0.98	**ENFP** N = 26 % = 11.56 I = 0.84	**ENTP** N = 13 % = 5.78 I = 1.03
EXTRAVERSION JUDGMENT	**ESTJ** N = 12 % = 5.33 I = 0.74	**ESFJ** N = 21 % = 9.33 I = 0.98	**ENFJ** N = 15 % = 6.67 I = 1.08	**ENTJ** N = 10 % = 4.44 I = 0.87

Notes: ■ = One Percent; Base Population = All Arts and Sciences undergraduates; N = 1053.

	N	%	I
E	117	52.00	0.90
I	108	48.00	1.14
S	97	43.11	0.88
N	128	56.89	1.11
T	92	40.89	0.95
F	133	59.11	1.04
J	108	48.00	0.98
P	117	52.00	1.02
IJ	50	22.22	1.06
IP	58	25.78	1.22
EP	59	26.22	0.87
EJ	58	25.78	0.92
ST	45	20.00	0.85
SF	52	23.11	0.91
NF	81	36.00	1.14
NT	47	20.89	1.06
SJ	62	27.56	0.90
SP	35	15.56	0.86
NP	82	36.44	1.10
NJ	46	20.44	1.13
TJ	51	22.67	0.92
TP	41	18.22	0.98
FP	76	33.78	1.04
FJ	57	25.33	1.04
IN	64	28.44	1.38
EN	64	28.44	0.93
IS	44	19.56	0.92
ES	53	23.56	0.86
ET	41	18.22	0.82
EF	76	33.78	0.95
IF	57	25.33	1.20
IT	51	22.67	1.09
Sdom	49	21.78	0.88
Ndom	60	26.67	1.02
Tdom	44	19.56	0.94
Fdom	72	32.00	1.13

I = self selection index
* = p > .05
** = p > .01
*** = p > .001

Table 3.13

consider other professional pursuits. In that case, their attrition may be educationally appropriate, and working to reduce that attrition may be inappropriate. Type data can offer an effective mechanism for understanding general trends in attrition and for working with students in making appropriate choices about their educational commitments.

Another example may illustrate the usefulness of such retention data. Analysis of the TRAILS data suggest IF types are at risk in the business program. On the one hand, it may be that their pursuit of other options is an appropriate response to their awareness of the kinds of rewards and challenges of, for example, an accounting major and/or career. On the other hand, perhaps their attrition is a reflection of the type of social climate characteristic of the business school at a predominantly commuter campus, where there are few opportunities for personal interaction or affiliation with either faculty or other students. Either way, there are a host of interventions to consider in responding to the students' needs. Relating type data to attrition allows educators to begin to consider the dynamic interactions of types of students with types of academic and social environments, and thereby begin to respond appropriately to enrollment management tasks.

Retention Action Strategies

The Tinto model implies that improving retention is not a goal in itself but rather the outcome of an institution's efforts to increase students' academic and social integration. Any action plan that results from an institution's retention research should attempt to maximize the quality of the student's experience at every point of contact between the student and the institution. This, of course, is easier said than done. Difficult choices must be made about how to make good use of limited resources in such efforts.

Information is the fundamental ingredient in mobilizing any

successful enrollment management strategy. In retention programs, information without action is empty and action without information is blind. Information management becomes the necessary prelude to any retention program, as well as a necessary ingredient for appropriate assessment and evaluation of enrollment management strategies. This is the value of the TRAILS project, which illustrates one process for building that information infrastructure.

Describing actual retention action strategies using the MBTI instrument, however, is not an objective of this chapter. Using the MBTI tool to improve an institution's responsiveness to students and its sensitivity to the individual characteristics of students is certainly one means of improving students' academic and social integration within the various environments they encounter at the college or university. A wide variety of avenues exists for using the MBTI assessment tool for such ends: academic advising and educational planning, career development, environmental management in residence halls, faculty and staff development, and student involvement opportunities. The use of the MBTI instrument in these areas is addressed in other chapters. This chapter has proposed that:

1. investing resources in information systems such as that illustrated by the TRAILS project is necessary for effective broad-based campus change using the MBTI instrument;
2. an information system with the MBTI instrument as the hub facilitates more effective use of the MBTI tool in the various ways discussed in the other chapters;
3. the MBTI instrument can be one important component in a campus retention strategy, and fits well with the premises of the Tinto model; and

4. to begin to make effective use of the MBTI instrument in campus retention efforts, ongoing research should be conducted to continuously monitor the academic and social integration students may experience in certain environments.

References

Bean, J. P. (1982). Conceptual models of student attrition: How theory can help the institutional researcher. In E. Pascarella (Ed.), *New directions for institutional research: Vol. IX, No. 4, Studying student attrition* (pp. 17–33). San Francisco: Jossey-Bass Publishers, Inc.

Davis, M., and C. Schroeder (1983). "New students" in liberal arts colleges: Threat or challenge? In J. Watson and R. Stevens (Eds.), *Pioneers and pallbearers: Perspectives on liberal education.* (pp. 71–80). Macon, GA: Mercer University Press.

Kalsbeek, D. H. (1986). *Linking learning style theory with retention research: The TRAILS project.* Paper presented at the Association for Institutional Research forum, Orlando, FL.

McCaulley, M. H. (1978). *Application of the MBTI to medicine and other health professions.* Gainesville, FL: Center for Applications of Psychological Type.

Myers, I. B. with P. B. Myers. (1980). *Gifts differing.* Palo Alto, CA: Consulting Psychologists Press.

Myers, I. B., and M. H. McCaulley (1985). *Manual: A guide to the development and use of the Myers-Briggs Type Indicator,* 2nd ed. Palo Alto, CA: Consulting Psychologists Press.

Pascarella, E. (1982). (Introduction). In E. Pascarella (Ed.), *New directions for institutional research: Vol. XXXVI, No. 4, Studying student attrition* (pp. 1–2). San Francisco: Jossey-Bass Publishers, Inc.

Terenzini, P. T. (1982). Designing attrition studies. In E. Pascarella (Ed.), *New directions for institutional research: Vol. XXXVI, No. 4, Studying student attrition* (pp. 55–71). San Francisco: Jossey-Bass Publishers, Inc.

Tinto, V. (1975). Dropout from higher education: A theoretical synthesis of recent research. *Review of Educational Research*, 43(1), 89–125.

Walsh, W. B. (1973). *Theories of person-environment interaction: implications for the college student.* Iowa City, IA: The American College Testing Program.

CHAPTER 4

Learning Styles

GEORGE H. JENSEN

The study of learning styles is a rather recent phenomenon, and, not surprisingly, the field is replete with the archetypes of an emerging science. At the core of the field are those who feel that their approach to learning styles is a virtual panacea for the current ills of education. At the borders are those who claim that learning styles do not exist, that the varied approaches students adopt to learning are purely random responses to their environment. Caught in between are those educators who sincerely want to become better teachers but who are confused by competing and conflicting paradigms (Kuhn, 1970).

These educators are confused with good cause. Since 1960, approximately thirty instruments of learning styles have appeared. Some of the more interesting and more frequently used are the *Hidden Figures Test* (1962), *Matching Figures Test* (1965), *Group Embedded Figures Test* (1971), *Student Learning Styles Questionnaire* (1974), *Cognitive Style Mapping Inventory* (1975), *Kolb's Learning Styles Inventory* (1976), and Dunn, Dunn, and Price's *Learning Styles Inventory* (adults, 1977; students, 1978). These and other instruments collectively measure about 20 aspects of learning styles (Keefe, 1982), but none is comprehensive or clearly superior.

The Myers-Briggs Type Indicator® instrument, while it cannot earnestly claim to be comprehensive, has important strengths that are not often found in the rest of these instruments. First, the MBTI®

The author wishes to acknowledge the assistance of John DiTiberio in writing this chapter.

instrument is better "normed" than most instruments of its kind. It was painstakingly developed over a twenty-year period. Second, the Indicator is more sophisticated and complex than most learning style assessments. Rather than identify a few "styles," for example, field-dependent versus field-independent, the MBTI instrument can identify sixteen types or sixteen approaches to learning.

Because of its sophistication, the MBTI instrument can, as Lawrence (1984) has documented, account for most of the traits identified by other widely used instruments. The most significant shortcoming is the Indicator's inability to identify preferences for visual, auditory, and kinesthetic channels of perception and communication (Grinder and Bandler, 1976). Lowen (1982) has hypothesized connections between Sensing and the kinesthetic channel, Thinking and the visual channel, and Feeling and the auditory channel, but his theory remains untested and has yielded mixed results in the clinic and classroom.

What is most striking about the Indicator, and what empowers it, is that the instrument was developed as, and primarily remains, an assessment of personality type. Most learning style inventories assess how the student is behaving or *how the student believes that he or she performs best.* With these instruments, teachers can better understand the patterns in a student's learning behaviors, but learning style inventories rarely provide clues as to whether student's behavior is truly his or her learning style or how each was taught to learn. Rather than assessing behavior, the MBTI instrument assesses personality type. Once the student's type is identified, teachers can make predictions about how that student learns best, which may or may not be consistent with his or her behavior, and suggest alternative methods of study. The MBTI instrument, as will be explained later, allows teachers to penetrate through the veil of behavior to underlying cognitive functions as can few other assessments of learning style.

The MBTI Instrument and Learning Styles

In developing fields, terms are often ambiguous or vague, and this is also true of the study of learning styles. "Learning styles" can mean anything from hemisphericity to one's method of sharpening pencils. Lawrence (1984) described four uses of the term "learning styles" as used in connection with the MBTI instrument:

1. Cognitive style in the sense of preferred or habitual patterns of mental functioning: information processing, and the formation of ideas and judgments.
2. Patterns of attitudes and interests that influence what a person will attend to in a potential learning situation.
3. A disposition to seek out learning environments compatible with one's cognitive style, attitudes, and interests, and to avoid environments that are not congenial.
4. A disposition to use certain learning tools and avoid others.

Lawrence states that the MBTI instrument can only predict "preferred or habitual patterns" or "dispositions." As will be explained in the following sections, a student's MBTI results can be used to predict, on a probability model, what kind of behaviors, instructional tools, and environments facilitate or hinder learning for that student. It cannot predict with certainty how that student will read, write, or study. How a student actually behaves will be determined by a number of factors: personality type, parental influence, instruction, learning environment, and maturity. A perfect correlation between personality type and learning style is not possible.

In the following section, a description of the connection between type and learning style is drawn from Lawrence (1982 and 1984), McCaulley and Natter (1974), and Myers (1980). See also Figure 4.1.

Type and Learning Styles

Extraversion (E)

Es learn best in situations filled with movement, action, and talk. They prefer to learn theories or facts that connect with their experience, and they will usually come to a more thorough understanding of these theories or facts during group discussions or when working on cooperative projects. Es tend to leap into assignments with little "forethought," relying on trial-and-error rather than anticipation to solve problems.

Introversion (I)

Since Is may be more quiet and less active in the classroom, teachers may feel the need to press them into taking part in group discussions. Such pressure, however, will often only increase their withdrawal. Teachers need to respect their need to think in relative solitude, for that is how they think best. Is will be more willing to share their ideas when given advance notice. This will allow them time to think about how they will become active in the classroom.

Sensory Perception (S)

Ss learn best when they move from the concrete to the abstract in a step-by-step progression. They are thus at home with programmed, modular, or computer-assisted learning. They value knowledge that is practical and want to be precise and accurate in their own work. They tend to excel at memorizing facts.

Intuitive Perception (N)

Ns tend to leap to a conceptual understanding of material and may daydream or act-out during drill work or predominately factual lectures. They value quick flashes of insight but are often careless about details. They tend to excel at imaginative tasks and theoretical topics.

Thinking Judgment (T)

Ts are most motivated when provided with a logical rationale for each project and when teachers acknowledge and respect their competence. They prefer topics that help them to understand systems or cause-and-effect relationships. Their thought is syllogistic and analytic.

Feeling Judgment (J)

Fs are most motivated when given personal encouragement and when shown the human angle of a topic. Fs think to clarify their values and to establish networks of values. Even when their expressions seem syllogistic, they usually evolve from some personally held belief or value.

Judgment (J)

Js tend to gauge their learning by the completion of tasks: reading "x"-amount of books, writing "x"-amount of papers, or making "x"-amount of reports. They thus prefer more structured learning environments that establish goals for them to meet.

Perception (P)

Ps tend to view learning as a free wheeling, flexible quest. They care less about deadlines and the completion of tasks. They prefer open and spontaneous learning environments and feel "imprisoned" in a highly structured classroom.

Figure 4.1

Extraversion–Introversion

The E–I dimension can indicate the degree of students' reliance on activity in the learning process and how students become involved in activity.

Extraverted students rely on activity more than Introverts. Since Extraverts tend to use their greatest strength, their dominant process, in the external world, they think best when talking, learn well in groups, and may have difficulty sitting in front of a book for a long period of time. They are usually able to concentrate more fully in classrooms that allow for group discussions or when they take frequent *and* active breaks from the typically solitary tasks of reading and writing.

Since they value active experience so highly, Extraverts tend to leap into academic tasks with little planning or consideration. Once actively involved, they use trial-and-error, which naturally suits their types, to complete projects. They prefer the trial-and-error process because it allows them to think while they are active. Thinking while acting or after acting is how Extraverts think best, which is why Jung referred to them as *Epimetheans,* (Greek for "after-thinkers").

Introverted students, on the other hand, need quiet time for concentration and study, for they think best when alone, or at least when their inner solitude is uninterrupted. They are more comfortable than Extraverts with teacher-centered or lecture-based instruction and long stretches of solitary study, but, unless they anticipate questions before hand, they may perform poorly during in-class discussions. Because Introverts do not always share what they know, teachers may be slow to appreciate their talents and depth of knowledge.

Jung called Introverts *Prometheans,* (Greek for "fore-thinkers") because they do most of their thinking *before* they act. They tend to plan extensively, anticipate problems, and develop solutions to these problems before ever becoming involved in a task or activity. If asked a question, Introverts will usually think about their answer, rehearse it, and only then deliver it to their audiences. Extraverts, on the other hand, are more likely to begin answering the questions immediately, thinking of what they want to say as they speak.

Sensing–Intuition

In general, the greatest contrast between Sensing and Intuitive students is how they direct their perceptions. Sensing students tend to focus on the concrete aspects of the here-and-now; they attempt to master first the facts and details of the learning environment. Intuitive students will seek general impressions, or the gestalt of what could possibly be; they will tend to master first the theories and concepts.

Sensing types also like to put into use what they have learned; they are, in general, practical and realistic. Learning for its own sake does not appeal much to them; usefulness does. They like teachers who give clear directions that are concise and to the point, and they tend to be detailed and precise in their own communications. Sensing students can accurately be described as artisans or surgeons. They like to learn a skill or procedure, perfect it, and then practice it without much variation. Thus, they are more likely to complete a task as they have refined it rather than be innovative for the sake of innovation.

Intuitive types are less likely to be patient with routine or overly structured mechanical approaches to learning. They desire and seek the opportunity to let their imaginative instincts work and thus tend to prefer open-ended assignments. Their greatest strength is a facility for learning concepts and mastering abstract theories; their greatest weakness is a reluctance to observe details and learn facts.

Thinking–Feeling

The T–F dimension is most useful for providing insights into the affective domain of learning styles.

Thinking types tend to perform to the best of their ability when given a clearly presented set of performance criteria. They also want to know that their learning will lead toward a greater understanding of the systematic way that the world works and of the principles that underlie systems. In contrast, Feeling types need to know that what they are about to learn can be put to work for people they are concerned about or in the service of personally held convictions and values. They are best motivated when their hearts are in their work. While all students certainly are at their best when both sets of conditions prevail, Thinking types are less likely to complain about dry, uninteresting tasks, as long as they are given a logical reason for doing them. Feeling types, unless given personal encouragement, may find any task boring and unrewarding.

Thinking and Feeling types also differ in how they solve problems and communicate. The talk of Thinking types usually reflects their thought process, which is rule—or principle—based and syllogistic. They often explain their decisions by counting off "reasons" on their fingers: "the first reason is . . . the second reason is . . . the third reason is . . . ." They also frequently punctuate their talk with the markers of an orderly, syllogistic thought: "thus," "therefore," "in conclusion." Their discourse is what Kinneavy (1971, p. 88) calls "thing-centered." They concentrate on content, the message of what is being said, rather than process, how the message is connecting with the audience. They may, as a result, come to their points too quickly or express it too bluntly.

Since the thought of Feeling types is based more on forming hierarchies of values, their talk is more likely to be expressive, filled with markers like "I feel," "I believe," or "I like." Their discourse is more "people-centered" (Kinneavy, 1971, p. 88); they are more concerned with *how* their message is connecting with the audience than with the message itself.

Judging–Perceiving

The J–P dimension is most useful for determining whether or not students prefer structured learning environments. Judging types, who tend to gauge their academic progress by their accomplishments, prefer the kind of structured learning environment in which goals and deadlines are set. Judging types can then take pleasure in accomplishing tasks, in writing papers, reading books, or making oral presentations. Perceiving types depend less on accomplishing tasks to feel comfortable with the learning environment. They tend to view learning as a freewheeling, flexible, and thorough quest that may never end. When in a highly structured classroom, they may feel "imprisoned" and restricted.

Due to their natural desire to reach closure, Judging types tend to be overachievers. They tend to meet important deadlines by keeping commitments limited and focusing on one task at a time. Teachers often view them as being more organized and motivated than Perceiving types. The natural style of Perceiving types, which leads them to overcommit themselves, work on several projects at once, and delay closure until the eleventh hour, may make them appear unmotivated or unorganized. Or they might be viewed as the exceptionally talented student who can program a computer as easily as he or she can compose a piano sonata. Teachers need to realize that the procrastination of a Perceiving type is often as productive as a Judging type's rush to meet a deadline. Perceiving types may delay beginning or finishing projects so that they can more thoroughly conceptualize or research them.

Type and Teaching Style

As any student knows well, teachers also have "styles." Extraverts tend to develop student-based classrooms. They prefer very active instruction full of talk, group projects, and experimental learning; they are also more likely to allow students choice about what to study and how to study it. Introverts, on the other hand, tend to develop teacher-based classrooms. They seem to prefer lectures to discussions and are more likely to structure the learning tasks from the textbook or other instructional materials or from their own plans for the course. Sensing types tend to keep instruction focused on a narrow range of choices and usually concentrate on factual and concrete questions. Intuitive types are more likely, when students can have a choice of assignments, to allow for a wide range of choices. They also tend to focus on questions that involve conjecture, often beginning their questions with "What if . . . ?" Thinking types are more likely to treat a class as a collective, whereas Feeling types are more likely to treat the class as individuals and attempt to attend to each student's needs. Thinking types tend to excel at challenging students, although they may offer little feedback, or at the other extreme, be so critical and harsh that they intimidate rather than motivate. Feeling types are more likely to motivate their students with praise and empathy. Judging types tend to develop orderly classrooms with schedules and deadlines. Perceiving types develop more spontaneous classrooms with more movement, open-ended discussions, and flexible schedules (Lawrence, 1982).

If students have learning styles and instructors have teaching styles, mismatches are clearly inevitable. What happens when an ISTJ instructor, who prefers an orderly and quiet classroom, prefers to lecture about facts and details, gives little feedback, and allows for few options on assignments has an ENFP student, who wants to talk about ideas, craves autonomy, wants to work on projects that are personally relevant, and feels imprisoned by structure and deadlines? Not much. The teacher teaches little, probably because he or she finds the ENFP a constant disruption, and the student learns little, probably because he or she is unmotivated, bored, or rebellious. The problem is one that almost every instructor, to some degree and in some fashion, faces with every class; there is always at least one student who seems impossible to reach, who either acts out or drifts off. Something must be done, but what? Should the teacher adapt to the student's learning style, or the student to the instructor's teaching style?

Initially, theorists of learning styles assumed that instructors should adapt their teaching styles to the students' learning styles. More recently, theorists have questioned the practicality and wisdom of this approach (Partridge, 1983). If an ISTJ instructor adapts his or her teaching style to an ENFP student, then what happens to the other students who may be ISFJs, ESFPs, INTJs, and other types? The teacher cannot adapt to a classroom of thirty students who may represent most of the sixteen MBTI types. Even if instructors could adapt to a diverse class, some theorists believe that students would be ill served. One purpose of education is to help students grow and mature, to adapt to the adult world. Exposing them to a wide variety of teaching styles, some argue, helps students to develop in ways that they could not if only exposed to the one teaching style that is compatible with their learning style (Partridge, 1983).

Perhaps the greatest condemnation of the matching strategy is that it violates some basic assumptions of type theory: that one's type does not change, that one functions best when acting in accordance with one's type, and that attempting to change one's type has dire consequences. By asking instructors to adapt to their students' learning styles, we are asking them to abandon their preferred behaviors, to hold their strengths in reserve, and to teach from their weaknesses. Jung felt that many of the failures of education result from instructors who teach from their weaknesses rather than their strengths. An ENTP instructor, whose strength is in leading discussions about concepts and theories, should not be forced to lecture on facts and details. The results of teachers falsifying their type,

Jung felt, are "educational monstrosities" (1954, 171).

As it is unwise to ask teachers to falsify their types, so too is it unwise to ask students to learn in a process and environment that is foreign to their natures. Yet, if teachers are true to their style and students true to theirs, how can learning occur? How can an ISTJ teach an ENFP?

Without attempting to falsify their types, or abandon their preferred teaching styles, instructors can be more flexible in how they teach. Even though Introverted teachers may prefer to lecture, they can allow some time for class discussion. Even though Sensing teachers may prefer to teach facts and details, they can discuss some theories and concepts. Even though Thinking teachers may like to challenge students, they can also express "pats on the back." Even though Judging teachers like the structure of goals and deadlines, they can also allow for unstructured learning and open-ended assignments. Instructors may not be able to restructure the classroom to meet the needs of each individual, but they can try to include a broad enough range of activities and approaches so that no one type of student feels left out.

When students perform poorly, instructors can also use MBTI results to reach an understanding of what that student needs to improve. For example, if an INTP's theoretical lectures bewilder an ISTP student, the instructor might arrange for the student to receive computer-assisted instruction on the topic; or when the ISTP student asks for a clarification of some point made in the INTP's lecture, the teacher can explain the theory again, this time including several concrete examples.

Finally, type theory can be useful in establishing contact with that student. To quote an educational aphorism, "You have to reach them to teach them." Whenever dealing with an individual student during tutorials, when answering an individual student's question, or when giving written feedback, instructors can attempt to establish contact with students as orators establish contact with audiences. Instructors do not have to match their teaching styles completely to their students' learning styles, as an effective orator does more than simply tell the audience what they want to hear. Rather, instructors can adapt their teaching styles to a particular student's learning style long enough to make contact, establish common ground, and pique interest. Instead of asking an Intuitive instructor with predominately Sensing students to teach facts, we can advise him or her to teach some facts as an entree to teaching concepts and theories. The Intuitive instructor can say, "Let me teach you some facts so that I can interest you in my ideas." Figure 4.2 can aid instructors in establishing contact with students of different types, as an example will illustrate.

Doug (an INFP) wrote the following essay on what bugs him about life, the first of a series of essays for a remedial composition course:

> There are many things in my life that I disapprove of. Not only do they affect my personal being, but also affect everyone in some way. Personally my biggest dislikes are ignorance and hatred towards each other. Everywhere you look you find good examples of this behavior. The situations range from something as simple as inconsiderate drivers of cars, to the superpowers of the world threatening each other. The single largest fault of people is that they won't accept each other. If everyone would try to work with human nature and understand it, then there would be a lot less chaos on this planet.

Unless an instructor was tuned into the student's type, he or she would probably respond only to the faults in the essay. The teacher might scrawl across the margin of Doug's essay: "You need better organization," "You need to develop your ideas," or "You need

Strategies for Making Contact with Students

Extraversion (E)

Making contact: The best way to make contact with Es is through their preferred channel of communication: talk. They usually respond better to oral than to written feedback. Since they value experience, they respond well to compliments about the vitality of their writing.

Words that appeal to Es: experience, vitality, lively, action

Introversion (I)

Making contact: Is will respond better to any situation when given advance notice and when not expected to "think on their feet." Before talking to Is, it is best to tell them what you want to talk about and then schedule an appointment. This will allow them time to think about what they may want to say. Is often respond well to teachers who acknowledge that they have more to say (or write) than they have offered. Is will talk (or write) more when they trust the teacher and when they are not forced to share their ideas.

Words that appeal to Is: thoughtful, serious, sincere

Sensory Perception (S)

Making contact: Ss prefer to process information inductively and attend better to communications that begin with the concrete. Facts, concrete examples, and practical solutions appeal to them. They respond well to compliments about being accurate, reliable, and precise.

Words that appeal to Ss: practical, realistic, solid, concrete, sensible, here-and-now, reliable, accurate

Intuitive Perception (N)

Making contact: Ns prefer to process information deductively and attend better to communications that begin with concepts, theories, or inferences. They love sentences that begin with "What if . . . ?" They value being innovative, original, and theoretical.

Words that appeal to Ns: innovation, possibilities, hunches, inspiration, fantasy

Figure 4.2

(continued)

Strategies for Making Contact with Students

Thinking Judgement (T)

Making contact: Ts value being logical and objective. They react most favorably to logical rationale and analytical thought. They prefer criticism that is to the point and delivered without much affect rather than criticism that is that is softened or indirect.

Words that appeal to Ts: objective, analytic, logical, valid, systematic

Feeling Judgement (F)

Making contact: Fs tend to respond best to communication after personal contact has been made. They prefer to chat informally before getting down to business. They respond well to any acknowledgment of them as individuals: learning their name, asking about their interests and values, a smile, a pat on the back, etc. They often respond well to an instructor saying that he or she enjoyed reading their essays.

Words that appeal to Fs: beliefs, values, personal, heart-felt, touching, interesting, us, we, together, share

Judgment (J)

Making contact: Js are particularly concerned about the passage of time, and usually respond well to compliments about how efficient, expedient, or punctual they are. Js also value being decisive. They tend to view their work, once it is submitted, as finished, and prefer to hear comments about how they can improve the next essay than about how to improve this essay.

Words that appeal to Js: complete, finished, decisive, hardworking, punctual

Perception (P)

Making contact: Ps are usually most concerned about being thorough, so they tend to view their work as ongoing. They prefer to hear about how to improve this essay rather than about how to improve the next essay.

Words that appeal to Ps: thorough, complete, extensive, in-progress, ongoing

Adapted from McCaulley and Natter (1974) and Lawrence (1984).

paragraphs." Doug's instructor, however, chose to use knowledge of type theory to make contact with Doug:

> Doug,
> I get the idea, very clearly, that there are some things about the world we live in that bug you. Me, too! The thing I like most about this essay is that sense of strong values you have, your feeling that there is something wrong out there. But I think that the paper is weak in one major way: you feel the need to mention all the things that bug you. I appreciate your need to be complete, but I think I would understand your feelings even better if you just selected one gripe and developed it more. Then I could get more connected with your values.

With knowledge of Doug's type, the instructor was able to connect with him by acknowledging and accepting Doug's "strong values," which evolve from his preference for Feeling judgment. Once contact was made, the instructor could suggest a revision—that Doug be less inclusive and further develop one or two ideas. Even when suggesting a revision, the instructor acknowledged the values or strengths behind the process that produced a weak text. Doug's preference for the Perceiving attitude led to the inclusion of too many ideas in his short essay. The instructor said that he appreciated Doug's "need to be complete" before suggesting a change. The instructor closed with another appeal to Doug's preference for Feeling judgment by saying, "Then I could get more connected with your values." Since Feeling types want to be connected with their audiences, the comment should provide additional motivation for change.

The effective use of type theory in the classroom, then, entails a seemingly contradictory application. Instructors should remain true to their type, teaching from their strengths, but instructors should also be flexible enough to allow students to employ their preferred approaches to learning. Instructors must not be asked to change their teaching styles, but they should be shown how to make contact with their students.

PROGRAM EXAMPLE

Division of Developmental Studies, Georgia State University

The Division of Developmental Studies at Georgia State University offers instruction in reading, composition, math, and study skills to students who are marginally prepared for college. The teaching is challenging since the students are placed into the program for diverse reasons and have a range of needs. Some of the students are capable but unmotivated; others are capable but the products of poor school systems. Some are motivated but have poor skills; others are motivated but not exceptionally capable. Several of the composition faculty have found the MBTI instrument useful in meeting the needs of this population, as will be explained after some background is provided.

Although composition theorists agree that writing should be taught as a process, they are unable to agree on what sort of process should be taught. For example, Rohman (1965) and others (see Young, 1976) believe that students should be taught prewriting strategies, which are typically questioning heuristics such as the "five Ws" of journalism. They feel that, if students decide what they want to say before writing, then the process of putting words on paper will be easier, and the finished text will embody more sophisticated thought. In direct opposition, Macrorie (1970), Murray (1978), and Elbow (1973) believe that writers should leap into writing with little planning and discover what they want to say as they put words on paper.

One might think that such obvious disagreements among theorists would lead to an uncertainty among teachers, but not necessarily. Of course, some well-informed instructors are uncertain of what to teach and thus give rather permissive advice. They might tell their students, "Some like to outline, others don't" or "Some like to think everything out before they write, others don't." Intuitive types generally find such open-ended advice satisfactory, but Sensing types usually want more direction and may become distressed, confused, and even paralyzed by a variety of options. Many teachers are seemingly unaffected by disagreements of theorists. They continue to issue "rules" of writing: "You must write an outline" or "You must develop a thesis before you write." The unfortunate end result of such dogma is the development of writing anxiety. As students are forced to write in a process that is incompatible with their personality type, writing becomes less natural, more laborious, and more stressful (Jensen and DiTiberio, 1983). As Jung has stated, whenever individuals are forced to function contrary to their type, to falsify their type, they will usually experience stress, acute exhaustion, or even neurosis (1921, p. 332).

The instructors in the Developmental Studies program are faced with the results of both the permissive and dogmatic approaches to teaching composition. Sensing types who were not given adequate direction in high school enter college feeling that there are definite ways to approach writing but that these have been hidden from them—that if only a teacher would tell them *how* to write then they could do it and do it well. These students generally perform better with more guidance, as long as the guidance is compatible with their personality type.

Students of all types who were taught dogmatically that they must write in a prescribed process enter college suffering from writing anxiety. Their anxiety can be relieved if they realign their writing process, and if they begin to write in a process that is more suited to their personality type. The Developmental Studies program instructor, then, needs to provide these distressed or misled students with guidance, but the kind of guidance that is appropriate for each individual student. It is in individualizing advice and instruction that the MBTI instrument is particularly useful.

Jensen and DiTiberio (1984) have shown that composition teachers can use results from the Indicator to make some assumptions about how individuals will tend to write best. Extraverts tend to generate ideas best when talking and prefer to leap into writing with little planning; Introverts, on the other hand, need solitude to think best and prefer to plan extensively—both what to say and how to say it—before writing. Sensing types tend to prefer prescribed organizational patterns, detailed directions, and factual topics; Intuitive types prefer original organizational patterns, general directions, and imaginative, abstract topics. Thinking types think best when they write from patterned structures, while Feeling types tend to write best when they just follow the flow of their thoughts. Judging types, in their rush to meet deadlines, often shorten the research phase and minimize revision. Perceptive types, in their need to keep discovering more about the topic, extend the research phase and revise extensively. For more information about this, see Figure 4.3 (pages 141–142).

Developmental Studies instructors use MBTI results to formulate a working hypothesis of how individual students tend to write best and use this hypothesis to individualize instruction. For example, an Extraverted student may be having difficulty writing because he feels that he must, as he was taught to do in high school, develop an outline before writing. Knowing that Extraverts usually write better when they leap into writing, the instructor can use the theories of Macrorie (1970), and Murray (1978), and Elbow (1973) to show the student how to write without outlines or extensive planning. If an Introverted student is having difficulty developing ideas, the instructor, using the theories of Rohman (1965) and others, might suggest that she use prewriting strategies to clarify her ideas before writing. The MBTI instrument, then, can be used to both resolve apparent contradictions in theory and to individualize instruction, usually with positive results. As students develop more effective and healthy writing processes, writing becomes easier, and the quality of their finished texts improves.

One word of caution should be issued. Even when instructors have their students' MBTI scores, they should not assume that a student who is scored as an Extravert will necessarily write as Extraverts typically do. The measurement of type is not always accurate, and, as stated above, people do not always act consistently within their type. It is best, therefore, to give advice carefully. Different writing contexts also demand that we write in ways that might not come naturally. If teachers have an Extravert who plans extensively before writing, they should not dogmatically insist that the student change his or her writing process. A teacher might say: "You might find writing easier if you just leap into it and write as you think. I'd like you to try this approach and see if it works better for you." After the student tries the approach, the teacher should talk to the student and assess whether or not the new approach was more comfortable and efficient.

As the MBTI instrument provides insight into individual students, so too can it provide insight into particular coteries of students. Since at least the 1950s, composition theorists have been trying to classify the kind of college students found in programs similar to Developmental Studies at Georgia State. These students have been labeled as subfreshmen, remedial writers, basic writers, unskilled writers, and developmental writers; they have been described as being concrete (Lunsford, 1979), unreflective (Pianko, 1979), and overly concerned with "error-hunting" (Perl, 1979). Even though these researchers feel that they are describing the same category of students, one should not assume that the description of "basic writers" (the

The MBTI and Individual Writing Process

Extraversion (E)

Es generate ideas best by talking about the topic, interviewing people, or actively experiencing the topic. They tend to leap into writing with little anticipation and then write by trial-and-error. They tend to develop a great deal of material as they write. As a result, their in-class essays and first drafts may reflect confusion in early paragraphs and clarity in later paragraphs. If they perform traditional prewriting strategies (such as outlining), they can often do so more easily after writing a first draft. Discussing drafts with others helps them to understand the need for revision and what needs to be revised. Some Es (esp. if also J) may not revise at all unless they receive oral feedback.

Introversion (I)

Introverts plan before writing and want most of their ideas clarified before putting words onto paper. When they begin to write, they stop frequently to anticipate the direction of the essay and where their ideas are leading them. They usually spend more time than Extraverts between drafts because they like to have time to consider their revisions. Throughout the writing process, they tend to write alone, asking for advice only from close friends or teachers that they trust.

Sensory Perception (S)

Sensing types prefer explicit, detailed, and specific directions. Their first drafts reflect their inductive thought and are often filled with facts that have not yet been related to a central idea or theme. They feel more comfortable when following a pattern prescribed by the teacher or one that is tried and true, one that they have used in the past. Even during a first draft, they may closely attend to mechanics (grammar, spelling, etc.). They may regard revising as merely correcting or proofreading.

Intuitive Perception (N)

Intuitive types tend to write best when given general directions that allow their imagination to work. Developing a unique approach to the topic is an important part of their prewriting phase. At their best, they tend to write quickly, letting one idea trigger another and paying little attention to mechanics. They tend to innovate organizational patterns. In their first drafts, they may present generalities without examples or concrete support.

Figure 4.3

(continued)

The MBTI and Individual Writing Process

Thinking Judgement (T)

Ts tend to select topics that can be written about with emotional distance rather than self-involvement. They tend to make organizational decisions by following a structure, such as an outline. When writing, they tend to focus on content rather than on how the message is affecting the audience. As a result, they may sometimes be overly blunt.

Feeling Judgement (F)

Feeling types prefer topics that they can care about; they often complain about topics that are dry or "boring." When writing, they tend to draw upon personal experience; for example, their introductions often begin with a personal example. They rely less on structure than Thinking types; they usually begin with a sentence and then follow the flow of their thoughts. They also tend to make organizational decisions by anticipating the audience's reaction to their text.

Judgment (J)

Js tend to limit their topics quickly and set goals that are manageable. They also tend to limit their research so that they can begin writing more quickly and complete the project. Their first drafts tend to be short and underdeveloped with ideas stated emphatically and often without qualification.

Perception (P)

Ps tend to select broad topics and dive into research without limiting them. Topics will usually be limited only as the deadline approaches. They want to thoroughly research or analyze a topic, often without a clear focus, before beginning to write and may feel that there is always one more book or article to read. Their drafts tend to be long and thorough. Their writing may ramble because they are inclusive of ideas and data.

Figure 4.3 *From Jensen and DiTiberio, "Personality and Individual Writing Processes," College Composition and Communication, 35 (October 1984), 285–300.*

most commonly employed label) at one university is similar to that at another university (Shaughnessy, 1976). Descriptions of basic writers are usually inaccurate when applied to the students in a particular program at a particular university or college (Jensen 1986).

A type table of the students in an instructor's class or in an entire program can provide data for refining the crude characterizations found in professional literature. Table 4.4 is a type table of 188 composition students in the Developmental Studies program. The table shows that the program seems to have a roughly equal distribution of Extraverts and Introverts, but significantly more Sensing types, Thinking types, and Judging types. From this data, one might predict that the typical student in this program is a very structured learner, which is generally true of STJs and consistent with instructors' hunches about their students. Should, then, the instructors in this program teach to the typical students? Should they, for example, have all students write on the kind of concrete, detailed, and structured writing topics that appeal to STJs?

The type table, again, provides useful information. If the instructors teach primarily to the STJs, what would happen to the Intuitive students? The Intuitive types are definitely a minority, but thirty percent of the population is a sizeable minority that would be ill served if instructors relied only on their hunches about the student population, or descriptions of basic writers in professional literature. By compiling type tables, the instructors in the Developmental Studies program can both understand the typical student and appreciate the diversity of the population. Table 4.4 shows an over-representation by STJs, but all of the sixteen types appear.

In the Developmental Studies program, these data have been used to make program-wide decisions, such as the selection of topics for an exit essay exam, which all students must pass in order to enter regular English classes. Since the students are predominately Sensing types, the

Students in Developmental Composition Georgia State University (Eleven Classes from Fall 1982 to Winter 1985)

N = 190

SENSING – THINKING	SENSING – FEELING	INTUITION – FEELING	INTUITION – THINKING	
ISTJ N = 40 % = 21.05 ■■■■■■■■■■■■■■■■■■■■■	**ISFJ** N = 12 % = 6.32 ■■■■■■	**INFJ** N = 2 % = 1.05 ■	**INTJ** N = 4 % = 2.11 ■■	JUDGMENT / INTROVERSION
ISTP N = 12 % = 6.32 ■■■■■■	**ISFP** N = 9 % = 4.74 ■■■■	**INFP** N = 4 % = 2.11 ■■	**INTP** N = 14 % = 7.37 ■■■■■■■	PERCEPTION / INTROVERSION
ESTP N = 16 % = 8.42 ■■■■■■■■	**ESFP** N = 5 % = 2.63 ■■	**ENFP** N = 10 % = 5.26 ■■■■■	**ENTP** N = 7 % = 3.68 ■■■	PERCEPTION / EXTRAVERSION
ESTJ N = 24 % = 12.63 ■■■■■■■■■■■■	**ESFJ** N = 16 % = 8.42 ■■■■■■■■	**ENFJ** N = 6 % = 3.16 ■■■	**ENTJ** N = 9 % = 4.74 ■■■■	JUDGMENT / EXTRAVERSION

	N	%
E	93	48.95
I	97	51.05
S	134	70.53
N	56	29.47
T	126	66.32
F	64	33.68
J	113	59.47
P	77	40.53
IJ	58	30.53
IP	39	20.53
EP	38	20.00
EJ	55	28.95
ST	92	48.42
SF	42	22.11
NF	22	11.58
NT	34	17.89
SJ	92	48.42
SP	42	22.11
NP	35	18.42
NJ	21	11.05
TJ	77	40.53
TP	49	25.79
FP	28	14.74
FJ	36	18.95
IN	24	12.63
EN	32	16.84
IS	73	38.42
ES	61	32.11
ET	56	29.47
EF	37	19.47
IF	27	14.21
IT	70	36.84
Sdom	73	38.42
Ndom	23	12.11
Tdom	59	31.05
Fdom	35	18.42

Note: ■ = One Percent
Georgia State University, Eleven Classes from Fall 1982 to Winter 1985

Table 4.4

instructors are careful to develop topics that are concrete and detailed, such as:

> When you receive this month's MASTERCARD and VISA bill, you notice, much to your horror, that you have been erroneously charged with $3,400 worth of merchandise that you did not purchase. Rushing to check your wallet, you are relieved to discover your credit card secure. Now, you can assume that the credit card company has made an error, or that someone has duplicated your credit card number. Write a letter to the credit card company notifying them of this serious error. You do not have to mention every item, but you should argue why it was impossible for you to make some of the following purchases:
>
> - $400 worth of clothing from Davison's on April 4
> - $1600 vacation to the Bahamas from Delta Airlines on April 5
> - $230 worth of make-up from J.C. Penney's on April 6
> - $170 worth of tires from Firestone on April 8
> - $500 videotape machine from Rich's on April 5
> - $60 worth of fishing equipment from K-MART on April 10
> - $42 dinner at Po'Folks on April 14
> - $350 stereo from Radio Shack on April 18
> - $47 worth of harp music records from Turtles on April 17

However, because Intuitive types make up a sizeable minority of students, the instructors also develop more conceptual and open-ended questions, such as:

> John Boulton, who recently lost his job as a welder, was walking down the sidewalk in Cabbage Town carrying a duffle bag when a police car pulled up beside him and two officers got out and demanded to see what was in the bag. They examined the contents and found nothing but his clothes. After explaining that there had just been a robbery down the road, they sped away in their car. Write a letter to William Daniels, Chief of Police, in defense of this man's rights or defending the policemen's actions. Before writing, you may want to imagine how Boulton looks and acts, and how the police actually treated him.

By being aware of the diversity of the students in the Developmental Studies program, the instructors are better able to serve the needs of *all* students.

PROGRAM EXAMPLE

The Academic Skills Program, Counseling Service, University of Illinois at Chicago (Health Sciences Campus)

The Academic Skills Program, a division of the Counseling Service of the University of Illinois at Chicago, provides both group and individual instruction in reading composition, and study skills. Since its clientele are predominately students from the health sciences, the staff in the program more frequently deal with skills at the other end of the spectrum than do the instructors in the Developmental Studies program. The clients of the Academic Skills program are generally bright and highly motivated; they also tend to have been successful students. However, when they are faced with the pressures of a health sciences curriculum, they find that their skills, which may have been adequate in high school or in undergraduate school, must be improved or refined. The setting of the Academic Skills program is also different. The Developmental Studies program is an academic unit, the Academic Skills program is a clinic. In a clinic, staff are able to spend more time diagnosing the causes of each student's difficulties and developing individualized interventions, and the MBTI instrument can be a useful diagnostic tool.

Most of the nursing students at the University of Illinois are capable and dedicated students. They are able to master course content with hard work, but they often have difficulty demonstrating their knowledge on objective tests. At many universities, staff may attempt to improve students' test-taking skills by giving what is ultimately platitudinous advice (for example, "Look for key words") or by teaching guessing techniques (for example, "If in doubt, pick the longest alternative"). Such interventions can be helpful, but they hardly address the fundamental problems that students have with taking tests. To move beyond mere advice and guessing techniques, one must obtain as many insights as possible into the thought process behind answering test questions. In the Academic Skills program, the staff have students "think aloud" as they read sample test questions. These protocols, when coupled with knowledge of the student's type, can provide useful glimpses into how a particular student analyzes test questions. The following examples of how Cheryl (an ISTJ nursing student) misread questions will illustrate this.

Nursing students must learn from two important media: lectures and clinical experience. For Sensing types, the clinical experience often assumes hegemony over the theory of a lecture, leading them to misread questions such as:

> **Question:** It would be appropriate to explain to a patient on a restricted diet why he or she cannot eat certain foods in order that he or she:

1. does not think his or her diet restrictions are punitive
2. will not eat incorrect foods appearing on his or her tray
3. can continue dietary patterns after discharge
4. feels that he or she has an active role in his or her care

Answers:

a. 1 and 2
b. 2, 3, and 4
c. 1, 2, and 4
d. All of the above

When Cheryl read this question, she felt that all possible alternatives were correct except number three. She eliminated number three because in her clinical experience, she had seen very few patients have restricted diets after leaving the hospital. While number three may have seemed irrelevant to the facts of her experience, it is nonetheless compatible with nursing theory. Cheryl's reliance on the facts of her experience (S), as well as her inability to accept number three as something that might possibly occur (which would be more typical of Ns), led her to select "c" rather than "d," the correct answer.

At other times, Cheryl's inability to view the "big picture" (typical of immature Sensing types) led her astray, as with the question below:

Question: Mr. S. is an 85-year-old man admitted to the hospital with arteriosclerosis (increasing rigidity of the blood vessels). Knowing these facts, you would expect to find:

1. decreased pulse rate
2. rise in systolic pressure
3. decrease in diastolic pressure
4. rise in pulse pressure
5. no change in pulse pressure

Answers:

a. 1 and 5
b. 2, 3, and 4
c. 1, 2, 3, and 5
d. 2 and 4
e. 1, 2, and 4

After reading the question, Cheryl felt that number one was a correct response. She reasoned that, since Mr. S.'s blood vessels were rigid, then less blood would be able to flow through them. The result would be a decreased pulse rate. Cheryl's thought process was basically logical, but she made the mistake of analyzing a question on histology, which is a science of body systems, too logically and specifically. While it is true that hardened vessels allow less blood to pass, the cardiovascular system still demands the same amount of oxygen. Therefore, in order to meet the body's demand, the heart must pump faster to supply the same amount of oxygenated blood through a rigidly narrow vessel.

Protocols, or "thinking aloud," can provide valuable information about how a student is reading test questions, but instructors can make more sense of a student's spoken thoughts if they use knowledge of type to interpret them. As the MBTI instrument is useful in diagnosing how students misread test questions (see Figure 4.4), so too is it useful in diagnosing their difficulties with reading (see Figure 4.5), study skills (see Figure 4.1, page 126), and time management (see Figure 4.6).

Conclusion

As stated earlier, the Indicator is not a panacea for the ills of education, but it is certainly a very powerful and useful instrument. It can be a catalyst for helping students to understand how they learn best, for helping teachers understand why certain students are performing poorly, and for helping teachers make contact with their students. Many learning styles instruments can offer similar aid, but the MBTI instrument does more. It can also help teachers to move past behaviors to cognitive processes in order to better understand the thought processes of students quite different from themselves.

The S–N Dimension and Test-Taking

Sensory Perception (S)

When Ss read test questions, they often have hunches as to the correct answer, but they rarely trust their hunches. Frequently, they begin to reread the questions repeatedly, looking for a concrete clue (a fact, underlined, something that relates to their experience, etc.). They often reread a question until they misread it. They may also answer theoretical questions with lived experience, fail to grasp the big picture or system behind the question, and generally lose points by changing answers.

Intuitive Perception (N)

Intuitive types tend to read test questions quickly, at times carelessly, trust their hunch and then move on to the next question. Because they trust their hunches, they are often better test-takers than Ss, but they can often pick up points by checking for careless errors. Their misreading of questions is usually due to a faulty inference, a line of thought that begins with "What if . . . ?" A single inference is usually appropriate, but Ns often make inferences from inferences and stray too far from the core of the question.

Note: Only the S–N dimension has been included because the effects of other dimensions on test-taking appear to be marginal.

Figure 4.4

The MBTI and Reading

Extraversion (E)

Some Es may have difficulty concentrating on reading for long stretches of time. They often understand difficult sections of texts better if they process them orally.

Introversion (I)

Although Is may be able to concentrate for longer stretches of time, they may sometimes lose concentration because they begin to contemplate what they read and become lost in a daydream.

Sensing (S)

When learning to read, Ss may have difficulty learning the code of written language. Sometimes, they benefit from the language-experience approach, phonics instruction or other techniques that can help to break the "code." Even when mature, Ss may focus on the facts of a text and neglect the concepts.

Intuition (N)

Since they tend to have a greater facility for symbols, Ns usually learn to read with less difficulty and tend to be more "bookish." Even when mature, they may focus on the concepts of a text and neglect the facts.

Thinking (T)

Ts often focus so fully on the message of a text that they may neglect the style or tone. They often have a greater tolerance for "dry academic treatises." They also tend to be more critical of what they read.

Feeling (F)

Fs tend to be very sensitive to tone and style. They may enjoy an author simply because they like his or her style. They often become bored with texts that do not engage their personal values.

Judgment (J)

Ts often focus so fully on the message of a text that they may neglect the style or tone. They often have a greater tolerance for "dry academic treatises." They also tend to be more critical of what they read.

Perception (P)

Ps tend to more thoroughly read and process texts. This may cause them to read more slowly or become bogged down in research.

Figure 4.5

The MBTI and Time Management

Extraversion (E)

Es are most motivated when approaching active tasks and may neglect more typically introverted tasks like reading and studying. They sometimes work inefficiently because they leap into tasks without planning and work by trial-and-error. They need to learn that tasks can sometimes be completed more efficiently if they attempt to plan a bit before acting.

Introversion (I)

Is may have longer attention spans for reading arid studying, but they often avoid more typically extraverted tasks, e.g., scheduling meetings, returning phone calls, etc. They naturally like to contemplate a task before beginning it, but they may think too long before acting. It is often more efficient to simply leap into a task.

Sensing (S)

Ss often avoid more theoretical tasks and can sometimes spend more time on the details of a task than necessary. Ss may also become locked into their routine approaches to tasks, even when these approaches are inefficient.

Intuition (N)

Ns often have to redo tasks because they neglected important details; they also tend to avoid routine chores. They may want to complete each task (even if it is writing a memorandum) in a unique way, which may be more time consuming.

Thinking (T)

Ts tend to schedule what they feel are the most important tasks first, even if these tasks are the most unpleasant ones. The unfortunate consequence is that Ts sometimes never get around to more rewarding and relaxing activities.

Feeling (F)

Fs tend to schedule the tasks about which they care the most, whether or not these are the most pressing ones. They may avoid tasks that are not connected to their personal values.

Judgment (J)

Js tend to be natural time managers, with one important caveat. They are good at making schedules and sticking to them, but they are not always flexible. They need to learn how to "plan to be spontaneous." They need to plan to stop at key intervals and re-evaluate their schedules.

Perception (P)

The more spontaneous Ps are often reluctant to make schedules. When they do, they often fail to follow them or conveniently lose their "list of things to do." Ps may also overcommit themselves and have trouble meeting important deadlines. Ps need to learn how to prioritize and concentrate on the most important tasks.

Figure 4.6

References

Elbow, P. (1973). *Writing with power.* New York: Oxford.

Grindler, J., and R. Bandler. (1976). *The structure of magic II.* Palo Alto, CA: Science and Behavior Books.

Jensen, G. H. (1986). The reification of the basic writer. *Journal of Basic Writing,* 5(1) 52–64.

Jensen, G. H., and J. K. DiTiberio. (1983). The MBTI and writing blocks. *MBTI News,* 5,14–15.

Jensen, G. H., and J. K. DiTiberio. (1984). Personality and individual writing processes. *College Composition and Communication,* 35, 285–300.

Jung, C. G. (1921). *Psychological types.* Princeton, NJ: Princeton University Press.

Jung, C. G. (1954). *The development of personality type.* Princeton, NJ: Princeton University Press.

Kinneavy, J. L. (1971). *A theory of discourse.* Englewood Cliffs, NJ: Prentice Hall.

Keefe, J. W. (1982). Assessing student learning styles: An overview. In *Student Learning Styles and Brain Behavior.* Reston, VA: National Association of Secondary School Principals.

Kuhn, T. S. (1970). *The structure of scientific revolutions* (2nd ed.). Chicago: Chicago University Press.

Lawrence, G. (1982). *People types and tiger stripes: A practical guide to learning styles.* Gainesville, FL: Center for Applications of Psychological Type.

Lawrence, G. (1984). A synthesis of learning style research involving the MBTI. *Journal of Psychological Type,* 8, 2–15.

Lowen, W. (1982). *Dichotomies of the mind: A systems science model of the mind and personality.* New York: John Wiley & Sons.

Lunsford, A. (1979). Cognitive development and the basic writer. *College English*, 41, 37–46.

McCaulley, M. H., and F. L. Natter. (1974). *Psychological (Myers-Briggs) type differences in education.* Gainesville, FL: Center for Applications of Psychological Type.

Macrorie, K. (1970). *Telling writing.* Rochelle Park, NJ: Hayden.

Murray, D. M. (1978). Write before writing. *College Composition and Communication*, 29, 375–81.

Myers, I. B. with P. B. Myers. (1980). *Gifts differing.* Palo Alto, CA: Consulting Psychologists Press.

Partridge, R. (1983). Learning styles: A review of selected models. *Journal of Nursing Education*, 22, 243–48.

Perl, S. (1979). The composing processes of unskilled college writers. *Research in the Teaching of English*, 13, 317–36.

Pianko, S. (1979). Reflection: A critical component of the composing process. *College Composition and Communication*, 30, 275–78.

Rohman, G. D. (1965). Prewriting: The stage of discovery in the writing process. *College Composition and Communication*, 16, 106–12.

Shaughnessy, M. P. G. (1976). Basic writing. Gary Tate (Ed.). In *Teaching Composition: Ten bibliographical essays.* Fort Worth, TX: Texas Christian University Press.

Young, R. (1976). Invention. In *Teaching composition: Ten bibliographical essays.* Fort Worth, TX: Texas Christian University Press.

CHAPTER 5

Diverse Learners in the 21st Century

DANIEL C. ROBINSON AND KAY ANN TAYLOR

> "*The chief reason why so many give such little attention to the background of the Negro is the belief that this study is unimportant . . . . To educate the Negro we must find out exactly what his [sic] background is, what he is today, what his possibilities are, and how to begin with him as he is and make him a better individual of the kind that he is. Instead of cramming in the Negro's mind with what others have shown that they can do, we should develop his latent powers that he may perform in society a part of which others are not capable.*"
> (Woodson [1933] 1999, 190–151)

Significant strides are being made in investigating, determining, and beginning to identify learning styles for diverse groups in the United States and internationally. Recent research utilizing the Myers-Briggs Type Indicator® (MBTI®) instrument demonstrates that, although progress is being made, much research and study remains to be done in an effort to level the educational playing field in teaching, learning, and opportunity for all of our children. Our focus in this chapter addresses the learning styles of African-American students in higher education. Further, this focus broadens to address the implications for all students of color, in the United States and globally. However, before we can understand college students and what benefits them, it is imperative that we first understand them at an early age, as children, so that they may receive the benefit of learning that is meaningful to them and experience success as a foundation upon which to build toward their college years. As noted by Janice E. Hale (1986):

> Attempts to understand the learning styles of Black children cannot advance without the development of an appropriate social-psychological theory of the educational process. This theory must identify the social, historical, and cultural forces that create and maintain them. It must seek to describe the cultural context out of which creative and intellectual responses occur. The thesis . . . is that psychology is social as well as personal and that we cannot separate an individual's cognitive (thinking) processes from his [sic] emotional processes. (Hale, 1986, p. 5)

It is toward this end that the MBTI instrument holds the potential to broaden opportunities for learning for African-American children in the United States. Further, ongoing research and study of the Indicator in identifying learning styles of African-American children, and other children of color, holds the promise of educating teachers and learners in unleashing not only the true potential of our children, but of opening the doors to a truly equitable education for all. With the increase in student populations of color, not only the future of our children is paramount, but so also is the future of our country and our world.

Overall U. S. national college enrollment trends show an increase in college enrollment from approximately 6 million in 1965 to a projected 16 million in 2009 with a total population of 270,299,000. Racial and ethnic distribution for this population is cited as American Indian, 0.9%; Asian, 3.7%; White, 82.7%; and Hispanic (may be any race), 11.0%. The proportion of those who speak a language other than English at home is 13.8%. Per-capita personal income is $26,412 and the poverty rate is 13.5% (The Chronicle of Higher Education Online, 1999). College enrollment since the mid-1980s for students of color increased 61.3% between 1986 and 1996. This includes a 22.2% increase since 1991. However, during the last several years, the rate of increase has slowed; from 1995 to 1996, students of color gained in enrollment by 3.2%. College enrollment rates for Whites have decreased by 6.9% since 1991, including a slight decrease in 1996. Enrollment gains were made by both men and women of color in higher education in 1996. In 1996, enrollment of students of color increased at each of the three major levels of higher education—undergraduate, graduate, and professional (Wilds and Wilson, 1998).

Review of the Literature

In the early 1920s, Katharine Briggs and Isabel Myers began studying Jung, became "type watchers," and started making their own observations to extend and develop Carl Jung's theory of psychological types. In 1951, Myers embarked on a longitudinal study of 5,355 medical students from forty-five schools. After Myers was invited as a seminar presenter at the Educational Testing Service (ETS) in 1956, ETS decided to publish the MBTI instrument and incorporated it into ongoing college student studies. Myers' *Manual* was first published in 1962, along with MBTI Form F, which was for research only. As such, the MBTI personality assessment tool, which identifies sixteen different personality types, or approaches to learning, has a history of almost eighty years (Center for Applications of Psychological Type,

1993). Kirby and Barger (1998) note that, "since the publication of the 1985 *MBTI® Manual*, there has been a rapid expansion experienced in the use of the MBTI personality inventory in international and multicultural settings" (367). Kirby and Barger provide examples of studies conducted in other cultures where the reliability and validity of the MBTI instrument was supported. In particular, studies conducted "in predominately English-speaking cultures report results very similar to those of validity studies conducted in the United States" (369). In contrast, there are cultural groups for whom the MBTI instrument may not be appropriate. For example, van Heerden (1997) translated the Murphy-Meisgeier Type Indicator for Children (MMTIC™) into Afrikaans and Xhosa and applied it to a group of 2,205 South African secondary pupils, standard 6 to 10, grades eight through twelve. De Beer (1997) reported a database of almost 6,500 South Africans, which included 930 Blacks. Concerns expressed by De Beer parallel those by U.S. researchers when considering social, cultural, and historical contexts of African Americans. Specifically, De Beer identified the concept of *ubuntu* in South Africa, "*ubuntu* is characterized by the following values: solidarity, cooperation, hospitality, tolerance, joyful service, harmony, dignity, compassion, consensus, trust, compromise, accommodation, caring about others, and readiness to 'go the extra mile'" (12). These characteristics and values are directly opposed to the dominant ideology in the United States; however, they are quite similar, if not identical, in nature to those discussed in the following paragraph.

Numerous researchers have identified that cultural, social, and historical contexts and experiences have a profound impact on the learning styles of African-American children and other people of color (Allen and Boykin, 1992; Boykin, 1992; Darling-Hammond, 1997; Donaldson, 1996; Hale, 1986 and 1994; Nieto, 1996; Shade, 1982). Asa Hilliard (1983, 1987) emphasizes this by stating:

> Misunderstanding of cultural behavioral style has been shown to lead to errors in the estimation of a student's or cultural group's: (1) intellectual potential (the consequences of which—mislabeling, misplacement, and mistreatment of children—are enormous); (2) learned abilities or achievement in academic subjects such as reading; and (3) language abilities.

Banks (1993) noted that more research is needed on learning styles of African-American children because research results lack clarity about race and socioeconomic class as separate variables that affect achievement.

The classroom organization for White children and the analytical style more common to them was contrasted with the relational style, reflective of African-American cultural strengths by Hale (1986) with Cohen's work (1969). In general, schools are analytical in approach and support this style of learning (Cohen, 1969; Hilliard, 1976) that emphasizes conformity, standardization, deduction and is atomistic and reductionist in philosophy and practice. In contrast, the relational approach typified by African-American children promotes flexibility, expressiveness, contextuality, humanism, inductiveness, and is more global and unique wherein sameness equals oppression (Hilliard, 1976).

African Americans and the MBTI

When these characteristics are translated into the MBTI instrument for African-American students, results are emerging that advance Battle's (1989, 1992, and 1994) research investigating the higher likelihood that more U. S. Black respondents than Whites misreport themselves on the Indicator, particularly in the direction of STJ. At the July, 1999, Multicultural and International Issues symposium, Pat Battle and Kim Battle focused their presentation on African-American students and type. Their research was part of a larger examination of type as it relates to African Americans. The data were presented comparing a number of diverse groups of students from Johns Hopkins University (master's degree level), Lincoln University (entering freshman), Coppin State College (honors students), Columbia, MD, (suburban seventh graders), and Howard University. Their research suggests a need to continue to study African-American students and the impact of culture, race, oppression, and other variables on how they respond to the MBTI instrument. Evidence has shown that generalizations derived from studies of White samples do not truly capture an understanding and appreciation of the uniqueness of African Americans. This has been substantiated by several researchers (Battle, 1984, 1989, and 1998; Carlson and Levy, 1940; Gurin, Gurin, Lao, and Beattie, 1969; Hedgegard and Brown, 1969 as cited in Robinson, 1999) who agreed that further research is needed.

Blacks in the U. S., South Africa, Trinidad, and Tobago

In discussing a comparative study of Blacks in the U. S., South Africa, Trinidad, and Tobago, Battle, Robinson, and Battle (1998) identified that through research, findings indicate that the MBTI assessment tool shows African Americans preferring a basic style that (1) values tasks as more important than relationships (T–F), (2) reports being precise and detailed vs. focusing on the big picture (S–N), has a predisposition for establishing rules and working with timetables and standard operating procedures (SJ). The study further demonstrated the impact of colonialism on African Americans and Afrocentric people. Battle, Robinson, and Battle note that African Americans overwhelmingly respond to the MBTI instrument with a preference of STJ. It has been posited that the way African Americans respond to the Indicator misses some of the essence of the individual. Binding identities in dichotomous terms must be avoided if the core identity is to be unraveled. Du Bois enlightens us in the direction of the twoness, or duality of the African American:

> It is a peculiar sensation, this double consciousness, this sense of always looking at one's self through the eyes of others, of measuring one's souls by the tape of a world that looks on in amused contempt and pity.
>
> One ever feels this twoness as an American, a Black, two souls, two thoughts, two unreconciled strivings, two warring ideals in one dark body, whose strength keeps it from being torn asunder. (Du Bois as cited in Battle, Robinson, and Battle, 1998)

Culture Shifting

Battle coined the term "culture shifting," which is the art of skillfully traveling between cultures. This "shifting" describes the adaptability of African Americans in negotiating the terrain between cultures. In the U. S., this particularly applies to the dominant White culture and African-American culture and how the individual relates to and interacts with others, depending on which paradigm they are negotiating at the time. Ames (1950), offers one example of "culture shifting":

- Got one mind for White folks to see
- Another for what I know is me.
- They don't know that they don't know my mind. (Ames 1950 as cited in Battle, Robinson, and Battle, 1998)

Masking

Battle and Harrison recently referred to a "masking effect" on type for African Americans. Battle explained how African-American culture instructed her to conform to a STJ culture because African-American males are nurtured to be social, or extraverted, for the purpose of being aware of what is happening around them from the standpoint of safety and self-protection. It further was noted that African American males value the present, Sensing, to align themselves with justice, not values; Thinking in order to think on their feet; Extraverted Thinking to act here and now, "because there are no guarantees," Judging.

Cultural masking is a result of cultural expectations that are verbal or nonverbal. Barlund (1975) noted how important the nonverbal portion of cultural communication is, "the most significant aspects of any cultural code may be conveyed implicitly, not by rule or lesson but through modeling behavior" (p. 4). A review of the literature on Asian Americans and type yielded a lack of data. One sample was drawn from high school through adult ages from the Asian-American community in the San Francisco Bay area and included 208 Asian Americans—54% Japanese, 26% Chinese, 10% Filipino, 0.5% Korean, 1.4% Asian Indian/South Asian, 6.3% Vietnamese, and 1.4% other (Southeast Asian). Results showed that Japanese Americans best fit the type ISTJ and had the most occurrence, 16.8% as compared with 14.0% adult college graduates. Japanese Americans also had higher occurrence of ISTJ than all other Asians; however there was no significance when compared with both U. S. adult college graduates and Asian Americans in the study. The broad implication of this study is that more research with the MBTI instrument and people of color is needed because of similarities among people of color responding to the Indicator, particularly STJ. Both masking and adaptability (culture shifting) factors pose challenges for future research. African Americans and all people of color, i.e., traditionally groups in the U. S., represent a changing U. S. society as their population continues to rise.

Lawrence and Robinson (2000) recently provided insight into using the MBTI instrument as building blocks in humane and effective approaches to education. Special focus and attention was given to psychological type as a window on students' intrinsic motivations for learning and development; responding to the changing demographics of college students—i.e., increased population in students of color—with specific focus on multicultural/cross-cultural applications of the Indicator; and lessons learned about adapting instruction to the ways children's minds work.

Recent research conducted by Posey, Thorne, and Carskadon (1999) opens the door to further research in testing Battle's hypothesis. As stated by Carskadon, "Although at present the differences found do not appear to be alarming, our hats are off to Pat Battle for successfully predicting where they would occur" (p. 3).

Type Distributions for Various Groups

Listed here are type distributions for various cultural groups.

South Africa

De Beer's (1997) South African database of 6,452 people demonstrates that ESTJ and ISTJ are the most common types for not only Black South Africans, but also for White South Africans. These two types represented almost 39% of the 5,000 White African group, whereas 930 Black South Africans, or 67.6%, reported these types. Interestingly, Malone (1988) reported that almost 38% of the sample of 302 Black, White, and Hispanic managers from a Midwest firm were either ISTJ or ESTJ. The group most likely to be TJ were Black, in contrast to their White counterparts and the combined sample as a whole.

Eskimo

An example of an application of the MBTI instrument in Eskimo culture, specifically Aleknagik students in Alaska, is found in Chapman's (1994) work. Through the assistance of MBTI consultants, the school environment was transformed into one that reflected student and staff preferences, as well as reflected the traditional Eskimo culture and values of cooperative, hands-on learning with community involvement. Ninety percent of the Aleknagik students reported a preference for Introversion, with 90% reporting a preference for Perceiving. Sensing and Intuition were split 50-50 between the students and 70-30 for Thinking and Feeling dichotomy. The combination of Sensing and Judging was not reported by any of the students.

Asian and Asian-American

The Japanese-American sample (N=142) and Caucasian sample (N=105) of college students of ancestry in Hawaii reported on by Levy and Ostrowski (1983) revealed MBTI types by the Japanese-American sample's significantly higher preference for Introversion and Judging compared to the Caucasian sample. Type distributions of 2,182 students representing ethnic backgrounds of Japanese, Caucasian, Chinese, Filipino, mixed ethnicity, and Hawaiians were reported on by Jones, Ukishima, Sakamoto, Tanouye, and Giron (1995). Preferences and combinations that were significantly higher at the .01 or .001 level included the following:

Japanese: Feeling (61%), IJ (38%), and FJ (34%)

Caucasian: Intuitive (66%), Perceiving (50%), NP (40%), and IN (37%)

Chinese: ST (32%), IS (38%), Sensing, (59%)

Filipino: Sensing (75%), Judging (73%), SJ (56%), and TJ (42%)

Hawaiians: Extraverted (59%), EJ (41%), and ES (34%)

Mixed Asian: Judging (75%) and FJ (44%)

The types of 687 University of Hawaii (UH) students were compared by Moody (1995) to the types of University of Florida freshmen (Myers and McCaulley, 1985). The group of students was considered to be a good representation of the student body. The comparison indicated similarities; however there were two major differences: (1) a significantly larger (<.001) percentage of Thinking types (50%) among the UH students; and (2) a slightly higher proportion of Judging types (<.05) among the UH students (53%). The most over-represented preference combinations in the different ethnic groups were as follows:

Chinese: TJ (47%), SJ (47%)

Filipinos: SJ (46%), FJ (38%)

Japanese: IJ (39%), NF (39%)

Hawaiians: ST (44%), SP (38%), TP (41%), ES (39%)

The groups' modal types were:

Chinese: ISTJ (20%)

Filipinos: ISTJ (17%)

Japanese: INFJ (14%), ISTJ (13%)

Hawaiians: ESTP (15%), ISTP (13%)

Moody further found in a comparison with three other samples—the Williams et al. (1992) mainland Chinese sample of college students and a study of Taiwanese (Hwang and Chi-en, 1991)—that similar patterns of over-representation of TJ were found among the three samples.

Native Americans

One hundred sixty-four (46 male and 118 female) Navajo students enrolled as freshmen and sophomore level courses in psychology, reading, human relations, and general business at the Tsaile Campus of Navajo Community College were given the MBTI by Huitt (1988) to provide guidelines for effective instructional methods. The Navajo students' results were compared with a sample of U. S. college students from the Center for Applications of Psychological Type (CAPT) data bank and were found to differ substantially on all four scales. ISTJ was the most frequent MBTI type for both male and female Navajo students, with their populations appearing more homogeneous than the non-Navajo population. The Navajo sample distributions were Introversion (65%), Sensing (84%), Thinking (males) (83%), Thinking (females) (60%), and Judging (66%), whereas the U. S. Student Sample Population distributions were Extraversion (57%), Sensing (60%), Thinking (males) 57%, Feeling (females) (61%), and Judging (55%).

All freshmen at Pembroke State University in North Carolina took the MBTI instrument and provided the base group for Simmons and Barrineau's (1994) study of MBTI results and SRTT analysis for 210 nonreservation Lumbee Indian Native-American college freshmen. There were 756 members in the total group with 59% White, 28% Native American, 12% Black, and 1% other, with 51% male and 49% female. Native-American students reported 78% Sensing, which was significantly higher at the .001 level than the base group. A higher preference for Feeling than the base group also was reported by the Native

Americans and was significant at the .05 level. The T–F differences were not significant when gender was controlled, but the S–N differences maintained a significance level of .05. Simmons and Barrineau cautioned that the Native Americans in their sample were not representative of all Native Americans, nor of all Lumbee Indians.

Nuby and Oxford (1998) used the MBTI instrument to identify learning styles of Native American and African-American high school students. Although both groups favored EST, judging was preferred by half of the African Americans but by fewer than 25% of the Native Americans. Instructional implications were noted in this study.

African Americans

African-American students in a study conducted by Johnson (1989) were significantly more Sensing and Thinking than their White counterparts. Johnson's report addressed the MBTI types and learning styles of Black and White college freshmen in Oklahoma. Race, gender, grade-point average, and size of high school were controlled. A multivariate analysis of covariance was used to determine if there were differences between the two groups.

MBTI results reported by Battle (1989) for 400 African Americans, most of whom were college graduates or who had attended college, indicated that they reported higher percentages of preferences for Sensing, Thinking, and Judging when compared to type distributions from mostly White respondents with a similar education found in the CAPT data bank. Battle (1994) further reported that the MBTI instrument indicates that most Blacks prefer STJ.

The MBTI was used by Melear and Pitchford (1991) with a sample of 134 African-American students, 78 females and 56 males, in science courses. The conclusion of the researchers was that more African Americans were Sensing than were the White students. They found that male African Americans in the sample were more Extraverted, Sensing, Thinking, and Perceiving when compared to Isabel Myers' sample and that the female African Americans in the sample were more Sensing, Thinking, and Perceiving.

Melear and Richardson (1994) reported research for a sample of 184 high school males and 212 sixth-grade male and female African-American students from eastern North Carolina regarding their learning styles by using the MBTI instrument. When compared to Myers' sample of mostly White high school males in college preparatory classes (N=3,503) and with a sample of male Howard University students (N=332), the African-American males were significantly more ISTJ and ESTP (<.001). The study indicated that African-American males preferred more Sensing, Thinking, SP, TP, and SJ. When compared to the Howard University males, the African-American high school males were significantly more ESTP (<.001) and ENTP (<.01).

These African-American high school students were compared to the results of an earlier study conducted by Melear and Pitchford (1991). The sixth-grade sample reported the preference for Feeling by 69% of the students, whereas 27% of the eleventh-grade sample reported the preference for Feeling. Melear and Richardson suggest that longitudinal studies of African-American children would provide clarification for the Thinking–Feeling dimension reported in their study. Kirby and Barger (1996) delineate some considerations addressing methodological issues in the interpretation of co-culture samples when attempting to determine differences in African Americans and more general U. S. type distributions.

A study conducted by Melear and Alcock (1999) demonstrated differences in learning styles between African-American youth and a population of White male students. Interestingly, African American learning styles were more heterogeneous than reported previously by

Campbell (1996) and Levy et al. (1972). Preferences were shown by African-American high school students for ST and SP. Melear and Alcock state that their study, along with studies conducted by Hale (1986) and other African-American researchers support the idea that differences do exist among African-American students and White students. Further, Melear and Alcock call for longitudinal studies and type development studies to confirm students reporting Thinking rather than Feeling preferences at the high school level.

Minorities in Higher Education in the U. S.

In their discussion of minorities in higher education, Wilds and Wilson (1998) identified several factors in college admissions that do not necessarily provide an accurate portrayal of African-American students' potential academic success in college. They state:

Standardized tests provide a relatively simple, convenient, cost-efficient, valid, and reliable means of determining and comparing academic achievement against a standard measure . . . . Other research from The College Board shows that test scores and high school grades better predict college performance in the sciences and mathematics (quantitative areas that make use of the skills measured by the SAT math score) and less well in areas that make less use of the verbal or mathematical skills measured by the test. (Ramist, Lewis, and McCamley-Jenkins, 1994, 49)

As further noted by Wilds and Wilson, the SAT and ACT scores were designed primarily as an indicator of academic achievement during the first year of college, whereas that emphasis is misplaced and retention and graduation should receive equal weight and focus. Less consideration is given to noncognitive variables in college admissions representative of personal and social characteristics such as positive self-concept, realistic self-appraisal, understanding and dealing with racism, successful leadership experiences, community, and nontraditional knowledge acquired. These characteristics and experiences are representative of experiential and contextual intelligence, rather than cognitive-analytical intelligence. As such, these recommendations and observations made by Wilds and Wilson further reinforce research cited above regarding learning styles and MBTI results for African Americans.

As the studies noted above indicate, more research is needed surrounding the learning styles of African Americans and people of color to create learning environments that foster growth and opportunity in a meaningful context. The representation of research addressing learning styles and MBTI profiles of African Americans and people of color in a multicultural setting both nationally and globally is increasing. Use of the MBTI instrument worldwide has met with relative success and is now published in twenty-seven languages and distributed in twenty-six countries.

Critical Race Theory, Learning Styles, and the MBTI Instrument

Critical Race Theory (CRT) locates its origins in the 1970s. More recently, CRT is emerging into the educational arena as a viable lens through which explanations are found for the vexing and ongoing racism in our society that cripples African-American children and children of color and continues to deprive them of their right to thrive. This emergence was evidenced at the American Educational Research Conference 2000 in New Orleans, where sessions included reference to CRT as well as sessions that were focused on CRT. In particular, three scholars are credited with initiating this body of thought. Derrick Bell, formerly a Harvard law professor and now at New York State, is a forerunner in the field, as are Richard Delgado and Kimberlé Crenshaw.

When we consider that education for African Americans and other people of color is riddled with legal cases, up to and including the Supreme Court, CRT becomes a powerful and provocative means through which we may examine racism in education and in U. S. society. There are three central tenets to CRT:

1. Racism is normal, not aberrant, in American society. Because racism is an ingrained feature of our landscape, it looks ordinary and natural to persons in the culture. Formal equal opportunity—rules and laws that insist on treating Blacks and Whites (for example) alike—can thus remedy only the more extreme and shocking sorts of injustice, the ones that do stand out.
2. CRT's challenge to racial oppression and the status quo sometimes takes the form of storytelling, in which writers analyze the myths, presuppositions, and received wisdoms that make up the common culture about race and that invariably render Blacks and other minorities one-down.
3. A third premise underlying much of CRT is interest-convergence. Developed by Bell, this idea holds that White elites will tolerate or encourage racial advances for Blacks and people of color only when they also promote White self-interest. This tenet is especially prevalent in issues surrounding desegregation. (Tate, 1997)

What does this have to do with learning styles and the MBTI instrument? Just as the research suggests that learning styles of African Americans and people of color nationally and globally emerge from their own contextual experiences embedded within their cultural, societal, and historical framework so, too, does CRT emphasize context and experiences. As such, CRT provides further substantiation that the educational needs of African Americans and people of color must evolve from within a setting that optimizes their innate abilities.

Another form of evidence supports a cultural approach to learning for African Americans. Black Feminist Thought evolves from the experience base of African-American women and their experiences that are unique to their society, culture, and history (Collins, 1991). In contrast White Feminist Thought generates from a point of privilege in the dominant group that being White designates in U. S. society. Just as Wilds and Wilson (1998) indicated the disparities that occur in college admissions for African-American students that are perpetuated through continued standardized criteria based largely on White norms, the experience base of African Americans in the U. S. differs just as greatly from that of Whites as expressed through the MBTI instrument CRT or Black Feminist Thought.

Although the MBTI instrument was developed within the United States culture that represented primarily White middle class educated Americans during the latter half of the twentieth century, its application and research continues to expand in multicultural settings both nationally and globally. Multicultural research using the MBTI instrument supports a cultural experiential contextualized setting. This is reiterated through the earlier references in this chapter through the research and work of Allen and Boykin (1992); Battle (1989, 1992 and 1994); Boykin (1992); Carlson and Levy (1940); Darling-Hammond (1997); Donaldson (1996); Gurin Gurin Lao and Beattie (1969); Hale (1986 and 1994); Hedgegard and Brown, (1969), as cited in Robinson (1999); Hilliard (1983 and 1987); Nieto (1996); Shade (1982); Wilds and Wilson (1998); and others.

African American and White Identity Racial Models

Chickering (1993) delineates a variety of more traditional theorists and identity models and categorizes them as psychosocial cognitive typology and person-environment interaction theories within a theoretical context for student development. Psychosocial theories are characterized as viewing development as a series of tasks or stages that include qualitative changes in thinking, feeling, behaving, valuing and relating to others and to oneself. Examples of psychosocial theories include Erikson's eight developmental crises, Chickering's seven vectors of development, Marcia's model of ego identity status, W. Cross' model of Black identify formation, Heath's maturity model life-span theories of adult development, and Josselson's pathways to identity development.

Describing changes in thinking and evolving frames of reference that structure values, beliefs, and assumptions characterize cognitive theories. Examples of cognitive theories include Perry's scheme of intellectual and ethical development; Belenky, Clinchy, Goldberger, and Tarule's women's ways of knowing; Baxter Magolda's epistemological reflection model; Kohlberg's theory of moral development; Loevinger's theory of ego development; Kegan's evolving self; Fowler's states of spiritual development; and Kitchener and King's reflective judgment model (Chickering, 1993).

Distinctive but stable difference in learning style personality type temperament or socioeconomic background as contexts for development are represented in typology theories. Typology theories include Kolb's learning styles; the Myers-Briggs typology; Keirsey and Bate's temperaments; and K. P. Cross' sociodemographic characteristics (Chickering, 1993). Person-environment interaction theories focus on how the environment influences behavior through its interactions with characteristics of the individual. These theories include campus ecology theories; Holland's theory of vocational personalities and work environments; and perceptual models (Chickering, 1993).

The Cross Model of Psychological Nigrescence, or resocializing experience, emerged during the late 1960s and early 1970s (Cross,

1971, 1991, and 1995). Cross revised this model in 1995. The five stages of the Cross model are: (1) pre-encounter, (2) encounter, (3) immersion-emersion, (4) internalization, and (5) internalization-commitment. Cross (1991) defines Stage 1, pre-encounter, as the person viewing the world from a White frame of reference. Thinking, actions, and behavior of individuals devalue and/or deny their Blackness. Pro-White and anti-Black attitudes are developed. Pre-encounter attitudes toward race include low salience, social stigma, and anti-Black. During Stage 2, encounter, the person experiences a "shocking" event that can be a negative experience with Whites or a positive experience with Blacks and that is inconsistent with pre-encounter views. Realization and personalizing, respectively, are the two phases of the encounter stage. In Stage 3, immersion-emersion, immersion is the first phase. Although the person has a high level of outward identification with Blackness, internalized security about one's Blackness is low. A better understanding of Black history and culture is developed during Phase 2, emersion. Internalization in Stage 4 is when individuals achieve a sense of inner security about their Blackness. The person moves toward a pluralistic perspective and begins to see the connections between other forms of oppression. Internalization-commitment occurs during Stage 5 when individuals translate their new internalized identity into activities that benefit the entire group. This identity model also may be conceptualized as a process of education wherein individuals move into their social, cultural, and historical contexts through a series of phases that culminates in a sense of community. This description further parallels learning styles of African Americans as they have been discussed throughout this chapter.

In order to better understand the Black Identity model described above, Helms' (1990, 1993) White racial identity development model further illuminates the constructs within which African Americans live, adapt, and are educated. Helms states:

> The development of White identity in the United States is closely intertwined with the development and progress of racism in this country. The greater the extent that racism exists and is denied, the less possible it is to develop a positive White identity. J. M. Jones (1972 and 1981) has identified three types of racism: (a) individual, that is, personal attitudes, beliefs, and behaviors designed to convince oneself of the superiority of Whites and the inferiority of non-White racial groups; (b) institutional, meaning social policies, laws, and regulations whose purpose is to maintain the economic and social advantages of Whites over non-Whites [CRT: interest-convergence]; and (c) cultural, that is, societal beliefs and customs that promote the assumption that the products of White culture (e.g., language, traditions, appearance) are superior to those of non-White cultures.

Because each of these three types of racism is so much a part of the cultural milieu, each can become a part of the White person's racial identity or consciousness ipso facto. In order to develop a healthy White identity, defined in part as a nonracist identity, virtually every White person in the United States must overcome one or more of these aspects of racism. Additionally, he or she must accept his or her own Whiteness, the cultural implications of being White, and define a view of Self as a racial being that does not depend on the perceived superiority of one racial group over another. (Helms, 1990, 1993, 49)

Phase I of Helms' model is abandonment of racism with status 1 that of contact, or the "happy racist" when the idea or the actuality of Black people and other people of color are encountered. Status 2 is disintegration, and status 3 that of reintegration. Phase II of the model involves defining a nonracist White identity, with status 4 that of pseudo-independence. Status 5 in Phase II is immersion-emersion, at which time the person can truly begin to tackle racism and oppression in its various forms. And, status 6 is autonomy—an ongoing process in which White individuals continue to be open to new ways of thinking about culture and race. Consider the implications of this model in concert with the Black identity model described previously. Situate a Black child or college student in a predominately White educational setting, or a Black child in a predominately Black school population but with White teachers. Or, alter this scenario as one for any oppressed group for a person of color, since the research is leading us in the direction that developmental aspects are similar among people of color. Add to this equation what the literature and research reveals to us about learning styles of African-American students and people of color in a culture dominated by White standardized, reductionist norms rather than a community generating from a different experience socially, culturally, and historically. A poem written by a Black college student at a predominately White, large Midwestern university (see page 189) and provides a powerful example of his perspectives on learning, education, and life as a young Black man today. The tenets of CRT and Black Feminist Thought solidify the implications of the enormity of the situation that has existed far too long already in the United States and mandates an overdue call to action to ameliorate the educational landscape of racism for our children and their futures.

Implications for Research and Practice

Of all the civil rights for which the world has struggled and fought for 5,000 years, the right to learn is undoubtedly the most fundamental . . . the freedom to learn . . . has been bought by bitter sacrifice. And whatever we may think of the curtailment of other civil rights, we should fight to the last ditch to keep open the right to learn, the right to have examined in our schools not only what we believe, but what we do not believe; not only what our leaders say, but what the leaders of other groups and nations, and the leaders of other centuries have said. We must insist upon this to give our children the fairness of a start which will equip them with such an array of facts and such an attitude toward truth that they can have a real chance to judge what the world is and what its greater minds have thought it might be. (Du Bois, [1949] 1970, 230–231)

The twenty-first century holds the promise and potential to be the learning age. Howard Gardner targets our challenge:

> Research indicates that most students in most schools including our best students in our best schools do not really understand . . . . Although we need teachers and textbooks they often are not enough. Unless you really confront students' notions about the world and figure out why they believe these theories and what could convince them they are wrong, they will continue to hold onto those ideas . . . . What's amazing about children's museums is that you can take kids who seem like total dolts in school and put them in children's museums and suddenly they become very intelligent. They inquire, explore, experiment. *They learn things, approach things in their own way and do their own kind of reflection* [italics added] about what is going on . . . . A lot of intelligences really can't be tested for in the sense we usually use the word 'test.' What we need to do is to create school environments where you can observe a lot about what kids are good at, what interests them, and where they show substantial growth . . . . Within the educational context, I believe we need to start with the child's strengths. (Steinberger 1994, pp.26–28)

Gardner's comments relate to MBTI theory. He speaks of understanding, inquiry, exploration, experimentation, approaching things in one's own way, environments, observation, and reflection. These are implications for different ways of learning and knowing for both student and teacher, not only for practicing teachers but also for teachers in preparation programs so that they become more aware of the learning styles of a diverse group of students. If we expect students to learn and to understand, as opposed to memorize, then we need to make better use of the knowledge and tools available to us to meet that end and make it a reality. As noted by Nieto (1996):

> Although not specifically related to cultural differences, Gardner's work on "multiple intelligences" has important implications for culturally compatible education . . . . The implications of the theory of multiple intelligences . . . may be significant because the theory goes beyond the limited definition of intelligence valued in the school. In Gardner's words, it centers on "breaking out of the hegemony of a single intelligence." In opening up our understanding of intelligence, this theory permits schools and teachers to look at their students with a different perspective and may be particularly helpful in helping them challenge current assessment practices that focus almost exclusively on logical-mathematical and linguistic intelligence. The danger, as always, lies in extrapolating from individual cases to an entire group. (p. 140)

Levine (1993) noted that "every college generation is defined by the social events of its age" (p. 8). Levine has observed students over the last twenty years. He decided to repeat his 1979 study, in which intentionally heterogeneous groups consisted of eight to ten students on each campus. For the repeat study, he raised the number of institutions to twenty-eight to reflect the changing character of higher education since 1979. Undergraduate groups were asked what social and political events had most influenced their generation. The Challenger explosion was the most frequent answer. The fall of communism was a second event that students cited. They spoke in terms of "pride," "hope," "drama," "energy," and "a closer world" (p. 12). The third event mentioned by students was the 1991 Gulf War, which they described as "our first war" and "Every generation has a war: this was ours" (p. 12). A fourth event noted by students was the AIDS epidemic, which has been a fact of life for this generation. The final event students cited was the verdict in the Rodney King beating trial and the riots that followed. "Minorities—African-Americans, Hispanics, and Asian-Americans—cited it most frequently, but by no means exclusively" (p. 12). The only commonality was their strong negative reaction, some who were appalled by the verdict, and others who were repulsed by the violence. Overall, students expressed that they felt that they were living in a deeply troubled nation where problems were multiplying and solutions were growing more distant. At the same time, more than 9 out of 10 were optimistic about our collective future—95 percent. "While they were rather negative about the future of the country, they were remarkably optimistic about the future of their communities. Today's students emphasize the local in their thinking and their action .... Above all, this is a generation torn between doing good and doing well" (p. 14). The implications from Levine's study are that our students care, and that they care deeply. They want to do both good and well—with a focus localized in the context of their community. It is from community that our students learn, grow, and develop in a country that continues to grow in its diversity. As such, it becomes the responsibility of educators to be sensitive to the varied contexts from which our students come to us so that their learning will be meaningful to them.

Schroeder (1993) launched a comprehensive, longitudinal, eight-year study called TRAILS, whose primary objective was to provide educators necessary institutional data on how student characteristics related to choice of major, academic "aptitude," academic performance in specific curricular areas, and attrition. The database included information such as MBTI scores, ACT/SAT scores, high school grade point average, demographic factors, and students' responses to a questionnaire. The project results suggested interesting relationships between learning patterns and variables such as academic aptitude, college achievement, and choice of major. "For example, the mean SAT score for concrete active (ES) learners was 932 compared to 1110 for the abstract reflective (IN) learners" (p. 25). The difference of 178 points was statistically significant and the patterns were consistent across several institutions. In fact, the relationship between learning patterns and scores appeared to be consistent on all standardized timed aptitude measures such as the GRE, MAT, LSAT, etc. INs scored the highest followed by ENs, ISs, and ESs. The evidence does not support the hypothesis that the differences indicate different intelligence levels. Other fascinating findings resulted from this study. The information provided by the MBTI results and TRAILS project suggested a number of perspectives for creating learning opportunities and academic programs that respond effectively to the diversity of learning characteristics revealed by today's students. Putting this information to use could achieve a better balance between teaching and learning styles. In speaking specifically to the MBTI instrument, Schroeder stated that "I am suggesting than an overall understanding of how students learn and where they are in the process can help us meet the needs of the new students who sit in our classrooms" (p. 28).

Darling-Hammond (1997) states that a system of schools in the U. S. that can educate people for contemporary society calls upon schools to do two things that they have never before been asked to do:

> *To teach for understanding.* That is, to teach all students, not just a few, to understand ideas deeply and perform proficiently.
>
> *To teach for diversity.* That is, to teach in ways that help different kinds of learners find productive paths to knowledge as they also learn to live constructively together.
>
> I suggest that this task will require a new paradigm for education policy—one that shifts policymakers' efforts from designing controls to developing capacity among schools and teachers to be responsible for student learning and to be responsive to student and community needs and concerns. This means (1) redesigning schools so they focus on learning, foster strong relationships, and support in-depth intellectual work; (2) creating a profession of teaching to ensure all teachers have the knowledge and commitments they need to teach diverse learners well; and (3) funding schools equitably so that they invest in the front lines of teaching and learning rather than in the side offices of system bureaucracies (p. 5–6)

Once again, the focus and emphasis is on recognizing and capitalizing on the diverse strengths that we find in multiple learning styles so that learning and teaching benefit each person. This can not take place in isolated contexts. For effective change to take place, it must permeate and saturate every level of education in U. S. society—from preschool through higher education. The MBTI instrument, as the growing body of research evidences, is a viable tool through which this change may be accomplished. Global evidence for increased understanding is seen in the work of De Beer (1997), Ismail (1993), Lim (1994), Sim and Kim (1993), and Williams et al. (1992).

As with the research and quotes cited throughout this chapter, Banks (1998) reinforces the challenge to education at all levels in the new century to "respect and acknowledge the community cultures and knowledge of students . . . with an overarching set of values to which all students will have a commitment and with which all will identify. He continues by noting that it is essential for this to occur in both learning and teaching:

> Teachers should help students examine and uncover the community and culture knowledge they bring to school and to understand how it is similar to and different from school knowledge and the culture knowledge of other students. Students should be helped to understand the ways in which their values undergird their personal and community knowledge and how they view and interpret school knowledge.
>
> Teachers, like students, also bring to the classroom personal and cultural knowledge that is situated within a set of deeply held values that result from their personal and professional experiences. However, the values that teachers hold, and their knowledge related to those values, are often unexamined. Teachers need to critically examine the value assumptions that underlie their personal knowledge, the knowledge taught in the curriculum, and the values that support the institutionalized structures and practices in the schools (p. 14).

Implications for research are summarized as follows:

- We should aggressively pursue the inclusion of additional populations from not only within the

United States, but also from outside the United States, as we work to create a truly stratified, random sample for all groups. This would allow us to make definitive comparisons of type distributions of ethnic or national cultures (McCaulley and Moody, 2000). This particular research should be undertaken by the publishers of the MBTI instrument to ensure that the integrity of the instrument is maintained.

- The literature lacks research studies that utilize both quantitative and qualitative research methodologies. The application of qualitative research methodologies would serve to enhance individuals' understanding and utilization of information reported by the Indicator.
- It also is critical that individuals who are using the Indicator with persons from different cultures have a thorough understanding of the underlying and influential theories that shape and define the nature of oppressed groups when using the complex and powerful tool that we call the MBTI instrument.
- We should strongly encourage revisions and contributions to the next *MBTI Manual* that greatly enhance our knowledge of the expression of type across cultures. Until research contributes to the larger body of knowledge through publication, its voice remains mute.
- More research is needed about the learning styles of African-American children, because research results lack clarity about race and socioeconomic class as separate variables that affect achievement (Banks, 1993).

- Research should continue concerning African-American students and the impact of culture, race, oppression, and other variables on how they respond to the MBTI instrument (Battle, 1984, 1989, 1994, and 1998; Carlson and Levy, 1940; Gurin, Gurin, Lao, and Beattie, 1969; Hedgegard and Brown, 1969, as cited in Robinson, 1999).
- Research should address cultural masking and adaptability (culture shifting) factors (Barlund, 1975; Battle, 1989, 1992, and 1994; Battle, Robinson, and Battle, 1998).
- Longitudinal studies and type development studies should be conducted to confirm African-American students reporting Thinking rather than Feeling preferences at the high school level (Melear and Alcock, 1999).
- Research addressing relationships within MBTI instrument, learning styles, and Gardner's multiple intelligences is crucial.
- MBTI studies with people of color in the U.S. and with global cultures should exercise caution in imposing interpretation of behavior in non-White cultures through a White lens.
- Further exploration of the influence of cultural values on an individual's ability to develop and use type preference should occur.
- Collecting type distributions within cultures can aid in a deeper understanding of the interactions and dynamics between individuals and their cultures.

There are many implications for practice, including the following:

- All MBTI qualifying programs should have as a part of their pre-study guides, specific information regarding the use of Indicator across cultures or with persons of color.
- Qualifying programs also should have as a part of the content, specific informational resources regarding the expression of type across cultures.
- Ongoing professional development and in-service opportunities for additional training in this area should be available through the offering of advanced workshops and programs as a part of local, regional, and international conferences.
- Enhanced use of technology via the Internet can make information available through CPP, Inc.; CAPT, the Association of Psychological Type, and other association web sites for clients who use the MBTI instrument with people of color.

There are numerous other topics specific to the use of the Indicator across cultures that would benefit from further research; for example, teaching for understanding; teaching for diversity; diversity training programs; balancing teaching and learning styles; pre-service teacher programs; increased contextual knowledge of students' cultures and experiences that influenced and informed their unique development, and educators who recognize different learning styles and capitalize on those strengths to provide an environment conducive to learning and success for every student and individual.

As noted earlier in this chapter, the overall U. S. population, as well as college enrollment, continues to increase for students and people of color. This is accompanied by an increasing social-class, racial, ethnic, and gender gap between learners and educators at all levels of education. Although it provides no unconditional guarantee, the MBTI instrument, as the emerging research bears out, offers a tool to begin leveling the educational playing field for all students through an indication of their learning styles. We must stress that this is not an instrument through which we sort, label, or stereotype people, but that it is one through which we may better create and implement optimized opportunities for both learning and teaching in an increasingly diverse culture, both in the U. S. and globally. The success, quality of life, and future of not only our children from preschool through higher education, but also that of the nation and the world, rest on meaningful learning and living for all in a global community. Through conscientious and ongoing practice and research efforts we can seek to illuminate, understand, and know what we can do better that will enrich and enhance a diverse population at home and throughout our global community.

The Right to Learn

The poem that follows was written by Marcus Goins, a Black undergraduate male student attending a predominately White, large midwestern public university. It was first submitted in addition to a required assignment for a 200-level education class. In another assignment, the group to which this student belonged focused their teaching around Paulo Freire's (1993) book, *Pedagogy of the Oppressed.* This poem was read to the entire class by the student as part of his contribution to the group project. The students in the class found it to be a powerful expression of a context, life, and thinking for which none of them shared any common experiences or frame of reference.

Some readers may find the content and language of the poem

strong. What is important to bear in mind while reading it is that we can all agree to disagree. It is possible that other Black college students may disagree completely with the contents of the poem. However, the words and the message in the poem are powerful and compelling. He speaks to learning, education, and the right to learn in a most provocative way. That the student found a level of trust and security in the class that encouraged him to express himself is equally important. This, in particular speaks to our ability to realize, recognize, embrace, and encourage different learning styles that originate from different life experiences and contexts as teachers and learners—the essence of this chapter—that we open the doors to learning and teaching for our diverse population in the U. S. so that each individual is valued and experiences success so that they may reach their full potential. Thank you, Marcus, for your brilliance and your bravery.

Words of Wisdom

Killing us one by one
In one way or another
America will find a way to eliminate the problem
One by one
The problem is
the troubles are in the black youth of the ghettos
And one by one
we are being wiped off the face of this earth
At an extremely alarming rate
And even more alarming is the fact
that we are not fighting back
Brothers, sisters, niggas. That's what they called us.
When I say niggas it is not the nigga we are grown to fear

It is not the nigga we say as if it has no meaning
But to me
It means Never Ignorant Getting Goals Accomplished, Nigga
Niggas what are we going to do
Walk blind into a line or fight
Fight and die if we must like niggas
This is for the masses the lower classes
The ones you left out, jobs were givin', better livin'
But we were kept out
Made to feel inferior, but we're the superior
Break the chains in our brains that made us fear you
Pledge allegiance to a flag that neglects us
Honour a man who refuses to respect us
Emancipation Proclamation, Please!
They just said that to save the nation
These are lies that we all accepted
Say no to drugs but the governments keep it
Running through our community, killing the unity
The war on drugs is a war on you and me
And yet they say this is the Home of The Free
But if you ask me it's all about hypocrisy
The constitution, it don't apply to me
Lady Liberty still the one lied to me
Steady strong nobody's gonna like what I pumpin'
But it's wrong to keeping someone from learning something
So get up, it's time to start nation building
I'm fed up, we gotta start teaching children
That they can be all that they want to be
There's much more to life than just poverty

This is definitely ahhh words of wisdom
AMERICA, AMERICA, AMERICA
I charge you with the crime of rape, murder, and assault
For suppressing and punishing my people
I charge you with robbery for robbing me of my history
I charge you with false imprisonment for keeping me
Trapped in the projects
And the jury finds you guilty on all accounts
And you are to serve the consequences of your evil schemes
Prosecutor do you have any more evidence
Words of Wisdom
They shine upon the strength of a nation
Conquer the enemy on with education
Protect thy self, reach with what you want to do
Know thy self, teach what we been through
On with the knowledge of the place, then
No one will ever oppress this race again
No Malcolm X in my history text
Why is that?
Cause he tried to educate and liberate all blacks
Why isn't Martin Luther King in my book each week?
He told blacks, if they get smacked, turn the other cheek
I don't get it, so many questions went through my mind
I get sweated, They act as if asking questions is a crime
But forget it, one day I'm gonna prove them wrong
Now every brother had to smother on the welfare line
The American dream, though it seems attainable
They're pulling your sleeve, don't believe
Cause it will strangle you

Pulling the life of your brain, I can't explain
Beg as you can obtain from which you came
Swear that your mother is living in equality
Forgetting your brother that's living her apology
Thought they had us beat when they took our kids
But the battle ain't over till the black man sings
Words of Wisdom
But the battle ain't over till the black man sings
Words of Wisdom
NIGHTMARE that's what I am
America's nightmare
I am what you made me
The hate and evil that you gave me
I shine of a reminder of what you have done to my people
for Four hundred plus years
You should be scared
You should be running
You should be trying to silence me
ha
But you can not escape fate
Well it is my turn to come
Just as you rose you shall fall
By my hands
America, You reap what you sow

Marcus E. Goins, 2000

References

Allen, B. A. and A. W. Boykin. (1992). *School Psychology Review*, 21(4), 586–596.

Banks, J. (1993, April). What does it mean to integrate race, ethnicity, class, and gender in theory and research? Paper presented at the Annual Meeting of the American Educational Research Association, Atlanta, GA.

———. (1998). The lives and values of researchers: Implications for educating citizens in a multicultural society. *Educational Researcher*, 27(7), 4–17.

Barlund, D. C. (1975). Communication in a global village. *Public and private self in Japan and the United States*. Tokyo: Simul Press.

Battle, P. C. (1989). The effect of race and culture on black MTBI type preferences. In *Proceedings of the Association for Psychological Type Eighth Biennial International Conference*, pp. 161–163. Kansas City, MO: Association for Psychological Type.

———. (1992). Two warring ideas in one dark body: A phenomenological journey toward appreciating the lifeworld of the African American experience. Unpublished doctoral dissertation, University of Maryland, College Park.

———. (1994). Two warring ideals in one dark body. In *Proceedings of the Third International Conference on Myers-Briggs Typology* pp. 147–152. Montreal: International Type Users Organization.

Battle, P. C., D. C. Robinson, K. P. Battle. (1998). A comparative study of Blacks in the United States, South Africa, Trinidad and Tobago. Presented at the Third Multicultural Research Conference of the Center for Applications of Psychological Type, Honolulu, HI.

Boykin, A. S. (1992). *Retention of African-American males in high school: A study of African-American male high school dropouts, African-American male seniors and white male seniors*. Lanham, MC: University Press of America.

Campbell, S. (1996). International understanding and exploration. *Bulletin of Psychological Type*, 19(4), 36–39.

Carskadon, T. G. (1999). A grand synopsis of 345 studies in psychological type, 1979–1999. *Journal of Psychological Type*, 50.

———. (1999). Challenging assumptions and extending applications: Race and indicator validity; type and teaching African American children; and the Group Zig Zag Model. *Journal of Psychological Type* 48, 3.

Chapman, M. (1994). The Aleknagik project: A success story of cooperative school restructuring based on traditional Eskimo learning patterns and Myers-Briggs type theory (an overview). In *Proceedings of Orchestrating Educational Change in the 90s: The role of psychological type* (pp.–10). Gainesville, FL: Center for Applications in Psychological Type.

Chickering, A. W. (1993). *Education and identity.* San Francisco: Jossey-Bass Publishers, Inc.

Cohen, R. (1969). Conceptual styles, culture conflict and nonverbal tests of intelligence. *American Anthropologist,* 71,828–856.

Collins, P. H. (1991). Black feminist thought: Knowledge, consciousness, and the politics of empowerment. *Perspectives on Gender*, Vol. 2. New York: Routledge.

The Chronicle of Higher Education. (1999). Almanac 1999. Available: http://chronicle.com/'weekly/almanac/1999/nation/nation.htm.

Cross, W. E., Jr. (1971). Toward a psychology of black liberation: The Negro-to-black conversion experience. *Black World*, 20(9), 13–27.

———. (1991). *Shades of black: Diversity in African American identity.* Philadelphia: Temple University Press.

———. (1995). The psychology of Nigrescence: Revising the Cross model. In J. G. Ponterotto, J. M. Casas, L. A. Suzuki, and C. M. Alexander (Eds.), *Handbook of multicultural counseling* (pp. 93–122). Thousand Oaks, CA: Sage.

Darling-Hammond, L. (1997). *The right to learn: A blueprint for creating schools that work.* San Francisco: Jossey-Bass Publishers, Inc.

De Beer, J. (1997). *Dealing with personal and cultural transitions.* Paper presented at APT XII, Twelfth Biennial International Conference of the Association for Psychological Type International Conference, Boston, MA.

Donaldson, K. B. M. (1996). *Through students' eyes: Combating racism in United States schools.* Westport, CT: Praeger Publishers.

Du Bois, W. E. B. (1970). The freedom to learn. In P. S. Foner (Ed.), *W. E. B. Du Bois speaks* (pp. 230–231). New York: Pathfinder. (Original work published in 1949)

Freire, P. (1993). *Pedagogy of the oppressed.* New York: Continuum Publishing Company.

Goins, M. E. (2000). *Words of wisdom.* Unpublished poem. Ames, IA.

Hale, J. E. (1986). *Black children: Their roots, culture, and learning styles* (Rev. ed.). Baltimore: The Johns Hopkins University Press.

———. (1994). *Unbank the fire: Visions for the education of African American children.* Baltimore: The Johns Hopkins University Press.

Helms, J. E. (1990/1993). Toward a model of White racial identity development. In J. E. Helms (Ed.), *Black and White racial identity* (pp. 49–66). New York: Greenwood/Praeger.

Hilliard, A. (1976). Alternatives to IQ testing: An approach to the identification of gifted minority children. Final report to the California State Department of Education.

———. (1983, 1987). 1998 Facilitator: Keynote sessions. Belief and research: Culture, context and dysfunctional paradigms. Available: http://www.mcrel.org/products/noteworthy/noteworthy98/belief.asp

Huitt, W. G. (1989). Personality differences between Navajo and non-Indian college students: Implications for instruction. *Equity and Excellence,* 24(1), 71–74.

Hwang, C .H., and H. Chi-en. (1991). *Chinese University Students on the MBTI: A Study from Tung-Hai University, Taiwan.* Paper presented at the Ninth Biennial International Conference of the Association for Psychological Type, Richmond, VA.

Ismail, Z. (1995). Typewatching along the crosswalks of cultures in Malaysia. In *Proceedings of Psychological Type and Culture—East and West: A Multicultural Research Symposium, 1993* (pp. 275–282). Gainesville, FL: Center for Applications of Psychological Type.

Jensen, G. H. (1987). Learning styles. In J. A. Provost and S. Anchors (Eds.) *Applications of the Myers-Briggs Type Indicator in Higher Education* (pp. 181–206). Palo Alto: Davies-Black Publishing.

Johnson, W. M. (1989). A comparative analysis of learning styles of Black and White college freshmen. (Doctoral dissertation. Oklahoma State University, 1989). *Dissertation Abstracts International*, 50, 3863.

Jones, J. H., J. Ukishima, K. Sakamoto, A. Tanouye, and G. Giron. (1995). Ethnicity and type of counseling center clients. In *Proceedings of Psychological Type and Culture—East and West: A Multicultural Research Symposium*, 1993 (pp. 77–98). Gainesville, FL: Center for Applications of Psychological Type.

Kirby, L. K. and N. J. Barger. (1996). Multicultural applications. In A. L. Hammer (Ed.), *MBTI Applications: A decade of research on the Myers-Briggs Type Indicator* (pp. 167–196) Palo Alto: Consulting Psychologist Press, Inc.

———. (1998). Chapter 14: Use of type in multicultural settings. In Briggs et al., *MBTI Manual: A guide to the development and use of the Myers-Briggs Type Indicator* (pp. 367–384). Palo Alto: Consulting Psychology Press, Inc.

Lawrence, G. D., and D. C. Robinson. (2000, July). *Student differences in psychological type: A bedrock reality for shaping the future of education.* Presentation at the Annual Conference of the World

Future Society, FutureFocus 2000: Changes, Challenges and Choices, Houston, TX.

Levine, A. (1993). The making of a generation. *Change*, 25(4), 8–14.

Levy, N., C. Murphy, and R. Carlson. (1972). Personality types among Negro college students. *Educational and Psychological Measurement*, 32, 641–653.

Lim, T. K. (1994). Personality types among Singapore and American students. *Journal of Psychological Type*, 31, 10–15.

Malone, O., Jr. (1988). Psychological type differences between minorities and majorities in an organizational setting. *Journal of Psychological Type*, 14, 15–24.

McCaulley, M. H. and R. A. Moody. (2000). Multicultural applications of the Myers-Briggs Type Indicator. In L. A. Suzuki (Ed.), *New handbook for multicultural assessment* (pp. 279–305). San Francisco, CA: Jossey-Bass Publishers, Inc.

Melear, C. T. and M. W. Alcock. (1999). Learning styles and personality types of African American children: Implications for science education. *Journal of Psychological Type*, 48, 22–33.

Melear, C.T. and F. Pitchford. (1991). African American science student learning style. In *Proceedings of the Ninth International Conference of the Association of Psychological Type* (pp. 4C–9C). Kansas City, MO: Association for Psychological Type.

Melear, C. T. and S. Richardson. (1994). Learning styles of African-American children which correspond to the MBTI. In *Proceedings of Orchestrating Educational Change in the 90s*, (pp. 11–22). Gainesville, FL: Center for Applications of Psychological Type.

Moody, R. (1995). Psychological type and ethnicity. How do ethnographic and type descriptions compare? In Moody, R. (Ed.), *Proceedings of Psychological Type and Culture—East and West: A Multicultural Research Symposium, 1993* (pp. 157–191). Gainesville, FL: Center for Applications of Psychological Type.

Nieto, S. (1996). *Affirming diversity: The sociopolitical context of multicultural education (2nd ed.).* White Plains, NY: Longman Publishers USA.

Nuby, J. F. and R. L. Oxford. (1998). Learning style preferences of Native American and African American secondary students. *Journal of Psychological Type,* 44, 5–19.

Posey, A. M., B. M. Thorne, and T. G. Carskadon (1999). Differential validity of the indicator for Black and White college students. *Journal of Psychological Type,* 48, 6–21.

Robinson, D. C. (1999, late Summer). Multicultural and international issues symposium. *Bulletin of Psychological Type,* 22(5) 32–33.

Schroeder, C. C. (1993, September–October). New students—new learning styles. *Change,* 25(4), 21–26.

Shade, B. (1982). Afro-American cognitive style: A variable in school success. *Review of Educational Research,* 52(2), 219–244.

Sim, H. S., and J. T. Kim. (1993). The development and validation of the Korean version of the MBTI. *Journal of Psychological Type,* 26, 18–27.

Simmons, G. and P. Barrineau. (1994). Learning styles and the Native American. *Journal of Psychological Type,* 23, 3–10.

Steinberger, E. D. (1994, January). Howard Gardner on learning for understanding. *The School Administrator,* pp. 26–31.

Tate, W. F., IV. (1997). Critical race theory and education: History, theory, and implications. In *Review of Research in Education* (pp. 195–247). Washington, DC: American Educational Research Association.

van Heerden, A. E. (1997, July). Providing for diversity in the education for a rainbow nation. Presented at the twelfth International Conference of the Association of Psychological Type, Boston, MA.

Wilds, D. J. and R. Wilson. (1998). *Minorities in higher education: 1997–98. Sixteenth annual status report.* Washington, DC: American Council on Education.

Williams, M. Q., T. F. Williams, Qisheng, X., and L. Xuemei. (1992). A glimpse of the psychological types of Mainland Chinese undergraduates. *Journal of Psychological Type*, 23, 3–9.

Woodson, C. G. (1933, 1999). *The mis-education of the Negro.* Trenton, NJ: Africa World Press, Inc.

Note: The Myers-Briggs Type Indicator bibliography and library are maintained by the Center for Applications of Psychological Type (CAPT) at 2815 N.W. 13th St., Suite 401, Gainesville, FL 32609. For bibliographic information or keyword searches, call CAPT's research librarian at (352) 375-0160 or e-mail requests to library@capt.org. On-line searches are available at **www.capt.org**.

Resources for Learning Styles

Baron, A., Jr. (1991). Counseling Chicano college students. In C. Lee and B. Richardson (Eds.), *Multicultural issues in counseling: New approaches to diversity* (pp. 171–184). Alexandria, VA: American Association for Counseling and Development.

Black, C., H. Paz, and R. DeBlassie (1991). Counseling the Hispanic male adolescent. *Adolescence*, 26, 223–232.

De Bello, T. C. (1990, July–September). Comparison of eleven major learning styles models: Variables, appropriate populations, validity of instrumentation, and research behind them. *Journal of Reading, Writing, and Learning Disabilities International*, 6(3), 203–22.

Dunn, R. and K. Dunn. (1992). *Teaching elementary students through their individual learning styles: Practical approaches for grades 3–6.* Boston: Allyn & Bacon.

Dunn, R. and K. Dunn. (1993). *Teaching secondary students through their individual learning styles: Practical approaches for grades 7–12.* Boston: Allyn & Bacon.

Dunn, R. and S. A. Griggs. (1995). *Multiculturalism and learning style. Teaching and counseling adolescents.* Westport, CT: Praeger Publishers.

Dunn, R., S. Griggs, and G. Price. (1993). Learning styles of Mexican-American and Anglo-American elementary-school students. *Journal of Multicultural Counseling and Development*, 21(4), 237–247.

Freeman, M. K., and D. L. Whitson. (1992, Spring). An overview of learning style models and their implications for practice. *Journal of Adult Education*, 20(2), 11–18.

Guild, P. (1994, May). The culture/learning style connection. *Educational Leadership*, 51(8), 16–21.

Hanson, J. R. et al. (1991). Square pegs: Learning styles of at-risk students. *Music Educators Journal*, 78(3), 30–35.

Hudgens, B. R. (1993). The relationship of cognitive style, planning ability and locus-of-control to achievement for three ethnic groups (Anglo, African-American, Hispanic). Doctoral dissertation, Southern Illinois University at Carbondale, 1992. Dissertation Abstracts International, A53-08, 2744.

Irvine, J. J. and D. E. York. (1995). Learning styles and culturally diverse students: A literature review. In the *Handbook of Research on Multicultural Education* (pp. 484–497).

Jalali, F. (1988). A cross-cultural comparative analysis of the learning styles and field dependence/independence characteristics of selected fourth-, fifth-, and sixth-grade students of Afro, Chinese, Greek and Mexican heritage. Doctoral dissertation, St. John's University, Jamaica, NY. Dissertation Abstracts International, 50(62), 344A.

Jones, S. (1993). Cognitive learning styles: Does awareness help? A review of selected writings. *Language Awareness,* 2(4), 195–207.

Keefe, J. W. (1991). Learning style: Cognitive and thinking skills. Instructional Leadership Series. Reston, VA: National Association of Secondary Principals.

Melear, C. T. (1995, April). Learning styles of African American children and NSTA goals of instruction. Paper presented at the Annual Meeting of the American Educational Research Association, San Francisco, CA.

Morgan, H. (1992). An analysis of Gardner's theory of multiple intelligence. Paper presented at the Annual Meeting of the Eastern Educational Research Association.

Philbin, M. et al. (1995, April) A Survey of gender and learning styles. *Sex Roles: A Journal of Research,* 32 (7–8), 485–494.

Riding, R., and I. Cheema. (1991). Cognitive styles: An overview and integration. *Educational Psychology: An International Journal of Experimental Educational Psychology,* 11 (3–4), 193–215.

Reiff, J. C. (1992). *Learning styles. What research says to the teacher series.* Washington, DC: National Education Association.

Saracho, O. N. (1997, Apr). Some implications of cognitive styles on young children's play. *Early Child Development and Care,* 131, 19–30.

Severiens, S. E., and T. N. G. Ten Dam. (1994). Gender differences in learning styles: A narrative review and quantitative meta-analysis. *Higher Education,* 27(4), 487–501.

Sims, J. (1988). Learning styles of Black-American, Mexican-American, and White-American third- and fourth-grade students in traditional public schools. Unpublished doctoral dissertation, University of Santa Barbara, Santa Barbara, CA.

Vasquez, J. (1990). Teaching to the distinctive traits of minority students. *The Clearing House* 63(7), 299–304.

Yong, F. L., and N. J. Ewing. (1992). A comparative study of the learning-style preferences among gifted African-American, Mexican-American and American born Chinese middle-grade students. *Roeper Review,* 14(3),120–123.

CHAPTER 6

Effective Teaching and Type: The Words of Outstanding Professors

JUDITH A. PROVOST AND BARBARA H. CARSON
WITH PETER G. BEIDLER

The ingredients of effective teaching are often as elusive as those of effective learning. This chapter reports on a study designed to explore type preferences and excellence in teaching. Outstanding professors are identified annually by the Council for the Advancement and Support of Education (CASE). A sample of these professors agreed to take the Myers-Briggs Type Indicator® instrument. Their preferences were then compared with their statements about their teaching philosophies and approaches found in *Distinguished Teachers on Effective Teaching* (Beidler, 1986). In this book Peter Beidler, a CASE finalist himself, has solicited and compiled written responses from CASE finalists.

The CASE professors' statements in Beidler's book were examined to pursue the following questions:

1. Among professors identified for their outstanding teaching records, are there similarities in personality types and in preferred styles of teaching and learning?
2. How have these professors capitalized in their teaching on strengths natural to their personality types?

3. How have they compensated for their lesser preferences, in areas where there is less likely to be natural strength?

Only one of the CASE professors was familiar with type theory at the time Beidler surveyed them. Therefore, this study is not an example of an application of the MBTI instrument but rather an *illumination* of type theory and the relationship of MBTI preferences to effective teaching. The implications of these findings suggest specific applications of the MBTI instrument in the teaching process.

Procedure

Peter Beidler was contacted and asked to support the study by introducing the authors to the CASE professors and by providing his draft manuscript of their teaching statements. Beidler also offered to provide additional unpublished responses from the CASE finalists to a query about why they thought they had been selected for this honor. After this introduction through Beidler, the authors sent letters to the CASE professors describing the study, the nature of the Indicator, the relationship of type to learning, the procedure for the study, and a postcard to return, indicating willingness or unwillingness to participate in the study.

Those respondents willing to participate in the study gave permission to use their MBTI results and teaching statements. Subjects were then mailed the MBTI Form G, with instructions. These were scored and the results compared with the professors statements in Beidler's manuscript and in the additional unpublished responses.

The Sample

CASE instituted the Professor of the Year program in 1981 to honor outstanding teachers of undergraduates, using the following criteria (according to a CASE brochure):

- extraordinary effort as a scholar or teacher
- service to the institution and/or the profession
- a balance of achievement in teaching, scholarship, and service to the institution
- evidence of impact and/or involvement with students
- evidence of achievement by former students the quality of nominations by former students
- the quality of nominations by former students

Each year, after the several hundred nominations from colleges and universities across the country have been narrowed to about 30, a panel chaired by the president of the Carnegie Foundation for the Advancement of Teaching chooses a small group of finalists and the National Professor of the Year. Of the 27 professors chosen as CASE finalists or Professors of the Year from 1981 to 1985, 20 contributed to Beidler's book by responding to questions about the way they taught, what they expected from themselves and their students, and their values about teaching.

Eighteen of these 20 finalists agreed to participate in the study. The sample included 14 men and 4 women, with equal representation from state universities, small private four-year colleges, and private universities granting doctorates. The professors represented a range of academic disciplines:

English 7
Religion/philosophy 3
Anthropology/sociology 2
Economics 2
Biology 2
Astronomy 1
Geography 1

Although the sample is a small and very select one and generalizations cannot be made concerning specific types and excellence in college teaching, several MBTI patterns are worth noting. Of the 18 professors, nine are ETJs; seven of these are ENTJs. The 4 women in the sample are INFJ, INFP, ENFJ and ENTJ. There are few Sensing types, consistent with a larger university sample tabulated by the Center for Applications of Psychological Type, (CAPT). There are four times as many ENTJs in the CASE sample than would be predicted based on the percentage of this type in the CAPT University Professors sample of 2,282. Compared to the percentages of each type in a sample of Danforth Associates, there are two times as many ENTJs and four and a half times as many ENFPs than would be expected. These findings are statistically significant, as noted on the type tables (tables 6.1 and 6.2).

Using Natural Strengths for Effective Teaching

How have these master teachers capitalized on strengths natural to their type preferences in their teaching? Their statements in Beidler's book reveal how their teaching styles have been shaped by their types. Most revealing were responses to Beidler's questions:

- "What qualities, skills, or attitudes do you want your students to have after a semester in one of your classes?"
- "How do students learn by example, by rote, by reading, by discussion?"
- "What do you feel you have done to earn your college's nomination and the CASE committee's selection of you?"—"What is most distinctive about your teaching?" (Note that this last question was not included in Beidler's final manuscript.)

Case Finalists Compared to Danforth Associates

N = 18

	SENSING THINKING	SENSING FEELING	INTUITION FEELING	INTUITION THINKING	
	ISTJ N = 1 % = 5.56 I = .70 ■■■■■	**ISFJ** N = 0 % = 0.00 I = 0.00	**INFJ** N = 1 % = 5.56 I = .66 ■■■■■	**INTJ** N = 0 % = 0.00 I = 0.00*	JUDGMENT INTROVERSION
	ISTP N = 0 % = 0.00 I = 0.00	**ISFP** N = 0 % = 0.00 I = 0.00	**INFP** N = 1 % = 5.56 I = .94 ■■■■■	**INTP** N = 1 % = 5.56 I = .80 ■■■■■	PERCEPTION
	ESTP N = 0 % = 0.00 I = 0.00	**ESFP** N = 0 % = 0.00 I = 0.00	**ENFP** N = 4 % = 22.22 I = 4.49* ■■■■■■■■■■■■■■■■■■■■■■	**ENTP** N = 0 % = 0.00 I = 0.00	PERCEPTION EXTRAVERSION
	ESTJ N = 2 % = 11.11 I = 1.73 ■■■■■■■■■■■	**ESFJ** N = 0 % = 0.00 I = 0.00	**ENFJ** N = 1 % = 5.56 I = .66 ■■■■■	**ENTJ** N = 7 % = 38.89 I = 2.18 ■■■■■■■■■■■■■■■■■■■■■■■■■■■■■■■■■■■■■■■	JUDGMENT

Note: ■ = One Percent
Base Population = University faculty selected as Danforth Associates (N= 202)

	N	%	I
E	14	77.78	1.60
I	4	22.22	.43
S	3	16.67	.69
N	15	83.33	1.10
T	11	61.11	.95
F	7	38.89	1.09
J	12	66.67	.91
P	6	33.33	1.25
IJ	2	11.11	.30
IP	2	11.11	.75
EP	4	22.22	1.87
EJ	10	55.56	1.52
ST	3	16.67	1.02
SF	0	0.00	0.00
NF	7	38.89	1.40
NT	8	44.44	.93
SJ	3	16.67	.82
SP	0	0.00	0.00
NP	6	33.33	1.46
NJ	9	50.00	.94
TJ	10	55.56	1.10
TP	1	5.56	.40
FP	5	27.78	2.16
FJ	2	11.11	.49
IN	3	16.67	.42
EN	12	66.67	1.84
IS	1	5.56	.47
ES	2	11.11	.90

I = self selection index
* = p > .05
** = p > .01
*** = p > .001

Table 6.1

Case Finalists Compared to University Professors

N = 18

	SENSING THINKING	SENSING FEELING	INTUITION FEELING	INTUITION THINKING	
	ISTJ N = 1 %= 5.56 I = 0.43 ■■■■■	**ISFJ** N = 0 %= 0.00 I = 0.00	**INFJ** N = 1 %= 5.56 I = 0.74 ■■■■■	**INTJ** N = 0 %= 0.00 I = 0.00	JUDGMENT INTROVERSION
	ISTP N = 0 %= 0.00 I = 0.00	**ISFP** N = 0 %= 0.00 I = 0.00	**INFP** N = 1 %= 5.56 I = 0.69 ■■■■■	**INTP** N = 1 %= 5.56 I = 1.03 ■■■■■	PERCEPTION
	ESTP N = 0 %= 0.00 I = 0.00	**ESFP** N = 0 %= 0.00 I = 0.00	**ENFP** N = 4 %= 22.22 I = 2.45 ■■■■■■■■■■■■■■■■■■■■■■	**ENTP** N = 0 %= 0.00 I = 0.00	PERCEPTION EXTRAVERSION
	ESTJ N = 2 %= 11.11 I = 1.71 ■■■■■■■■■■■	**ESFJ** N = 0 %= 0.00 I = 0.00	**ENFJ** N = 1 %= 5.56 I = 0.69 ■■■■■	**ENTJ** N = 7 %= 38.89 I = 4.03*** ■■■■■■■■■■■■■■■■■■■■■■■■■■■■■■■■■■■■■■■	JUDGMENT

	N	%	I
E	14	77.78	1.70
I	4	22.22	0.41
S	3	16.67	0.46
N	15	83.33	1.30
T	11	61.11	1.14
F	7	38.89	0.83
J	12	66.67	1.01
P	6	33.33	0.98
IJ	2	11.11	0.30
IP	2	11.11	0.66
EP	4	22.22	1.29
EJ	10	55.56	1.94
ST	3	16.67	0.75
SF	0	0.00	0.00
NF	7	38.89	1.19
NT	8	44.44	1.42
SJ	3	16.67	0.56
SP	0	0.00	0.00
NP	6	33.33	1.20
NJ	9	50.00	1.39
TJ	10	55.56	1.39
TP	1	5.56	0.41
FP	5	27.78	1.35
FJ	2	11.11	0.43
IN	3	16.67	0.52
EN	12	66.67	2.08
IS	1	5.56	0.25
ES	2	11.11	0.81
ET	9	50.00	2.21
EF	5	27.78	1.20
IF	2	11.11	0.47
IT	2	11.11	0.36
Sdom	1	5.56	0.26
Ndom	5	27.78	0.85
Tdom	10	55.56	2.40
Fdom	2	11.11	0.50

I = self selection index
* = p > .05
** = p > .01
*** = p > .001

Notes: ■ = One Percent; Base Population = University Faculty (N = 2882).

Source of Base: Atlas of Type Tables (p. 236) by Gerald P. Macdaid, Mary H. McCaulley, and Richard I. Kainz. Gainesville, FL: Center for Applications of Psychological Type, 1986. Used by permission.

Table 6.2

Quotations from professors' responses in Beidler's book are included here for each of the types in the sample.

ENTJ

There were 7 ENTJs in the sample of 18. Several in this group discussed their roles as teachers in terms of power. None of the other types referred to their roles in a similar way.

Basic Style

An English professor said:

> I love the power knowledge gives me. I know how uncomfortable and reverential I feel in the presence of people who have more knowledge than I have, and I like knowing that others feel slightly uncomfortable and reverential in my presence. When I discuss two pieces of freshman writing with my freshmen we generally both know which piece is better, but they think they are just guessing, whereas I know that I know which is better. I also have the power of knowing that I can find the words to explain why one theme is better. My freshmen often cannot do that, for they are going by true, but to them unexplainable, instinct when they pick one theme over another. I like knowing more than my freshmen do because knowing puts me in control, gives me the power not to sound like a fool when I try to talk about writing. (p. 44)

A biology professor talked about power this way:

> I am the "Vince Lombardi" of modem biology. I am the "'Godfather" of biochemistry. Winning is everything. Contracts must be fulfilled by both parties to that contract

> ... or else! As I flog, so do I caress. I know I alienate as I gain respect. (Unpublished)

He goes on to speak of several awards for his teaching by saying, "It says I am winning more than I am losing. I am still not satisfied. I want to win more" (unpublished).

It is clear that both of these professors convey a great deal of vitality and most likely inspire their students with it. Their language of power gives some clues to the motivations and values behind this vitality. The other ENTJs commenting on their teaching styles also reveal aspects that type theory would suggest for dominant Extraverted Thinking types (objective decisiveness, tough mindedness, logical structure). One English professor reported that her colleagues described her as a "compassionate hard-ass":

> Students who want Mickey Mouse courses are unlikely to enroll in mine. On the other hand, I try to be exceptionally clear. I try to allow students ample time to adjust to my expectations, and I try through midterm evaluations to adjust my expectations to any specific group of students. (Unpublished)

An astronomy professor reflects the tendency of ENTJs to take a strong leadership role. In answering the question about why he was chosen as a CASE professor, he said, "I was among the leaders in innovation of our general education program which became a very important part of the curriculum here" (unpublished).

Extraverted Teaching

The extraverted energy of the 7 ENTJs' teaching approaches is apparent in all of their statements:

> "I generally learn best and most permanently by doing something. It is useful in some ways to have someone tell me what to do or show me how to do it, but it is still theirs when they are finished. It is mine when I have done it myself. In my classes, then, I almost never lecture. When I do, I never lecture for more than fifteen minutes. I am not much good at lecturing anyhow, so no one is missing much when I refrain from doing so. I suppose I could learn to be better at it by doing more of it, but my heart would never be in it. There are better ways for students to learn what I have to teach. (pp. 51–52)

This same English professor gives an example of involving students in "doing" during a composition class. Instead of using a published handbook on writing, he had them collectively create their own handbook for the class.

A biology professor comments, "When I stand before my class they know that they are being exposed to the real me . . . I go 'all out' to make the course powerful and relevant. I expect them to go 'all out in the' learning process" (unpublished).

An English professor puts it this way: "I am able to translate my own love for literature into an energy level which allows me to be 'on' in what has been called a contagious way for the hour(s) of class time" (unpublished).

A professor of geography emphasizes his belief in the value of "doing" to learn:

> Facts, concepts, and relationships are meaningless unless students know the places in which these elements of the natural and cultural environments are located. I have tried to facilitate their knowing about such places by developing

> what I call the audiovisual-tutorial independent method of learning . . . . I have also conducted field trips by air so that my students can see for themselves . . . . (p. 24)

The astronomy professor further illustrates this extraverted orientation: "So for me, field work . . . in the observatory or on-site among the ancient Mexican ruins is the best way I can help students to learn by doing" (p. 55). Extraverts prefer to learn by externalizing so they can manipulate ideas through talking and action; this preference is clear in the previous statements.

Thinking Judgment

> "I suppose that one reason for my good teaching ratings, as far as students are concerned, is that they know I spend a lot of time preparing my courses" (unpublished).
>
> "I regularly distinguish between the 'facts' of literature and the 'interpretations' which must be based on those facts. I am alert to boredom and adapt techniques accordingly" (unpublished).
>
> "I feel that students learn best from carefully prepared and well delivered lectures" (p. 55). This same professor continues later, "During the preparation, I type up notes, draw diagrams, synthesize relevant literature, and consider examples from current events. The morning of the lecture I write three to six key thoughts on a five-by-eight card" (p. 69).

These are examples of the ENTJ's emphasis on preparation and structure (J) and on use of facts and objectivity (T) to evaluate theories and interpretations (N). The ENTJs put more stress on grades and a system of grading than the Feeling and Perceiving types did. They used language such as "principles," "systems," and "objectivity," and relied on structured evaluation through carefully scheduled testing.

An English professor discusses his grading system:

> The grading process was more successful than before, in part because those freshmen, in writing the criteria themselves [also Extraverted doing], had "bought into" them. These were not principles of good writing that came down from high in some egghead lectures or from some grand principle-maker in the sky. No, these were their principles, principles at least half-understood because they had discovered and articulated them themselves (p. 53).

This same professor gave daily quizzes on the assigned reading *before* discussing the reading because he felt this structure involved them more actively (Extraversion). Students were allowed to ask as many questions as they wanted to before the daily quiz. As the term progressed, the quiz was given closer and closer to the end of the class period. This strategy reflects expression of both the professor's Extraversion in getting the students to do the work of learning, and Judging preference in structuring these daily evaluations and markers of progress.

ESTJ and ISTJ

The two ESTJs also revealed their Extraverted Thinking in their statements but with more of an emphasis on practical applications and public service (Sensing instead of Intuition). They share the ENTJs' preferences for learning by doing (E). It is interesting to compare the ESTJs' with ISTJs' teaching statements here and see how the dominance of introverted Sensing shifts the TJ focus.

ESTJ Style

One of the CASE professors who is also an academic administrator explains CASE's recognition of his teaching:

> . . . because I put so much effort into communicating the importance of the subject, because my syllabi are organized, clear, detailed, because I work like hell in preparing every class, because I have published enough to win the respect of my colleagues, I have managed to convince a lot of students and fellow teachers that what I do is important, is good and will have a life-long influence (Unpublished).

This same professor also says, "My courses are pretty traditional, large lectures on general humanities subjects with no prerequisites. I am not an innovative teacher" (p. 56). He indicates that he stimulates participation, although the classes are large, by throwing out "about 10 questions with the intent of provoking" (p. 56). He continues:

> In my classes students seem to get the most out of the material when I succeed in getting them to think about their place in the scheme of things. I love to take them back, to place them in a historical context, to make them feel that it is important to understand their place in this grand scheme (p. 56).

His comments illustrate a desire most ESTJs have to place information in a sequential and historical context and to bring immediacy to material by connecting students' lives to this material. His advice for successful teaching is, "Be scared. Be a worrier. Be afraid of failure. Then translate these feelings into energy, careful preparation, and ambition" (p. 81). These words reflect a prevailing ESTJ style that is painstakingly conscientious, concerned with tradition and maintenance of existing structures, and reliant on sensing data.

An ESTJ anthropology professor states his beliefs about teaching succinctly:

> The most important way students learn is by being involved in a research project. If it is in a laboratory science, they learn more by being in the lab and working with junior and senior or graduate level students as well as faculty. They learn equipment techniques and are in a position to listen to discussions about a particular field and its problems (p. 55).

An interesting quotation from this same professor may not be so relevant to his teaching as to type expression through his chosen field:

> I have difficulty separating teaching from public service. Because I am a forensic anthropologist who identifies decayed 'bodies' or skeletons for law enforcement agencies, I make public service a part of my work (p. 22).

ISTJ Style

An ISTJ professor of sociology shares many of the STJ characteristics of the ESTJs, such as reliance on facts and structure, but with two distinct differences. With the Introverted attitude, the emphasis is not placed on externalized energy and doing. The dominant function is introverted Sensing, resulting in a different emphasis from the ESTJs:

> I like to try new arrangements of information .... My talent is less a matter of performance . . . than an ability to assemble resources in support of the efforts of others who I respect greatly as colleagues (Unpublished).

The language of the Thinking preference is apparent in this IS quotation:

> Students learn by measuring their ideas against those of others. As a consequence, the effective teacher starts by recognizing that students already know a good deal and simply provides a yardstick and some things to measure. (pp. 56–57)

ENFP and INFP

The NFPs provide a dramatic contrast to the TJs. This group uses different language to talk about teaching and emphasizes different motivations and strategies. The ENFPs exemplify a high energy level and focus on doing, as the ETJs do, but the style of that energy is dissimilar. An ENFP English professor writes:

> I believe Alice in Wonderland was essentially right when she said, "How can I know what I think until I see what I say". We learn about experience of others by reading, but we best learn about ourselves by writing (p. 58).

The first sentence shows the extraverted way of sorting ideas. His comment about writing is one way ENFPs can access their introverted auxiliary Feeling to understand their own inner worlds. The statement reflects an appreciation for the importance of ways of learning both in the external and the internal "worlds." He further stresses his preference for Extraversion: "It is hard for me to see how anyone can stand still and be interesting . . . to teach, move" (p. 81).

Student-Centered Focus

To remain stimulated intellectually an ENFP professor says, ". . . keep the focus upon the student as much as possible, rather than on the material taught. As a teacher I try to assist the students on their route to self-knowledge" (p. 66).

The previous quotation and the one following show EN characteristics of process rather than outcome orientation, student-centered versus teacher-centered focus, and desire to be a catalyst or facilitator. "I prefer another image, that of the teacher as a wise but lonely wanderer, a kind of singing peddler, who comes upon a group of innocent and ignorant youngsters and convinces them the sparkling rocks he carries in his old buckets can enlighten their lives . . ."(p. 66).

Several of the ENFP teachers reflect a theme of mutuality:

> I do not have a two-camp image of education—"We and They." I see us all as learners. Some of us are simply further along the path than others and only a cooperative effort on the part of all participants will ensure a successful outcome to the process (Unpublished).

A naturalist describes a shared experience during field work by saying, ". . . [I] lie there in the grass like any human, and reach out to them. And then, with friendships established, I can help guide their university experience" (Unpublished). Elsewhere he claims, "When two minds are caused to meet, then all flows from that bonding" (p. 61). A philosophy professor asserts, "The teacher-student relationship is much like a master-apprentice relationship" (p. 59).

Spontaneity and Performance

According to type theory, the EPs and particularly the ENFPs, often exhibit a flare in their presentations and thrive on spontaneous response to people and the environment, often producing their best work under such conditions. A naturalist illustrates these qualities: "Out in the field, also, my students can see me in unrehearsed action, learning and doing and failing" (p. 23).

An economics professor reveals his ENFP style:

> . . . the most distinctive thing about my teaching is my enthusiasm . . . . I must admit that I have a streak of "ham" in me and I don't mind some of that showing in the classroom: it helps keep the students awake and they certainly can't learn while asleep. I treat students as adults; have confidence in them, as Gandhi put it, to realize his or her potential. Finally, I am willing to "lend an ear," which means a lot of office time is spent with students who are not dropping by to get help in economics (Unpublished).

Perhaps the clearest contrast of the ENFP teaching style with the TJ style is the following:

> First of all I work hard—every day—and as a rule I teach with abandon. I despise lesson plans, overhead projectors, and indeed any device that is supposed to aid the teacher in the classroom. I know this is utterly rejected today, but I feel that all a teacher needs is a decent text and a piece of chalk, perhaps only a piece of chalk if he knows enough. I do use a syllabus and frequently pass out bibliographies which makes me in a way, I suppose, as dependent on machines as anyone else.
>
> In class I have to admit I frequently "perform," though I don't intend to be eccentric or a "character" . . . . I will use any technique that is legal to try to get the students to perform . . . . I frequently feel absurd in the classroom, but never ashamed of what I'm doing. In absurdity there is abandonment and with abandonment quite often a good deal of fun (Unpublished).

This last comment about feeling absurd is in striking contrast to the ENTJ's comment about wanting "the power not to sound like a fool" in the classroom.

INFP

An INFP English professor shares many stylistic similarities with the English and economics professors who are ENFPs. The main difference is much less emphasis on classroom performance; instead, there is persuasiveness expressed through a gentle, almost seductive approach:

> . . . I make it clear that it is their enjoyment that I am after, not their grade . . . . My aim is to make them comfortable with the (to them) strange manner of writing that poetry is; and then, when they are used to that, to enable them to perceive the means the poet is using to enact experience (Unpublished).

Again the gentle approach is illustrated:

> If your students are hostile to your subject, that is probably because they were taught it badly in high school, were frightened of it because of its terminology . . . . In any case, the thing is to present it as enchantingly and interestingly as possible, without reference to any of their hostility. Refer to your subject always as if it were irresistible and full of gaiety. Soon your students will find it so (p. 78).

Notice the NF language and especially the expression of dominant introverted Feeling in the above passage. The INFP, like the ENFPs, sees herself as a facilitator to student learning. A last quotation from the INFP reveals the introverted orientation to learning, in contrast to that of the Extraverts:

> I do not think it is possible to learn without reading. It

> consolidates what one hears in lectures and many people take in material better through the eyes than through the ears. I think studying is better done when it is focused by practical assignments. I find that students "get more" out of a poem when they are asked to think about several questions while they read it, in preparation for discussion in section meeting (p. 58).

ENFJ and INFJ

The two NFJs in the sample are women who teach English. Their language reflects much of the idealism and romanticism of the other NFs' words, with some specific differences. The ENFJ and INFJ use extraverted Feeling in their classroom. They also prefer more structure than the NFPs do.

Extraverting Feeling in the Classroom

The ENFJ has dominant extraverted Feeling, clearly shown both in word choice and in approach described here:

> When I was young I harbored a dream of becoming an Aimee Semple McPherson kind of evangelist. I think what I wanted as much as redeemed souls was the sense that I had redeemed them . . . . I think I have kept the evangelism. I want to make a difference in people's lives. I believe in teaching I do that. I teach, too, because it makes me feel good (p. 90).

An INFJ's reference to "faith" has a similar ring:

> Have faith in the greatness of teaching as a vocation. Have faith in your students. Have faith in yourself. Bishop Tutu said no Christian can be anything but an optimist. He

> would not mind, I think, if I said that of the teacher (p. 81).

None of the other CASE professors talked about teaching with this kind of "religious" flavor.

> I would like to think that in my courses some students develop a view of life that can accommodate loss and suffering, an awareness that love almost always calls for self-sacrifice, an ability to be joyfully surprised by a single flower of the horse chestnut tree, a reverence for words . . . (p. 48).

While the ENFJ has a dominant extraverted Feeling function illustrated earlier, the INFJ has as dominant introverted Intuition. The difference of the INFJ in the dominant function, though similar on three preferences, causes a shift in emphasis or tone from Feeling to Intuition. Dominant introverted Intuition is represented by the metaphor of a net:

> I teach in a liberal arts college where one discipline touches another, meshes with it, and becomes, paradoxically, a great net to hold an infinite number of questions, and at the same time to release possibilities, intuitions, sometimes even answers to the problems of the "real world" (p. 25).

Many professors struggle to achieve some kind of balance between the demands to publish and to teach well. For the dominant extraverted Feeling professor this conflict is poignantly expressed:

> There is a painful conflict for me, because I enjoy teaching more than research and writing. I am better at it, and I get more praise for what I do in the classroom than for what I do in print. It strikes me as nearly impossible to be the kind of teacher I want to be, have a family life I value, and be the kind of published scholar . . . (p. 39).

Structure

A major difference in teaching style of NFJs compared to NFPs is one of structure:

> I have a purpose and a theme in mind for each part of a course. I enter almost every class with either a detailed lecture or a very careful outline. Then I try to let my students discover these ideas themselves. As I ask questions, provide the framework, clarify, and fill in the background, they create the analysis, building up evidence, connecting, comparing, synthesizing . . . . This tension between order and creativity, between the given and the discovered is, it seems to me, the source of learning (Unpublished).

INTP

The last type in the sample is an INTP professor of English. His motivations for teaching are described here:

> My earliest and highest aspiration was to be a writer. I turned to college teaching because I guessed that I might have a better chance of earning a living by doing it than by writing. Much later, after much writing and teaching, I found out that I had chosen rightly but for the wrong reason. I realized I could not have pursued the solitariness necessary to being the kind of writer my aspirations would want me to be. I realized that some strong part of me needed the interchange with other people over things we were interested . . . (p. 91).

Academic involvement seems to have provided him a way to exercise his introverted dominant Thinking through writing and at the same time provide him with stimulation through "interchange" for his extraverted auxiliary Intuition, so that his life does not become too solitary. He has a long list of publications to his credit, serves on many committees, and describes his teaching as having "good solid, scholarly work behind it" (unpublished).

The INTP's approach to teaching is to "be flexible."

> Do not pay much attention to someone who has only one piece of advice about how to teach. It is both a curse and a blessing of teaching that there is no one way. Teaching continues to delight me because the ground is always shifting under my feet (pp. 80–81).

Summary of Strengths

These CASE professors demonstrate the various strengths of their types in their own words. Their assumptions about how students learn best are influenced by their types. Their words provide a clear contrast and comparison of type styles. The variation in language—the word choice—is most striking. Language reflects internal processes, value systems, and overall style. Their metaphors also reflect preferences: the religious metaphors of the NFJs; the teacher as father from several ENTJs; images of "bonding" and mutuality from the NFPs; and "yardstick" and the "entrepreneur" packaging ideas from the STJs. Readers may make additional connections between the statements and type theory.

These teachers seem able to capitalize on their natural preferences to develop successful teaching styles and to find an arena in which these preferences could be best expressed and encouraged to develop. An ENFP philosophy professor makes this point elegantly: "I suppose that the best one can do is find one's strengths and nurture them" (p. 34).

The next step is to ask if these master teachers are sufficiently self-aware and well developed (having competence in using their dominant and auxiliary and ability to use their less-preferred functions when needed) to compensate for areas outside their natural strengths and preferences. Do they acknowledge learning styles other than their own and how do they respond to other learning styles? These questions cannot be completely answered by examining their statements, but the statements may provide clues. It is interesting to note that many in the sample reported preference scores above 39, some at the outer range. Although one cannot put too much weight on scores in themselves, a natural question to ask is whether individuals who cast all or most of their "votes" for a certain preference will consistently avoid engaging in the opposite preference.

Awareness and Type Development

The question of how aware these master teachers are of their strengths and limitations has actually been partially answered in many of the previous quotations. For example, the ENTJ who discussed the positive aspects of his challenging and demanding approach and at the same time the potential for intimidation and alienation of some students. The ISTJ professor is clear about his strengths lying in organizing resources and serving the team effort instead of in a brilliant classroom performance. In some of their statements, the CASE professors have also demonstrated flexibility to adapt their approach and expectations to student needs. In this section their comments can be examined for additional indications of good type development.

ENTJ

One of the characteristics of some ENTJ professors is their conception of power within the teaching role. One of these professors demonstrates awareness of the limitations of this role and shows his attempts at compensating:

> My job as a teacher is to empower my students, to demystify a subject for them and so give up my power over them. If I am doing my job, by the end of the semester my students are independent of me. I strive every semester to give my students power, even though when I succeed I inevitably disempower myself. I hate that feeling of powerlessness at the end of the semester. I love it (p. 44).

There is a lovely paradox in his statement, illustrating both his natural inclination and his balanced response, and finally his delight in being able to go beyond his natural preferences.

An ENTJ reveals the alteration of his teaching style in response to students' reactions:

> I teach technique and seeing and criticism and writing and self-awareness and how to ask questions and, occasionally, little side dishes like honesty and virtue and truth and beauty. I used to try to lecture about such subjects, but I have come to see that my students will learn what I have to teach not by my telling but by their doing . . . . Gradually, sometimes painfully, I have come to understand that only doing will convince my students (p. 52).

The ENTJ who said he was the "Vince Lombardi" of modern biology also realizes that he "alienates" as he "gains respect." "I know I cannot be all things to all people." He also says, "I reach out to them in every possible mode that I know" (Unpublished).

The ENTJ who had been called a "compassionate hard-ass" shows the following awareness:

> In providing such a lively, focused, challenging atmosphere

> I am troubled by the chance that students may come to depend upon me and not engender their own pace and excitement (Is my strength my weakness?) (Unpublished).

This comment sounds much like the earlier ENTJ comment about striving to give up "the power" to the students. An ENTJ English professor's comment contains the classic T–F polarity of hard honesty versus tact. She shows sensitivity to her inferior function here:

> Evaluate others and yourself as honestly as you can, given the evidence you have honestly worked to collect. Then be forgiving of mistakes (including your own) and rest in Chaucer's assurance that the intention is all. One more word: do it all with tact (p. 78).

Her flexibility to use functions other than her preferred ones is also demonstrated in this statement, "I try alone or with students to create some spectacle, some mutual project or challenge or event which, in a creative and at times outrageous way, serves to embody our learning and be 'fun'" (p. 72). None of the Perceiving types placed the word fun in quotation marks; this may reflect a Judging attitude.

An economics professor shows his appreciation for both his favored Thinking orientation and the least-preferred Feeling function in his comment, "I want them to appreciate that they cannot solve problems unless they marshall facts, sift through data, and establish a framework for solving them. But I also want students to incorporate compassion and values into the solution of a problem" (p. 46).

There seems to be a "mellowing" with maturity of these ENTJs. One advises, "Show that you are human . . . . As young Ph.D.s we often feel like experts ready to hang out a shingle and practice the art of teaching . . . . But pride goes before a fall" (p. 80). Another counsels,

"You should be human, interested in students, and willing to poke fun at number one" (p. 79).

Another example of developed flexibility to use functions other than the preferred ones is this comment:

> To be "responsible" to society seems to require some "irresponsible" behavior: neglecting committee assignments, common sense security, dependable colleagues, and the fruits of predictability (p. 24).

He advocates a deliberate letting go of structures when doing so will bring about a rich learning experience. He goes on to give examples of creative and unusual learning experiences he developed which involved not only his students but also his family. This same professor discusses his relationship to students this way: "I have to force myself to listen to them, to find out what they are thinking, singing, longing for. It is so easy to become out of touch, obsolete, a vestigial remnant of the '40s, '60s, Vietnam, graduate school, yesterday" (pp. 69–70).

Occasionally some language more frequently heard from NFs emerges in ENTJ comments about teaching, suggesting development of Feeling:

> But unexpected (yet dependable) flashes of intuition or dogged discoveries or familiar ideas enlighten and warm me and make my joy complete. Every day. But I must mention also one special pleasure of the profession: friends we could give everything to cultivate if we were not on the campus, friends we take for granted day after year and discover anew each time an occasion makes dialogue possible (p. 89).

An ENTJ's appreciation for diversity can be seen in the following:

> Surely we must insist on the value of diversity in the professorate, that there is more than one way to show success or progress in a profession as complex as ours (p. 41).

This professor also points out:

> There is no one most important way that students learn, though it may well be that for each student there is at any one moment one best way. Our job as professors is to discover the one best way for as many of our individual students as we can. For most of our students we shall not fully succeed . . . . Helping a student find the best way to learn is sometimes called love (p. 61).

ESTJ and ISTJ

The ESTJs in this study are similar to the ENTJs in their development of an appreciation for the Feeling dimension and a willingness to use less-preferred functions as needed and to adjust teaching style to students. The professor-administrator expresses it this way:

> I love college life. I love being near a gymnasium and being able to work out with the varsity baseball team. I love being able to order books for the library and then being the first person to read them. I love being with young people who are the same age I was thirty years ago . . . . I love making lights go on in people's heads (p. 87).

Another ESTJ shows modification of his teaching style to accommodate the students:

> I lecture not from notes but only from an outline. I

> encourage students to ask questions and to a certain extent I allow students to lead me in the subject that we discuss in class. I have found as the years go by that attitudes and interests of the students change, and I try to keep abreast of these changes by following a basic outline, but not necessarily teaching exactly the same thing each quarter. (p 69).

In this quotation the effort to balance control and structure with flexibility and responsiveness to students' needs is apparent. Later he comments, "I think education should be fun and I try to make my lectures as interesting as possible" (Unpublished).

The ISTJ who spoke modestly of his strengths shows his self-awareness in his interactions with others and in his academic pursuits:

> I am not foolhardy enough to venture too far into someone else's backyard [academic area], less out of a respect for turf than the recognition of his or her superior knowledge. The solution to MY ambition and my caution is to enlist the help of others to looking at common problems. I am fortunate to work at a college where others share my concerns and penchant for teamwork (Unpublished).

ENFP and INFP

If the TJs have shown good type development through appreciation of diversity and of interpersonal issues as well as by becoming flexible, how have the NFPs shown development? Do they develop beyond strengths such as classroom performance and facilitation? The same economics professor who identified his primary teaching asset as enthusiasm shows development, especially a blending of Sensing and

Thinking functions, with his preferred functions:

> I hope my course will help produce a person who has acquired a knowledge of analytical concepts and who can think straight, communicate ideas, evaluate conditions, and discriminate between the important and the unimportant. We do not want skilled barbarians. We want graduates who have technical skills but who know what to do with these skills (p. 47).

The ENFP English professor seems sensitive to the Sensing student's way of learning in his approach to poetry:

> I tell my freshmen and sophomores that explicating a poem is much like looking at a car that one is thinking of buying. Though a poem and a car are very different, some crucial questions are the same in evaluating them (p. 26).

He then involves students in evaluating the usefulness of cars and poems.

The naturalist uses a variety of teaching approaches:

> Most lectures can lose some students, so I put an outline on the board and point to it now and then to show where I am in the text [J]. And I watch the audience to see how they are receiving things [ENF]. I try to involve the audience, to get them to ask questions [E]. I tell a story about some class member who has done an interesting thing [SF] (p. 77).

Elsewhere he adds, "I'm a popular and interesting classroom teacher, though I have my lapses, and sometimes simple organization eludes me" (Unpublished). This professor with a preference for Perceiving is conscious of his natural style and tries to balance this in the ways described above. He describes himself as an effective lecturer but "my best teaching by far is in nature, where I become an - orchestrator of events for students" (p. 23).

INTP

The INTP professor acknowledges that many of his personal academic interests may be too esoteric for his students. ". . . my specialized inquiries become of great interest to me but leave the students behind. Knowing too much is as sure a way to be boring as any" (p. 70). He goes on to muse:

> In the end, it is the variety of human life—in the students, in the literature, in myself—that is my subject. One of the advantages we older teachers have is that we can be much freer than younger ones. We can be more ourselves and have more self that is of interest to students (p. 70).

This last sentence speaks to type development and individuation as people mature. His comments also suggest expression of his inferior Feeling, an appreciation for the human, subjective values.

ENFJ and INFJ

The INFJ's comment illustrates the ongoing nature of development as teacher and person: "Patience, hard thing! But I think I am learning to be patient, to wait—believing in the student—her, his potential" (Unpublished).

Perhaps the appropriate way to end this line of inquiry into the awareness and development of these master teachers is with a quotation from the only one of the sample with a prior knowledge of type and the MBTI This ENFJ sums up the issues:

For years, I thought there was only one way of learning. That it happened to be precisely the way I learn best never struck me as odd. I catch on easily by reading and by imitation through writing. While not particularly creative, I am good at analysis, at seeing central ideas, identifying supporting specifics, and synthesizing what I have just learned with old knowledge. Expecting my students to do the same, I constructed writing assignments and examinations requiring these skills. Now I know that there are a number of different kinds of learner from the linear learner who needs step-by-step practical guidance, to the global learner who seems capable of skipping all intermediate stages and with dazzling (and to us more orderly folk, sometimes messy) creativity arriving at a new idea. This recognition of diversity made me rethink many of my writing assignments. I now try to provide choices enabling students to learn and to express ideas in a variety of ways. So, while I require all my American literature students to write an original critical analysis of some work, I now give them options. The global learners can discover and display their knowledge of Poe by writing a short story imitating him, while the more linear learners might begin by summarizing and evaluating major critical articles on "The Fall of the House of Usher." I also try to recognize different learning styles in exams, combining long essays requiring synthesis or original insights with shorter one-paragraph responses based on more specific knowledge of the works studied (p. 59).

Summary

One *cannot* generalize from this very select sample that most outstanding teachers will be a certain type, or have a specific preference. This study does show how type affects teaching style, assumptions about the learning process, and attitudes about what aspects of teaching are valued and seen as rewarding. The master teachers' own words are like a vivid field study of type dynamics. Although generalizations cannot be made regarding type and teaching excellence, it is interesting to note the distribution of types in the sample and to speculate as to how type might have factored into the selection process, given the nature of the CASE selection procedure.

More interesting than the distribution of types is the way the master teachers have expressed their types through their work and through the language and choice of words used to describe their work. It is evident that they have capitalized on their strengths and natural preferences. At the same time these master teachers have been able "to speak" to other types and to appreciate diversity in students and colleagues. This study suggests that good type development is a primary factor in the sample subjects' recognition for their contributions to teaching.

Implications

Introducing type theory and its implications for learning and teaching early in the careers of faculty can facilitate their personal and professional growth. They can be supported in developing their natural strengths and at the same time encouraged to experiment with a variety of teaching modes to reach students different from themselves. Through knowledge of their MBTI preferences, they can become aware of their own natural biases about the best way to learn. They can realize that there are many other ways to learn and that frequently individuals are more comfortable and successful learning in one of these other ways. By understanding their own natural preferences, teachers can choose work conditions and projects which support and enhance the development and expression of these preferences. Especially in the earlier years, they can also be more tolerant of their shortcomings when they can relate these to their lesser preferences; type gives them a "map" of how they need to develop over a lifetime.

It follows that knowledge of type can influence curriculum development, teaching strategies and assignments, course structure, and method of student evaluation. One of the CASE professors, upon learning his MBTI results, was quick to point out the usefulness of this information in deciphering previously puzzling student evaluations of his teaching. He had received conflicting reviews over the years about "such things as organization of material, clarity of argument, etc." With the knowledge of this MBTI results he realized that the positive and negative comments about the same teaching approach were probably a result of his ENFP style appealing more to the students with preferences for Intuition and less to the students who preferred Sensing. He said, "It casts a whole new light on reviewing student evaluations" (personal correspondence, August 1986).

Administrators can also be shown that there are many models of excellence among faculty based on productive expression of professors' natural strengths; the CASE finalists provide such models. Therefore, the institution should be prepared to recognize and reward more than one model of excellence. For example, the institution valuing teaching may decide that the ENFJ professor who thrives on classroom interaction and is loved by students for her dedication to teaching should be supported to the same degree as the INTP who, although available to the students, places a higher priority on research for publication.

Those of us not involved directly in the classroom can help students clarify their own learning styles and the relationship of their styles to their success and failures in certain teachers' courses. The examples given by the professors in the sample increase our understanding of differing motivations, value systems, and approaches among faculty. If we are to be effective in the academic community, we must be able to understand and talk the language(s) of the faculty.

Peter Beidler's own comment about the job of professors deserves restatement; he says it is their job to discover the one best way individual students learn. "Helping a student find the best way to learn is sometimes called love" (p. 61). For those interested in a thorough exploration of these themes and others related to college teaching, a complete reading of Beidler's book, *Distinguished Teachers on Effective Teaching* (Beidler, 1986), is recommended.

A special note of appreciation to the CASE Finalists, 1981 to 1985: Robert G. Albertson, University of Puget Sound; Anthony F. Aveni, Colgate University; William M. Bass III, University of Tennessee; Peter G. Beidler, Lehigh University; Barbara Harrell Carson, Rollins College; Kenneth Eble, University of Utah; Sister Maura Eichner, College of Notre Dame of Maryland; Julienne H. Empric, Eckerd College; Sol Gittleman, Tufts University; Robert J. Higgs, East Tennessee State University; Parker Grimes Marden, St. Lawrence University; Kenneth S. Norris, University of California at Santa Cruz; Charles E. Ratliff, Davidson College; Benjamin Richason, Carroll College; Paul Saltman, University of California at San Diego; Daniel G. Sisler, Cornell University; Lawrence P. Ulrich, University of Dayton; and Helen Vendler, Harvard University.

Reference

Beidler, P. (1986). *Distinguished teachers on effective teaching.* San Francisco: Jossey-Bass Publishers, Inc.

CHAPTER 7

Academic Advising

SCOTT ANCHORS

Uses of the Myers Briggs Type Indicator® personality assessment tool in academic advising have changed significantly over the past two decades. In the 1980s, advisors and other educators used the instrument for institution-wide administration to incoming students. Large amounts of data were collected, and campus-wide programs were developed. Special advising programs were created at a variety of institutions, including Mercer University, University of Maine, Mississippi State, Rollins College, and St. Louis University to name a few. The emphasis on uses of the MBTI® instrument paralleled the national movement focusing on the first-year experience in colleges and universities. However in the 1990s, uses of the MBTI personality assessment tool in colleges and universities have changed and appear to have decentralized. The result is counselors and advisors viewing the Indicator as one of many tools they can use with individual students, and mass administration seems to be declining.

Regardless of how or when the MBTI instrument is administered on a campus, the advising process can utilize type information to help students by teaching them a useful framework for decision making and assisting them in the development of perception and judgment. While the MBTI instrument is not the answer to all the challenges advisors face in assisting students, it can serve as a useful tool for guiding students through what is often a frustrating and confusing process. This chapter discusses the importance of advising, type and decision-making styles, a model program for advising, and the use of type to plan a student's course load.

Importance of Advising

Few experiences in students' university or college careers have as much potential for influencing their lifelong development as academic advising. Through continual contact with students, whether face-to-face, through the mail, on the telephone, or e-mail, advisors gain meaningful insights into students' academic, social, and personal experiences and personal development needs.

Advisors can use these insights to help students understand themselves, develop sound academic and career goals, and ultimately be successful making life decisions. Increased interest in advising has resulted in the creation of a national advising association, the National Academic Advising Association (NACADA), and the proliferation of workshops, seminars, and numerous publications on the topic. NACADA grew out of the first National Conference on Academic Advising in 1977 and currently has more than 4,800 members representing all fifty states, Canada, Puerto Rico, and several other countries. Members represent higher education institutions across the spectrum of Carnegie college classifications and include professional advisors/counselors, faculty, administrators, and students whose responsibilities include academic advising.

In addition to this nationwide organization, national surveys of college presidents rank academic advising as a leading factor in student retention (Beal and Noel, 1980). The advising process can have a tremendous impact on students, their satisfaction with the institution, their academic performance, and ultimately upon retention.

Despite this heightened interest in advising and its potential value, little has been written about using the MBTI instrument for this purpose. Gordon and Carberry (1984) presented an overview of how the MBTI instrument could be used as a resource for developmental advising. They explained that students can benefit from understanding how they process information, and that the MBTI instrument can be used in group advising to help students understand their reactions in certain situations. Tom Carskadon of Mississippi State University, a leading researcher on the MBTI instrument, and a frequent user with first year advisees says, "the MBTI [instrument] continues to be the most practical tool I use in helping students to understand and explore the challenges of selecting courses and ultimately a major and life work" (2001). Others such as McCaulley (1981) and Laney (1949) have discussed the use of the MBTI instrument in career planning, and its implications for improving academic advising.

Research by Crockett investigated the relationship of Myers-Briggs Type Indicator preference scores to advising styles. She found that students who prefer Intuition have a stronger interest in including a wide scope of activities in the advising process. As one might expect, she found these interests to be in future possibilities, and less in the mundane details of planning an educational program. In contrast, the Sensing type students were interested in the practical details of educational planning and implementation. The broader picture was of less interest to them.

The advising relationship should be maximized since it is generally one of the few institutional contacts required of students. This contact has potential to help a student explore a variety of issues that are pertinent to college success. The advisor can use type information to help the student gain greater self-insight and select an appropriate program of study.

How do different students proceed through the process of selecting a program of study? Are there characteristic decision-making styles, and do these styles impact academic choices? The next section will address these questions.

Decision-Making Styles

Students vary tremendously in the way they approach the educational planning process. Patterns can be identified among students who are undecided or decided about a college major related to their types and to the combinations of their attitudes (Extraversion–Introversion and Judging–Perceiving). These combinations are: Extraversion Judging (EJ), Extraversion Perceiving (EP), Introversion Judging (IJ), and Introversion Perceiving (IP). For example, EJ students tend to be found more frequently among the decided students, and IP students tend to occur more frequently among the undecided students. Myers and McCaulley (1985) described these combinations of attitudes in the *MBTI Manual.* Anchors, Gershman, and Robbins (1989) in a study of characteristics of undecided students found Extraversion–Introversion and Judging–Perceiving to be related to students' "sense of purpose." As students' scores on the Developing Purpose task of the Student Development Task Inventory (SDTI) (Winston, Miller, and Prince, 1979) increased, so did the strength of their preference for Extraversion and Judging. Table 7.1 shows these intercorrelations in a sample of 946 students who were administered both the MBTI instrument and the Student Development Task Inventory. By looking at the direction of the correlation of these scale correlations, it is clear that on the SDTI, students with preferences for Extraversion, Sensing, and Judging are the most comfortable in the accomplishment of tasks having to do with planning. Although it might be easy to conclude these students are more "developed," the complexity of decision making must be viewed from a framework that views the entire type and their path and pitfalls to deciding upon a major.

Table 7.2 shows a trend in relationships between the MBTI attitudes and SDTI scores. On the Appropriate Educational Plans subtask of the SDTI, the EJs ranked first, with well-defined and personally meaningful educational goals. They were followed in descending order by the EPs, IJs and finally the IPs. On this subscale students with high scores are described as goal-oriented and self-directed learners. They seek in-depth educational experiences, enjoy college and take advantage of available resources to enhance learning.

Pearson Correlations Among the SDTI-2 and MBTI Scales (N=946)

Scale	Appropriate Educational Plans	Mature Career Plans	Mature Lifestyle Plans
EI	–.21**	–.21**	–.24**
SN	–.02	.04	–.01
TF	–.05	–.09*	–.01
JP	–.15**	–.12**	–.19**

* P .01
** P .001

Table 7.1 *Anchors, S., Gershman, E., and Robbins, M. (1989)*

These findings will be elaborated upon through the following detailed descriptions of the four combinations of MBTI attitudes in relation to decision-making and the advising process.

Mean SDTI-2 Subtask Scores for Attitude Combinations

Mature Lifestyle Plans: The ability to balance vocational, advocation, and family plans (maximum score 20).

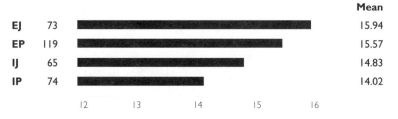

Appropriate Educational Plans: A high score indicates the individual has well defined and personally meaningful educational goals (maximum score 20).

Mature Career Plans: Involves a tentative commitment to a chosen field (maximum score 20).

Table 7.2

Extraversion and Judgment: The Decisive Extraverts

Extraverted Judging types have a judging function (Thinking or Feeling) extraverted and dominant, while their perceiving function (Sensing or Intuition) is introverted and auxiliary. Extraverted Judging types are characteristically decisive, confident, and enjoy closure and making things happen. Their preference for structure and closure makes deciding on a college major an easier task for them, relative to other types. Extraverted Judging types place high priority on completing the task. One EJ advisee said about selecting a major, "I just want to hurry up and get it over with."

Students who express Extraversion and Judging preferences have dominant Feeling or Thinking. This dominant judging process provides a system of order (Thinking) or a set of personal values (Feeling) that shapes the decision to choose a major. Many EJs progress toward graduation through an orderly sequence of studies and milestones (completion of core courses, etc.) that mark their progress. Extraverted Judging types are often uncomfortable when these markers are absent. The absence of these markers or structures can cause distress. For example, one EJ advisee was filled with anxiety and could not sleep because her master's degree program of study could not be approved until her entire committee met to approve her plan. In her case this meant waiting several stressful weeks to finalize her program. Another student said "I get extreme satisfaction from making decisions; they help me mark my progress and way to accomplishing things in my life".

Extraverted Judging types are the most likely types to make early career decisions. McCaulley (1981), in her research on medical students, found that EJ types were most frequent among those medical professionals who knew they wanted to be a doctor as early as ages ten through thirteen. Otis (1972) in other research found that ES types were early deciders about medical specialties and that Extraverts,

Sensing types, Thinking types, and Judging types were associated with earlier decisions than Introverts, Intuitive types, Perceiving types.

Extraverted Judging types Potential Pitfalls and Strategies

Extraverted Judging types, as one might predict from type theory, may have difficulty with premature foreclosure. In other words, they may not take enough time to gather information and perceptions, and they may fail to consider the possibilities. They may operate in their dominant function without the benefit of their auxiliary. Although the institution may allow or encourage them to put off their decision for several semesters, their discomfort with this may lead to premature closure. Teaching them the value of brainstorming processes and various information-gathering approaches can be of value. The dominant Thinking types can be motivated by showing the logic of gathering more information, which will make the formula of selecting a major more complete. Feeling types can be motivated to use their auxiliary by stressing that the resulting decision will be a *better* one for themselves and for others.

When advisors find EJ students who are undecided, they should be alert to the possibility that these students may need help in the development of the Thinking or Feeling function. As Grutter states in the chapter on career development, lack of differentiation may suggest lack of identify formation—a prerequisite for career decision-making. Advisors can make an assessment: In general how easy is it for these students to make a decision? What guides them in their decisions (personal values or logic)? Does head or heart rule? These questions can be a useful way to begin the process of identifying one function as a guide in their decision-making. Of course the advisor should always consider the possibility that Thinking or Feeling is not actually the dominant function, but the auxiliary. This possibility may be suggested by a low preference score on any of the attitude scores (E–I and J–P).

If an EJ is uncertain about the Thinking or Feeling preference, ask him/her to think of a situation in which he/she is having a hard time making a decision. Inquire as to why the decision is not being made: Is more information needed? Are the consequences too difficult? Are values in conflict, or is the issue just not worthy enough for consideration?

Extraverted Judging types can be assisted in strengthening their dominant Thinking or Feeling through values clarification exercises, learning about force-field analysis, and other such focusing processes. They can benefit from learning to introvert through quiet reflection and meditation. Advisors can suggest students ask themselves such questions as what other majors might exist besides my present one? Or will I really be satisfied with engineering as a career?

Extraverted Judging types also can be aided by taking career planning courses that involve a high level of activity, such as student presentations, group projects, and out-of-class experiences. Occasionally I have found career planning courses frustrating to EJ students. The exposure to additional possibilities they receive in these courses can disrupt their already conceived educational plans.

Various programs, which can give EJs, especially ESJs, hands-on learning about majors and careers can be very helpful. Traditional work co-op programs, where students are placed in job settings for periods of time, can prove beneficial. These programs ground the student in the real world of work, making it less abstract and conceptual. Since these approaches often require more time than most students have, less time-consuming programs should also be offered. Programs can include visiting work settings, interviewing workers, and other related activities that expose students to new options and perspectives.

Introversion and Perceiving: The Adaptable Introverts

Introverted Perceiving types have a judging function (Thinking or Feeling) that is introverted and dominant, while there perceiving function (Sensing or Intuition) is extraverted and auxiliary. Introverted Perceiving types are often described as reflective and looking inward for guidance and direction. Although adaptable in many areas, they stand firm on issues that are important to them.

Those who prefer Introversion and Perceiving have characteristic styles radically different from EJs. While EJs tend to be the executive decision makers, the IPs are often at the other end of the continuum, hesitant and reflective, often enjoying the process. Many IPs I advise lack information about careers, rarely obtain information about majors as expediently as their EJ peers, and are generally not comfortable making decisions. Decision making for many IPs can be a confusing and difficult process. Since their dominant function is introverted, and their auxiliary function is extraverted, they may be in a struggle between responding to the outer world and yet being true to their inner world of personal values or logic.

The challenge for IFPs is to select a major that is true to their inner spirit and values. Advisors can help them explore who they are, so they can find a fit with a particular major. As Jung said of introverted feeling types, "Still waters run deep." They can be difficult to understand because of an inability or reluctance to express what is going on internally. Their judgments are grounded in a self often not easily expressed. Extraverted advisors may have more difficulty drawing out IP advisees. The advisor should allow plenty of time for a response from the introverted student during individual sessions. An advisor might also consider sending the student an informal meeting agenda ahead of time to encourage reflection prior to the meeting.

Introverted Thinking types need an environment that allows and encourages them to construct their own system for selecting a major. Are there plenty of interesting books available? Has the advisor explained various career development models? One INTP advisee after three years of exploration of self and majors said, "I have finally put it all together into a neat formula that makes perfect sense." The student used a diagram to put together considerable details that explained his past interests and experiences. The diagram showed how factors had shaped and influenced his college attendance and future direction. Diagramming his past, present, and future was crucial in affirming his choice of a major. The creation of a logical formula was needed by this student to implement a decision. Although this can be a frustrating and complex process, once this formula is developed, it may continue to serve as the backbone for career decision making for years.

Introverted Perceiving Types: Potential Pitfalls and Strategies

Introverted Perceiving types may put off until tomorrow what needs to be done today. In an academic setting this may result in taking five years to complete a four-year program. Their extraverted auxiliary process (Sensing or Intuition) is continually drawing in new and interesting information. They may have a feeling that there is never enough information or time to explore all of the options. In fact when many of them do decide on a specific program of study, the advisor may have to support them while they mourn all of the majors they might have had.

Occasionally an advisee's dominant judging process has not had an opportunity to develop. Reliance on the auxiliary perceiving function without use of the dominant may cause problems requiring more in-depth assistance than an advisor can offer. (See chapter 1 to understand the dynamics that may occur in this developmental pattern.) Of all the types, IPs and INFPs in particular, are reported to be the most frequent seekers of career assistance (Myers and McCaulley, 1985). When special advising programs are set up that provide opportunities for support and exploration, INFPs are often first in line to join. This high response by INFPs reflects their interest in programs focused on growth and development.

The same strategies and methods developed by IPs for the selection of a major might be used for other future decisions. Helping them find a decision-making model that works for them is one of the most valuable advising activities. Lawrence's (1982) Zig-Zag decision-making model is easy to understand and helps students use their strengths and weaknesses positively.

The Zig-Zag model begins with the Sensing function. When presented with a problem, a natural beginning step is the gathering of concrete, relevant facts that can be validated through the senses. The second step is the intentional use of the Intuitive function. What do these data mean? What possibilities do they suggest? After Intuition, Thinking is engaged to analyze and evaluate the logical consequences of acting on the facts and possibilities. Finally we use our Feeling to judge how these consequences will affect others, and the effect of the decision on interpersonal harmony and personal values. This model when applied step by step uses all four functions to achieve a more complete and informed decision. Feeling types respond positively to this approach because of the gestalt-like quality of the process, and Thinking types appreciate the logic in the model.

One of the difficulties many IPs have in selecting a major comes from distractions and preoccupations with other areas of student life. Thus many can benefit from learning time management and goal-setting strategies. For example one IP said that "to-do" lists were frustrating to her. While many people said these lists freed them to work on matters of importance, she said lists were only physical manifestations of what she already knew. The problem, she said, was that the items on the "to-do" lists swim around and things get accomplished as they come to the top regardless of their importance. Teaching IPs some simple strategies for goal setting and planning can help prevent a last-minute rush that may not reflect their talent and abilities. Advising on these matters can increase an IP's ability to control his or her outer world, a world that seems too demanding at times.

The IP, more than the other attitude combinations, may profit from a lower advisor/advisee ratio. They often are more confused about decision-making and may need more time. More advising time is offered at the University of Maine through an advising program that utilizes faculty advisors, peer helpers, and a special residential program to be described later.

Introversion and Judging: The Decisive Introverts

Introverted Judging types are usually reflective, enduring, and tenacious about plans. Their judging function (Thinking or Feeling) is extraverted and auxiliary, while their perceiving function (Sensing or Intuition) is introverted and dominant. Introverted Judging types are likely to base their decisions about majors on a deep, solid accumulation of perceptions. Their depth of conviction may come from their enduring and persistent reflection about issues of concern to them.

The combination of the introverted dominant perceiving function with extraverted judging function often results in an advisee who appears decisive, yet prefers to reflect before acting. Thus they can feel confused if rushed to make a decision. Some IJs report a need for "worry time" when making important decisions. This "worry time" helps them work things out internally before they verbalize. Once something is verbalized, many IJs feel it should be adhered to. Time for reflection gives them a sense of completion and rightness, although this need for time (as with the IPs) can prolong the decision-making process.

Introverted Judging types who are dominant Sensing types select a college major using common sense and practicality as their yardstick. They may ask themselves: Why should I major in Accounting? Is English going to land me a job?

Introverted Judging types who are dominant Intuitives may evaluate a major by how well it helps them to achieve their dream or inner vision. They may ask themselves: Does this major provide me with a steady flow of interesting ideas in my life? Is the choice sufficiently complex and filled with opportunities?

Some IJs may appear to be both decisive and hesitant about the same issue. Their Introversion encourages reflection and information gathering, while the extraverted judging auxiliary works for closure in the outer world. Introverted Judging types preference for laying a solid foundation before finalizing decisions often results in a process that is frustratingly slow. Their dominate function, whether Sensing or Intuition, may overload them with perceptions that are conflicting or difficult to sort out. One ISTJ came to me in total confusion about what to select as a major. He was bewildered as to how to sort through all the papers he had collected. He had visited each academic department on campus and organized respective brochures and flyers neatly in cross-referenced folders. Like many ISJs, he had thought that gathering and organizing information was the same as understanding it. He had failed to see the trends and patterns among majors and was only focusing on discrete facts. Introverted Judging types often are perceptual "sponges," and the advisor can serve an important role in helping them sort out what is really important in the decision-making process.

Introverted Judging type students can benefit from a variety of strategies. Advisors can help them become aware of their style of making decisions. The Zig-Zag decision-making model can highlight their strong and weak points. Advisors can help them understand and trust their dominant functions. Validation of the importance and the richness of the perceptions that IJ students gather give them new confidence in their decision-making.

Extraversion and Perceiving: Adaptable Extraverts

Extraverted Perceiving types are characteristically energetic, sociable, adaptable, and searching for new experiences. They extravert the perceiving function (Sensing or Intuition) and introvert their judging function (Thinking or Feeling).

Extraverted Perceiving type advisees generally have a wide breadth of interests in subjects, majors, and careers. They generally adapt to most advising approaches and respond enthusiastically. Extraverted Perceiving types at first appear to be decisive. Although EPs may decide quickly, they are likely to change when their dominant function (Sensing or Intuition) receives more information. These advisees are likely to come regularly into an advisor's office with a new major and/or changing academic interest. Within one week, an ENFP advisee told me she had decided upon pre-law, physics, math, and psychology. It was no coincidence that she was also taking these courses during the current semester. The dominant function of ENPs can cause them to be enchanted by and drawn to almost any new subject. Most majors hold an element of excitement, surprise, and fun. Although changing majors may cause concern for advisors, parents, and others, it is a very natural and comfortable trial-and-error process for EPs. For many EPs, decisions are not particularly things to live with, but ways of responding immediately to the world.

Extraverted Perceiving Types: Potential Pitfalls and Strategies

At their worst, Extraverted Intuitive types can appear to be "in the clouds," unrealistic, scattered, and changeable in selecting a major. Occasionally unrealistic views of themselves and a major or career can result in the development and nourishment of an inflated notion of their own skills and the demands of a particular major or career. Realistic perceptions can be encouraged by such activities as simply examining a college catalog that describes course requirements or through interaction with a professor who is demanding of them. For example, an ENFP advisee may take a basic math course and be challenged by the professor to be accurate and use a step-by-step process. This experience can help the ENFP realistically evaluate his/her skill related to this learning activity. While the ENPs may idealize the future, the ESPs (Extraverted Sensing types) may fail to consider sufficiently the long-range impact of their decisions about a major. They tend to value short-term results. For example, a student may decide to join the military but fail to consider how it might impact a family in a few years. The advisor can help this student think through his/her decision by probing the effect of this decision on the future.

Helping EPs through the decision-making process can be one of the most challenging activities for any advisor. While IPs may decide silently and the EJs may act decisively and firmly, the EP may decide with fanfare, only to change soon after. The EPs can truly benefit from the traditional values clarification exercises that many academic advisors use. These exercises challenge them in a fun, playful way to develop their introverted auxiliary judging process while learning to prioritize. They can also benefit by setting deadlines for gathering information. A peer with a dominant judging function can be a useful model; these students can be encouraged to work together.

A word of caution seems appropriate at this time about strategies and approaches academic advisors can use in working with students. Most advisors are not trained as psychologists or therapists. Academic advisors should use their skills in advising and their interest in type as a way to help students conceptualize their decision-making process and make course selections. When students appear to have needs which go beyond this advising process, advisors should refer those students to counseling or other appropriate professionals.

The following program was designed for freshmen, applying the type patterns just described. The program reflects an integration of type theory, student development theory, and environmental management in the provision of advising to students. Created in 1983 at the University of Maine, the program was phased out in the early 1990s, and replaced by a variety of institutional programs that apply the MBTI instrument individually, rather than programmatically.

Arts and Science in KNOX (ASK): A Model Advising Program

Some programs and services for advising students have too narrow a focus or approach. This multifaceted approach impacts the total development of first-year college students. The program was based on the assumption that entering students need a balance between challenge and support (see chapter 9 Designing Residential Environments). The designers of the ASK program assume that the residence hall environment is a logical place to address the notion of balancing challenge and support.

The ASK program was created in the spring of 1983 through the joint efforts of the department of Residential Life and the College of Arts and Science at the University of Maine. The American College Personnel Associations Commission III recognized the program in

1983 across the country as one of the "outstanding residence programs."

The course goals included helping students think through why they came to college, providing information about prospective careers and majors, establishing positive advisor-advisee relationships, and using the course to identify potential academic and motivational problems.

Students who took the course were assigned to live together on the same wing of a residence hall. They were assigned to roommates using the complementary strategy in chapter 9. Students shared the same advisor, a common course, a similar roommate and a supportive environment. This approach along with a supportive liberal arts faculty encouraged students to use their perceiving and judging functions for good decision-making. Students were encouraged in the ASK program to use the first few years of college to gather information (perceiving) about programs of study and careers.

The success of the Freshman Seminar Advising class was discussed in Gershman, Anchors, Dryfus, and Robbins (1986). They reported that undecided students participating in the course showed statistically significant progress towards selection of a major after one semester.

This program evolved over the years and was replaced by a series of institutional initiatives on advising. The campus initiative that uses the MBTI instrument most frequently is the Academic and Career Exploration (ACE) Program. It is based upon the premise that it is common for students entering college to be undecided about a major or to have several areas of academic interest. Such students are encouraged to apply for admission to the ACE Program rather than to one of the baccalaureate degree colleges at the University of Maine. The ACE program provides students the opportunity to assess their abilities, interests, and goals while systematically investigating the university's various academic programs. The MBTI instrument is frequently presented to class seminars with ACE students, with an emphasis on self-awareness and implications for the selection of a major.

Through special seminars and close contact with advisors that characterize the program, ACE students engage in structured activities, which enable them to make informed choices of a major and consider potential careers. Under the guidance of their advisors, ACE students select courses to investigate disciplines of interest as well as to fulfill general education requirements.

Using Type in Guiding Course Selection

The MBTI instrument can be used to help students select a beneficial course load for the academic term. Students need to achieve a balance in the kinds of courses and workload selected in any one term. Examples of course selection issues are the amount of reading required, labs, assigned papers, and teaching format (lecture, discussion, independent study). Students' types should be considered along with interests and abilities. Examples of some of the considerations follow.

Reading. Courses can vary considerably in the amount of reading required. Examples of subjects typically requiring more reading are literature, history, and philosophy. The student who is a slow reader and the student who does not enjoy reading may suffer academically if he or she schedules more than one or two of these courses a term. Myers (1980) pointed out that reading involves translating symbols, and that this process seems to be easiest for Introverts with Intuition. Introverted Intuitive students are generally more comfortable with a heavy load of reading assignments than many of the other types.

For example, Extraverted Sensing students' natural orientation towards action in the practical world may cause the world of words and symbols to be less appealing. Extraverted Sensing students may need to consider the amount of reading they can comfortably do in a semester, and the importance of balancing reading and lecture courses with action-oriented courses with labs, discussions, field work, etc. See chapter 4 for additional information on reading and type.

Writing. With the current emphasis on improving writing skills of students, it is likely that most advisees will be taking courses that stress writing. Research by Jensen and Ditiberio (1983) indicated that the MBTI preferences influence approaches to writing and the nature of writing difficulties. Chapter 4 gives clear examples for the types. The amount and nature of writing required in specific courses should be considered in helping plan academic schedules for different types of students.

Discussion/High Participation. Discussion-centered classes and those requiring active participation and presentation tend to appeal more to certain types than to others. Extraverts often thrive on this kind of learning environment. Some Introverts may find these classes stressful. The advisor can help the student evaluate the learning environment of various classes to make balanced selection. The goal should not be to avoid all challenges to one's type, but rather to achieve a balance between the number of classes that challenge development of less-preferred areas with courses that allow further development of one's natural strengths and preferences.

Lectures. Lecture classes may be the mainstay of many students' educational experience. Lectures offer Introverts the opportunity to be quietly receptive and digest material being presented. Morgan (1977) found that Introverts in particular preferred the lecture format because it gave opportunity to sort things out within themselves. Extraverts may become restless and have difficulty holding their concentration in lecture courses unless these are balanced with more participatory forms of learning.

Knowing the impact of different kinds of classes on different types of students can help advisors guide students in choosing a realistic course load. Of course, caution must be used in applying these general type tendencies to individual students, since there may be wide variations due to degree of type development, previous educational experiences, and so forth. Course selection should consider students' preferences *and* challenge development of the other functions and attitudes.

Career Exploration Uses

Staff at the Career Center at the University of Maine use the MBTI instrument in individual career counseling and advising sessions with students and classroom presentations for individual faculty. They describe it as an excellent assessment tool that students find interesting and enlightening. Primarily, the MBTI instrument is used in working with students who are undecided about their college majors and/or career directions. They do not use it with every student who seeks out career counseling, but for those students who are open to doing several different self-assessment activities as part of their exploration and decision-making, the MBTI instrument works very well. They find the Indicator helps students gain a better understanding of themselves which, in turn, helps them make better decisions on choice of college major, choice of elective courses, choice of activities and internships, and ultimately, better career choices that fit with their personality type.

Summary

The MBTI instrument can help the advising process in a variety of ways. It can serve as a useful tool in understanding how students view the college environment, how they gather and process information about course selection and related areas, and how they make important decisions about majors and careers. Knowledge of type can assist advisors in developing rapport with their advisees. Undoubtedly students will feel more relaxed and open if such a relationship is characterized by a sense of understanding.

Developmental advising as emphasized here focuses on understanding students from their perspective and offers them an appropriate balance of challenge and support so that they can learn to use their unique talents and abilities.

Uses of the MBTI instrument in college and university advising have changed significantly in the last two decades. The shift has been towards the integration of the Indicator into the advisor's tool chest, rather than an institution-wide administration, a reflection of the popularity of the MBTI instrument within the advising community.

References

Anchors, S., E. Gershman, and M. Robbins. (1989). Developmental and personality-type differences among first year undecided and decided college students. *Journal of Psychological Type*, (17), 17–25.

Anchors, S. (1985). Unpublished research, University of Maine.

Carskadon, T. (2001). Personal Correspondence, Mississippi State.

Gershman, E., S. Anchors, S. Dreyfus, and M. Robbins. (1986). The effects of differential programming on undecided first year college students. *College Student Affairs Journal* 6, 39–39.

Gordon, V. (1981). The undecided student: A developmental perspective. *Personnel and Guidance Journal,* 59, 433–439.

Gordon, V., and J. Carberry. (1984). The Myers-Briggs Type Indicator: A resource for developmental advising. *NADADA Journal,* 2, 75–81.

Jensen, G., and J. K. DiTiberio. (1983). The MBTI and writing blocks. *MBTI News,* 5, 14–15.

Lawrence, G. (1993). *People types and tiger stripes: A practical guide to learning styles.* Gainesville, FL: Center for Applications of Psychological Type.

Laney, A. (1949). Occupational implications of the Jungian personality function types as identified in the Myers-Briggs Type Indicator. Unpublished master thesis, George Washington University.

McCaulley, M. H. (1978). *Monograph I: Applications of the Myers-Briggs Type Indicator to medicine and other health professions.* Gainesville, FL: Center for Applications of Psychological Type.

Morgan, M. (1977). Relating type to instructional strategies. In *People types and tiger stripes: A practical guide to learning styles* by G. Lawrence (pp. 52–53). Gainesville, FL: Center for Applications of Psychological Type.

Myers, I. B. with P. B. Myers. (1980). *Gifts differing.* Palo Alto, CA: Consulting Psychologists Press.

Myers, I. B., and M. H. McCaulley. (1985). *Manual: A guide to the development and use of the Myers-Briggs Type Indicator* (2nd ed.). Palo Alto, CA: Consulting Psychologists Press.

Otis, G. (1972). Types of medical students. Contract No. 71-4066. USPHS, National Institute of Health.

Winston, R. Jr., T. Miller, and J. Prince. (1979). *Assessing student development: A preliminary manual for the Student Development Task Inventory.* (2nd ed). Athens, GA: Student Development Associates.

CHAPTER 8

Student Involvement and Activities

JUDITH A. PROVOST AND SCOTT ANCHORS

Anyone involved in student activities programming has observed different patterns of participation. Not all students participate in academic and social opportunities to the same degree. The same group of students consistently appears at certain kinds of events, while other students are seldom seen. Certain organizations tend to draw certain kinds of students. We all know that some students are not reached by activity programming. Perhaps their needs are not being met by opportunities, perceived or real, within the institution. Personality type can be helpful in understanding some of the aspects of students' extracurricular behaviors and responses to activities programming.

This chapter reviews briefly the importance of Astin's (1975, 1977, and 1984), Tinto's (1975), and Chickering's (1969) theories to the topic of involvement and activities. Research studies and data concerning student activity patterns and the Myers-Briggs Type Indicator® instrument are included to show how the Indicator can help in understanding students' needs and behaviors. From this data some general observations about types and involvement are made with recommendations for those working with student activities and setting institutional policy.

Theories of Involvement

Student involvement is a key construct in student development theory. Astin (1984) defines student involvement as the amount of physical and psychological energy that the student devotes to the academic experience. He goes on to state, "Thus, a highly involved student is one who, for example, devotes considerable energy to studying, spends much time on campus, participates actively in student organizations, and interacts frequently with faculty members and other students" (p. 297). Astin's research indicates that the more involved students are, the less likely they are to drop out of college. Other theorists and researchers have also pursued the relationship between involvement and retention.

One of these theorists is Tinto (1975). He correlates the degree of student integration with the retention rate of the college or university. Kalsbeek's chapter 3 about campus retention research describes this model thoroughly. Tinto distinguished two kinds of integration, academic and social. Both are equally important and interdependent. Social integration indicates involvement in campus activities and relationships. Academic integration includes embracing the educational goals of the institution as well as personal educational goals and participating fully in academic programs offered by the institution.

These concepts of involvement and social and academic integration complement Chickering's vectors described in chapter 1. Consider the vector of competence as it applies to social and academic integration. Students need to develop social and interpersonal competence and intellectual and instrumental skills. Without this development, integration will not occur. Chickering emphasized the importance of out-of-class experiences; the "student culture." He saw residence halls and extracurricular activities as providing opportunities for growth within his seven developmental vectors.

We can all, therefore, recognize the importance of involvement and social/academic integration to the individual student and to the institution: for the institution, student retention and a sense of educational community; for the individual student, success and satisfaction in the college experience.

Extracurricular activities provide a way for different types to express themselves and a way for their development to be stimulated. For example, suppose a young ENTJ arrives at college hungry for a leadership role and thrives on the challenge of reorganizing a floundering student organization. She is expressing and developing her natural interest in leading. In terms of Chickering's vectors, she is developing competence.

Additional value is placed on student activities because of their importance in providing a balance with academics and in providing leisure outlets. Many needs are met through leisure such as relaxation and socialization. Balance and effective use of leisure time can mitigate student stress and enhance well being.

An example of the importance of balance is the experience of many Extraverted students who channel much of their energy into intramurals and varsity sports, aerobics, and other physical activities. After sitting passively in classrooms and studying, many Extraverted students become restless and unfocused. These activities provide an outlet and balance so they can later return to their studies refreshed and able to focus again.

These theories and what we know about psychological types allow us to speculate about patterns of student involvement and strategies to foster that involvement. However, research is necessary to determine more accurately the needs and appropriate approaches for the sixteen types. Some of the basic questions are:

- Which activities appeal to which types?

- Which formats or structures for activities are comfortable for different types?
- How can the reluctant types be encouraged and supported to participate?
- How should programs and activities be "marketed" to appeal to a variety of types or to a targeted group?
- How does the nature of balance between academic and social activities vary because of type?

The following research reflects attempts to answer some of these questions.

Research on the MBTI® Instrument and Patterns of Involvement

The first research on type and involvement patterns may have been done by Harold Grant (1965) at Auburn University. After obtaining MBTI results, Grant surveyed students about out-of-class behaviors such as frequency of drinking, likelihood of joining a fraternal organization, and frequency of dating. He compared these behaviors to types and found certain patterns. Table 8.1 shows some of these patterns. The Extraverts, for example, indicated a preference for extracurricular activities that involved social groups. The Introverted Sensing types most frequently reported they would "definitely not join" a Greek organization.

In 1967, Stalcup continued this kind of inquiry at Auburn University by comparing MBTI type with 229 extracurricular activities. Subjects checked activities in which they participated during the freshman–sophomore years, the term in which they participated, and the average number of hours per week spent at that activity. Stalcup found the largest numbers of non-participants among

Extracurricular Activities of Auburn University Freshmen Classified According to MBTI Type			
ISTJ	**ISFJ** Movies	**INFJ** Movies	**INTJ** Lectures Drama Music
ISTP Athletic Events	**ISFP**	**INFP** Movies	**INTP** Lectures Drama Music
ESTP Social Events	**ESFP** Social Groups	**ENFP** Social Groups	**ENTP** Social Groups Athletic Events
ESTJ	**ESFJ** Athletic Events	**ENFJ** Movies	**ENTJ** Athletic Events

Table 8.1 *Source:* Behavior of MBTI Types *by W. Harold Grant, Auburn University, 1965.*

Introverts and a higher frequency of certain activities reported for certain of the sixteen types.

Provost (1980) surveyed seventy-three sophomores, juniors, and seniors to explore possible relationships among type, grade point average, and leisure interests, and amount of time spent on academic and paid work. Several statistically significant patterns between leisure interests and type occurred. Extraverts reported significantly higher interest than Introverts in social amusements (going to parties, going to popular music concerts, visiting amusement parks) and in intellectual activities (chess, reading mystery stories, playing guitar). Type theory would predict the higher interest in social amusements but not in intellectual activities. The Perceiving types reported significantly higher interests than the Judging types in competitive activities (running races, racquetball, backgammon, handball), in social games (softball, frisbee, volleyball, board games), and in social amusements. Analyses of variance for SP, SJ, NF, and NT groupings revealed significantly higher interest in competitive activities by the SPs.

In terms of work and leisure, the Judging types were significantly higher in reported hours of academic and paid work. Theory would predict that Judging types would generally place a higher priority on work completion before engaging in leisure, while the Perceiving types would be more likely to mix work and play and be open to more leisure experiences. Judging types tend not to play until work is completed, unlike the Perceiving types. Judging types are more concerned with structured time and completion of tasks before taking on new activities. Thus response patterns of Js and Ps to extracurricular activities tend to differ.

Provost (1982) studied the relationship of type to attrition, grade-point average, leisure satisfaction at college, and extracurricular activities pursued. The study involved surveying sophomores; the sample size was 189 (84 male, 105 female). The Leisure Satisfaction

Survey (LSS) measured student responses on six subscales:

- Psychological—satisfies a need for freedom, enjoyment, involvement, and intellectual challenge.
- Educational—satisfies a need for intellectual stimulation and information about themselves and their environment.
- Social—satisfies a need for rewarding relationships with people.
- Relaxation—satisfies a need for stress reduction.
- Physiological—satisfies a need for physical fitness, weight control, and general physical well being.
- Aesthetic—satisfies a need for involvements that are pleasing, beautiful, and well designed.

Table 8.2 shows the mean scores on each of these subscales for each of the sixteen types. Three of the six subscales have significantly different scores for the sixteen types. Of the three remaining subscales, Relaxation was above the nationally norm mean for all types, indicating the high need among college students for this type of extracurricular activity. The other two scales, Aesthetic and Physiological, were lower for all types. Age is an interactive factor here, since the sample of nineteen- to twenty-two-year olds is less likely than an older population to be concerned with these aspects of leisure.

Readers can draw their own observations from the data in Table 8.2, but several patterns are worth noting here. The SJs reported higher satisfaction than other type combinations on the Psychological and Educational subscales and total LSS score. Sensing may be more conducive to identification and utilization of the leisure resources on campus. It also may be that Sensing types are more easily satisfied than Intuitives, who tend to be restlessly anticipating the future rather than

College Sophomores: Mean LSS Subscale Scores and MBTI Types (N=189)

MBTI Type	Psychological Mean	Psychological SD	Educational Mean	Educational SD	Social Mean	Social SD
ISTJ	17.45	1.75	16.82	1.83	15.36	2.77
ISFJ	17.14	2.85	17.86	2.27	16.86	2.34
INFJ	15.71	3.15	16.14	2.73	15.86	2.67
INTJ	17.00	2.06	16.11	1.17	15.56	3.78
ISTP	14.67	3.72	13.67	1.86	12.50	1.52
ISFP	14.40	2.12	13.60	3.20	14.80	2.39
INFP	13.73	2.84	14.67	3.02	14.80	2.78
INTP	16.44	3.17	14.56	3.97	15.67	2.29
ESTP	15.38	2.39	15.75	3.28	15.50	3.42
ESFP	15.27	2.52	15.73	2.66	16.13	2.64
ENFP	14.66	2.46	14.47	2.44	15.91	2.87
ENTP	16.00	2.08	16.07	3.27	14.79	2.75
ESTJ	16.87	2.90	16.87	2.90	17.80	1.78
ESFJ	16.90	2.64	16.30	1.70	16.60	1.65
ENFJ	16.00	2.28	15.82	2.86	17.55	1.92
ENTJ	15.20	1.69	16.40	1.78	16.30	1.77
	F Ratio = 2.37**		F Ratio = 2.07*		F Ratio = 2.21*	

* Significant .05
** Significant at .01

Degrees of Freedom = $\frac{15}{173}$

Range of LSS Score = 4–20

Table 8.2 (continued)

College Sophomores: Mean LSS Subscale Scores and MBTI Types (N=189) *continued*

Relaxation Mean	Relaxation SD	Physiological Mean	Physiological SD	Aesthetic Mean	Aesthetic SD	Total Score	SD
16.27	2.28	15.36	3.47	14.82	2.79	96.1	9.8
16.14	4.22	14.29	5.02	16.86	2.54	99.1	15.2
18.29	1.80	14.14	3.39	16.43	2.37	96.6	13.0
16.89	3.06	13.56	4.50	15.00	2.06	94.1	8.9
15.17	2.32	12.00	3.35	12.67	1.51	80.7	5.5
15.50	2.76	14.40	2.88	13.90	2.60	86.6	12.8
16.60	2.92	13.07	2.84	14.40	2.72	87.3	11.6
15.44	4.33	15.11	2.85	14.33	2.24	91.6	10.5
16.25	2.76	15.25	2.76	16.00	2.45	94.1	12.8
16.47	2.61	14.80	3.53	14.20	2.34	92.6	12.9
15.81	2.44	13.78	3.13	13.88	2.27	88.5	9.4
16.57	2.71	15.86	3.35	15.07	2.81	94.4	11.8
18.27	2.12	16.20	3.30	16.13	2.83	102.1	10.9
15.90	1.97	15.40	2.99	15.10	2.81	96.2	10.3
18.82	1.08	14.55	5.84	15.27	2.76	98.0	11.8
16.90	1.66	15.50	2.59	14.80	2.04	95.1	5.6
F Ratio = 1.78		F Ratio = 1.07		F Ratio = 1.75		F Ratio = 2.59**	

* Significant .05
** Significant at .01

Degrees of Freedom = $\frac{15}{173}$

Range of LSS Score = 4–20

Table 8.2

experiencing the present. Judging types may be better at organizing their time and following through so that they can be involved in activities. The EJs scored highest on Social satisfaction, and the TPs lowest, followed by the IPs. The IPs ranked low on many of the subscales and may have more difficulty than other types in becoming involved in student life.

In the same study sophomores were asked, "Please list the three activities you most like to do in your leisure time at college." Table 8.3 shows the most frequently reported activities for each type and also those activities reported exclusively by one type.

The MBTI patterns of involvement in campus activities were again studied in the same college for the purpose of exploring a possible relationship to attrition and grade point average (Provost, 1985). Types who had the lowest and highest rates of persistence at the college four years after matriculation were interviewed about their college involvements. These seniors were asked about campus activities outside of classes and aspects of the college experience that had been most helpful.

The types with the lowest rate of persistence at the college were ISTP, ISFP, ESTP, and ENFJ. The persisting ISPs reported very little involvement during the four years except in intramural sports and small informal gatherings. They were influenced to persist at the college primarily because of personal and informal relationships with faculty, the small campus, and their study/travel abroad experiences. The ENFJs reported being very active in student organizations and, to a lesser extent, in varsity sports. ENFJs found campus resources (facilities, faculty, and student personnel staff) most helpful.

The types with the highest rate of persistence were ESTJ, ENTJ, ESFJ, and ESFP. These types all reported heavy involvement in student government and/or the Greek fraternity and sorority system. Many played varsity sports, and all had had leadership roles. Aspects of the

Most Frequently Named Activities of College Sophomores by Type (N=189)			
ISTJ Film	**ISFJ** Reading Sports Friends Volunteer Work*	**INFJ** Playing Piano	**INTJ** Jogging Writing*
ISTP Sports Friends	**ISFP** Sports Sunbathing at Pool	**INFP** Friends Sports Playing Guitar*	**INTP** Sports
ESTP Sports Friends	**ESFP** Sports Friends	**ENFP** Sports Greek Activities Friends Sewing Quiet Time*	**ENTP** Sports Parties Friends
ESTJ Sports Jogging	**ESFJ** Sunbathing at Pool Greek Activities	**ENFJ** Sports Parties	**ENTJ** Sports Reading Acting*

Table 8.3 **Reported only by this type, but not frequent.*

Activity Patterns by Type

Extraversion (E)

- focus on variety and doing
- discharge of energy through physical activity and action
- opportunities for multiple interactions with others

Introversion (I)

- opportunity for small group, one-on-one, and individual activities
- space for private leisure (e.g., contemplation)
- opportunities for renewal through solitude, nature, passive activities (e.g., a lecture)

Sensing (S)

- physical activities and sports
- established social structures

Intuition (N)

- opportunities to use imagination and originality
- more naturally see possibilities for activities outside established channels

Thinking (T)

- opportunities for mastery
- development of technical or specialized skills

Feeling (F)

- community service activities
- "cheerleading"/persuasive activities
- interpersonal focus

Judgment (J)

- structured and established activities
- leadership
- concern for time (to get academics done), limit-setting on leisure time

Perception (P)

- spontaneous, unplanned activities and parties
- sometimes over-involvement without follow-through
- play first, work later?

Figure 8.1

college seen as most valuable to them were Greek organizations, friends, student services staff, and relationships with specific faculty. One ENTJ summed up well the high persister group's attitude, "Getting involved in activities and clubs gives students a reason to stay. Doing something for the college made me feel I had an impact." (Provost, 1985, p. 19)

This last study reflects findings similar to those in the other Provost studies, particularly in regard to IP and EJ patterns of involvement. These patterns are consistent with type theory and suggest that activities programming for the IPs should be different than for the EJs.

Summary of Involvement Patterns

A few general trends among traditional-age college students can be noted by preference, remembering that these trends may not be true for all individuals.

Each of the sixteen types has some distinctive activity patterns. Some observations of these are clustered under the four attitude combinations. The attitudes seem especially significant to involvement because they shape the level of activity and the dimension of time management or spontaneity.

Introversion with Perceiving. The types with IP orientation tend to be the least involved in established, structured activities. Their involvements tend to be sporadic. They seem to prefer informal, unstructured, and small group formats. They may not respond to opportunities around them unless "dropped in their laps." The ISPs especially may appear "lost" among the maze of campus activities or may randomly respond to an activity, which confronts them. All the IPs responds best to an individualized "marketing" approach.

Introversion with Judging. The IJ combinations may be no more active than the IPs on campus but are generally more deliberative;

therefore, they tend to be very selective in their involvements. Completion of academics or other work obligations takes priority over leisure and may result in very little time given to extracurricular activity, unless this activity is seen as a "responsibility." This attitude about priorities may lead to isolation, especially for the ISTJs and INTJs. The ISJs prefer well-organized and established campus organizations. INJs may welcome the challenge of an intriguing leadership position or other activity that gives them a chance to explore their intuitive interests. IJs will respond best to programs that appear well organized and time limited and are willing to attend if they know the activity is structured (as opposed to "whatever happens, happens").

Extraversion with Judging. Students with this combination tend to be most visible in campus organizations in leadership roles. They often choose a variety of activities based on action, for example, community service, or the orientation week task group. They are most attracted to organizations where they can have impact and see results. They will tend to "schedule in" lectures and other cultural events, which fit with their motivations and interests.

Extraversion with Perceiving. Students with this combination of attitudes may have cycles of activity followed by overload and then withdrawal to complete academic work. Many activities may attract them, but they may not be able to follow through on all. They may be selected as leaders by their peers and begin their leadership with flashes of brilliance, only to sputter out when overload sets in. They generally enjoy a high level of activity (physical and social) and may need help in becoming selective, taking workload into account. The ESPs are most attracted to pleasurable experiences such as a party with good food and music. All EPs seem attracted by exciting and/or adventurous experiences that provide multiple stimulation to their perception preferences (either S or N). A cultural event with the format of lively discussion will be more appealing than a structured lecture/presentation.

CIRP Data and Type

The above involvement patterns are reinforced by research through the Cooperative Institutional Research Project (CIRP). This national survey, when correlated with type can reveal some useful and enlightening profiles of entering students. At the University of Maine, Hedlund (1985) found significant relationships between anticipated involvement in academics and activities and MBTI preference. Anticipated involvement was measured by entering students' reported intentions to participate in specific academic and social activities. Her research used factor analysis to identify relationships between certain items on the CIRP survey and type.

Student-anticipated involvement was found to correlate with several of the MBTI preferences. In comparing the Extraversion–Introversion preference, she found that Extraverts predicted that they would become more involved in the traditional aspects of campus life, such as living in a coeducational residence hall, having Greek affiliation, and acquiring a bachelor's degree. In contrast the Introverts planned to work while attending the university.

Students with a preference for Sensing maintained a practical posture and were likely to foresee marriage as part of their college experience. The Intuitive students anticipated involvement with academic achievement, career achievement, traditional activities, work, and the possibility of interrupting school for other activities. Perceiving type students predicted career exploration and the possibility of dropping out of college. Many of these results are predictable from the type descriptions developed by Isabel Myers (Myers, 1980).

In summary, significant relationships exist in the Hedlund study between MBTI types and anticipated involvement in various aspects of college life. More research must be done to sharpen these observations and improve our ability to plan activities for all types of students. The following is an example of the application of type principles to activities planning on one campus.

Program Applications at the University of Maine

The University of Maine has administered the MBTI instrument to more than 18,000 students from the fall of 1980 to 1989, leading to the development of numerous programs and research projects. Due to the large size of this group (usually over 1,600 students at a time) and the lack of an opportunity to administer the MBTI on campus, the MBTI was mailed home with explicit directions on how the results would be used. The confidential nature of the results was emphasized. Return rate on this form of administration was more than 98 percent. To check the accuracy of this procedure, and to assure that parents and others are not influencing the students' responses, several mini-research projects were conducted to crosscheck the accuracy of reported types. Students' agreement with their MBTI description proved to be high (Anchors, 1983). Seventy-eight percent of the students agreed with all four of the preferences on their profile. During the past ten years, financial challenges and staffing changes resulted in the University's changing its strategy from large group administration to the use on an individual basis. Currently, there are less programmatic uses of the MBTI, and more use in individual counseling and advising.

During the period of large administrations at the University of Maine the MBTI instrument was used to match roommates, to design programs, to market programs, to track various types' use of campus programs, and to construct a framework for planning, organizing, and involving students on campus. Following is a review of some of the ways the university has been using type.

Peer Helpers

Currently, peer helpers in Student Affairs at the University of Maine are routinely administered the MBTI instrument. The peer helpers range from resident assistants, hall directors to peer programmers in the areas of sexuality and personal skill adjustment. MBTI results are often the major tool in helping these students conceptualize who they are, as well as in helping them in their roles as peer counselors/advisors on campus. Type is used with these students as a way to confirm their strengths and to help them recognize how others may perceive them. It is often helpful for peer counselors to view their type distributions as a group compared to the distribution among students receiving their services. For example, resident assistants at the University of Maine are likely to prefer Extraversion, Intuition, and Feeling (von Hoffman, 1986). Knowing that these types are attracted to this campus role has caused the professional staff to structure the recruitment process to attract other types and to assure that these student helpers are able to communicate effectively with peers having different preferences.

Encouraging Freshman Adjustment

Psychological type is used as part of a campus-wide focus to encourage freshman involvement, retention, and adjustment in a variety of activities at the University of Maine. The foundation of this approach was a publication, *Row by Row* (Stone & von Hoffman, 1986), given to entering freshmen. *Row by Row* is based on the theories of Jung, Perry, and Chickering. It is an attempt to provide a guided tour of the challenges, activities, and opportunities at the university. The publication is illustrated graphically, with clear directions for Sensing types and opportunities for Intuitives to explore possibilities within a general suggested structure. All preferences were considered in designing the presentation of materials. The publication encourages students in a direct, yet fun manner to get involved in the following: locating classes; understanding learning style; becoming acquainted with roommates, and getting prepared for their first vacation home. Self-guided instruction and group experiences are suggested for addressing these issues.

Type is used in facilitating academic adjustment, with special programs for students undecided about majors and careers (see chapter 7, Advising Chapter). Those students most attracted to academic support activities, such as selecting a major or career, prefer Introversion, Intuition, Feeling, and the Perceiving attitude. This finding suggests to staff that the marketing of these activities needs to be evaluated to see if the program description may "turn off" or not attract other types.

In recent years the Academic Career Exploration program and the Career Center use the MBTI instrument extensively to provide self-awareness information to new students. In small seminars and through individual interpretations, students are provided MBTI feedback that relates to major choices, study styles, and implications for fitting into work environments.

Design of New Residence Facility

The MBTI instrument was a major tool used by the building committee for the construction of Doris Twitchell Allen Village, a residence facility opened on campus in 1992. All members of the search committee, including the architectural team, were administered the MBTI instrument and asked to provide input on various building and community needs based upon their own type and other types. The result was the creation of public spaces that were designed to meet the needs of Extraverts with open spaces able to accommodate larger number for mingling and to allow students to see one another coming and going. For Introverts, special attention was given to the creation of spaces that allowed privacy. Small areas of seating in corners and an increased number of private rooms were created.

A major premise of the building committee was that community is experienced differently by various types, and thus spaces needed to be designed to accommodate these differences. The goal was to create a building that has personal space, creates humane interaction, and supports the development of community in natural ways (Anchors and S. Moore, 1992). In 1993, this 200-bed residency facility received a design award by the America Association of Architects.

Fitness program, sports and activities

The Hilltop Health Club (Anchors and Arsenault, 1984), located in the basement of a college residence hall, is a comprehensive health facility available to all campus residents, faculty, and staff. The club provides a program that focuses on encouraging the physical development of members through goal setting, assessment, and instruction. The facility houses weight-lifting equipment, sauna, steam room, whirlpool, and a variety of aerobic equipment. In addition to individual involvement, over twenty noncredit courses are offered ranging from weight training to stress reduction. The program was recognized in 1982 as one of the "Outstanding Residence Hall Programs" across the nation.

The entire environment of the health club is inviting, stimulating, action-oriented, and filled with lots of possibilities for health exploration. More than 67 percent of the members have a preference for the Perceiving attitude, which is proportionally more than that in the larger student body. Forty percent of the members prefer Intuition and Perceiving, with ESFPs and ENFPs being over represented among those who join. These findings are not surprising when viewed within a program that is designed for stimulation and action. A positive consequence of this program has been a reduction in student damage and discipline referrals in the residence halls adjoining the Hilltop Health Club.

Several of the university major sports teams have used the MBTI instrument for self-awareness in teambuilding and communication between athletes. Teams have used their MBTI results as a tool in understanding different ways of planning game plays and communicating under stress. Some coaches have attempted to use the information to help motivate athletes and give feedback that is constructive and useful.

Senior administrators in the athletics, development, fund raising, cooperative extension, and life long learning are using the MBTI instrument as a tool in strategic planning. As they learn to understand their own styles, as well as the styles of their numerous constituents, they are trying to be more deliberate in the diversity of styles in which they communicate and respond to external and internal needs.

Although the MBTI instrument is not used in all aspects of campus life, it has impact on the appreciation of differences campus wide. The university can approach issues and problems using the Indicator as a research and educational tool.

Conclusions and Recommendations

Student involvement has been stressed as a means to academic retention, student satisfaction, and personal development. Type theory gives some insights into the motivations and behaviors of students in regard to extracurricular activities.

Research should continue to address the questions identified early in the chapter. Higher education professionals would do well to record type distributions within selected activities and organizations and to survey the sixteen types to determine what their needs are. These needs may vary from one academic setting to another because of other variables at play such as socioeconomic characteristics.

All professionals engaged in helping students succeed in college should be sensitive to the importance of balancing academics with leisure/extracurricular activity and should also be aware that "balance" will be defined differently among the sixteen types. Some types will need encouragement to experiment with activities, while others will need help in limiting themselves and setting priorities. Professionals can help students evaluate their need for balance, for various kinds of activity (such as physical), and for leisure involvements that foster development. Professionals can apply their skills such as time management, assertiveness training, role play (for reluctant participants), program planning, advocacy, and so forth, to facilitate individual student involvement on campus.

References

Anchors, S., and N. Arsenault. (1984). Hilltop health club: A model program for health education in residence halls. *Journal of College Student Personnel.*

Anchors, S. (1983). Unpublished research. University of Maine, Orono, ME.

Anchors, S. and S. Moore (1992). Doris Twitchell Allen Village: The University of Maine's response to housing needs of the future. Presented at the convention of the Association of College and University Housing Officers International, Boston.

Astin, A. W. (1975). *Preventing students from dropping out.* San Francisco: Jossey-Bass Publishers, Inc.

Astin, A. W. (1977). *Four critical years.* San Francisco: Jossey-Bass Publishers, Inc.

Astin, A. W. (1984). Student involvement: A developmental theory for higher education. *Journal of College Student Personnel,* 25(4), 297–308.

Chickering, A. (1969). *Education and identity.* San Francisco: Jossey-Bass Publishers, Inc.

Grant, W. H. (1965). *Behavior of MBTI types.* (Research report, Student Counseling Service, Auburn University.) Gainesville, FL: Center for Applications of Psychological Type.

Hedlund, J. B. (1985). Entering freshman input at the University of Maine at Orono: A conceptualization of the relationship between personality preferences and motivation, influences, goals/values, and potential involvement. (Doctoral dissertation, University of Maine, Orono). Dissertation Abstracts 46(11), 3262A. (University Microfilms No. 85-2 & 793).

Myers, I. B. with P. B. Myers. (1980). *Gifts differing.* Palo Alto, CA: Consulting Psychologists Press.

Provost, J. A. (1980). Work/leisure patterns of college students, personality, and college students, personality, and college grades. Unpublished paper, Rollins College, Winter Park, FL.

———. (1982). Personality type and leisure satisfaction as factors in college attrition (Doctoral dissertation, University of Florida). Dissertation *Abstracts,* 43(09), 2894A. (University Microfilm No. 83-02289).

———. (1985). Type watching and college attrition. *Journal of Psychological Type,* 9, 16–23.

Stalcup, D. K. (1967). An investigation of personality characteristics of college students who do participate and those who do not participate in campus activities (Doctoral dissertation, Auburn University). Dissertation Abstracts, 28(11), 4452A. (University Microfilms No. 68-5897).

Stone, G., and I. von Hoffman. (1986). *Row by row.* Orono, ME: Department of Residence Life, University of Maine.

Tinto, V. (1975). Dropout from higher education: A theoretical synthesis of recent research. *Review of Educational Research,* 45(1), 89–125.

von Hoffman, I. (1986). Unpublished research. Orono, ME: University of Maine.

CHAPTER 9

Designing Residential Environments

CHARLES C. SCHROEDER AND SMITH JACKSON

Overview

As noted in previous chapters, the Myers-Briggs Type Indicator® is an extremely powerful tool for understanding and facilitating student development. This chapter describes a number of practical and proven strategies for using the MBTI® instrument in college and university residence halls. For readers not familiar with some of the inherent challenges in residential living, a brief review is provided. A conceptual framework is then presented as the primary model for utilizing the Indicator to enhance the "fit" between students and their living environments at three different institutions. By following two students, Willard Wilson and Sam Hudson, the reader is subsequently introduced to the role that individual differences play with regard to understanding and resolving roommate conflicts. A variety of practical intervention strategies, along with research findings, are shared which illustrate the efficacy of using the MBTI instrument in pairing roommates for satisfaction and personality development. The chapter concludes with sections on practical administrative considerations and implications.

Inherent Challenges in Residential Living

Colleges and universities have undergone considerable changes in recent years. As the baby boom generation reached college age, enrollments expanded at staggering rates. To cope with the sudden demand for student housing, many institutions launched extensive building programs. Since cost and ease of maintenance were primary design considerations, modern complexes and high-rise buildings were constructed with corridor upon corridor of small, cell-like rooms, complete with built-in furniture and institutional decor. A building's long and narrow hallways often house 50 to 60 students, and it is quite common for as many as 500 students to occupy one building.

Since many residence halls were constructed without adequate attention to individual needs and interaction patterns, it is certainly not difficult to understand why many students find residence halls a bit overwhelming and, at times, downright aversive. This is particularly true today when very few traditional-age students entering college have ever shared a room. Imagine, for example, the predicament of a new student assigned to a 168-square-foot room with a stranger who is totally different in basic needs and interpersonal style? Or consider the difficulty students experience when they are assigned to live on a hall of 50 students with whom they have very little in common and yet must share a communal bath? And picture the frustrations students experience because of built-in furniture, lack of space for privacy and reflection, and institutional policies that prohibit decorating or otherwise limit students' ability to express their individuality.

Undoubtedly, architecturally hard and interpersonally dense and diverse residential environments present numerous challenges to students and staff alike. In an attempt to meet these challenges, college and university housing programs have changed their goals and priorities. Dormitories are now called residence halls. House mothers have been replaced by highly trained and skilled residence educators. A multitude of organizations and new programs proliferate, including the creation of learning communities and residential colleges (Smith, 1994; Schroeder, Minor, and Tarkow, 1999). Developmental programs are offered on assertiveness training, human sexuality, time management, etc.; discipline has become an intervention point to identify and resolve developmental problems through counseling with students; and community development is fostered through students' participation on programming councils, student governance committees, and judicial boards (Schroeder and Mable, 1994). These efforts have significantly contributed to improving the quality of residential life for many students.

Nonetheless, there is considerable evidence that students continue to become disenchanted with residence hall living within a relatively short period of time. Major reasons for student dissatisfaction include inability to control personal space, lack of privacy, roommate conflicts, forced sociability, and few opportunities to personalize the institutional environment (Heilweil, 1973; Winston and Anchors, 1993). Many of these concerns are related to a basic mismatch between students and the social and physical environments of their living units. Even though it may not be feasible to tear down buildings and construct new ones or to reduce the interpersonal density in the residence halls by reducing occupancy, it is possible to implement strategies that will help overcome or at least reduce the negative impact of these factors (Kalsbeek, 1982; Anchors, Douglas, and Kasper, 1993; Schroeder and Mable, 1994).

The Myers-Briggs Type Indicator instrument has proven to be an extremely useful tool for structuring conditions that enhance the "fit" between students and their residence hall environments. The Indicator has been successfully utilized in matching roommates, suitemates, and floor mates. These interventions have been beneficial because they have been applied within a conceptual framework that can be adapted and made operational for particular residential populations. This overarching framework is Sanford's (1966) notion of the relationship between challenge/support and development.

Balancing Challenge and Support: A Conceptual Framework

According to Sanford, the personality does not just unfold according to a plan of nature. Instead, students must be confronted with challenges sufficiently strong to trigger new ways of thinking and behaving. Once motivated, however, students must feel significant support so they may proceed to experiment with new ways of thinking and behaving. Sanford emphasized that a delicate balance of challenge and support must be achieved before development can occur. If an environment is overly supportive, students may be satisfied but not adequately challenged to grow. On the other hand, if an environment is overly challenging students may be so overwhelmed and overstimulated that they will not be satisfied and development will not occur. It is particularly important to note that the amount of challenge one can tolerate is a function of the support available. Challenges that might otherwise be maladaptive may become growth inducing when moderated by support.

In order to design residential environments that will allow for student satisfaction and development, the relative degrees of challenge and support that are characteristic of a specific setting in a specific student population must first be assessed (Rodgers, 1980; Strange and Banning, 2001). Since students are most affected by their immediate surroundings, it is best to analyze the smallest social unit possible. If the setting is highly supportive, then more challenge, less support, or both would need to be introduced to achieve a developmental balance.

If, on the other hand, the setting is found to be overly challenging, then more support, less challenge, or both would be needed (Kalsbeek, Rodgers, Marshall, Denny, and Nicholls, 1982). The following section describes how the MBTI instrument has been effectively used to balance the ratio of challenge and support in various residential environments.

Using the MBTI to Balance Challenge and Support in Residence Halls

Humanizing the Environment in a High-rise Complex

At Ohio State University the MBTI instrument was used to balance the challenge/support characteristics of a high-rise residence complex. The complex was assessed as an overly challenging environment as evidenced by exceedingly high damage rates, numerous mental health referrals, and very low retention rates (historically 1 to 4 percent). The complex consists of two 24-story towers with six suites per floor. A suite typically houses 16 students in a cluster of four rooms, resulting in 96 students living on each floor. Beyond the density of students assigned to suites and floors, other challenging factors that were identified included: the developmental levels of the residents; the significant heterogeneity of the students' cultural backgrounds; built-in furniture; and the overwhelming size and complexity of the multiversity itself. Few elements of support were present for mediating the excessive amount of challenge. For example, the student staff to resident ratio per floor was 1 to 96, the professional staff to student ratio was 1 to 900, and there were very few upper-class role models. This particular situation called for an intensification of the degree of support.

Kalsbeek et al. (1982) assigned suitemates according to their degree of similarity on the MBTI instrument. Prior to their arrival in the fall, first-year students desiring to participate in this project were mailed the Indicator. Students were then assigned to suites in the following fashion: (a) they were identical on all processes (Pure Strategy suites); (b) they had their most-preferred process in common (Dominant Strategy suites); (c) they had in common their second most preferred process (Auxiliary Strategy suites); or (d) they had in common the same process they preferred for dealing with the external world (External Strategy suites). In principle, these suites represented different points on a continuum of support, with "degrees of support" being defined by different degrees of commonality on the MBTI instrument. This relationship is depicted in Figure 9.1 and Table 9.1. As expected, it was found that the more similar suitemates were in their mental functioning, the more support they perceived in their environment.

The Ohio State intervention suggests that the living group can serve as a source of support and mediate between students and environmental factors. The MBTI instrument was used to foster mutually supportive suitemates, thereby humanizing a complex, impersonal, and challenging setting. Assigning students to floor units according to MBTI functions has produced similar results.

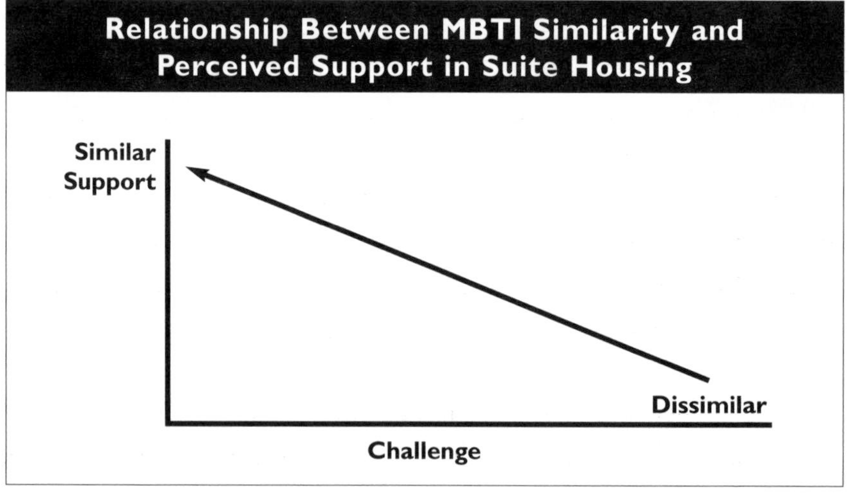

Figure 9.1

Degrees of Challenge/Support for MBTI Suitemate Groupings

MBTI Grouping Strategy	Description	Highest Degree of Support Lowest Challenge
Pure	All four preferences are identical	↑
Dominant	Identical dominant personality functions	
Auxiliary	Identical auxiliary personality functions	
External	Identical functions with which one deals with the external world	
Random	Maximum heterogeneity of personality types by random assignment	↓
		Highest Degree of Support Lowest Challenge

Table 9.1

Transforming an Aging Complex into an Exciting Community

At Auburn University, the MBTI instrument was used to pair hall mates and roommates in the Magnolia Dormitories residential community. Prior to the intervention, this complex was operating at an occupancy rate of approximately 80 percent and retention, from spring to fall, was less than 30 percent. Resident behavior was characterized by overt hostility toward the environment as evidenced by considerable damages, numerous roommate conflicts, and a full docket of discipline cases.

Two change strategies were implemented that served to reverse the downward spiral in both the physical and interpersonal environments of the complex (Schroeder, 1976 and 1981). First, residents were encouraged to paint, decorate, and otherwise personalize their rooms and hallways to suit their tastes and needs. Second, roommates were matched on the basis of common personality dimensions using MBTI scores obtained during summer orientation sessions. On some floors students were assigned to the units based upon commonality in dominant MBTI personality functions. One floor unit, for example, was composed of dominant Sensing types, another of dominant Intuitive types, and so forth. Housing students together with the same personality function resulted in predictable and stable social environments with behaviors that could be forecast from type theory.

Not surprisingly, the residents of a floor unit composed of dominant Intuitive types were found to tolerate a great amount of diversity in behavior without social sanction, to prefer less formal structure and organization in the residence halls, and to be quick to get involved in a multitude of activities. At first glance, however, it might seem curious that the Intuitive types, more than any other dominant type grouping, emphasized a traditional social orientation as measured by the University Residence Environment Scale (Moos and Gerst, 1974). And yet, the Intuitive types initially expected this emphasis, eventually found it in their living unit, and ideally preferred it. It appears that the Intuitive types created a social climate emphasizing dating and ceremonial activities. Formal social situations became creative outlets for the collective imagination of the residents. A costume party for Halloween was a sure bet for the Intuitives!

A major advantage associated with grouping floor units by dominant types is that not only does this strategy permit insights into type behaviors, but it also allows developmental programs to be more easily fitted to the living units. For example, many Intuitive types tend to be energetic and ambitious. Because some of them (particularly NPs) exhibit poor time management, they often feel they have far too much to do. Thus, staff can focus on time management programming to address this particular need of some of the Intuitives.

The overall results of utilizing this strategy in the Magnolia Dormitories were quite dramatic. Within a period of three years, retention from spring to fall terms increased by 30 percent and damages decreased by 360 percent. Further, occupancy during the same time period exceeded 100 percent each year with many prospective residents being turned away as waiting lists became excessive. Of special interest in this regard were the observed friendship patterns that emerged. When asked to indicate where their friends lived, students living on the MBTI-matched floors had a much higher percentage of their friends living on their same floor than did those students randomly assigned to floors. Thus, grouping students on floors according to the MBTI instrument was an effective strategy for facilitating supportive interactions, friendship patterns, and group cohesiveness (Schroeder, Warner, and Malone, 1980; Schroeder, 1994). The same results may also be achieved by encouraging students to self-select into living units. When given the opportunity, students migrate toward residential groups with whom they share personality styles and create interpersonal environments with unique characteristics.

Creating Floors with Unique Characteristics

During the spring semester of each academic year, residents in Saint Louis University residence halls described the social climates of their floors. These descriptions were compiled into a publication, *Choices*, which was distributed to prospective residents. Residents were also given the opportunity to assign new residents to their floors for the following fall term as a first priority in the assignment process. One of the annual descriptions that the residents of 13G composed was as follows:

> The word that best describes our floor is FUN! Sometimes we may seem pretty disorganized, but when we all want to do something, somehow we all pitch in and it gets done. There are lots of different types of girls on the floor—with different interests and activities, music and friends which make us really interesting! Most of us study and work in the early evenings and do a lot of our considerable socializing in the later evening hours, when doors are often open and popcorn popping. We enjoy playing intramural sports and recently got red sweatpants with "13G" appliquéd on the bottom—which we all wore together to the cafeteria for dinner on the day we got them.

The women assigned to this floor were dominant Intuitive types (N) with Feeling (F) as their supporting mental functions. The following year the demand for this floor by Intuitive types exceeded many times over the number of spaces available. The composition of the floor is illustrated in Table 9.2. The description the women gave of their floor's personality was predictable from knowledge of the MBTI composition. Since retention in this living unit was so high, the few new residents attracted to and assigned to this floor were paired with roommates with whom they had complementary MBTI types, a roommate matching strategy to be discussed later.

The social climate of another floor in the same building had several parallels yet was distinctively different from that of the women of 13G. The women of 9G described their floor in the following fashion:

> Most of us returned to the floor this year and the new girls fit in perfectly. We all contributed to painting our floor in a twilight design with a silhouette and setting sun design (which placed second in the Room Personalization contest).

> We are mostly Physical Therapy majors and put a big emphasis on our class work. We often study together as our schedules are similar. We are also athletic as a group, and many of us work out together and several girls work at the Rec Center. We are well on our way to winning the overall women's Dorm League Championship—a hot contest between us and 4 Walsh. We do a lot together and really pride ourselves on our involvement and support.

Whereas the women of 13G had a wide range of academic majors, 67 percent of the women living in 9G majored in physical therapy and nursing one year, and 84 percent majored in the same fields the following year. Even though it was primarily the grouping variable of majoring in physical therapy that retained and attracted residents to 9G, an after-the-fact view of the women's MBTI profiles, as displayed in Table 9.3, is enlightening.

As revealed in chapter 3, academic majors and academic schools are predominated by students of certain psychological types and thus these settings often create an environmental "press" on an individual's

MBTI Composition of 13G

Preferences	Percentage	Preferences	Percentage
Extraversion	82	Introversion	18
Intuition	88	Sensing	12
Feeling	83	Thinking	17
Perception	73	Judgment	27

Table 9.2

MBTI Composition of 9G

Preferences	Percentage	Preferences	Percentage
Extraversion	80	Introversion	20
Intuition	20	Sensing	80
Feeling	90	Thinking	10
Perception	50	Judgment	50

Table 9.3

behaviors (Strange, 1993). It is not surprising then to find that a living unit predominated by students majoring in physical therapy would also have a high percentage of Extraverted Sensing Feeling types; hence, one would expect that certain behaviors would be valued and perpetuated from year to year. The women of 9G won the All Sports Dorm League Championship for two consecutive years; they won at least one blood drive competition in each of the drive's existence; and they repainted their hallway each year. Contrasted with the spontaneous, fun-loving atmosphere described by the Intuitive types of 13G, the description of 9G portrays a more serious, structured, and achievement-oriented atmosphere. Even though physical therapy is a highly competitive curriculum, the interactions and activities described by 9G residents suggest a supportive living environment. New students to this floor were assigned to roommates as similar as possible in MBTI types in order to further enhance the degree of support exhibited by returning residents.

All of the preceding strategies demonstrate that grouping students in floor units or suites according to similar personality styles increases the probability that friendships and a sense of community will emerge in a natural fashion. Since students with similar personality characteristics view a situation (perception) and respond or draw conclusions about it (judgment) in the same manner, they find more support in living groups with whom they share the dominant group interests or personality. The same reasoning also applies to the roommate situation. The behaviors and attitudes of a roommate with a similar personality style can provide the student with evidence that he or she is functioning in a consistent and meaningful manner; the interpersonal environment is perceived as predictable and understandable. If, however, roommates differ radically in their perceptual and response patterns, they may threaten each other, clash frequently, and in general, utilize energy that could be better spent on things they value.

Using the MBTI to Understand and Resolve Roommate Conflicts

The Case Study of Willard and Sam

The role that individual differences play with regard to the quality of student/environment interactions can be further understood by viewing this issue from the perspective of two typical students.

> Two eighteen-year-old freshmen, Willard Wilson and Sam Hudson, arrive at Any University, USA. Everything has been done for them—they have been assigned to a nice, clean room on the fourteenth floor of "The Towers," their resident assistant has informed them about various policies and procedures, and they are now ready to embark on their college careers.
>
> Willard, raised in a rural community seventy miles from the nearest city, is basically an aggressive, practical, analytical type who possesses a great knack for managing

facts and details. Willard has already taken great pains to systematically organize his personal belongings—books are neatly arranged on the shelf, clothes are smartly hung in the closet, and his bed is routinely made each morning before he departs for class. To be sure, Willard likes to live his life according to a plan! He manages his time wisely and completes his studying promptly at 10 p.m. each night, and then retires for a minimum of eight hours sleep. Willard reasons that since he is paying $1200 per semester in room rent, he should be able to sleep and study in a distraction-free environment. For Willard, his room is primarily a work environment—he does his socializing with one or two close friends from a neighboring residence hall.

Sam Hudson grew up in a large city of over three million. He is sociable, outgoing, warmly enthusiastic, and highly creative. Because he prefers to think about imaginative possibilities, he has real difficulty with details and always appears to be disorganized. His bed and study area are cluttered with notebooks, dirty clothes, athletic equipment, half-eaten sandwiches, and candy wrappers—in short, it appears to be pure chaos. Because of his natural tendency to work in bursts of energy, Sam's study habits are erratic. It is not unusual for him to postpone unpleasant tasks, and he may wait until the last minute to complete an assignment. Hence, he frequently pulls "all-nighters." Sam has no trouble with distractions, actually preferring to study with his favorite rock music emanating from a CD player and stereo system. For Sam, his room is primarily a play environment—he enjoys socializing with a wide variety of friends at all hours of the day and night.

> Willard and Sam's relationship deteriorates rapidly. Sam is really beginning to get on Willard's nerves. Willard seems to be constantly studying, but not making the grades he would like—and Sam, who hardly ever puts in any time, is making all *A*'s." Sam is inviting his friends into the room late at night for parties and other social events.
>
> Willard hopes things will get better but he is pretty convinced they won't. It seems to Willard that he can't even move around his room without bumping into Sam. The built-in furniture and inflexible arrangements seem to force confrontation. Anytime he and Sam write a paper, they have to sit right next to each other at the built-in desks along one wall of their room. When Willard tries to sleep at night, Sam almost invariably has the lights on. Everything is so crowded, so complex, so unpredictable that Willard is really beginning to feel the stress of being confined to a tight space with someone much different than himself. He is becoming increasingly nervous, tense, and overtly hostile in his interactions with others.

It doesn't take much imagination to visualize the potential conflicts inherent in Willard and Sam's relationship. From the description of Willard's personal characteristics, one can assume that he has a basic need for structure. He prefers to structure his room in ways that demonstrate order, clarity, organization, and predictability. Willard finds freedom in structure; planned, systematic ways of doing things help him feel in control, influential, unrestricted, and important. Because Willard is naturally skilled at planning and organizing things, he just can't understand why Sam is so disorganized. Why doesn't Sam clean up his side of the room? Why can't Sam meet deadlines? Why doesn't Sam develop a study schedule? How can Sam study with the stereo on? Why does Sam spend so much time socializing? Maybe Sam is just basically aimless and irresponsible!

From the description of Sam, it appears that his basic needs are opposite and antagonistic to Willard's. Sam has a basic need for freedom. He enjoys living life in an independent, spontaneous fashion and flexibly adapts to unexpected changes in his environment. Whereas Willard seeks to structure and control almost every aspect of his environment, Sam would much rather understand than control things. In an attempt to satisfy his need for freedom, Sam avoids uninspired routines and established ways of doing things. He feels a sense of influence and control by living in accord with his spontaneous, imaginative inspirations and prefers to keep his options open by avoiding closure. Because Sam's basic needs are in opposition to those of Willard, Sam cannot understand why Willard has to organize everything or why Willard spends so much time studying. Why doesn't Willard loosen up? He always seems to have his nose to the grindstone, all work and no play! Sam reasons that maybe Willard's basic problem is that he is too rigid, inflexible, and task oriented.

Obviously, Willard and Sam are opposite types—Willard is an ISTJ and Sam is an ENFP. According to type theory, they have no mental process in common. They perceive things differently, formulate decisions from different perspectives, and tend to prefer to live their lives in opposite ways. Although Willard and Sam are expressing their natural tendencies in trying to meet their conflicting needs, they probably view each other as purposefully irritating. If, however, someone could help Willard and Sam understand their natural differences, they might not only allow for each other's preferences but perhaps appreciate and benefit from them. The MBTI can be very useful in this regard as it can help us understand in advance many of the basic living style preferences that can limit satisfaction between roommates.

Understanding Basic Living Style Differences Between Roommates

Some very basic differences in living styles must be overcome before roommates will be satisfied. Three of the most potent dimensions on which roommates must be compatible are study habits, sleeping conditions, and bedtimes. Differences on these dimensions are repeatedly the source of annoyance for roommates, yet are predictable from knowledge of MBTI profiles (Jackson, 1984; Schroeder and Jackson, 1987).

Differences in preferences for sleeping conditions and study habit can readily be explained when roommates' abilities to concentrate or relax with different amounts of background noise—music, talking, TV, etc., are understood. Some students (screeners) are able to "tune out" distractions even in a highly loaded setting such as a residence hall. These are the students who can literally sleep or study in a crowded and noisy bus depot. Other students (nonscreeners) are not able to be selective in what they focus their attention on and are attuned to minor subtle changes in the environment (Mehrabian, 1976). These students have difficulty in achieving and maintaining necessary levels of privacy in a residence hall. In their attempts to establish desired level, students like Willard may sometimes appear overly controlling and unfriendly. These students often pay a very high cost for achieving privacy.

The screener-nonscreener dimension is highly related to the MBTI preference for dealing with the outer world in a perceiving or judging way; Perceiving types tend to be screeners and Judging types, nonscreeners. The time that students go to bed is also related to the Judging–Perceiving preference. Perceiving types, particularly NPs such as Sam, tend to go to bed later than Judging types both during the week and on the weekends. Since Perceiving types often become consumed in a activity or thought that interests them, it is no wonder they stay up late and, because they are often oblivious to time, may not go to bed according to a schedule. There is even some observational information to suggest that Perceiving types tend to be "late night" people and that Judging types are often "morning" people. It is apparent that differences on the Judging–Perceiving preference could generate difficulties between roommates such as Willard and Sam, particularly when they must function in space as tight as a 120-square-foot room.

Another basic living style issue that roommates must resolve is their preferences for neatness. Neat students like Willard prefer neat roommates while clutterers such as Sam prefer other clutterers. This dimension is related to the MBTI preference for Extraversion or Introversion; Extraverts tend to see their roommates as neat while Introverts often view their roommates as messy (Jackson, 1984; Schroeder and Jackson, 1987). The Extravert, by definition, simply needs a greater amount of external stimulation than the Introvert. Certainly a messy room is more stimulating than a neat one! The Extravert's craving for stimulation has also been denoted in residence halls; Extraverts tend to paint their rooms in highly exciting colors such as Pixie Green and Dark Regal Purple while Introverts often paint their rooms in colors such as Blue Cloud or Lemon Meringue (Jackson, 1983). The way students personalize and keep their living space often reflects whether they prefer to orient themselves to the outer world (Extraversion) or toward the inner world (Introversion). As with the Judging–Perceiving dimension, roommates who vary greatly in their preferences for Extraversion and Introversion may find it difficult to feel at home and simply be themselves with one another.

The mental processes, Sensing and Intuition, and Thinking and Feeling, are also predictive of some disparities to which roommates must accommodate. For example, Feeling types tend to be less concerned with boundaries and have a broader range of acquaintances. In contrast, Thinking types tend to be more territorial and have a tighter circle of a few, close friends. While these and the other type-related behaviors associated with roommate conflicts have been verified empirically (Schroeder et al., 1980), residence educators knowledgeable of the MBTI instrument can derive many others. Since a major source of all interpersonal problems is the failure to communicate, the multiple uses of the MBTI instrument as a counseling tool, as presented in chapters 8 and 11, can be successfully applied to resolving roommate conflicts.

Helping Roommates Accommodate Natural Differences

A proven mechanism for resolving roommate conflicts is for roommates to develop a behavioral contract, a process that can help roommates function effectively regardless of their degree of dissimilarity in personality styles. Important issues to resolve include cleanliness, study habits, sharing personal belongings, bedtimes, where each keeps his/her things, entertaining guests, and attitudes toward social behaviors. Resolution through compromise on these matters would be of great benefit to Willard and Sam. For example, Willard and Sam might agree on certain hours for sleeping, studying, and socializing in their room. During designated study hours, Sam could use headphones if he wished to listen to music; conversely, Willard might study in the library during the designated socializing hours. Sam could agree to keep his clothes off the floor and in his closet and Willard might agree to cleaning the entire room only twice a week. In addition to these kinds of behavioral accommodations, it might be possible for Willard and Sam to structure their room to further allow for their differences. Willard might find that installing privacy curtains around his bed would allow him to sleep more easily when Sam pulls an all-nighter. To deal with the noises that interfere with studying, Willard might try reading a magazine with a fan running until he becomes so accustomed to hearing the fan that it is no longer distracting. The fan would serve to block out other distracters so that he could focus his attention on study materials. All these efforts should increase the probability that Willard and Sam could accommodate each other's natural differences.

Over time, roommates like Willard and Sam may even be able to understand and appreciate each other's differences. The amount of time and effort required to make this relationship work, however, may leave little time for accomplishing academic, social, and personal goals. Without any similarities in interests, values, motivations, and living habits, it is difficult, if not impossible, for roommates to establish a meaningful relationship. In conjunction with using the MBTI instrument as a counseling tool to help roommates understand each other and themselves, the Indicator can also be used to match roommates on the basis of personality compatibility.

Pairing Roommates for Satisfaction and Development

The MBTI instrument was first used at Michigan State University as a tool for understanding the dynamics in the roommate situation (Eigenbrod, 1969). No attempt was made to assign roommates by personality type. Instead, freshman roommates living in a six-story, coeducational residence hall of 600 students were classified into the following three broad categories of compatibility: (a) compatible—both the perception (Sensing or Intuition) and judgment (Thinking or Feeling) functions of roommates were alike; (b) complementary—either the perception or the judgment functions of the roommates were alike; (c) incompatible—*neither* the perception nor the judgment functions of the roommates were alike. As predicted, the greater the similarity or compatibility between roommates, the greater the expressed satisfaction with not only their roommates but also with their room assignments. Increased satisfaction with the living situation resulted in greater investment and involvement in maintaining and improving the physical condition of the residence hall. Thus, the roommate relationship mediated the quality of students' interactions with both the social and physical environments of the residence halls.

The MBTI instrument has been used to actually assign roommates together on the basis of personality similarity. At Auburn University roommates in the Magnolia Dormitories were matched according to commonality in dominant mental functions indicated by the MBTI instrument (Schroeder, 1976). The conditions in the community at the time were stable and there were numerous support systems in place. Since the spring to fall retention rate was more than 70 percent, there was a high percentage of upper-class role models for the first-year students. In addition, the student population overall was fairly homogenous. Single rooms had been introduced to reduce the density per floor so that most floors did not house more than 30 students. Students were encouraged to personalize their rooms and hallways and, in general, felt very influential and unrestricted in their behaviors. Public areas had been zoned for specific psychological-type behaviors to accommodate natural differences in environmental preferences. A recreation area with pinball machines, table games, loud music, and exciting colors was created to provide students with easy access to a variety of novel, intense, and complex stimulation; a woodworking shop was provided to encourage various practical, sensing behaviors; other areas were zones for privacy and so forth (Jackson and Schroeder, 1977). Hence the overall residential community was characterized by a high degree of support.

In this setting, matching roommates using the MBTI instrument had a startling effect. The first year this strategy was implemented, requests for roommate changes declined by more than 65 percent. In addition, twenty-one of the twenty-four roommate pairs who had self-selected their roommates had the same dominant functions—the same assignment criteria the housing staff had employed. These results clearly indicate that matching roommates with similar MBTI functions resulted in compatibility. In such a secure and predictable environment, however, pairing roommates by commonality in dominant functions may have created an overly supportive environment. The students were obviously satisfied with their living situation, but it was never determined whether or not there was sufficient diversity or challenge between roommates to stimulate their development.

A central question in roommate assignments is whether satisfaction and development are mutually exclusive or whether satisfaction is a requisite to development. Most studies of the goals and processes of roommate pairings have assumed satisfaction as the only desired outcome (Garrison, 1973; Strange, 1993). The prevailing assumption has been that satisfaction is a prerequisite to academic and personality development; however, the relationship between satisfaction and development had not been investigated. In a campus-wide study at Auburn University, the interrelationship of variables in the roommate situation that might affect not only satisfaction, but also academic and personality development, was examined in the early 1980s (Jackson, 1984).

After assignment by the university's standard procedures, freshmen were classified according to their degree of similarity in MBTI profiles. Roommates were classified into the following four groups that ranged from identical roommate pairs as the most similar to opposite roommate pairs as the least similar: (a) identical—roommates with both dominant and auxiliary functions in common; (b) complementary—roommates with the same dominant function and different auxiliary functions; (c) tangent—roommates with different dominant functions and the same auxiliary function, or roommates with the dominant function of one the same as the auxiliary function of the other; (d) opposite—roommates with both the dominant and auxiliary functions in opposition. Based on previous research studies and theoretical considerations, it was expected that similarity between roommates' MBTI profiles would be related to roommate satisfaction. Further, it was expected that a satisfying roommate relationship would provide a supportive context in which development would occur. Thus, it was expected that similarity between roommates' MBTI profiles would lead to satisfaction which, in turn, would lead to development, both academic and personality. The actual results of the study are quite provocative and are illustrated in Figure 9.2.

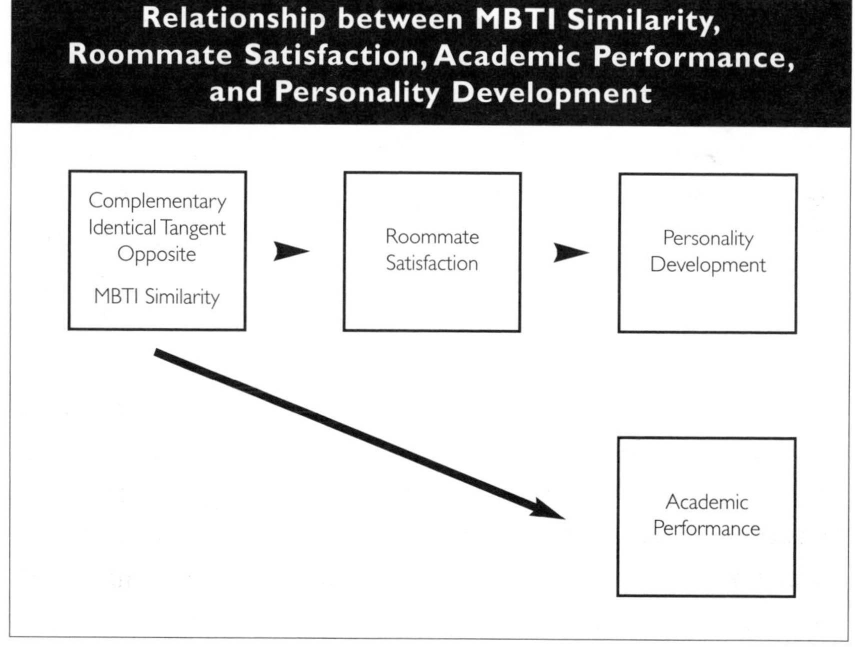

Figure 9.2

Contrary to previous studies, similarity between roommates' MBTI profiles was not related to roommate satisfaction. Roommates' degree of similarity on the Indicator, however, was related significantly to academic performance, as defined by grade point average. Further, roommates with the highest grades had complementary MBTI profiles, followed in descending order by roommates whose MBTI profiles were identical, tangent, and opposite. It appears that the complementary pairing provided the incongruence in the roommate relationship necessary for stimulating academic development. Consistent with this finding is Schroeder's (1981) notion that roommates sharing the same dominant function are provided with a common basis for understanding and interpreting actions while having different auxiliary functions helps each roommate, through modeling, develop behaviors corresponding to the roommates' auxiliary function.

Though roommates' similarity in MBTI profiles was found to be a requisite for academic development, it was not a requisite for personality development. Roommate satisfaction, however, was related significantly to personality development, as defined by selected scales of the Omnibus Personality Inventory (Heist and Yonge, 1968). The traditional goal of pairing roommates with the desired outcome of satisfaction was thus confirmed as very worthwhile; the interpersonal environment formed by satisfied roommates provides a medium for personality development.

Collectively, studies of the MBTI instrument in roommate, suitemate, and hallmate pairings point to the same general conclusion—assigning students to living units according to similarity in MBTI profiles increases the likelihood that students will be compatible and satisfied (Winston and Anchors, 1993). The Auburn study (Jackson, 1984) demonstrates that the MBTI instrument may be promising for creating a dynamic equilibrium in the roommate relationship—one that will not only facilitate satisfaction and thus personality development, but academic achievement as well. This strategy of balancing challenge and support to achieve maximum development may also be applied to residence hall neighbors (Ingalls, 2000), by matching roommates, podmates, or suitemates with the same or complementary MBTI profiles (highly supportive), while varying the MBTI types of the suite or floormates to provide challenges within a floor or living community. While researchers have used the MBTI in different ways to define the degree of challenge and support in interpersonal environments, all investigators agree that dominant pairings (see Table 9.4) are effective as assignment criteria. The pairings to the left are identical and become progressively less similar moving to the right. To determine which of the four dominant pairs to use, the practitioner should first assess the relative degrees of challenge and support within the area of assignment (floor or building) and the students to be assigned. When students are in developmental transition, not yet integrated into social groups, and/or the residence hall environment is extremely challenging, students should be assigned as similarly as possible. When students are not in developmental transition, have support groups to help mediate their college challenge and/or when the residence hall environment allows for a high degree of predictability, students should be paired less similarly. Hence, as previously suggested, the MBTI instrument can best be utilized as a mechanism for balancing the elements of challenge and support in the resident environment. However, when using the Indicator for various assignment purposes, there are a number of practical administrative issues that must be considered.

Practical Administrative Considerations

When using the MBTI instrument for assignment purposes, one of the first issues that must be considered is the most appropriate way to gather type data on resident students, an issue that has been addressed in various ways. At Auburn University, for example, all freshmen students who participated, in the summer pre-college counseling program completed the Indicator prior to attending one of eight orientation sessions scheduled from mid-June through the last week of July. After the Indicator was scored, the housing staff obtained type scores for incoming freshmen from Student Development Services, the department that provided leadership for managing MBTI data.

At Saint Louis University, incoming resident students were mailed the Indicator as part of the housing contracting process. New students were encouraged to complete and return the Indicator within a three- to four-week period during the summer. Once the information was received in the housing office, answer sheets were hand scored by trained student assistants. The MBTI type scores, along with academic information and data, recorded on a Personal Information Sheet, were utilized to match roommates. It is important to note that at Saint Louis University, MBTI information generated by the housing office was combined into an integrated database with type scores obtained through freshman orientation, Counseling and Consultation Center testings, and various personal development workshops. The value of integrating this information for retention purposes has been addressed in chapter 3.

Obviously, there are a number of ethical considerations that must be addressed when using the MBTI to match roommates, floormates, and suitemates. First, students must clearly understand why this approach is beneficial and they must consent to the utilization of the data for matching purposes. At Saint Louis University, this was communicated to incoming resident students when they received the MBTI booklet and answer sheet. Naturally, all MBTI information generated for matching purposes was handled in a confidential

Dominant MBTI Pairings for Each Type

	Identical	Complementary-1	Consonant	Complementary-2
Dominant Sensors				
ESTP	ESTP	ESFP	ISTJ	ISFJ
ESFP	ESFP	ESTP	ISFJ	ISTJ
ISTJ	ISTJ	ISFJ	ESTP	ESFP
ISFJ	ISFJ	ISTJ	ESFP	ESTP
Dominant Intuitives				
ENTP	ENTP	ENFP	INTJ	INFJ
ENFP	ENFP	ENTP	INFJ	INTJ
INTJ	INTJ	INFJ	ENTP	ENFP
INFJ	INFJ	INTJ	ENFP	ENTP
Dominant Thinkers				
ESTJ	ESTJ	ENTJ	ISFP	INTP
ENTJ	ENTJ	ESTJ	INTP	ISTP
ISTP	ISTP	INTP	ESTJ	ENTJ
INTP	INTP	ISTP	ENTJ	ESTJ
Dominant Feelers				
ESFJ	ESFJ	ENFJ	ISFP	INFP
ENFJ	ENFJ	ESFJ	INFP	ISFP
ISFP	ISFP	INFP	ESFJ	ENFJ
INFP	INFP	ISFP	ENFJ	ESFJ

Table 9.4

manner. Room assignments were made by trained, professional staff. No information on a student's type was released without his or her expressed, written consent. Students were encouraged, but not required, to participate in the process. Students chose to participate by signing an informed consent form. In addition, the roommate selection and assignment process was highlighted in the following fashion in the SLU housing brochure:

> From choice of roommate to selection of a floor unit, you have the freedom to associate with whomever you choose. Our application process provides information which will help you choose living arrangements where you will feel most at home. If you do not indicate a preference for a particular roommate, the information obtained through the application process will be used to make assignments.

In applying these strategies at Auburn University, Mercer University, and Saint Louis University, housing staff utilized type scores for matching purposes—no attention was given to strength of preference scores. However, since other information (academic goals, living habits, etc.) was combined with MBTI information, the housing director obtained a fairly accurate picture of a student's personality prior to the actual assignment.

Costs associated with administering an assignment program of this nature include purchasing a supply of MBTI booklets and answer sheets and mailing and scoring the instrument. Since it is common for 10 to 15 percent of the students to fail to return their booklets and answer sheets, these items must be replaced at additional cost. Similarly, if the Indicator is handscored, student assistants or clerical support staff must be paid for their time. For housing staff desiring a different scoring option, CPP, Inc. and the Center for Applications of

Psychological Type offer a low-cost, rapid, efficient computer scoring service that provides individual scores and profiles. CAPT offers a composite profile by preference for various groups as well.

One final consideration—staff should be aware of the politics associated with using a personality instrument for roommate matching purposes. Unless the program is effectively communicated to student affairs staff, faculty, key administrators, and students, the approach could be viewed as a deliberate attempt to manipulate the environment in order to change the behavior of students without their knowledge and consent. We are certainly not advocating such an approach for residence educators. Rather, we are advocating that the MBTI instrument be used to help students understand themselves and others and to avail themselves of the opportunities for development which campus environments offer.

Implications

Throughout this chapter, we have described various strategies for applying the MBTI personality assessment tool in residence halls—strategies that, in many cases, have served to improve the quality of life for students. Some of the strategies, however, may challenge the traditional approaches to student development used by many college housing staffs. On most campuses it is quite common for residence-hall staff to spend considerable time and energy reacting to problems, mediating roommate conflicts, responding to discipline problems, implementing developmental programs, and working with resident assistants (RAs). Although some of these roles are both necessary and appropriate, they appear to suggest a crises management perspective akin to hospital emergency room treatment. In this chapter we have suggested an alternative role—environmental management—a strategy more akin to preventive medicine. Instead of expecting students to adjust or accommodate themselves to prevailing social environments, residence educators can use the MBTI instrument as one means of structuring environments that respond to the diversity in students' needs and preferences. Hence, we hope that residence educators will recognize the value of environmental management as a principle for promoting student development and thereby embrace a central tenet of the Student Learning Imperative (ACPA, 1996). The SLI states that " . . . the key to enhancing learning and personal development is not simply for faculty to teach more and better, but also to create conditions that motivate students to devote time and energy to educationally-purposeful activities, both in and outside the classroom" (p. 118).

Although the MBTI instrument is definitely not a panacea for all the problems students and staff experience in residence halls, when properly applied it is an extremely useful tool for creating the conditions in the residence halls that promote various dimensions of student learning and development. Perhaps it goes without saying that any tool must be applied with care; its user must recognize both the possibilities and limitations associated with its application. Almost everyone has witnessed great works produced by knowledgeable and experienced craftsmen using primitive tools and, conversely, inferior products created by novices utilizing sophisticated, state-of-the-art tools. Likewise, the Indicator can be used most effectively when in the hands of a knowledgeable practitioner—one who possesses not only a thorough understanding of the MBTI instrument and how to apply it, but also grasps the complex interactions between students and the physical and social environment of his/her own campus. For example, an MBTI roommate-matching strategy that is effective at a large multiversity, such as Ohio State University, may be totally inappropriate at a small Catholic women's college. Therefore, prior to utilizing the MBTI instrument as an intervention strategy, residence educators should systematically assess sources of challenge and support in their residential settings and then adopt an MBTI strategy for their local circumstances (Sahuh, 1981).

Finally, almost all colleges and universities are experiencing much more competition for traditional college-age students. In response to this situation, most institutions are being challenged to improve their retention rates. Fortunately, housing officials are in a favored position for impacting the retention of their students. The results of over 30 years of research have clearly shown that the on-campus living experience can mediate students' satisfaction, functioning, and persistence with virtually all aspects of their undergraduate experience (Astin, 1977 and 1993; Pascarella and Terenzini, 1991; Winston and Anchors, 1993; Schroeder and Mable, 1994). While these benefits have always been goals of residential programs, they have infrequently been directly linked to staff interventions. The MBTI instrument can be used to intentionally create conditions in the residence hall that promote student academic achievement, personal growth, and satisfaction—student development objectives related to retention.

Whether by design or by default, residence educators are managers of the social ecology of students. With increasing knowledge that the social environments in residence halls can be purposefully structured, college housing administrators have not only the opportunity for influencing students' learning and development, but also the obligation to reduce or eliminate the inhumane conditions that residence hall environments sometimes create for students. When appropriately applied, the MBTI instrument is a sound, useful, and efficient tool for these purposes.

References

American College Personnel Association (ACPA). (1994). *The student learning imperative: Implications for student affairs.* Washington, DC: Author.

Anchors, S., K. Douglas, and M. Kasper, (1993). Developing and enhancing student communities. In *Student housing and residential life.* R. Winston and S. Anchors (Eds.), San Francisco, CA: Jossey-Bass Publishers, Inc.

Astin, A. W. (1977). *Four critical years.* San Francisco: Jossey-Bass Publishers, Inc.

Astin, A. W. (1993) *What matters in college: Four critical years revisited.* San Francisco, CA: Jossey-Bass Publishers, Inc.

Eigenbrod, F. A. (1969). The effects of territoriality and personality compatibility on identity and security (Doctoral dissertation, Michigan State University). Dissertation Abstracts International 30(06), 2329A.

Garrison, R. (1973). Roommate selection: A plan for community growth. *The Journal of College and University Student Housing,* 3, 15–18.

Heilweil, M. (1973). The influence of dormitory architecture on resident behavior. *Environment and Behavior,* 5, 377–411.

Heist, P., and G. Yonge. (1968). *Omnibus Personality Inventory* (Form F). New York: The Psychological Corporation.

Ingalls, Z. (2001, August 18). The art, science, and framework of pairing roommates. *Chronicle of Higher Education,* Washington, DC, A 41–43.

Jackson, S. and C. Schroeder. (1977). Behavioral zoning for stimulation seekers. *Journal of College and University Student Housing,* 7, 1, 7–10.

Jackson, S. (1983). The relationship between psychological type and color preferences. Unpublished manuscript, Saint Louis University, St. Louis, MO.

Jackson, S. (1984). The impact of roommates on development: A causal analysis of the effects of roommate personality congruence, satisfaction and initial developmental status on end-of-quarter developmental status and grade point average. (Doctoral dissertation, Auburn University, AL).

Kalsbeek, D., R. Rodgers, D. Marshall, D. Denny, and G. Nicholls. (1982). Balancing challenge and support: A study of degrees of similarity in suitemate personality type and perceived difference in challenge and support in a residence hall environment. *Journal of College Student Personnel,* 23(5), 434–442.

Mehrabian, A. (1976). *Public places and private spaces.* New York: Basic Books.

Moos, R., and M. Gerst. (1974). *The University Residence Environment Scale Manual.* Palo Alto, CA: Consulting Psychologists Press.

Pascarella, E. T. and P. T. Terenzini. (1991). *How college affects students: Findings and insights from 20 years of research.* San Francisco, CA: Jossey-Bass Publishers, Inc.

Rodgers, R. (1980). Theories underlying student development. In D. Creamer (Ed.), *Student development in higher education: Theories, practices, and future directions.* Cincinnati, OH: American College Personnel Association.

Sanford, N. (1966). *Self and society: Social change and individual development.* New York: Atherton.

Schroeder, C. (1976). New strategies for structuring residential environments. *Journal of College Student Personnel,* 17(5), 386–391.

———. (1981). Student development through environmental management. In G. Blimling and J. Schuh (Eds.), *Increasing the educational role of residence halls* (pp. 35–51). New Directions for Student Services Sourcebook No. 13. San Francisco: Jossey-Bass.

———. (1994). Developing learning communities. In C. Schroeder and P. Mable (Eds.) *Realizing the educational potential of residence halls*, (pp. 165–189). San Francisco, CA: Jossey-Bass Publishers, Inc.

Schroeder, C. and S. Jackson (1987). Creating conditions for student development in campus living environments. *NASPA Journal*, 25, 1, 45–53.

Schroeder, C. and P. Mable (1994). *Realizing the educational potential of residence halls.* San Francisco, CA: Jossey-Bass Publishers, Inc.

Schroeder, C., F. Minor and T. Tarkow (1999). Learning communities: partnerships between academic and student affairs. In J. Levine (Ed.), *Learning communities: New structures, new partnerships for learning* (Monograph No. 26). Columbia, South Carolina: University of South Carolina, National Resource Center for the First-Year Experience and Students in Transition, 56–69.

Schroeder, C., F. Minor and T. Tarkow (1999). Promoting student success through freshman interest groups. In J. Schuh and L. Whitt (Eds.) *Student and academic affairs partnerships.* San Francisco, CA: Jossey-Bass Publishers, Inc. New Directions in Student Services, No. 87.

Schroeder, C., R. Warner and D. Malone (1980). Effects of assignment to living units by personality types on environmental perceptions and student development. *Journal of College Student Personnel*, 21(5), 443–449.

Schuh, J. (1981) Staff training. In G. Blimling and J. Schuh (Eds.), *Increasing the educational role of residence halls* (pp. 81–93). New Directions for Student Services Sourcebook No. 13. San Francisco: Jossey-Bass.

Smith, T. (1994). Integrating living and learning in residential colleges. In C. Schroeder and P. Mable (Eds.) *Realizing the educational potential of residence halls* (pp. 241–266). San Francisco, CA: Jossey-Bass Publishers, Inc.

Strange, C. (1993). Developmental impacts of campus living environments. In R. Winston and S. Anchors (Eds.), *Student housing and residential life* (pp. 134–166). San Francisco, CA: Jossey-Bass Publishers, Inc.

Strange, C. and J. Banning. (2001). *Educating by design: Creating campus learning environments that work.* San Francisco, CA: Jossey-Bass Publishers, Inc.

Winston, R. and S. Anchors (Eds.). (1993). *Student housing and residential life.* San Francisco, CA: Jossey-Bass Publishers, Inc.

CHAPTER 10

Using the MBTI® Instrument for Student Career Development

JUDITH GRUTTER

The typical college student can expect to spend at least half of his or her waking hours working. And yet many college students expect their first professional career move to be decided by a few brief meetings with recruiters during on-campus interviews just prior to graduation. College and university career professionals have long been aware that career development activities should be a part of the entire college experience—from high school matriculation, to freshman orientation, to academic major selection, to internship placement, to post-college decision making (Williamson, 1939). Motivating students to buy into this kind of developmental philosophy, however, continues to be a major challenge to career development offices, career planning and placement centers, and psychological services departments—all vehicles for career services delivery. This challenge is even greater as the nature of college student populations continues to change, reflecting stop-out options, patterns of life-long learning, and an increasing number of first generation college students and under-represented groups.

The career counseling framework most commonly used on college and university campuses is the best-fit model, which can be traced back almost a century to the person-environment fit writings of Frank Parsons (1909) and E. G. Williamson (1937 and 1939). As early as 1909, Parsons suggested three aspects of vocational choice that can easily be recognized in the more recent research of John Holland (1959) and the empirical evidence behind such systems as the Strong Interest Inventor® (1994), the Self-Directed Search (1994), and the Myers-Briggs Type Indicator® occupational data bank maintained by the Center for Applications of Psychological Type (Macdaid, McCaulley, and Kainz, 1986). These aspects are:

1. a clear understanding of yourself and of your aptitudes, abilities, interests, ambitions, resources, limitations, and their causes;
2. a knowledge of the requirements and conditions of success, advantages and disadvantages, compensation, opportunities, and prospects in different lines of work; and
3. true reasoning on the relations of these two groups of facts (1909, p. 5).

In today's educational settings, this process most often takes the form of administering interest and personality assessments, and "matching" students' results to suitable career fields and college majors. Not without merit, this approach still works when the assessment results point in a clear direction, the student is motivated, and the job market is cooperative. However, it is not always correct to assume that the student is ready for the "matching" process when he or she arrives on the college doorstep.

Recognizing the efficiency of this approach to career counseling, this chapter presents a best-fit framework based on MBTI® applications.

It is presented, however, within a developmental continuum. Career development tasks and issues, which are representative of the college student experience, are discussed. Practical MBTI strategies and resources that can be addressed on both an individual and group basis are suggested.

Two Illustrations

Barbara is a twenty-year-old sophomore at a major university. She is an excellent student and expresses particular interest in science and math. Her mother is an art teacher and her father is an engineer. She has been encouraged from an early age to explore any and all opportunities with which she has come into contact; she began to focus her interests while still in high school. She is considering a premed major, possibly with a specialization in psychiatry, although special education and art are also of interest to her. Barbara asks to take some career assessments to help her to pinpoint her interests. She recognizes that a career in medicine requires an earlier commitment than a career in education, and she does not want to waste time. She is given the MBTI and the Strong Interest Inventory instruments, as well as a values questionnaire and several other pencil and paper exercises. Barbara verifies her type as INFP, and her Strong Theme code as IAS (Investigative-Artistic-Social). She learns that in a rank ordering of 208 occupations for INFPs, fine artist ranks first, psychiatrist ranks second, and special education teacher ranks 102 (Hammer and Macdaid, 1992). Barbara's Strong results confirm that work environments that involve researching and analyzing, creating art, and/or helping others would all appeal to her, but that her interests are much more similar to those of physicians and psychologists than they are of fine artists and special education teachers. Barbara's personality and interests appear to be quite well differentiated, and she appears ready and well informed to choose a college major. She chooses premed with a possible minor in psychology, representing her personality and acknowledging her valuing of helping others and high earnings over artistic creativity.

Tim is twenty-three and just about to graduate from a small liberal arts college. As a liberal studies major, he thought at one time that he might want to teach, but his highest priority now is to make a lot of money. He dropped out of college after his sophomore year to teach skiing and sell sporting goods, but the job quickly bored him, and he quit to travel around Europe. Tim's father is an attorney, and his mother volunteers in the local schools and fills in as a teacher's aide when she is needed. Both parents "just want Tim to be happy." He comes to the career center to sign up for on-campus interviews, but isn't really interested in any of the employers on the list—mostly pharmaceutical and insurance companies or retail chains that won't pay him enough, he says. A career counselor suggests that Tim take some career assessments to help him to better define what he is looking for, and he readily agrees, relieved that there is something available that will give him the answer. It won't surprise the experienced career counselor to learn that Tim's assessment results are undifferentiated. He reports clear MBTI preferences for E and P, but only slight preferences for N and T, which he is unable to verify. His Strong results are flat, and the only values that he is sure of are high earnings and independence.

Barbara and Tim are at very different career development stages. Although the MBTI instrument is a useful tool for both, it is not useful in the same way. For Barbara, it helps in the matching process. Her perception and judgment functions (N and F) are well enough developed for a pattern of interests to have emerged, and for her to be able to narrow them down. In Tim's case, his unverified perception and judgment preferences (N and T) suggest a lack of identity formation—a prerequisite for career decision making (Bluestein and Noumair,

1996; Bluestein, Devenis, and Kidney, 1989). The MBTI instrument is used more in the diagnostic vein, to encourage developmental activities.

The MBTI Instrument and Career Development

The framework presented in this chapter is based on two widely-held assumptions: 1) that career decision making is a life-long process of discovering, learning, and changing rather than a one-time event (Super, 1953 and 1994); and 2) that the development of personality, represented here by type, is also a lifelong process (Myers, McCaulley, Quenk and Hammer, 1998; and Myers and Kirby, 1994)[1]. The two processes naturally parallel each other and can be guided through developmental stages by various structured interventions (Grutter, 1990 and 2000). The table that follows outlines the various stages of career, life, and type development, along with their career development focus, suggested strategies, and desired outcomes. The exploration and commitment stages, most applicable to college and university students, are addressed more fully in the following sections with student case studies and program applications for both individual and group career counseling settings.

The Career Counseling Process

There are almost certainly as many career-counseling frameworks presented in the literature as there are textbooks on career counseling.[2] All of them contain similar components, which are outlined here. The model can be applied to either an individual or group format, examples of which appear in the following sections.

1. Establish the counseling relationship and identify career issues.

   What is the student's presenting problem?

   What is the student's developmental stage?

Stage	Time of Life	Type Development Task
Identity Formation	The early years	Experience with all four mental functions Discovery of the dominant and the auxiliary
Exploration	Middle and high school, college entry	Formulation of the core identity Focus on perception function
Commitment	The college years	Development of J–P balance Focus on judgement function
Career Entry	Post college	Specialization of the dominant and the auxiliary
Career Advancement	Mid-20s through 40s	Emergence of tertiary
Career Refinement	Late 40s through 50s and 60s	Integration of the tertiary Emergence of the least preferred function
Career Disengagement	The retirement years	Integration of the least preferred function

Table 10.1

Career Dev. Issues	Strategies	Desired Outcomes
Discovery of interests and awareness of abilities Possible foreclosure	Varied play and school experiences Role playing Unconditional support	Awareness of unique self Emergence of positive self concept
Initial separation from parents Development of interest and unique abilities Examination of values	Varied play, school, and work experiences Interest and personality assessment Assessment of abilities	Alignment of interests and abilities Preparation for work or additional education
Narrowing of interests Interests/values conflicts Focus and commitment Finding a sense of purpose Possible diffusion	Prioritizing and decision-making training Values clarification Testing of interests/values conflict	Alignment of interests and values Refinement of appropriate skills Initial career decision
Search for congruence Clarifying commitment Securing position	Clarification of purpose Job search techniques Coaching for induction	Initial career position Successful induction
Competition Career adjustment Career satisfaction	Self-promotion Networking Strategic alliances	Certification of position Promotions or satisfying lateral moves
Balance Career change Life/career enrichment Preparation for retirement	Self-assessment (values shift) Evaluation of opportunities Transition	Re-pacing of lifestyle Job redesign Ultimate congruence
Deinstitutionalization Role change Personal enrichment	Identity re-evaluation Self-assessment (new interests)	Successful deceleration Institutional disengagement New interests

Table 10.1 *Adapted from Grutter, J.* Developmental career counseling. *In J. M. Kummerow (Ed.),* New Directions in Career Planning and the Workplace *(pp. 273–306). Used with permission.*

What are the barriers to reaching the goal(s) of career counseling?

2. Determine career-counseling strategies.

   How much does the student know about him or herself, the world of work, college?

   What strategies will appeal to the presenting personality style?

   How much time does the student have to accomplish the goal(s) of counseling?

3. Set the career-counseling contract.

   Drawing upon student and counselor input, agree upon the counseling goals and strategies, and a reasonable timeframe.

4. Collect self-information.

   Administer typical performance assessments—personality/interests/values.

   Evaluate evidence of ability and achievement, or administer maximum performance tests.

5. Interpret assessments.

   Select a framework for integrating the assessments, for instance RIASEC or a schematic of academic departments or college majors

   Interpret each assessment and combine the results.

   Resolve discrepancies.

   Assign summarizing activities.

6. Explore possibilities and target a range of alternatives.

   Assign research and activities to narrow the possibilities.

7. Make a preliminary decision and develop an action plan

   Discuss next steps and long-range goals.

8. Evaluate and revise the decision as necessary.

Establishing the counseling relationship. Most students who seek career counseling assistance during the college years state as their primary concern finding a job after college, choosing a major, or identifying career fields for majors already selected. On the other hand, the counselor may see the student's concern differently. For instance the counselor may detect such issues as a lack of identity formation and decision readiness, or incongruence between interests and demonstrated ability, or an expectation that career choice is provided by outside "experts." A key to successful career development counseling is reaching agreement between the student's stated concern and the counselor's judgment.

Martha is a case in point. She comes to a community college career center in response to a job board announcement for a receptionist/technician in an animal care facility and requests assistance with her resume. Her counselor notes that Martha plans to transfer to a four-year university in the fall and has declared a history major on her application. He suggests that she might want to consider part-time and summer jobs more suitable for history majors and offers to help her in an appropriate job search. He also notes that the college offers a guidance class that is beginning the next week, and that it might be advisable for Martha to enroll to clarify her career goals. Martha thanks the counselor for his time and leaves. She finds help with her resume on-line and gets the job she is seeking. Martha might have benefited from career planning assistance, but she shut out the possibility when her immediate concern was discounted. Another approach might have been to assist her with the animal care resume and use the resume objective section to begin to talk about other possibilities. Martha may also be considering a change of major so exploring that possibility in the moment rather than referring her to an upcoming class might hold her interest.

In Martha's case, like many other college students, the actual career issue is often a function of their stage of career development. The student may clearly state that she is ready for career commitment, but the counselor may question the completion of identity formation and exploration. In the developmental framework, successful future outcomes are dependent upon the completion of previous developmental tasks. Career decisions can be fleeting if options have not been explored and evaluated beforehand. On the other hand, exploration can be prolonged if commitment is not encouraged at the appropriate time. It is during the initial meeting between student and counselor that the developmental stage is evaluated, and next steps are agreed upon. Questions for Martha might be:

- What is it about the animal care position that appeals to you?
- Tell me a little about how you decided on history as a major when you transfer.
- How do you think this job would help you in the future?

The counselor is looking for evidence of prior exploration and evaluation activities that would demonstrate a readiness for commitment. In addition to incomplete developmental tasks, the counselor is also listening for other common barriers to the career development process. Students often express such barriers as not having time to commit to the exploration process, the need for immediate employment, a conflict between their own career interests and family expectations, and the attractiveness of short-term high earnings.

Using type concepts in establishing the counseling relationship can be very helpful. At this point in the career counseling process, the student's type has not usually been established. The goals of the session are to connect with the student at his or her place in the process and to encourage further work together. The best way to do this is to ensure that all of the MBTI preferences are covered in the conversation

Encourage discussion as well as thought and reflection (E–I).
Be factual and concise as well as suggesting possibilities (S–N).
Be logical and objective as well as caring and supportive (T–F).
Present a plan of action with plenty of room for flexibility (J–P).

As students' reactions to these various MBTI communication styles are observed, response patterns will begin to emerge as predominant. Hammer (1993) suggests that some students will need specific action plans right away (EJs). Others will need time for thorough research and reflection (IJs). EPs will want to experience every option fully and talk about them. IPs will want to wander and wonder at their own paces. The second stage of the career counseling process begins when the counselor-counselee relationship is established, and it is clear that the student wishes to continue.

Determining career-counseling strategies. Most college and university career centers have many options available to them for career development work with students. Most typical are computerized career guidance systems, standardized assessments, career information systems, credit guidance classes, structured groups, and individual counseling sessions. The selection of appropriate strategies for a particular student depends largely upon how much the student knows about himself or herself (identity formation), the world of work and college (the perception functions), decision making (the judgment functions), and how much time the student has to accomplish the goal(s) of counseling. Very often a standardized assessment or structured questionnaire is administered to explore with the student which career development strategies will be the most motivating. The MBTI instrument is particularly helpful for this purpose.

Students who have not yet formed preferences for Judging and Perceiving, and thus an identity core, will require the most time and attention. Standardized assessment results will most likely be flat, motivation will be low, and decisions will be elusive. Even values and needs will be undifferentiated. Often making the process even more challenging to counselors are some students' other-directed convictions that "the answer" lies not within themselves, but in the hands of an outside expert—the counselor. Such students will benefit the most from retracing and mastering the tasks of the earlier stages of development: identity formation and exploration. Varied directed experiences with all four of the MBTI mental functions, combined with structured counselor-student discussion and caring support, may be necessary to help students to identify their function core.

One efficient way to encourage the process of vocational identity formation at the college level is to align student experiences with the MBTI function columns. Have them begin with the column of their choice and proceed through the columns, following each set of experiences with an evaluative debriefing session. Encouraging students to experience activities in each of the columns will develop their awareness of perception; evaluating their experiences will help them with judgment. Depending on the setting and the nature of your students, activities might include discussions with alumni, meetings with faculty advisors, visits to classrooms, visits to web sites, reading books, or leisure activities. Career resources are numerous, and often untapped. Connecting the resources to a system of personality characteristics promotes as much understanding of self as the world of work. Suggested activities representing each of the function cores follow in Table 10.2.

When students are given the opportunity to experience a variety of activities and evaluate them based on their likes and abilities, they begin to acquire the self-information necessary to proceed successfully

Activity	ST	SF	NF	NT
Discussions with alumni	Accountants Police officers Computer professionals Military Business managers Gov. workers	Nurses Elementary school teachers Social workers Child care workers Office managers	Religious workers Counselors Psychologists Artists Writers Musicians Physicians	Architects Lawyers Management consultants Engineers Scientists Sales managers
Meetings with faculty advisors	Departments of Business, MIS and Computer Science, Law Enforcement, Math	Departments of Nursing, Education, Social Work, Business Education	Departments of Religion, Fine Arts, Counseling, English, Music, Creative Writing	Departments of Business, Engineering, Science, Math, Law, Architecture
Visits to classrooms	Business management and MIS	Social work and early childhood education	Counseling and the creative arts	Engineering, science, and law
Web sites	Business	Education	The arts	Science
"Careers in Books"	Business	Education	The arts	Science
Leisure Activities	Collecting and tabulating; sports, ROTC	Visiting a hospice, volunteer service	Church activities, volunteer counseling	Environmental protection club, astronomy

Table 10.2

with the more traditional career exploration strategies of assessment, guidance groups and classes, and computerized information systems.

Students who have accomplished the tasks of identity formation and a portion of exploration are more likely to be able to verify MBTI function preferences than those who have not. An initial MBTI assessment session will help to narrow down the many exploration options available to them.

STs	Want practical information and facts that are accurate and make sense.	Use standardized assessment results and research to chart self and employment information. Respond well to computer-assistance guidance systems.
SFs	Want practical information and facts that are accurate and can be related to personal experience.	Use standardized assessment results and personal stories to chart self and employment information. Provide encouragement and personal support.
NFs	Want to use their creativity to explore ideas and options that are personally meaningful.	Use journaling, metaphors, and values clarification activities. Emphasize the personal growth aspect of assessments.
NTs	Want logical strategies for investigating options.	Analyze patterns in assessment results. Encourage options beyond the data. Strategize the improbable.

In addition to the identity core, the MBTI E–I and J–P orientations are also helpful for determining the most motivating career development strategies. Extraverts will want things to talk about and time to share; Introverts will want things to think about and time to reflect. Judging types want activities to be organized and results-oriented; Perceiving types want activities to be open and flexible, to go with the flow (Grutter and Lund, 2000).

Setting the career-counseling contract. Once strategies have been discussed, mutually agreed upon goals for counseling and a suitable timeframe need to be understood. This process ranges in some settings from an informal statement of the plan with agreement on both sides, to other settings that use a written agreement that is signed by both the student and the counselor. In any case it is critical that both student expectations and counselor intentions be clarified. One of the most frequent misunderstandings in career counseling is that standardized assessments will provide the one right answer to career questions, and are a short cut through the process. Clarifying this misunderstanding up front will help to avoid the disappointment of unmet expectations later. Keeping student MBTI preferences in mind during the agreement process will help to insure commitment and follow through.

MBTI Preference	Make sure the agreement includes . . .
For Extraverts	Action and discussion
For Introverts	Thought and reflection
For Sensing types	Clearly stated instructions and expectations
For Intuitive types	Opportunity to do it differently
For Thinking types	Logical reasoning
For Feeling types	Personal meaning
For Judging types	Results and closure
For Perceiving types	Flexibility

Collecting self information. Almost all college and university career development programs use some form of assessment to help students explore their career options. Many prefer formal assessments such as the Strong Interest Inventory, the Self-Directed Search, the Career Assessment Inventory, and the Campbell Interest and Skills Survey. Others use informal checklists, narratives, and computerized questionnaires. Some form of type assessment is commonly used as a framework for the assessment of interests, values, and abilities; some might say even a *precursor* to the assessment of interests, values, and abilities.

No single assessment can cover all of the components of career choice. Interest inventories measure likes; ability tests measure potential and demonstrated *skills*; values inventories help to prioritize work-related needs. All these are important to career satisfaction. What sets the MBTI instrument apart is that it is the best indicator we have of the core personality—the mental functions that comprise our preferences for perceiving and judging. From these preferences we can infer potential interests, values, and even ease of skill development and behaviors. The verified INFP senior, for instance, who is drawn to the arts, values creativity and independence, and is a talented painter. From MBTI preferences for perceiving and judging functions, we can also infer a potential misdirection and unique applications of type: the verified INFP sophomore, for instance, who declares an accounting major, struggles with math, and is unsure of his values. With the MBTI instrument, we have a baseline from which to evaluate all of the other assessments, each one reconfirming a verified type, adding clarity to an unverified type, or providing valuable information for the discussion of discrepancies.

As it is not appropriate to administer the MBTI instrument as a single career indicator, it is crucial to its interpretation that students understand what it does and the specific purpose for which it is being used. The Indicator, like any psychological assessment, will be most valuable when administered in an atmosphere of trust and confidentiality. If the previous steps in the counseling relationship have been pursued, students will be more likely to give honest responses than if they are unsure about the circumstances for testing. It is well worth the time spent establishing rapport, discussing career exploration strategies, and understanding what assessments can and cannot do, in order to obtain the most accurate possible indicator of true type.

The most common misunderstanding that students have about the MBTI instrument and other typical performance indicators is that they are measures of ability. Explain when administering the MBTI instrument that it gives us a picture of healthy personality preferences for exploring and making decisions and for energizing and orienting our lives—information that will be helpful in the career search itself and in identifying potentially satisfying work environments and jobs. Encourage students to respond in their most natural ways and assure them that:

- there are no right or wrong answers;
- they will receive a full interpretation of their results with the opportunity for questions and feedback; and
- their results are confidential; that no one will have access to them without their permission and that they will be given their profiles and interpretive materials to keep.

To preserve the reliability of the Indicator, the MBTI instrument, like any formal assessment, should be taken in one sitting. If the Indicator (and other assessments) are being administered on-line, be sure that these points have been covered beforehand. These guidelines will help to provide the student with the best possible information in subsequent interpretation sessions.

Interpreting the assessments. Not unlike the selection of personally motivating career counseling strategies in the previous sections, test interpretation strategies may also be individualized to tap into type-specific motivators. Some suggestions based on the MBTI core functions follow:

STs Work out interpretation details in advance.
Be concrete; stress usefulness of the information.
Anchor examples in real life experiences.
Emphasize the practical application of results.
Provide specific job title and work task resources.

SFs Work out interpretation details in advance.
Be personable and friendly; stress helpfulness of the information.
Anchor examples in personal experiences of the student.
Emphasize the personal value of the information presented.
Provide specific job title and work task resources.

NFs Work out a holistic picture for presenting the results.
Be warm and supportive; stress the uniqueness of the student.
Anchor examples in the personal framework of the student.
Emphasize creative possibilities; draw upon the imagination.
Provide motivation to explore personal and professional fulfillment.

NTs Work out a holistic picture for summarizing major points.
Be objective; stress the logic of the information.
Anchor examples in logic.
Emphasize patterns and relationships.
Provide motivation for analysis and introspection.

Whatever test interpretation strategy is selected by the counselor, it is important that students have the time and resources necessary to process the interpretive information and verify their types. This is often accomplished in a group discussion format but can also be done through the use of various checklists, booklets that introduce type (Hammer, 1993; DiTiberio and Hammer, 1993; and Myers, 1998), and other career center materials.

If the MBTI instrument has been administered in combination with other career inventories, each assessment requires its own interpretation and verification, as well as integration with the others. For logistical reasons, it is often convenient to interpret the MBTI instrument first. This works particularly well if the Indicator has been hand scored or self-scored, and the other assessments are being scored by their publishers. However, the main reason for verifying MBTI results first is that it is an indicator of *genetically predisposed personality preferences*—preferences that can subsequently be evaluated against the more socially influenced interests and values. In either case, the MBTI instrument describes characteristics of the whole person. It is only when these characteristics have been verified that we can begin to attach them to career concepts.

Counselors will first want to help students to verify the accuracy of each reported MBTI dichotomy based on general personality characteristics and then assist in translating their two preferred attitudes and two preferred mental functions into work environments, job tasks, college majors, and career fields. This process will broaden students' understanding of type and personality and expand their knowledge of work beyond their immediate experiences. The process also provides an opportunity for counselors to observe type development issues that are particular to career development. A worksheet such as "Verifying Your Type Preferences" (Kummerow, 1987) is often helpful. Table 10.3 provides selected examples of the application of type preferences to work.

Preference	General Characteristics	Preferred Work Environment	Sample Job Tasks
E	Outgoing, sociable Broad interests Active	People contact Involvement in a variety of projects at the same time Lots of things happening at once	Interviewing Helping others Public speaking
I	Reflective, introspective Deep interests Thoughtful	Quiet, time alone Concentrate on one project at a time Private space	Researching Writing Developing ideas
S	Practical Factual Experiential	Efficient, detail oriented Established procedures Hands-on	Accounting Data management Building, fixing
N	Theoretical Abstract Original	Holistic, idea-oriented Intellectual Appreciative of new ways of doing things	Solving complex problems Strategic planning Developing future possibilities
T	Logical Objective Firm-minded	Task-oriented, serious Fair, rewards based on merit Principled	Quality control Analyzing legal precedents Project management
F	Personal Subjective Compassionate	Friendly Harmonious Person-centered	Helping people with problems Working as part of a team Employee development
J	Organized Scheduled Decisive	Structured, hierarchical Goal-oriented Opportunity to finish tasks	Supervising and directing Establishing timelines Keeping projects on task
P	Adaptable Spontaneous Open to new experiences	Flexible Fun Open-ended projects	Facilitating change Trouble-shooting Crisis management

Table 10.3

For an expanded discussion of the relationship of each of the preference scales to work, it is recommended that the counselor consult "Effects of Preferences in Work Situations," a document that is included in many type publications (e.g., Hirsh and Kummerow, 1998; Myers, 1998; Myers, McCaulley, Quenk, and Hammer, 1998.)

As students are learning about themselves through the lenses of their MBTI results, the career counselor will want to be listening for evidence that the identity core of perception and judgment functions has indeed been formed. Two potential career development issues tend to arise in the career decision-making process. The first is with students who have not developed perception preferences, but who have over-used their judgment preferences. Referred to as the "vocationally foreclosed," (Bluestein, Devenis, and Kidney, 1989), these are students who decide on careers without any exploration. They are often rigidly following parental, cultural, or religious expectations, or geographic limitations; and learn as young children to screen out any perception that might disagree with their decision. They arrive at college with their majors decided and their career plans cut in stone. In a sense they are a career counselor's dream. They present no problems and rarely ask for career counseling or enroll in guidance classes. This is not an unusual occurrence with students who are focused on highly technical or medical careers. Their focus is highly rewarded and will not be interrupted unless the unexpected occurs.

Phil is an example of a foreclosed student. He is twenty-one, a first semester transfer student at a small liberal arts college. He completed his two-year degree at a community college the previous June, and chose the college for transfer because of its excellent Navy Reserve Officers' Training Corp (ROTC). He has to declare a major immediately.

Phil has always planned to be an officer in the Navy, and has been in ROTC since high school. His father and grandfather are Navy men, and his younger brother is in the Air Force. A month ago Phil was diagnosed with a twenty-five percent hearing loss and declared ineligible for the military. His reported type is ISTJ, but he is unable to verify either Sensing or Intuition. He is almost totally unable to relate to the concept of career exploration at all.

Phil required some concurrent therapy to help him to deal with what he perceived to be the loss of his future. In cooperation with the therapist, his career counselor designed a very structured exploration program for Phil, using Holland's (1995) six categories of personalities and work environments: Realistic-Investigative-Artistic-Social-Enterprising-Conventional (RIASEC). Each week he was assigned a new corner of the hexagon to experience—which included attending specific classes, observing workers, watching specific television programs, reading specific books and articles, talking to teachers and alumni in the field, and anything else that would expand his awareness of careers in each of the RIASEC categories. It was crucial to Phil's confidence that the activities be structured, the instructions be clear, and each category be discrete. At the end of each week he shared his impressions with his therapist and career counselor. Eventually he was able to determine that his interests, in addition to the military, were in the areas of applied technology and business—mostly Realistic and Conventional. He is currently evaluating the options of marine technology and accounting.

Phil's case is not too different from that of Joe, a forty-eight-year-old Chinese-American male. He has been in the banking industry for twenty-five years, and was "out-placed" six months ago. He has been unable to find suitable employment.

Joe knew that he wanted to go into banking when he was ten. His father and two uncles were both in banking, and although they were not college graduates, they advanced in their careers and enjoyed their work. Joe obtained his bachelor of science degree in finance and started right away as a bank teller with a large branch in the Midwest. He progressed rapidly through several branch manager and loan officer training positions, and in ten years was in charge of small business loans for the branch. Four years later he was offered an assistant bank manager position with a small community bank in Northern Michigan and took it, enjoying the opportunity for more responsibility with a smaller bank and wanting to get away from the growing competitive atmosphere in the larger banking industry.

Joe did well for six years. Then the bank was acquired by one of the largest commercial banking institutions in the country, and he found himself back in a loan officer position. His responsibilities were much more sales-oriented than he was accustomed to, and he became nervous and depressed. He was offered the opportunity to return to college to study computer science, but refused. College did not appeal to him at his age, he said. He was laid off shortly thereafter. Unable to find employment, he enrolled in a career exploration class for re-entry students at his local university. His assessment results reinforce his banking interests, and his options seem bleak.

Fortunately, Joe has some non-work interests that provide some starting points for the development of his Sensing perceptive process, movement out of foreclosure, and career exploration. He is active in the Air Force Reserves, and enjoys building model planes and solving mathematical puzzles. He may be able to redirect his banking experience toward civilian administrative support for the military or clerical work with the government. The important thing for Joe is that he expands his options beyond the narrow focus of foreclosure.

Joe's situation happens often in the corporate world. Companies are closed, industries are eliminated, businesses are merged, and employees are downsized. The unexpected can do nothing but disrupt the complacency of decisions made too early.

The second concern in the identity core is the opposite lack of type development from foreclosure: vocational diffusion (Bluestein, Devenis, and Kidney, 1989). Career counselors see these students more frequently than the foreclosed. They wander from major to major and counselor to counselor, always seeking the answer from someone else. They often verify ENP preferences and share little evidence of prior decision-making activity in their lives. Even when forced to declare a major, they run the other direction, seeking another "expert" to lend them their judgment. Hattie is a case in point.

Hattie is thirty years old. She dropped out of college at twenty to marry her high school sweetheart. She has three children, ages four to nine, and is faced with the probability of a divorce. She would like to return to college so that she can "make a decent living and support her children," but has no idea what to major in.

Hattie's original major was sociology, but she dropped out at the end of her sophomore year. She enjoyed all of her general education classes with the exception of an orientation to computers class, which she found very difficult. She admits that she was more interested in the social aspects of college than the academics but says that she is more serious about school now. The career center offers a two weekend career exploration group that excites her. She enrolls immediately.

Hattie's work experience is limited. She worked in a department store during high school and college, selling women's fashions and demonstrating make up. She has also been a Mary Kay representative and a teacher's aide in her daughter's kindergarten classroom. She says that she would like any kind of work that would involve people. Hattie's verified MBTI type is ENFP; her Strong Interest Inventory Profile is elevated beyond the valid range, and her RIASEC code is undifferentiated. She dropped out of the career exploration group before it was completed.

Hattie subsequently met with a career counselor who designed an approach not unlike the approach taken by Phil's counselor. Similar

RIASEC experiences were assigned but with a different focus. She was to live each week as if she had already made the decision to commit to that particular corner of the hexagon. She was to tell everyone with whom she came into contact that she had made her decision, repeating it out loud as often as possible. At the end of each week, Hattie met with her career counselor and reported on her experiences, practicing the use of her Feeling judgment as she evaluated her options. Hattie was close to risking all of her options, out of fear of committing to the wrong one. What she soon learned was that by making an initial commitment, other doors began to open to her. She decided on a psychology major with a concentration in early childhood development. As she progressed through her courses, she was given the opportunity to work on an important research project with her major professor, and eventually decided to complete a graduate degree and credential in school psychology.

Even more interesting to students than their personal identification with the four MBTI dichotomies, is the best career match for their four-letter type. It is typical for students to want to know what is the right career for them, expecting the MBTI instrument or any other inventory to give them the right answers. This can be a very delicate subject. There is evidence that each of the sixteen types appears in certain career fields more often than other types and more often than one would expect from its representation in the general population. The Center for Applications of Psychological Type (CAPT) has collected data since the mid-1970s on type and occupational membership, and published numerous tables of type frequencies within occupations (Macdaid, McCaulley, and Kainz, 1986). For example, in a sample of 673 vocational and educational counselors, ENFPs comprise 16.79%, and ESTPs only 1.04%. These data are valuable in two ways. First, we might surmise that ENFPs are found in the field of vocational and educational counseling much more often than ESTPs. Second, we can compare the percentage of ENFPs in the occupation (16.79%) with the percentage of ENFPs in the general population (8.1%) (Myers, McCaulley, Quenk, and Hammer, 1998), and see that there are more than twice as many ENFPs in the field of vocational and educational counseling than there are in the general population. This self-selection ratio of 2.07, as it is called, supports the construct that certain types are attracted to certain occupations more often than is likely to occur by chance.

The subject is a delicate one because we can see from the frequency tables that all types are found in every occupation. Different types will approach the same job in different ways and find satisfaction in different work environments and corporate cultures. The ESTP career counselor, for instance, may be working in an on-campus one-stop career center, assisting clients with job search strategies; while the ENFP career counselor may be working in the counseling center dealing with identity formation issues. They both hold the same job title, and may even have the same educational preparation, but they are attracted to different aspects of career counseling work. It is for this reason that we cannot say to students for certain, "this type goes into this field, and that type goes into that field." We *can say*, however, that if students choose to enter career fields where they are significantly under-represented, they may experience more tension while finding their niches than students whose type is more frequently represented. This situation may occur when students are experiencing a conflict between their personality, interests, and their values, such as the INFP student who is interested in the arts, but who expresses high earnings as his primary value. This student may enter the corporate world, where he is clearly under-represented, and experience a sense of "not fitting in." With guidance and a great deal of self-awareness, this same student may find his way into the arts acquisition department of a major corporation or into arts management of a large gallery. But this progression does not happen easily and usually not with the first career position. Table 10.4 lists the career fields and work characteristics that are most attractive to each of the sixteen types (Myers, McCaulley, Quenk, and Hammer, 1998, p. 294). Students who have their MBTI instruments scored for a Career Report receive a list of 208 occupations prioritized for their type (Hammer, 1992).

An alternative approach to exploring MBTI-related occupational information with students is the career-design approach used in many organizations, an advantage when students and/or counselors feel limited by the job title information available in the data banks. It also encourages student self-reliance skills, which are necessary to manage their own careers, rather than relying on outside "experts." The system is particularly applicable when type and other personality characteristics don't seem to fit (Grutter and Lund, 2000). In this system students use their MBTI results to explore the answers to four very basic questions about their career plans:

- WHO am I?
- WHY do I want to work?
- WHAT do I want to do?
- WHERE do I want to do it? (Grutter and Lund, 2000, p. 23)

The answers given below are for Donna, a nineteen-year-old sophomore who is considering career alternatives prior to declaring her major. The worksheet was designed for use in a career planning class on campus. Donna has verified her type as INTJ, although prior to this exercise she was still hesitant about her Thinking function. She has been considering law and medicine as career possibilities. Citations in italics refer to words and phrases that Donna has taken directly from commonly used published resources.

Occupational Trends of the 16 Types			
ISTJ Management Administration Law enforcement Accounting Or any other occupations where they can use their experiences and attention to detail to get the task done.	**ISFJ** Education Health care Religious settings Or any other occupations where they can draw on their experience base to personally help people in a behind-the-scenes manner.	**INFJ** Religion Counseling Teaching Arts Or any other occupations where they can facilitate emotional, intellectual, or spiritual development.	**INTJ** Scientific or technical fields Computers Law Or any other occupations where they can use their intellectual creativity and technical knowledge to conceptualize, analyze, and get the task done.
ISTP Skilled trades Technical fields Agriculture Law enforcement Military Or any other occupations where they can use their hands-on analytical work with data and things.	**ISFP** Education Business Law enforcement Or any other occupations where they can use their gentle, service-related attentiveness to detail.	**INFP** Counseling Writing Arts Or any other occupations where they can use their creativity and focus on their values.	**INTP** Scientific or technical fields Or any other occupations where they can use their solitary, objective analysis of problems based on their technical expertise.
ESTP Marketing Skilled trades Business Law enforcement Applied Technology Or any other occupations where they can use their action-oriented focus to attend to the necessary details.	**ESFP** Health care Teaching Coaching Childcare worker Skilled trades Or any other occupations where they can use their outgoing nature and enthusiasm to help people with their practical needs.	**ENFP** Counseling Teaching Religion Arts Or any other occupations where they can use creativity and communication to help foster the growth of others.	**ENTP** Science Management Technology Arts Or any other occupations where they have the opportunity to take on new challenges continually.
ESTJ Management Administration Law enforcement Or any other occupations where they can use logic and organization of the facts to get the task done.	**ESFJ** Education Health care Religion Or any other occupations where they can use their personal concern to provide service to others.	**ENFJ** Religion Arts Teaching Or any other occupations where they can help others with their emotional, intellectual, and spiritual growth.	**ENTJ** Management Leadership Or any other occupations where they can use tough-minded analysis, strategic planning, and organization to get the task done.

Table 10.4 *From* MBTI® manual: A guide to the development and use of the Myers-Briggs Type Indicator, *Third Edition (p. 290) by I. B. Myers, M. H. McCaulley, N. L. Quenk, and A. L. Hammer, 1998. Palo Alto, CA: Consulting Psychologists Press. Reprinted by permission.*

Question	MBTI Answers
WHO?	I am insightful, logical, analytical, independent, theoretical, conceptual, and creative (with ideas). (*Introduction to Type*®)
WHY?	To apply my intellectual creativity to find new ways to do things. (*Introduction to Type and Careers*®) To increase my understanding of others' ideas and relate them to my own in some practical way. (Student statement from her understanding of INTJ)
WHAT?	Solving scientific and technical problems, perhaps in the life sciences. (*Introduction to Type and Careers*)
WHERE?	For an employer that values independence and achievement, and that allows me to set my own structure. Independent consulting of some kind might be interesting later. (Student statement from her understanding of INTJ)

In addition to clarifying certain aspects of type for students, questions like these also help to integrate MBTI results with the results of other assessments. They are particularly helpful when there is a discrepancy between assessment results, as we see in the case of Donna. Donna's RIASEC code is SEI (Social-Enterprising-Investigative). Here she adds her Strong Interest Inventory answers to her chart:

Question	Strong Answers
WHO?	I am caring, helpful, responsible, cooperative, kind, understanding, idealistic, ambitious, persuasive, assertive, energetic, self-confident, optimistic, thoughtful, analytical, intellectual, independent, self-motivated, curious, original, introspective, problem-focused, insightful. (*General Occupational Themes*)
WHY?	To empower others, to lead, to research. (*General Occupational Themes*)
WHAT?	Encouraging others, teaching, training, facilitating, solving problems, leading discussions, organizing, debating ideas, leading groups, giving presentations, conducting research, collecting data, designing, analyzing, computing. (*General Occupational Themes*) My interests are similar to social science teachers, speech pathologists, human resources directors, dental hygienists, investments managers, college professors, dietitians, mathematicians, science teachers, psychologists, and sociologists. (*Occupational Scales*)
WHERE?	A work environment that is collaborative, changing, fast paced, research oriented, scholarly, and task oriented. (*General Occupational Themes*) Perhaps in a college or university, a corporate training department, a research institute or scientific foundation, a high-tech industry. (Suggested by *Basic Interest Scales*)

Several discrepancies can be seen between the two assessments. Noting Donna's type and self-descriptors such as *self-motivated, analytical, creative with ideas, introspective,* and *insightful,* her counselor suggested that she might want to take some time by herself to blend her two charts into summary statements that would include the most important concepts from each. Donna enjoyed doing the activity and came up with the summary statements that follow:

Question	Combined Answers
WHO am I?	I am analytical, insightful, logical but helpful, curious, idealistic, creative with ideas, independent, self-motivated, self-confident, introspective, problem-focused, and responsible.
WHY do I want to work?	To apply my intellectual curiosity and creativity to find, through research and practical application, new ways to empower others.
WHAT do I want to do?	Solve behavioral or social science problems by debating ideas, conducting research, teaching.
WHERE do I want to do it?	A work environment that is intellectually collaborative, but that values independent thinking. Probably a university setting, a research institute or foundation, or organizational development consulting firm.

Although NTs are often attracted to Investigative and Enterprising (Strong) work environments, it is not common for NTs to report Social interests on the Strong as Donna did (Myers, McCaulley, Quenk and Hammer, 1998, p. 309; Hammer and Kummerow, 1996). A review of the characteristics that she chose to include in her summary statements tends to reinforce an NT/Investigative pattern more than her primary Social code from the Strong instrument. For Donna this activity confirmed her Thinking judgment—the preference that was in question during her initial MBTI interpretation.

In exploring discrepancies between assessment results similar to

Donna's, it is advisable to consider possible socialized influences such as family, gender, and cultural expectations. These influences can affect both MBTI and RIASEC results, but often are more obvious on empirically derived interest inventories such as the Strong. Donna's results not only showed an NT/Social incongruity, but her Social Strong Theme was not consistent with the majority of occupations with which she showed a great deal of similarity, which were mostly Investigative. Donna shared with her counselor that she came from a very traditional family. Her mother is an elementary school music teacher, and her father is a corporate attorney. She has two older brothers, one of whom is a medical student, the other a high-school social studies teacher. She shared a very distinct memory with her counselor of a family discussion when her brother decided to enter teaching rather than law. It was clear that her parents and older brother thought that teaching was "girl's work." They were not happy with her brother's choice. In this situation, the counselor would want to explore just how much of an impact this family message has on Donna's preliminary career interests.

There are many workable systems for integrating the MBTI instrument with other career assessment results that are often more appealing to students with preferences for Sensing. Many campus career centers use interest assessments based on Holland's (1985) RIASEC categories and employ the same system for accessing career resources. It also makes sense for these centers to use the RIASEC hexagonal framework as the backdrop for characteristics that emerge from other assessments. An example might look like Sam, illustrated below.

Sam attends a large university on a full basketball scholarship. He is majoring in communications, although he did not give much thought to the choice. Sam was headed for the pros and had considered no other career options. During his junior year, a torn Achilles benched him for most of the season. At twenty-one, he realizes for the first time in his life that he has to consider career alternatives to basketball. At the university career center, his career advisor suggests that he take an MBTI instrument, a Strong Interest Inventory instrument, and the Work Values Checklist (Grutter, 2000) to help. Sam agrees, and anxiously awaits his results. He verifies his type as ESTP, and his RIASEC code as ERS (Enterprising-Realistic-Social), with high Basic Interest Scales in Sales, Public Speaking, Merchandising, Athletics, and Religious Activities. His highest values are Competition, High Earnings, Influencing Others, Moral Fulfillment, Power and Authority, Public Contact, Recognition, Risk Taking, Status, and Working with Others. To summarize Sam's results, he was given a copy of his Personal Hexagon from the Strong Interest Inventory Interpretive Report (Grutter and Hammer, 1994), and asked to "plug in" his other assessment results where he thought they belonged. His expanded hexagon looked like this:

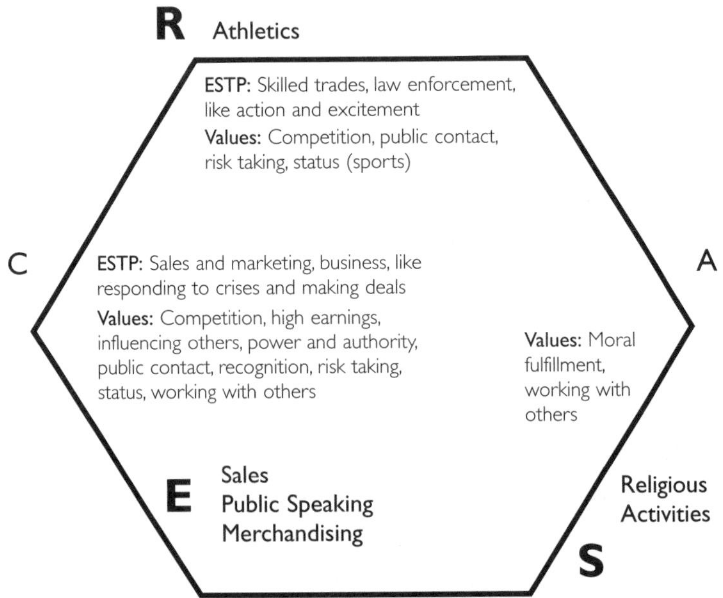

Figure 10.1

Exploring possibilities and targeting a range of alternatives. The career exploration process is not finished until possible options have been considered and evaluated. This phase of career counseling will be more difficult for some than for others. Students with preferences for Judging, for instance, may become impatient with the gathering of information and the lack of closure. Perceiving types have an easier time with the ambiguity that often comes with exploration.

Diverse types will also approach the exploration tasks quite differently, just as they are attracted to different kinds of careers. The choice of career exploration strategies can be directly related to students' preferences for Sensing or Intuition. Donna (INTJ) enjoyed a rather abstract, analytical process of designing her own unique career picture. It was only after her dominant Intuition had been engaged and challenged that she was interested in the specifics of job titles and majors. As of this writing, she was researching various fields of psychology—educational, clinical, and organizational—by reading journal articles, talking with professors, and participating in Internet discussions and listservs.

Sam (ESTP), on the other hand, wanted specifics right away. He consulted lists and charts and compiled his hexagon from very practical resources. Nor was he likely to be motivated to do the kind of research that appealed to Donna. He is much more outgoing and action oriented and would be bored by analytical investigation. Sam's advisor helped him to link his interests and personality to several majors on campus, and arranged interviews with alumni who had been successful in related fields. He added a business minor to his communications major and began exploring the possibility of sales and marketing for a major sports products manufacturer.

Dividing the sixteen types into combinations of Orientation of Energy and Perception (IS, ES, IN, EN) is also helpful for recommending exploration strategies to students. The table that follows describes the four energy-perception quadrants (Myers, McCaulley, Quenk, and Hammer, 1998, pp. 54–57), and suggests strategies for each.

	Descriptors	Career Exploration Strategies
ISs	Factual, careful, unhurried, quiet, persistent	▪ Time for reflection ▪ Specific research assignments in printed materials and on the Internet ▪ Charting information in workbooks
INs	Introspective, academic, philosophical, serious	▪ Plenty of time ▪ Reading, researching ▪ Journaling ▪ Documenting patterns and relationships between career options
ESs	Active, realistic, practical, enthusiastic, optimistic	▪ Specific activities with immediate follow-up ▪ Visiting work sites ▪ Job-shadowing ▪ Group discussions ▪ Visual depictions of work
ENs	Action-oriented, innovative, future-oriented, change agents	▪ Networking and information interviews ▪ Group discussions ▪ Talking with professors ▪ Frequent feedback ▪ Deadlines

Table 10.5

The successful exploration of career options depends on students' motivation to do it, and knowing when to use their judging function to stop. Employing strategies from the MBTI quadrants, combined with frequent follow-up activities, helps to overcome potential barriers. Hammer and Kummerow (1996) suggest obstacles for the counselor to watch for with students. Extraverts, for instance, may socialize too much and not want to do necessary research. Introverts, on the other hand, may try to do everything by themselves, and not ask others for help. Sensing types may take things too literally and see too few options. Intuitive types may not be literal enough and see too many options. Eventually possibilities and options will need to be focused as students realize that they have to make decisions.

Making a preliminary decision and developing an action plan. To complement career exploration, which draws upon the perception functions of Sensing and Intuition, career decision making draws upon the judgment functions: Thinking and Feeling. The completion of both of these career development tasks helps students find a balance between perception and judgment in their identity cores. This is the core that they will take with them through the later stages of their career development, refining it to advance their careers, broadening it to enrich their careers, and risking their less-preferred functions as they begin to disengage.

Just as the exploration phase of career counseling is more difficult for some than for others so is the decision phase. Students with preferences for Perceiving, for instance, may want to continue the exploration phase indefinitely, anxious that they will commit too soon. Judging types, on the other hand, will feel relief as they begin to reach closure.

During the previous exploration phase, students have been clarifying the criteria that are important to them in their career choices. Donna and Sam will most likely base their decisions on a logical analysis of the information that they gathered and integrated, Donna by answering four questions about herself, and Sam by filling in his personal hexagon. Earlier in the chapter we met Barbara, an INFP, who was deciding between majors in premed, special education, and art. Barbara also engaged in a rational decision-making process, but she used criteria that were more person-centered than logical, defined by her own personal value system and what is important to others.

For students, career decision making requires a thorough job of clarifying their own decision criteria, based on either Thinking or

Feeling judgment. Some students, usually those with a preference for Judging, will want to rush to this point too quickly, to reduce the anxiety of ambiguity. Others will want to continue the exploration phase indefinitely, anxious that they are committing too soon. Still others, whose judgment preference is not clear, may experience some conflict between what is logical and what is personally valuable in their careers.

The four MBTI attitude combinations, corresponding to the four rows of the type table (Myers, McCaulley, Quenk, and Hammer, 1998; DiTiberio and Hammer, 1993), are helpful in understanding how students choose careers. Each of the IJ, IP, EP, and EJ pairings may require a different kind of reassurance as they reach this point in the career process. Table 10.6

Once students are fairly clear about their identity cores and make their preliminary career decisions, they often think their career development processes are complete. The college and university career counselor will want to be available to revisit the decision.

Evaluating and revising the decision as necessary. This stage of the career counseling process takes many forms. Sometimes a student will make a decision about a major and then need to revise the decision based on new information about the job market. Almost as frequently, students will decide on career fields based on the assessments and activities completed in career exploration classes and then discover during the college experience that they have changed. Very often they grow into an awareness of their "true types" as they experience extended separation from parents and childhood influences. As this awareness grows, they need to revisit their initial career decisions and revise them accordingly.

At the decision evaluation points during college, the process is a little different from students' initial career exploration and commitment. As students' identity cores become clearer, they learn to base

	Career Decision Patterns	Assure them that . . .
IJs	▪ Carefully consider information ▪ Appear decisive, but often experience internal indecision ▪ Make decisions and then change their minds when new or better information becomes available ▪ Need next steps and long range goals	▪ They are using the best information available to them ▪ Taking responsibility for their own decision-making is the best way to make the right one
IPs	▪ "Try out" decisions internally ▪ Appear flexible, but often experience internal guilt over lack of commitment ▪ Very firm about what they believe to be important ▪ Need long range goals and next steps	▪ This decision is only one of many on their quest for more information and knowledge ▪ No decision is final
EPs	▪ Put off as long as possible while they experience more and gather more information ▪ Change their minds often ▪ Talk about a decision in order to experience it ▪ Need to commit to next steps	▪ Decisions open more doors than they close ▪ Career is a journey of discovery that unfolds with each decision
EJs	▪ Make decisions confidently and expect things to go according to plan ▪ Tend to reject information that doesn't fit into their plan ▪ Stick to their decisions once they are made ▪ The next step *is* the goal	▪ Taking charge of their own decision-making is the best way to ensure a positive outcome ▪ Slowing down to take in more information now will ultimately hasten the goal

Table 10.6

their decisions on a continuous dynamic balance between perception and judgment: experience and evaluate experience and evaluate. They learn when it is appropriate to obtain more information and how to narrow it down. Many even begin to learn when it is appropriate to use *both* kinds of perception, Sensing and Intuition, and both kinds of judgment, Thinking and Feeling. The college senior, for instance, when approaching the job market, is often learning to consider the facts about the job market, imagine how his or her major might possibly be adapted, set out a logical plan for making it happen, and then evaluate the impact of the plan on those he or she cares about.

Most colleges and universities implement career counseling frameworks such as the one discussed in this chapter in a group format, supported by individual counseling sessions as needed. Table 10.7 suggests group activities and time lines for a career guidance class or career exploration group that parallel the model.

Career Counseling Task	Group Activities	Time
▪ Establish the counseling relationship and identify career issues ▪ Determine career counseling strategies ▪ Set the career counseling contract	▪ Orientation ▪ What are the students' expectations? ▪ What are students' previous experiences with career exploration ▪ Overview of program ▪ Review objectives and assignments ▪ Introductory participation activity to introduce them to each other and generate interest in program objectives—a walking RIASEC hexagon followed by small-group discussion	First meeting 2 hours
▪ Collect self information	▪ Assign and administer assessments	Second meeting 2 hours
▪ Interpret assessments	▪ Brief overview of MBTI ▪ Group activities for each scale ▪ Living Type Table with focus on relationship of columns to career choice ▪ Complete group type table ▪ Assign MBTI booklet for individual type verification review	Third meeting 2 hours
	▪ Indicate changes on group type table following individual review and discuss reasons ▪ Interpret RIASEC and values assessments ▪ Group values clarification activity—values auction ▪ Assign worksheet for combining results	Fourth meeting 2 hours

Table 10.7 **(continued)**

The College Years

As students progress through the college experience, they are likely to seek career counseling at different points and with different issues. Career counselors cannot assume that the exploration and commitment process will be the same at each stage. The individual and group career counseling framework presented in the previous section is applicable to all of the college years if students' career issues are

Career Counseling Task	Group Activities	Time
▪ Explore possibilities and target range of alternatives	▪ Form triads and brainstorm possibilities from student worksheets ▪ Assign research with individualized type-related strategies ▪ Have each student share what they are going to investigate and how	Fifth meeting 2 hours
▪ Make a preliminary decision and develop an action plan	▪ Present a decision-making model and simulation activity ▪ Re-assign triads and have them work their options through the model ▪ Remaining in triads, have each student summarize next steps and long-range plan(s) and submit in writing ▪ Assign follow-up strategies—another group meeting or triad "buddy" system	Sixth meeting 2 hours
▪ Evaluate and revise the decision as necessary	▪ Arrange individual follow-up session with every student and revise plan accordingly	One hour per student

Table 10.7

identified and strategies are appropriately adapted. This section presents an overview of the college years and potential opportunities for career and type development.

Year	Career Development Task	Type Development Task	College Activity
Freshman	▪ Identify formation ▪ Exploration	▪ Pairing of judgment and perception functions ▪ Use of Perception	▪ Freshman orientation ▪ Initial advisement ▪ Career exploration groups
Sophomore	▪ Exploration ▪ Preliminary commitment	▪ Use of Judgment	▪ Internships, cooperative education, and volunteer experiences ▪ Career exploration groups ▪ Choice of major
Junior	▪ Commitment	▪ Balance of Judgment and Perception	▪ Internships, cooperative education, and volunteer experiences ▪ Refinement of major
Senior	▪ Career entry	▪ Use Judgement	▪ Job search and interviewing ▪ Preparation for mentoring
Re-entry	▪ Exploration ▪ Advancement/ Refinement/ Disengagement	▪ Balance of Judgment and Perception ▪ Emergence of less preferred functions	▪ Career exploration groups ▪ Individual counseling ▪ Assessment

Table 10.8

The Freshman Year—Exploration

The first year of college should be a time of exploration for students, beginning with freshman orientation and continuing through initial meetings with advisors, the completion of lower division courses, and preliminary scheduling of second-year classes. During orientation, students are often given the opportunity to take the MBTI instrument or other assessments, followed by brief interpretation sessions with counselors in preparation for later formal advisement meetings. These interpretations are often for large numbers of students and include tips on learning styles, studying, choosing majors, and considering career fields. Another way of covering the interpretation materials is for key lower-division faculty members to be trained in the assessments and include the interpretation in an early class session. This general information that is provided to students becomes the foundation for later meetings with academic advisors and career counselors. Students who have completed the tasks of identity formation prior to entering college will quickly recognize the usefulness of the MBTI instrument and be ready to evaluate their new experiences against the knowledge of who they are. They will benefit from early career exploration classes. Others will experience and explore their ways through their first year, developing their perception functions as they go. EJ types will be the most likely to want to rush to closure and want to make appointments with their advisors and counselors before the end of freshman orientation. EP types will relax in the comfort of the full year of experience ahead of them.

The Sophomore Year—Exploration and Preliminary Commitment

The second year of college usually begins the commitment stage of career development for students. It is a beneficial time to offer career exploration groups and credit guidance classes, as students are preparing to declare a major or make adjustments to decisions made the previous year. The assessment results and self-knowledge obtained in the groups can then be applied to specific subject areas for study and the selection of appropriate courses. Students' MBTI core functions are also useful in determining internship placements and volunteer experiences, which will help to narrow down their choices. The decisions of the sophomore year are exercises in judgment as students learn to prioritize objective and personal criteria.

The Junior Year—Commitment

During the third year of college, students are testing out decisions made earlier and further defining their types. They learn that life is a continual balancing of taking in new information and adjusting decisions or making new ones. Earlier commitments to majors may be revised to include new information obtained during internships and volunteer experiences, from new classes, and from increased knowledge of self and the job market. Many times it is the addition of an employable minor to a more academic major. For some, a complete change may be warranted. This possibility can be extremely stressful for some types, particularly EJs, who tend to view their decisions as irrevocable. Counselors may not even be aware that EJs are questioning earlier decisions, unless adequate steps for follow-up are implemented after initial meetings. Young EJs are more likely to respond to the possibility of negative consequences than they are to new information (Myers, McCaulley, Quenk and Hammer, 1998) and, therefore, may require a very directive approach to changing their direction.

The Senior Year—Career Entry

During the last year of college, students should be preparing to apply their previous experiences and decision making to the beginning of their professional careers. Some arrive at college and university career centers ready to sign up for on-campus interviews and off-campus job searches, but many others do not. Career centers need to be prepared to meet seniors' career development needs at all levels—from identity formation, to exploration, to commitment, to career entry. Career groups might include assessment and self-information (formation), an overview of the job market and employment trends (exploration), career focus sessions (commitment), and job search and interviewing skills. No one is more important in this "issue sorting" process than the front-line career center staff—often receptionists, career technicians, and on-call counselors and advisors. For students in their senior years, all of the first steps in the career counseling process, establishing rapport and identifying issues and barriers, often take place at the career center counter when they are signing up for groups, interviews, and counseling and assessment appointments. For this purpose, a working knowledge of the MBTI instrument and career development is as vital for these staff members as it is for professional career counselors.

For seniors who are ready to begin searching for their first professional positions, Hammer and Kummerow (1996, reproducible master 9) suggest these type-related pointers among others:

Extraverts may	Not be thorough enough in their preparation for interviews
	Need to pause and think before talking
Introverts may	Be slow to "warm up" in interviews
	Over think questions and appear too serious

Sensors may	Take interview questions too literally Have trouble responding to hypothetical situations
Intuitives may	Make factual errors Not focus on the question being asked
Thinkers may	Overanalyze interview questions Be too direct in stating opinions
Feelers may	Be easily discouraged and feel rejected Be hesitant in stating skills and competencies
Judgers may	Become impatient with job search process and commit too soon
Perceivers may	Experience information overload and miss out on opportunities

Adapted from the Strong *and MBTI Career Development Guide by J. M. Kummerow and A. L. Hammer,*

The senior year is also an appropriate time to introduce students to educational and career mentoring, teaching them how to assist in the exploration process of younger students, and new graduates when they later become seasoned alumni. Liaison relationships between career development centers and university alumni associations can provide "experts" who will share their experiences with newly graduating seniors and serve as role models for future experienced workers to return to their campuses and mentor the next generation preparing for career entry.

The Re-entry Years—The Process Begins Again

One of the factors that has changed the face of higher education the most in the past two decades is the concept of life-long learning. There are several potential scenarios for older students, each one requiring a careful assessment of his or her stage of career development, issues, and barriers. They include students who:

- "Stop out" of formal education for a few years to test out their career commitments
- Find college irrelevant and leave for paid employment
- Are encouraged by their employers to broaden their skills and/or earn higher degrees
- Want to enrich their work and/or lives by exploring new interests and skills
- Return to education after raising a family
- Want to change careers entirely
- Attend college indefinitely for their own personal growth and love of learning

For these students, special adult re-entry career exploration groups are particularly necessary and helpful, especially when groups are brought together around common concerns such as older students updating technical skills, women re-entering the work force, outplacement, and life enrichment.

Individual sessions with career counselors who specialize in returning students are also vital. The anecdotes of re-entry students who first really "discover" themselves when they are introduced to the MBTI instrument are infinite: The INFP hospital admitting clerk who never finished college and has been working out of her less-preferred functions for twenty years; the ESFP engineer who is out placed during a corporate downsizing, facing up to ten years of depression, and newly excited about the possibility of going into sales; the ENTJ homemaker who had never before considered that she was qualified to earn a living. These kinds of "discoveries" do not happen accidentally. They require extended interpretive sessions and the opportunity to "try out" newly revealed identities, often in safe groups and classes with others like themselves.

Summary

The MBTI instrument is at the core of student career development. In the hands of qualified users, the Indicator can provide the information and potential understanding that are necessary for successful identity formation, career exploration, career decision making and commitment, as well as addressing many later-life career development issues. The career counseling framework, the student situations, and the type-related techniques presented here are meant to serve as reminders of the immense value of type understanding at all stages of life, particularly for young people as they begin their careers. But they are also meant to serve as a beginning for counselors who want to deepen their knowledge of type beyond the simplistic method of matching type with job titles and career fields. Career counseling is, indeed, "real" counseling, and each student deserves the motivation and support unique to his or her developmental needs and type preferences.

References

Bluestein, D. L., and D. Noumair (1996). Self and identity in career development: Implications for theory and practice. *Journal of Counseling Psychology*, 74(5), 433–441.

Bluestein, D. L., L. I. Devenis, and B. A. Kidney (1989). Relationship between the identity formation process and career development. *Journal of Counseling Psychology*, 36(2), 196–202.

Brown, D. and L. Brooks. (1991). *Career counseling techniques.* Boston: Allyn and Bacon.

Campbell, D. (1992). Campbell Interest and Skill Survey. Minneapolis: National Computer Systems.

DiTiberio, J. K. and A. L. Hammer (1993) *Introduction to type in college.* Palo Alto, CA: Consulting Psychologists Press.

Golden, V. J. and J. A. Provost. (1987). The MBTI and career development. In *Applications of the Myers-Briggs Type Indicator in higher education* (pp. 151–180). Palo Alto, CA: Consulting Psychologists Press.

Grutter, J. (2000). Developmental career counseling. In J.M. Kummerow (Ed.), *New directions in career planning and the workplace* (pp. 273–306). Palo Alto, CA: Davies-Black.

Grutter, J. (1990). The MBTI and super's styles of career "maintenance." *Career Planning and Adult Development Journal*, 6, 13–17.

Grutter, J. and A. L. Hammer. (1994). *Strong Interest Inventory Interpretive Report.* Palo Alto: Consulting Psychologists Press.

Grutter, J. and S. L. Lund. (2000). *Making it in today's organizations using the Strong and the MBTI facilitator's guide.* Palo Alto, CA: Consulting Psychologists Press.

Hammer, A. L. (1992). *MBTI career report.* Palo Alto: Consulting Psychologists Press.

———. (1993). *Introduction to type and careers.* Palo Alto: Consulting Psychologists Press.

Hammer, A. L. and Kummerow, J. M. (1996). *Strong and MBTI career development guide.* Palo Alto, CA: Consulting Psychologists Press.

Hammer, A. L. and G. P. Macdaid. (1992). *MBTI career report manual.* Palo Alto: Consulting Psychologists Press.

Hirsh, S. K. and J. M. Kummerow (1998). *Introduction to type in organizations.* Palo Alto: Consulting Psychologists Press.

Holland, J. L. (1959). A theory of vocational choice. *Journal of Counseling Psychology*, 6, 35–45.

———. (1985). *Making vocational choices: A theory of vocational personalities and work environments.* Englewood Cliffs, NJ: Prentice-Hall.

———. (1994). *The self-directed search.* Odessa, FL: Psychological Assessment Resources

Johansson, C. B. (1993). *Career Assessment Inventory.* Minneapolis: National Computer Systems.

Kummerow, J. M. (1987). Verifying your type preferences. Gainesville, FL: Center for Applications of Psychological Type.

Macdaid, G. P., M. H. McCaulley, and R. I. Kainz. (1986). *Atlas of type tables.* Gainesville, FL: Center for Applications of Psychological Type, Inc.

McDaniels, C. M. and N. C. Gysbers. (1992). *Counseling for career development.* San Francisco: Jossey-Bass Publishers, Inc.

Myers, I. B. with L. K. Kirby and K. D. Myers (1998) *Introduction to type.* (6th ed). Palo Alto, CA: Consulting Psychologists Press.

Myers, I. B., M. H. McCaulley, N. L. Quenk, and A. L. Hammer. (1998). *MBTI manual: A guide to the development and use of the Myers-Briggs Type Indicator* (3rd ed.). Palo Alto: Consulting Psychologists Press.

Parsons. F. (1989). *Choosing a vocation.* Boston: Houghton Mifflin, 1909.

Savickas, M. L. and W. B. Walsh. (1996). *Handbook of career counseling theory and practice.* Palo Alto, CA: Davies Black.

Sharf, R. S. (1997). *Applying career development theory to counseling.* Pacific Grove, CA: Brooks/Cole.

Strong Interest Inventory (1994). Palo Alto, CA: Consulting Psychologists Press.

Super, D. E. (1994). A life-span, life-space perspective on congruence. In M. L. Savickas and R. W. Lent (Eds.), *Convergence in Career Development Theories* (pp. 63–74). Palo Alto, CA: Consulting Psychologists Press.

Super, D. E. (1957). *The psychology of careers.* New York: Harper and Row.

Williamson, E. G. (1937). *Student personnel work.* New York: McGraw-Hill.

Williamson, E. G. (1939). *How to counsel students.* New York: McGraw-Hill

Yost, E. B. and Corbishley, M. A. (1987). *Career counseling: A psychological approach.* San Francisco: Jossey-Bass Publishers, Inc.

Zunker, V. G. (1994). *Career counseling: Applied concepts of life planning.* Pacific Grove, CA: Brooks/Cole.

[1] See chapter 1 for a full discussion of type development and student development.

[2] Examples include Sharf, 1997; Savickas and Walsh, 1996; Zunker, 1994; McDaniels and Gysbers, 1992; Brown and Brooks, 1991; Golden and Provost, 1987; and Yost and Corbishley, 1987.

[3] For a full discussion of using the MBTI instrument in academic advisement, see chapter 7.

CHAPTER 11

Psychological Counseling

JUDITH A. PROVOST

Within colleges and universities, there has been an increasing use of the Myers-Briggs Type Indicator® instrument by counseling professionals. Use by counselors and counseling centers includes outreach, education, consultation, research, prevention, and treatment or intervention. The term *counselor* is used here in the generic sense to include all professionals involved in psychological counseling. Many counselors work within counseling centers, but some are found in less traditional organizational divisions within institutions of higher education. Although organizational structures suggest differing strategies for setting up and implementing programs using the MBTI® instrument, the basic processes and programs described here have relevance, no matter what the institutional structure.

This chapter begins by showing how the MBTI instrument fits within the counseling process and continues with a detailed description of one counseling office's program. Counselors should get an overview of the range of MBTI uses and hopefully be stimulated to further applications. Within the counseling process, the MBTI instrument is used as a tool for establishing rapport, understanding a variety of student problems, setting goals for counseling, and designing interventions or strategies. The description of a comprehensive program using the MBTI instrument, developed by the author while director of Personal Counseling at Rollins College, includes initiation of the program, procedures for administration and interpretation, identification of potential adjustment concerns through early outreach, developmental considerations, and MBTI uses beyond that of direct counseling.

The MBTI Instrument as a Conceptual Framework

The MBTI assessment tool provides a language for student and counselor to discuss strengths and preferences for dealing with the world and one's inner life, less-preferred or weaker areas, communication patterns, and so forth. If the concepts are explained accurately and ethically, this language is an objective or neutral one. The objectivity of the Indicator gives both parties a comfortable reference point from which to look at the student's present life and personal development. These concepts can be referred to throughout the course of counseling. Students will use MBTI concepts to varying degrees depending on their type and priorities. For example, Intuitive types generally want to work with the theory more extensively than the Sensing types.

The MBTI instrument validates the individual. When students already have a fairly good sense of who they are, their MBTI results are often experienced as a triumphant restatement of themselves. When students are somewhat unclear about themselves, the MBTI instrument provides a language to explore aspects of themselves that previously were too elusive to name. The Indicator can also validate students' tentative life decisions. If the MBTI instrument is interpreted properly, students invariably go away feeling better about themselves, whether they have further counseling sessions or not.

The Indicator is a conceptual framework that makes a useful map of individual type development. This map indicates preferred and least-preferred functions and the probable sequence of function development. Therefore, this map can guide counselors in assessing functioning and in setting counseling goals consistent with where students are developmentally and with where they are likely to go in their future development.

Multiple Uses in Counseling and Therapy

One of the most valuable applications of type is in counseling new students about adjustment to college. This topic is explored later under the discussion of outreach to freshmen. Another frequent application is self-exploration and personal growth through individual counseling. Students are eager for self-knowledge, and the MBTI instrument is one tool to assist in this process.

Understanding communication patterns of various types is valuable in relationship counseling. Intimacy is one of the critical developmental tasks of the traditional student. Counseling frequently focuses on relationships with roommates, boy or girlfriends, close friends, and groups such as one's sorority or fraternity, as well as with family members. A student's type can be discussed in relation to family conflicts and communication patterns. Often students' families are too distant to participate in family counseling, but through use of *Introduction to Type®* (Myers, 1987), *Please Understand Me* (Keirsey and Bates, 1984), other materials, and discussions, students may be able to estimate family members' types. Knowing there are sixteen different types with different ways of communicating and approaching issues is a revelation to most young people. Students are often locked into struggles with their families for independence and for their own identities. They are relieved and encouraged by these insights about type. Even when students can't be certain what types their families are, they often acquire a new sensitivity and respect for personality differences. They may be able to look at emotional conflicts in a more objective way. The MBTI instrument thus becomes a tool to improve communication, with the counselor serving as coach and guide.

Counselors employ the Indicator when helping students with self-management. Many students seek help in managing their time and learning to set priorities. They also may lack confidence in making decisions for themselves and need assistance in developing decision-making skills. *Introduction to Type* (Myers, 1998) has a clear description of the importance of using all four functions in making decisions. Counselors can use this description and other strategies based on MBTI concepts to teach this skill. Procrastination and work paralysis, when the student can't function because of fear that the outcome will not be perfect, are other counseling problems on which the MBTI instrument can shed some light on the individual's personality dynamics.

Another group of students who seek counseling do so not because of college adjustment problems per se, but because of emotional problems of a more serious nature. Depression, severe anxiety, tension, and acute crises are frequently seen problems. Knowing a student's type suggests possible personality dynamics and strengths that may be engaged by the counselor in the therapeutic process. Type can also suggest counseling approaches and language that may be effective in working with clients.

The term *language* here means word choice, use of metaphor, selection of images and content, and style of speaking. For example, an ESTJ client will relate better to a concrete and concise description of the counseling process with specific examples of what the counselor will do and specified outcomes. An INFP client might be put off by such language and prefer a description with a broader, more abstract picture of what might be accomplished in counseling.

Type may suggest areas to probe to determine underlying

problems; for example, exploring the quality of a young depressed INTP's intimate relationships. An INTP might not initially reveal relationship concerns; these deeper concerns might not be admitted to the counselor until after many sessions. Certain types are more likely to present specific behaviors when under emotional stress. For example, the EPs may become very excitable and even hysterical in behavior. Space does not permit a more detailed discussion of types and presenting problems in psychotherapy, nor is there a need to duplicate existing materials in print. The chapter references cite these additional resources.

The Counseling Process

Myers-Briggs Type Indicator concepts should be brought into the counseling process at the appropriate time, in accordance with a student's needs and readiness. Unless a student has made an appointment expressly to learn about the Indicator, the first counseling session (in the author's practice) is usually for establishing rapport, gathering information about why the student has sought counseling at this time, and beginning to set some counseling goals. The MBTI instrument is not usually introduced until the second or even later sessions, when it fits into the counseling process. Counselors may have access to students' scores from previous group administration, yet not introduce the MBTI instrument explicitly in counseling. For example, when a student presents a crisis with no expressed interest in counseling beyond solving his or her immediate problem, the counselor may formulate hunches about the student's coping style and possible interventions without explicit mention of the Indicator. Students in crisis or in a fragile state of mind are not asked to take the MBTI instrument; however, later when they have stabilized, they may take the MBTI instrument if it seems relevant to the counseling process.

If counselors refer to MBTI results obtained several years earlier, they should keep in mind that some students will report change in one or more preferences during their college years. The *MBTI® Manual* (Myers and McCaulley, 1985, 1998) gives test-retest reliabilities for the four scales and also reports various studies of how many preferences subjects changed over varying periods of time.

Counselors should explore with students, especially those who had reported slight or moderate preferences, whether they see themselves as the type they reported several years earlier. The basic strategies for establishing true type are discussed in the *Manual* and may be employed in these situations.

The sixteen types have varying expectations about counseling. Goals and duration of counseling vary also. The following are examples of these varying expectations from the author's clinical experience:

- The SJs often expect direct intervention and advice from the counselor, who is perceived as the authority and expert. They usually want to complete counseling in a few sessions, unless there is a long-term problem such as an ISFJ with chronic depression. The ESJs are most likely to expect concrete suggestions and a brisk pace.

- The INPs frequently are vague in their expectations and goals but hope that counselors will be patient and take time to help them articulate their thoughts. Instead of looking to the counselor as an authority, they tend to need a guide to help them search out the internal and external meanings. They may be put off by a counselor who is too directive.

- The NTs tend to watch for signs of competence in the counselor before trusting the relationship. They are skeptical of the counseling process unless the counselor can speak their language and explain the process in terms of logic and expertise.

Many other observations can be made; the point is that different types tend to have different attitudes and expectations about counseling, no matter what the presenting problem. Counselors must make their best efforts to join with students and talk the language of their types, almost as if the counselor acts like each student's type. This joining facilitates rapport and trust and assures that counseling goals are appropriate to the student, not just to the counselor. Counselors, and other helping professionals as well, have a built-in bias about what being helpful is all about because of their own types. ENFP counselors tend to talk about counseling in terms of change, self-actualization, connecting with people, etc. The MBTI instrument is a good reminder to counselors that their vision of the world is not the only vision. Counselors must guard against imposing their standards of mental health and positive outcomes on their clients. On the other hand, once counselors have joined with students and counseling is progressing, counselors can gradually pull back somewhat to their own styles and encourage students to experiment with their less-preferred functions. When the counselor and student are very different in their preference, the student may become discouraged about changing in the direction suggested by the counselor. The counselor's behavior may seem too far from where the student is, too far to reach. Counselors need to remember this in modeling behaviors such as assertiveness with clients very different from themselves.

The basic principle remains: start with the client's strengths and work from there. After a few small successes, counselors can then begin to challenge and encourage use of the other functions, working toward a goal of balance, in the complimentary sense, between the dominant and auxiliary, and ability to use the function necessary in a given situation. Of course, the latter goal is one that will probably extend long past the counseling experience and perhaps well into middle age.

Multicultural Considerations

Cautions about assuming that counselors' worldviews are the same as those of clients particularly apply when working with clients who are different culturally from their counselors. Multicultural counseling is a prominent movement within the field that urges counselors to be aware of differences that may be present because of socioeconomic, ethnic, sexual orientation, gender, regional, religious, and other cultural factors. Many counselor-educators believe that all counseling is multicultural because of personality and background differences. Furthermore, clients' culture may influence variations on the usual way type preferences are expressed. For example, an Asian-American client with a preference for Extraversion may look more like an Introvert in many situations. Occasionally clients may report out a type different from what they later identify as their actual types because of pressure from the dominant culture. For instance, an African-American student client in a predominantly White school may report type as ESTJ, while disclosing that in the client's own community the client would identify as ESFP. Other considerations besides culture pressure are degree of acculturation, language, and context. The *Manual* (Myers, McCaulley, Quenk and Hammer, 1998) has an excellent chapter on multicultural issues and type.

Often the MBTI instrument may be a bridge between counselor and client when they are culturally different. Clients' types give clues as to ways in which counselors can begin to connect with clients, mirroring some of their styles in the counseling process. If both share one or several MBTI preferences, this may provide a common ground despite significant cultural differences. Where clients' identified types are different from their family members' types and different from the expected way of being within their culture, the MBTI instrument can be an explanatory tool to use in working through tensions between the family and the client.

Examples of Counseling Strategies and Type

College students, especially Intuitive types, tend to be overly intellectual and prone to rationalization. Often they try to keep counseling interaction on this level. Therefore, it can be quite productive to use some noncognitive and perhaps nonverbal interventions with them, after trust has developed. Gestalt and body work are examples of interventions that may serve to cut through the layer of intellectualization.

Feeling types may need to learn how to use their Thinking function to balance their reactions and decisions. Rational Emotive Behavior Therapy can offer them a model for developing their Thinking. Again, cautiously introduce these interventions, or the student will be turned off by the "cold, impersonal approach."

Many students have difficulty making decisions and using their Thinking and Feeling judgment. Values clarification strategies; guided imagery, such as visualizing "the wise old one who knows"; Gendlin's (1981) focusing technique for inner awareness; and writing assignments are examples of ways to help students access their Thinking and/or Feeling. Counselors should keep in mind whether the function they are trying to encourage is extraverted or introverted, because these functions work differently in these two attitudes. Therefore, the strategies would vary as well. For example, journal writing would be a useful way for a busy ENFP to access the auxiliary introverted Feeling.

The student trying to develop extraverted Feeling might prefer some activity involving others in some helpful or expressive way or an "assignment" to request feedback from specific individuals.

A majority of counselors are Intuitive types (Myers and McCaulley, 1985) and often favor strategies requiring abstraction and imagination, such as guided fantasy, dream interpretation, and metaphor. When working with Sensing students, counselors should introduce their favorite strategies cautiously, so as not to create more confusion in the student. An ISTJ, for example, has a dominant and introverted Sensing function, and the least-preferred function is Intuition. Using guided imagery to help this student work through some difficult problem might increase confusion and instability because the imagery demands use of the least-preferred function. That function might be quite primitive and emerge in a frightening or exaggerated way. Introverted Sensing is a fascinating and difficult function for Intuitives to grasp (this is especially so for extraverted Intuitives). ISJs and ESJs may respond well to guided imagery that is more carefully structured with concrete, sequential instructions so that the student plays out sensory impressions and memories like a projector showing an internal film. This can be a rich experience for the student, yet one where the richness cannot be captured through verbalization. Counselors need to respect the nonverbal quality of the client's experience and not assume that the lack of verbal production indicates a minimal response to the intervention.

In summary, counselors need a repertoire of strategies to work effectively with a variety of students and to stretch students to use not only their favorite function but their less-preferred ones as well. Also counselors need to be alert to the bias of their own type in the selection of counseling goals and strategies.

Suggested Research about Counseling and Type

Numerous studies can be designed to examine aspects of the counseling process, student adjustment and mental health, and type. These projects usually require institutional support and certainly necessitate preservation of students' confidentiality. The following are some basic research questions other counselor-researchers have begun to address, but which need further study and replication.

- Is there a relationship between type and presenting a problem?
- Is there a relationship between type and number of sessions seen for counseling?
- Are certain interventions preferred and more effective with certain types?
- Is there a relationship between type and outcomes, perceived and actual, of counseling?
- Do students' types influence their selection of specific counselors and/or other student service assistance?

One Comprehensive Program Using the MBTI Instrument

The following pages will describe the comprehensive program for using the MBTI instrument developed by the author through the personal counseling office at a private, residential, four-year, liberal arts college in Winter Park, Florida. Rollins College has an approximate enrollment of 1400 and a traditional student body (ages 17–22). The positive nature of the Indicator and its focus on preferred ways of functioning make the Indicator a versatile tool for education about individual differences, personal and academic adjustment, and counseling intervention.

Beginning a Program for All Entering Students

After using the MBTI instrument with individual students in personal and career counseling for a number of years, it became apparent that a more systematic administration of the Indicator would be valuable to the college. The frequency of types on the campus and within certain subgroups would then be known. Faculty and staff were not likely to attempt changes in the campus environment without data such as type distributions of specific student groups. There was campus-wide concern about reducing the attrition rate and identifying factors influencing students' withdrawal from the college. Previous attrition research had focused on traditional variables, such as SAT scores, distance from home, and nature of the high school attended. None had examined personality factors; the MBTI instrument might identify significant new variables. Furthermore, the counseling office could operate more effectively if it had students' MBTI results on file *before* students requested counseling.

This background illustrates the attitude and prevailing climate in which the proposal was made to administer the MBTI instrument to the entering class during orientation week. The proposal necessitated a budget increase to finance the MBTI materials and scoring. The proposal also necessitated some accommodation in the scheduling of orientation activities. The proposal was made to the chief student affairs officer and to the president of the college. This expanded use of the MBTI instrument was presented as a way to determine what, if any, personality factors influenced attrition patterns. If research revealed a relationship between type patterns and attrition, counselors and other college staff could institute preventive measures. The well-documented uses of the MBTI tool for improving reading and study skills and guiding career decisions were emphasized. At this writing, the MBTI instrument has been administered to new students for about twenty years.

Other professionals seeking to administer the MBTI instrument to a student body should determine carefully their institution's needs and word their proposals to address those needs. It is useful to include some research data from other institutions demonstrating the validity of the MBTI approach.

Procedures for Administration of the MBTI Instrument

Orientation week was chosen for new students to take the MBTI instrument because there is no other time when the whole class is easily convened. Plans to convene the class later in the semester would result in a much lower percentage of participation. The instrument is given along with several short placement tests and a national college survey. The MBTI Form F was used the first few years, and Form G in subsequent years. About forty-five minutes is allowed for answering the questions. Students may take longer if needed.

In two large auditoriums, the counselors introduce the counseling services and the MBTI concepts. Students are told that information from the Indicator can be helpful to them in adjusting to college, developing appropriate study techniques, selecting courses and an academic major, exploring careers, and gaining more knowledge about themselves. Students are told that their results will be released only to them and will be kept on file in the counseling office until such time as they make appointments to go over their results. These two points, the usefulness of the information and the confidentiality of results, are important to stress in obtaining full cooperation. The standardized instructions on the question booklet are reviewed.

Some students miss this group administration. Transfer students and others take the MBTI instrument on an individual basis as needed through the counseling or career and placement offices. Some students want to retake the Indicator during their four years at the college.

These answer sheets are hand-scored, in contrast to the group sheets which are computer scored.

Procedures for Interpretation

The counseling office sends out a memo to each student after the MBTI instrument has been computer scored. The memos invite students to make appointments at their convenience to learn their results. They are told that their results will be held on file in the counseling office while they are students at the college. The usefulness of MBTI information is restated in the memo. A similar memo is sent to all faculty advisors to inform them that their advisees may benefit from making an appointment with the counseling office to review their results. Advisors may find this step especially helpful in working with advisees with academic difficulties or questions about career directions. Several other key student services staff are notified when the scores are available: those in the academic skills center, career and placement center, and academic advising. This outreach increases the visibility of the counseling office to the faculty and other student personnel and encourages referrals.

During the first two months after freshmen receive the memo, appointment requests are very heavy, then taper off. The counseling staff is usually able to provide individual interpretation time of approximately 45 minutes. At the very busy times students are given the choice of joining up to three other students in receiving their results. This small group obviously cuts down on individual time, but is a realistic way to deal with peak demand. The basic concepts are explained to the small group and a few minutes spent on each computer printout. Students are told that they can return for individual follow-up appointments if they would like a more personal and in-depth discussion. Students do not object to this approach and seem to enjoy this informal way to be with several other new students.

Many students do not seek their results until the sophomore year when there is more pressure to declare a major and a career direction. Some wait until their senior year, hoping their MBTI results may give them some idea about how to conduct a job search. Although it may sound like an onerous task to offer interpretation to all first year students, in reality a large percentage will not make appointments immediately.

Those who do make appointments early in their college career often have a need to make this contact with the counseling office or other student services. There may be hidden agendas or needs beyond obtaining results. Counselors can take the opportunity to explore this possibility. These interpretation appointments give new students a legitimate reason for meeting with a counselor. Appointments are voluntary, not compulsory.

Because the MBTI instrument gives students an easy reason for scheduling an appointment with a counselor, the MBTI program is an excellent outreach device. Another aspect of the outreach is the opportunity to explain the various student services during the appointment. At Rollins this means clarifying the role of personal counselors and giving examples of how they work with students. Other services emphasized are the learning and study skills center, career and placement services, and faculty advisors. Additional college resources can be identified as appropriate. After years of use with college students, counselors become practiced in stressing certain services and information for different MBTI types. Certain types are more likely to have difficulties in given areas, and these can be checked out directly or indirectly as appropriate. These difficulties are described in the following section.

Identifying Potential Adjustment Concerns in New Students

Student development literature describes the psychological, social, and academic tasks of college students, 17–22 years of age. These tasks will differ for the nontraditional, older students. Chapter 1 highlighted developmental issues that provide a context for using the MBTI instrument with college students. There is variation within this developmental pattern, and some of this variation can be explained by personality type differences. After years of observing types on a residential campus and comparing observations with those of counselors on other campuses, the author has observed some general tendencies among types. The term *general tendencies* is used to mean a set of behaviors more likely to be seen in a specific type than in others, but the term does not mean that certain types will have certain difficulties. Knowing some of these tendencies towards specific adjustment concerns can signal areas to explore in initial counseling sessions, information and resources to offer students, and directions for preventive programming. Some observations for each of the sixteen types follow, many of which may be more accurate for the traditional than the older student.

ISTJ

The ISTJs (and ESTJs) are less frequently seen for counseling than many of the other types. New students with ISTJ preferences who do seek counseling are often concerned about academic performance. Some have expressed perfectionist attitudes about the need to get all *A*s to consider themselves successful. Others have been extremely frustrated that study techniques employed in high school do not bring desired results with the more abstract, theoretical material in college, where evaluation often is done with papers and essay tests. Most ISTJs report being more comfortable with objective tests and homework problems. These students may study most of the night, memorizing material and painstakingly outlining the text. They study slowly and methodically; they often complain of insufficient time to handle a full course load and be as thorough as they feel they need to be. Those who do not seek counseling have probably adapted their style to the college's requirements, but may need assistance in learning new study approaches and techniques for handling essay tests. The college writing center can provide support to students like these ISTJs who may be anxious about writing papers. Counseling may also include cognitive restructuring of some of the perfectionist self-talk, such as, "I am a failure if I don't get all *A*s."

ISTP

The ISTPs who come to the counseling office in their first year usually do so in crisis. They express initial concerns about making new friends and fitting in. In counseling they often report difficulty managing their time, getting homework done, handling semester-long assignments, and reading abstract material. They tend to be easily distracted by outside events and other students. This type is one of several that seem to have more difficulty in the four-year liberal arts setting. Those who receive early assistance with time management and study skills and emotional support during the transition to college seem to do better. They also express a need for recreational and social activities on an informal scale and may shy away from large, highly organized student activities and events. Meaningful extracurricular activities seem crucial to their social adjustment to college.

ESTP

Few ESTPs seek counseling. Some are very curious about their MBTI results because of questions about career direction. For example, after half a term in college, several premed students began questioning whether they had the stamina and self-discipline to handle the heavy science and math load. They found the MBTI instrument a helpful framework for exploring their strengths and their goals. ESTPs may also need help with time management and study skills. If they receive some help with goal setting, immediate and long range, they are more likely to be successful in college.

ESTJ

Like the other ST types, ESTJs are not frequently seen for counseling. They do welcome the MBTI information as part of their need to set career and academic goals early in their college careers. Occasionally they are too hasty in formulating these goals without first sampling a variety of courses and learning more about the work world. They tend to be methodical in their studies, like the ISTJs, but usually work faster than the ISTJs. Some help in adjusting to abstract material, written papers, and essay tests may be needed.

ISFJ

Many ISFJs come to the counseling office during their first year. They explicitly name concerns about adjusting to the academic life and the separation from home and friends. They, along with the ESFJs, seem to express homesickness more frequently than the other types. Many ISFJs seen in counseling are nonassertive, dependent, and unsure of themselves. These students compare themselves unfavorably with their classmates, thinking they may be "too dumb" to be there. They often have trouble communicating their likes and dislikes to roommates. They seem to struggle more than many of the other types with the transition from dependence to independence. They may be looking for a surrogate parent in the counselor or upper-class resident aide. Emotional support, education about the transition phase (especially focused on moving toward independence), assertiveness training, and other such interventions are well received by these students who are highly motivated to become more comfortable with themselves at college. Since their study approaches tend to be as slow and methodical as the ISTJs, they may need some guidance with study techniques, especially with reading.

ISFP

ISFPs new to college may have difficulty adjusting to the academic load. Their new friendships and social activities usually take precedence over studying. A comfortable social environment is a top priority before they are willing to invest in academic work. Like the ISTPs, they often need assistance with time management and study skills. They may be alienated by NT professors who do not demonstrate personal warmth and interest. Their motivations are personal; for example, they may be more concerned about failing because of the great disappointment they will cause their parents than from any desire to achieve for themselves intellectually. Counselors can help them identify valid motivators for achieving in college. Counselors can also assist them to select courses with content of personal significance to them and taught by professors who will stimulate them through a personal approach.

ESFP

Few ESFPs make appointments during the first term to learn their MBTI results or for personal counseling. Many young ESFPs on campus have told the author that when they feel "down," they go do something to cheer themselves up or talk to a friend. They don't often consider counseling as a primary solution. These students seem to rely primarily on friends for advice about academics and problems of living. Sometimes professors, frequently Feeling types, have great impact in a mentor or helper role. The ESFPs who do come for counseling during the first year usually are struggling with some relationship concern, family or boy or girlfriend. They have difficulty focusing on schoolwork when their relationships are not in harmony. Although many young ESFP students could probably use some techniques in study and time management, their interests and motivations often seem more focused on social adjustment and involvement. They feel they can "get by" academically and generally have confidence that "things will turn out fine."

ESFJ

More ESFJs than ESFPs use the counseling office. They seem to take their "responsibilities" as students more seriously and therefore are more quick to want to "fix" problems and improve their position than the ESFPs. Many of their initial concerns at college involve social adjustment. Getting along with roommates and friends and working out conflicts are essential. Many may struggle overtly with letting go of family and the security of home. They need to ventilate feelings about home and friends left behind and receive support for their feelings. They respond well to information about the developmental stage of leaving home. They may also wish some guidance on course selection and modifying study techniques. Because they tend to be conscientious about doing the best work they can, they can become very frustrated if they don't do as well as they "should" do. A predominance of lecture and abstract courses the first few terms of college can discourage the ESFJ learner. A balanced course load, with some discussion classes and personally meaningful material, is more compatible with the ESFJ learning style.

INFJ

Some general patterns seem to hold for all the IN types. They use the counseling office more than the other types. Their concerns tend to certain themes, with some variation because of the other two preferences. New students with IN preferences are likely to express a lot of doubt about who they are, why they are at college, whether this is the right college for them, whether they will ever find a meaningful relationship with the opposite sex, and so on.

The inner world of INFJs is rich and complex because of dominant introverted Intuition. They need opportunity to express that inner world to a supportive, interested counselor; this may be their first experience in articulating that inner world. Through expression, INFJs can hear and modify any distortions or inner constructions not founded in reality.

In counseling, INFJ males raised with traditional gender roles are often trying to distinguish family values, especially those of the father, from their own values. If the father has lived the traditional male role and has expected this of the son, the student may be confused by developing personal values that don't seem to fit with the father's. The counselor can use values clarification to explore identity issues, goal formation, and career planning. Some of these INFJ males may have interests in design, languages, and the arts. These interests may have been discouraged by family as being "impractical" and "feminine." If the INFJs are comfortable with themselves, they do not usually need help with academic adjustment.

INFP

Some have called the prime dilemma of the young INFP "working through the existential pain of aloneness." INFPs frequently have many unanswerable questions. They relate well to a counselor who acts as a guide, not an advice giver. Their search is spiritual, social (finding an authentic relationship), and idealistic (a career they can believe in). If their lives are too caught up in their inner realities and questioning, they may have trouble focusing on studies. Organization may be a problem. Like INTPs, they may have serious problems with procrastination. Coming from high school where many assignments were on a daily or short-term basis, the self-directed term-long assignments can create a difficult adjustment. Completing term papers on time tends to be one of the biggest problems. Compounding this procrastination is a kind of perfectionism in which the INFPs have set such high personal standards and expectations for themselves that it is hard to write the first line of a paper. That first line is never good enough, and what if the paper isn't "brilliant"? Although serious procrastination may be spotted in these students early, they may not be ready to engage in efforts to change this pattern until later in their college careers when they have become very tired of this repetitive and destructive pattern. Often it is their professors who make this later referral to the counseling office. Of course, not all INFPs have a problem with procrastination. The more developed the two functions, Intuition and Feeling, and the more balance between them, the less likely there will be a problem with procrastination. In any case, many INFPs make contact with the counseling office early in their college career because of these kinds of issues. They are usually eager to work in counseling, but may need some help articulating the issues because of the vagueness of their searchings and inner questionings.

ENFP

The INFPs and ENFPs are the most frequent types in the student body at Rollins College and at many other liberal arts colleges. ENFPs are generally comfortable with the notion of talking with a counselor. As new students they may face problems with personal organization, focus, the social environment, and new relationships. A common pattern is ENFP students who think they have their academic and career goals set but quickly change their minds the first term. For example, like the ESTPs, they may start a premed program and after a few months question whether they have the motivation to do all the science and math. They feel like they are "missing out" on the social life of the college because of being in labs "all the time." Their parents are displeased that they want to change from premed to English. They want to live up to their parents' expectations and please parents and professors, yet their social needs are also very important. They may feel torn or at least confused. ENFPs may be interested in so many academic and career areas that they have difficulty focusing, and many bounce from one goal to another. They can benefit from early discussions about goals and from comprehensive career counseling later in the first year or early in the sophomore year. They may need help in setting priorities among academic and social demands. They may take on too many extracurricular activities before they have gotten a handle on their academics. If they are "burning the candle at both ends," they are likely to develop illnesses such as mononucleosis, strep throat, and colds. ENFPs are often so busy focusing outside themselves that they don't pay attention to internal stimuli about their own physical state. Through counseling they can learn to identify early signs of overload.

ENFJ

ENFJs, with their organized approach, generally take the academic side of college more seriously than ENFPs. When they seek counseling in their first year, it is usually because of social adjustment or family concerns, not academic adjustment. Some of the ENFJ female students may express unhappiness at the "meat market" mentality of some males at the large "keg" parties. Their values about authentic relationships and the need to be respected by the opposite sex may be in conflict with parts of the social environment. They may need help in clarifying their concerns and in finding other social outlets and ways of forming relation ships. If they are having difficulties settling in at college, they may have unresolved family concerns, such as mediating between two parents in a nonfunctional marriage. There may be a pull to be home where they can "help." ENFJs who seek counseling for family problems eagerly work for change and better understanding.

INTJ

The INTJs tend to have many of the seeking, questioning and perfectionist characteristics often found in the other INs, but seem less patient with themselves than the other INs. They want closure and some measures of progress. They seem to take their performance, whether in social leadership or in academics, more seriously than any of the other types. They are often impatient with themselves for their internal questioning, which they see as getting in the way of their performance. Mastery and competence are high values; measurement of these values through grades, athletic accomplishments, etc. is demanded of themselves. These themes and the resulting inner conflicts may not emerge in the first year. As students they may buckle down to serious studying and not allow themselves "the luxury" of focusing on questions of meaning, identity, and so forth, until these questions later force themselves into the foreground. In their first year, they may be concerned that their peers at college are not serious enough about academics and don't live principled lives ("too much superficial partying," etc.). If they judge their peers in this way, they may become alienated. They need to gain a better understanding of their own type and that of others. As a group, they have the highest grade-point average of all the types at the college, and have the profile most like that of the faculty. Although often academically successful, they may struggle with relationship issues or intrapersonal conflicts.

INTP

The INTPs are more likely to make an appointment to learn their MBTI results than to talk about a personal concern. Since they tend to value independence and to believe they can puzzle out issues on their own, they are less prone to seek ongoing counseling. They are often very curious about their MBTI results. This contact for MBTI interpretation is a good opportunity to build a relationship for the future, when personal concerns may cause them to remember the earlier positive experience with the counselor. INTPs, like the other INs, have many complex questions about the world. They bring their questions and doubts with them to college but may be very reserved about revealing these to a stranger.

These students may have gotten through high school with minimal studying. Often they are test-wise and do not need to study as much as others for tests. College may be a shock to them because they will not succeed solely on natural abilities without studying. Since they have not had to develop study techniques up to this point, they may flounder the first year. The shock of this may undermine their confidence in themselves unless they understand this process and the differences between high school and college. There may be a problem of motivation; if they've never had to face tough academic obstacles, their first responses may be to give up or change directions. Like some of the INFPs, they may procrastinate to a painful degree. These issues can be worked through with counseling and study skills assistance.

In the social and relationships arena, INTPs may have unresolved family or relationship issues when leaving home for college. Feeling is the least-preferred function. Some INTPs leave home without confronting feelings of loss and separation or without expressing their love to family and old friends. Away at college, these feelings come welling up and throw them off balance. They do not have a framework for dealing with these powerful emotions, which refuse to be manipulated in the manner of objective facts and will not stay "shelved." Counselors can assist INTPs in learning how to explore feelings safely and find expression for them.

ENTP

Like the ENFP students, ENTPs may have some difficulties getting focused in college. They may be prone to change majors and career goals frequently. They are usually curious about their MBTI scores and come in readily to learn about themselves. This is an opportunity to probe for their ability to set priorities and organize themselves. ENTPs seen in counseling tend to be restless; the classroom seems too confining to them. They often need the balance of a part-time job, volunteer work, or other outside activity. They must be cautioned not to let these outside activities take up too much time, however. Many ENTPs seen for counseling have eventually flunked out or dropped out to follow enterprises they had begun while students. Counselors can appeal to their future orientation to help them shape goals and manage the frustrations of their current restlessness. Career planning coupled with "real world" experiences, such as job shadowing or internships, can help focus these students. They do not often express social adjustment concerns.

ENTJ

The few ENTJs who seek counseling during the first year usually have interpersonal difficulties. For example, in some cases their tendency to take the lead and organize the world through extraverted thinking may be over used, and, thus, they may be perceived as over controlling and even arrogant. They may be puzzled about why people are irritated with them. They may also be troubled by family conflicts that were not resolved before coming to college. They do not have a natural way to process the subjective and emotional data from relationships. Counselors can help them develop a "vocabulary" for talking about and sorting out family relationships. Their energies need to be directed into academic areas where they can be successful and into student organizations where they can express their leadership. They are often quite responsive to their MBTI results. Again this gives counselors a chance to begin building a relationship, which later can be valuable to ENTJs.

Type Development and College Adjustment

These descriptions of potential adjustment concerns for each of the sixteen types are meant to be brief. It would take several volumes to do justice to the fascinating variability of each type. Besides variability in cultural background, life experiences and socioeconomic backgrounds that influence response to the college environment, type development and age are major factors. It is not the intent of this chapter to explain the theory of type development, but rather to show the theory's relevance to college adjustment.

By the time students come to college, they should be comfortable with their dominant function. Many may also be fairly successful in using their auxiliary functions, especially the Introverts who must use their auxiliaries to deal with the external world. One function is used to deal with the outside world, the dominant function for Extraverts and the auxiliary for Introverts, and one function is used to deal with the inner world of self, the auxiliary for Extraverts and the dominant for Introverts. To function well individuals must relate to both worlds; yet it takes time and maturation for both functions to develop. Eventually there should be a balance between the introverted function and the extraverted function, with the dominant function guiding the individual. Balance does not mean both functions are used equally. The two functions are like left and right hands. One hand is favored over the other, but most activities are better performed when both hands are used.

This concept has relevance in considering adjustment issues and other problems students may have. Students with both dominant and auxiliary functions developed appear to be more balanced individuals with more personal resources to draw upon than those who have only developed and favored one function. The EPs are a good example; they have a dominant perceiving function, either Sensing or Intuition. Their focus is outward. Without a developed auxiliary judging function, either Thinking or Feeling, to help them weigh and select from many perceptions, they may be rudderless, moving from one activity or stimulus to another. They have difficulty focusing or following through on their actions. Therefore, adjustment concerns among unbalanced EPs are more likely than among those with developed auxiliaries. The latter types have learned to select from all their perceptions, prioritize, and evaluate what is important for themselves.

Over a lifetime people also develop some use of their least-preferred functions, the third and fourth or inferior function. Individuals vary considerably in their ability to use these lesser functions; some never approach any comfort in using the third or fourth functions. A developmental goal is to be aware of and comfortable enough with all four functions to be able to use the one appropriate in a given situation. This goal requires ability to extravert and introvert, since some functions are used with the outer world and others with the inner world of self. Naturally, older individuals will have had more opportunity to develop the functions than freshmen eighteen year olds. Generally older students have better development and therefore more personal resources than young students. However, this assumption must be checked out in counseling, since there are incidents of unusually well-developed young people and of older students with impeded development.

Additional Applications through the Counseling Office

In addition to direct counseling with the MBTI, the Counseling Center has facilitated other interventions to support student adjustment and success. These interventions involve other college staff and college programs.

Learning and reading skills. Rollins College has a separate learning skills center that works with the counseling office in cross-referral. When counselors identify students with reading difficulties and lack of study skills during initial MBTI interpretations, they explain the services of the center and make the referral. Not all students will follow through, but many will at the time of referral, and some will at a later date. Students with a preference for Sensing, especially ISFJs and ISTJs, may be more likely to have reading difficulties. Since most courses require extensive reading, often abstract in nature, improved reading speed and comprehension are important. In the previous section of this chapter several types were identified that tend to have more trouble organizing themselves; these students can benefit from consultation with the learning skills center. Another chapter in this book deals with this subject in greater depth.

Training in peer counseling and leadership. The counseling office is heavily involved in the training of resident aides, head residents, house managers, rush counselors, and some other ad hoc groups of students. The office also teaches a credit course on interpersonal communications. The MBTI instrument is effective for increasing sensitivity to differences and for inspiring appreciation of the contributions of different types. Students learn how their preferences influence the way they listen, the way they respond, the pace of their responses, the language they use, their values and attitudes, and so forth. This learning is connected to peer counseling techniques. They are encouraged to identify their own biases and "blind spots" and discuss ways of controlling for these.

Because resident aides work in teams, the MBTI can be helpful in team building. They learn each other's preferences and least-preferred ways of functioning and discuss the implications for the role of resident aide. They explore ways they can complement each other. These same principles are used when working with student organizations that have asked the counseling office to help them with leadership training. Sometimes that help is a response to an organizational crisis. The request may also take the form of a consultation between a counselor and one or several leaders of a group; the MBTI preferences of these leaders may be explored in light of their concerns. On the basis of such consultation, future workshops may be planned for the organization, sometimes involving the MBTI instrument. Students are usually eager to increase their interpersonal competence and find information about the varying motivations and work approaches of different types especially helpful.

Consultation with faculty. It often takes time for counselors to establish the trust and respect of an analytical faculty; sometimes misperceptions of counseling functions and methods exist. They tend to be suspicious of personality measures, in general, and are initially skeptical about the MBTI instrument. Over the years, faculty have expressed bewilderment and frustration when seemingly capable students do not perform well in the classroom and on tests. Other faculty have referred to counseling students who seem paralyzed about writing papers despite their being very bright. These expressions of frustration by many faculty became the basis for several MBTI workshops presented in the format of faculty colloquia. Faculty were encouraged to take the Indicator prior to the presentations, and most who attended did. After explanation of type theory and MBTI interpretation, the applications to teaching and learning styles were discussed and energetically debated.

It is interesting to note that the predominant type among the faculty at Rollins College is INTJ, the same type among the students with the highest GPA. Yet a large percent of the students are ES. This contrast in faculty and student types, presented in type table form at a colloquium, had the strongest impact on faculty in causing them to reconsider their teaching approaches. A revelation for most faculty was that students who show the most promise on Scholastic Aptitude Test (SAT) scores often do not have the personality style that seems to perform most industriously (the way faculty desire students to be) at the college. Many faculty began to realize that simply pushing the admissions office to recruit students with higher SAT scores, without looking at other variables such as personality, was not addressing the issue of how students managed once they got to college.

These discussions with groups of faculty have led to increased referrals of individual students for MBTI interpretation. Some faculty have requested a group MBTI interpretation with implications for learning. In these cases a general explanation of the preferences is given, students estimate their own preferences, and then each is given his or her own results. Sometimes this is followed by class sharing, to the extent that students are comfortable. Faculty may also share their MBTI results.

Another interesting request some faculty have made is for consultation about a problem class. The counseling office has provided a type distribution (without student names) for the class from the class roster. This distribution is examined with the professor in light of his or her own type and teaching methods. The group dynamics are explored and recommendations made. After several years of exposure to the Indicator, some faculty are making additional requests. For example, the basketball coach arranged for the counselors to do team building with the MBTI instrument.

Research on attrition. Since the office of personal counseling has MBTI data on the student body, it seemed logical that this office might investigate whether certain types were more likely to persist or drop out of the college. Two graduating classes were tracked, with interesting results. A table showing the persistence rates for one of those classes appears in the appendix (see tables 5 and 6). For a thorough discussion of this research see Provost (1985). Chapter 3 also presents a fine discussion of attrition research. This research gives the counseling office a better idea of students at risk and suggests preventive programs. Some of the implications for counseling were included in the discussion about early outreach to first year students and potential adjustment concerns of the sixteen types.

Other research projects can be stimulated and supported by the counseling office. While controlling for the confidentiality of individuals' scores, counselors can provide MBTI data of some designated group, working with faculty of staff researchers. For example, one year the staff member in charge of academic advising provided a list of entering students who had performed poorly on verbal SATs. The counseling office was able to examine the type distribution of this group and identify SJs as over-represented. The math department has considered using its math placement test (given during student orientation) in conjunction with the MBTI instrument to make the appropriate placement in a math course. These are some examples of possible collaborative research projects with others at the college. In addition to the responsibility of protecting the confidentiality of individual scores, counselors should take care that overgeneralizations or labeling do not result from the research.

Conclusion

A detailed description of one counseling office's multiple uses of the Indicator in working with students and the broader college community has been presented. The MBTI instrument has been shown as a useful tool in the counseling process for establishing rapport, identifying counseling goals, and designing appropriate interventions. Programs in other counseling centers indicate wide use of the MBTI instrument and endless possibilities for helping students to become successful in college and to develop as individuals. The counselor can employ the Indicator and type theory to advocate for respecting and accommodating differences among students (and other college community members). MBTI data should be handled appropriately in terms of ethics, confidentiality, and positive application, with special care that type labeling does not occur.

References

Gendlin, E. (1981). *Focusing.* New York: Bantam.

Keirsey, D. and M. Bates. (1978). *Please understand me.* Del Mar, CA: Promethean Books.

Myers, I. B., with L. K Kirby, and K. D. Myers, (1998). *Introduction to type.* (6th ed). Palo Alto, CA: Consulting Psychologists Press.

Myers, I. B., M. H. McCaulley, N. L. Quenk, and A. L. Hammer. (1998). *MBTI Manual: A guide to the development and use of the Myers-Briggs Type Indicator.* (3rd ed). Palo Alto, CA: Consulting Psychologists Press.

Myers, I. B. and M. McCaulley. (1985). *Manual: A guide to the development and use of the Myers-Briggs Type Indicator* (2nd ed.). Palo Alto, California: Consulting Psychologists Press.

Provost, J. (1993). *A casebook: Applications of the Myers-Briggs Type Indicator in counseling.* (2nd ed.). Gainesville, Florida: CAPT.

Provost, J. (1985). "Type watching" and college attrition. *Journal of Psychological Type,* 9, 16–23.

Additional Resources

Hammer, A. L. (Ed.). (1996) *MBTI applications: A decade of research on the Myers-Briggs Type Indicator.* Palo Alto, CA: Consulting Psychologists Press.

Myers, I. B. with P. B. Myers. (1980). *Gifts differing.* Palo Alto, CA: Consulting Psychologists Press.

Quenk, N. L. (1993) *Beside ourselves.* Palo Alto, CA: Davies-Black.

Quenk, A. (1984). *Psychological types and psychotherapy.* Gainesville, FL: CAPT.

CHAPTER 12

Research Approaches Using the MBTI® Instrument

GERALD P. MACDAID

The brightest flashes in the world of thought are incomplete until they have been proven to have their counterparts in the world of fact."[1] Landmark works in the field of student development, such as Chickering's *Education and Identity* (1969), are built upon this principle, thus enriching the insight of the student development practitioner with the depth and substance of empirical observation. Good research has been an important foundation for the growth of the student development movement.

The Myers-Briggs Type Indicator® instrument has been generally available to practitioners since 1975, and while quite a number of applications within higher education have been explored and researched, much more still remains to be done. One problem with the research to date is a lack of systematic and thorough exploration of areas within student development. Initial research has been done in a random fashion reflecting the interests of the early researchers. Therefore, practitioners must determine which applications have been tested and are empirically sound and which are simply theoretical speculation.

Practitioners and educators in higher education are in a position to improve upon the body of research concerning the relationship between type and student development. Research can be done in simple straightforward ways and yield valid results. Small studies with a narrow focus can contribute valuable information to the field. Complex research projects have their place, but often serve to scare away the busy practitioner without strong research skills. Yet it is these same professionals who could generate important research from their daily contact with students.

By June 27, 2002 the Center for Applications of Psychological Type's MBTI Bibliography had 7,987 entries. This is a an eight fold increase since the 1985 edition. Table 12.1 shows the results of a literature review conducted by Jean Reid, where she identifies the frequency of topics pertinent to student development professionals.

Frequency of Relevant Topics in CAPT Bibliography

Topic	Frequency	Topic	Frequency
Education	1156	Values	46
Student	702	Intelligence	43
Teach	517	Academic Achievement	41
Learn	509	Self-Esteem	33
Teacher	320	Team Building	30
Career	273	ADHD/ADD	20
Learning style	240	Academic Prediction	18
Counseling	229	Drug/Substance Abuse	18
Cognitive Style	150	Distance Education/Online	17
Communication	141	Intimate Relationships	17
Team	140	Residence/Residential	16
Spirituality	107	Standardized Tests/SAT	16
Decision Making	91	Moral Development	15
Creativity	84	Teamwork	12
Religion	73	Learning Disabilities	10
Career Development	70	Career Success/Satisfaction	9
Development, Type	70	Interpersonal Relationships	9
Problem-Solving	61	Sex Roles	8
Teaching Style	61	Roommate	6
Reading	57	Gradepoint Point Average	6
Marriage/Marital	51	Memory	5
Career Counseling	48	Group Dynamics	4
Conflict	46	Privacy/Personal Space	2

Table 12.1

Table 12.1 shows that large global topic areas have the most research while smaller more specific areas have much less. Many pertinent topics are relatively unstudied. This illustrates the dilemma facing practitioners wanting to develop programs in such unstudied areas—the literature often is not solid enough to support the development of applications. This problem not only occurs in the quantity of studies but in the quality of studies as well. Many studies are just starting to describe the relationships between type and a topic area, providing a simple overview but lacking substance. Other studies are just poorly done, often showing the researchers' lack of understanding about the properties of the MBTI instrument.

This chapter examines how the practitioner can contribute valuable and pertinent MBTI research. First, I will present the notion that every MBTI user is a researcher. Then, I will examine the tools and strategies that lend themselves easily to the analysis of type data. As I discuss the various research approaches, I will give specific examples and the appropriate data presentation and reporting conventions.

Every MBTI User Is a Researcher

With the dramatic growth in the number of MBTI users, the potential for collecting large amounts of data is staggering. In 2000, CPP, Inc., the publisher of the MBTI instrument, sold approximately 3 million answer sheets. A reasonable estimate is that 90 percent of those are template scored by professionals, thus there are desk drawers across the country teeming with potential but untapped research data. Data are being collected every day within institutions of higher education. Individual feedback sessions with students, career exploration groups, and mediations of roommate conflicts are examples of opportunities to contribute more data on how personality functions in these various areas. Every MBTI user has valuable data (Carskadon, Lawrence, and McCaulley, 1983).

These unutilized data are important, because right now there are more MBTI users than active researchers. More and more people are using the MBTI instrument and doing so in more varied and creative ways. Yet the documented research to substantiate and transmit these findings lags far behind. Often other researchers are looking for data about these kinds of applications and cannot find anything in the literature. Often the "wheel is reinvented" because no record of another practitioner's discovery exists. Furthermore, today's standards of validity require us not only to demonstrate the validity of the instrument itself, but also to gather data on the validity of the applications of the instrument.

In addition we have a new challenge with the advent of Form M, a revision of the MBTI instrument. While initial research supporting Form M improvements look promising, our obligation is to continue research to deepen and broaden the support for this new version as well as detect any potential hidden flaws so corrections can be made.

For the body of research to grow, it will require contributions from the practitioners. All of us should document our discoveries so others may verify and amplify them. Each user taps into unique samples and contributes something no other person can. Even the simplest observations and findings add to our body of knowledge, especially as these various studies are replicated. This is particularly important for work with small specialty groups. Often these populations are not large enough to make clear or definite statements about type relationships, but when combined with other small groups, patterns become more apparent and the body of research grows.

Simple First Steps to Research

Since data are collected by many practitioners on a day-to-day basis, a valuable database often accumulates without much effort. However, the data often remain unanalyzed. Identifying simple, manageable, and appropriate methods can make data analyses less intimidating and more accomplishable for busy non–research-oriented practitioners.

The simplest approach is for someone else to analyze the data. While this statement is purposely facetious, it is also perfectly serious. There are a number of ways to get outside data analyses services. One way is to use the CAPT computer scoring service. This scoring service provides the researcher with a three page narrative report for each subject in the study, one page subject score summary report for the researcher, a group type table, and an alphabetical list with the subjects' types. The results of this scoring are archived in the CAPT data bank. Using the scoring services is a way of participating in large-scale assessment of the psychometric properties of the MBTI instrument as well as generating estimates of normative populations and occupational groups. This databank was started in 1970 by Isabel Myers and Mary McCaulley expressly for the purpose of facilitating research on the Indicator.

The size of this databank is in excess of one million cases. The answer sheets that pushed the number over a million came from MBTI users who scored cases from five students seen for academic advisement to users who administer the MBTI instrument to their entire freshman class every fall (as well as cases from practitioners in areas outside education). Each addition is important, because the power of this databank comes from the cases in aggregate. The databank is particularly valuable because it provides an opportunity to perform analyses that would be otherwise impossible on such a scale. Studies of the databank completed for various publications such as the second edition of the *MBTI® Manual* (Myers and McCaulley, 1985), *Atlas of Types Tables* (Macdaid, McCaulley, and Kainz, 1986), *Career Report Manual* (Hammer and Macdaid, 1992), *Looking at Type and Careers* (Martin, 1995), as well as conference presentations and papers by CAPT (Macdaid et al, 1983–1999) revealed many important facts about the Indicator and produced informative tables showing type distributions across various populations.

Practitioners who use the CAPT computer scoring services get the added benefit of being able to receive the scored data on diskette in a computer readable format for research. This can save the hours and expense of having to enter large data sets into the computer by hand.

The typical starting point in research is reviewing the literature. Some practitioners may not be sure what aspects of their practices may be pertinent to research. Others may be sure about their topics but unaware of what others have examined in their topic areas. Having a sense of what has been published and what is known helps get a researcher off to a solid start. The CAPT Bibliography is a very useful resource for this task.

The researcher can track down references of interest for themselves by using the CAPT web site (www.capt.org/research/bibliography search) or by purchasing a diskette. Additionally, literature review services can be purchased by contacting the CAPT librarian. Once either process is completed then the references can be found through local libraries, interlibrary loan, University Microfilms International (for dissertations), and, of course, the Isabel Briggs Myers Memorial Library at CAPT.

Descriptive Studies of Type

One basic kind of research study that can be done is a *descriptive* study. In a descriptive study the researcher examines a sample, describing one or more characteristics of interest, the nature of the sample, and the population it was drawn from. For example, for a descriptive study of freshmen, two variables that we could collect data on are gender and psychological type. In MBTI research the frequency distribution of types in a sample is not only used to describe a sample's characteristics but can also be used to explore the concept of self-selection. The basic notion behind self-selection is that people select for themselves different opportunities and situations that are satisfying, and these selections will be congruent with their type preferences.

Research in type self-selection asks the question: If type truly makes a difference in what is perceived by people as interesting, enjoyable, or attractive, then what differences would we find in various samples such as academic, career, and recreation groups? For example Sensing types are expected to be found in situations involving use of the senses and practical realities, and Intuitive types in situations where abstraction and hypothesizing are demanded.

Self-selection data are reported using the type table. Isabel Myers designed this format of data presentation as a standard way for representing type distributions of groups. With a type table, one can get a visual impression of the frequency distribution of that group, as well as determine more carefully the precise breakdown of the percentages and numbers of the types and type groupings.

The reporting of frequency distribution data is valuable on two levels. First, it provides further insight into the nature of the self-selection process for each of the types. There are limits to how much one can safely predict from theory, and self-selection data allow us to expand upon what is known about the attractions and behaviors of each type. With data in a type table format the practitioner can compile a compendium of activities, interests, programs, etc., by type. This can facilitate the targeting of programming efforts.

Second, self-selection data provide a test for type theory itself. Since the underlying theory is what every application of the MBTI instrument is founded upon, the theory deserves rigorous testing. The confidence we can place in the Indicator is related to our confidence in the validity of our applications. Practitioners are in the best position to contribute valid studies of their own applications.

Leaders in Student Government Activities

N = 225

SENSING: THINKING	SENSING: FEELING	INTUITION: FEELING	INTUITION: THINKING	
ISTJ N = 11 % = 4.89 ■■■■	**ISFJ** N = 6 % = 2.67 ■■	**INFJ** N = 9 % = 4.00 ■■■■	**INTJ** N = 2 % = 0.89	JUDGMENT INTROVERSION
ISTP N = 8 % = 3.56 ■■■	**ISFP** N = 3 % = 1.33 ■	**INFP** N = 8 % = 3.56 ■■■	**INTP** N = 6 % = 2.67 ■■	INTROVERSION PERCEPTION
ESTP N = 8 % = 3.56 ■■■	**ESFP** N = 13 % = 5.78 ■■■■■	**ENFP** N = 27 % = 12.00 ■■■■■■■■■■ ■■	**ENTP** N = 18 % = 8.00 ■■■■■■■■	PERCEPTION EXTRAVERSION
ESTJ N = 47 % = 20.89 ■■■■■■■■■■ ■■■■■■■■■■	**ESFJ** N = 16 % = 7.11 ■■■■■■■	**ENFJ** N = 8 % = 3.56 ■■■	**ENTJ** N = 35 % = 15.56 ■■■■■■■■■■ ■■■■■	EXTRAVERSION JUDGMENT

	N	%
E	172	76.44
I	53	23.56
S	112	49.78
N	113	50.22
T	135	60.00
F	90	40.00
J	134	59.56
P	91	40.44
IJ	28	12.44
IP	25	11.11
EP	66	29.33
EJ	106	47.11
ST	74	32.89
SF	38	16.89
NF	52	23.11
NT	61	27.11
SJ	80	35.56
SP	32	14.22
NP	59	26.22
NJ	54	24.00
TJ	95	42.22
TP	40	17.78
FP	51	22.67
FJ	39	17.33
IN	25	11.11
EN	88	39.11
IS	28	12.44
ES	84	37.33
ET	108	48.00
EF	64	28.44
IF	26	11.56
IT	27	12.00
Sdom	38	16.89
Ndom	56	24.89
Tdom	96	42.67
Fdom	35	15.56

Note: ■ = One Percent; Data Collected by Alice Hadwin of Florida Community College at Jacksonville during October 1983. Subjects were 44% male and 54% female.
Data used by permission.

Table 12.2

Table 12.2, which shows a sample of 225 college leaders from the *Atlas of Type Tables* (Macdaid, McCaulley, and Kainz, 1986), is an example of type data being displayed in this fashion. The table displays the frequencies and percentages of the sixteen types plus thirty-six common type groupings; in addition, a symbol is used to convey a visual impression of the frequency distribution of the sixteen types. In Table 12.2, we can see that the two most frequent types in this sample are ESTJ and ENTJ. The most frequent preference is for Extraversion.

Table 12.3, which shows a sample of 2,678 Florida Future Scientists, is an example of data from a twenty-four-year longitudinal study that has been aggregated. The subjects were high school students recommended by their schools to attend summer programs for scientifically gifted students to work with the University of Florida faculty. The most frequent type is ENFP at 13.7% and the most frequent grouping in NT at 13.7%.

Short descriptive studies are often published in many of the professional journals. Practitioners may contribute to their field by submitting for publication simple descriptive studies of this kind. Information about sharing data with CAPT as well as information about submitting articles to the *Journal of Psychological Type* can be found at the end of this chapter.

Hypothesis Testing with Statistical Tools

So far I have described a method for reporting and collecting descriptive data. Now I would like to turn to the issue of hypothesis testing and statistical inference. Usually research has the very specific goal of discovering the answer to a very exact question. This question is the hypothesis. Hypothesis testing uses statistical tests to see if collected data support a belief.

Florida Future Scientists: 1974–1997

N = 2678

	SENSING THINKING	SENSING FEELING	INTUITION FEELING	INTUITION THINKING	
	ISTJ N = 184 % = 6.87	**ISFJ** N = 97 % = 3.62	**INFJ** N = 130 % = 4.85	**INTJ** N = 274 % = 10.23	JUDGMENT / INTROVERSION
	ISTP N = 98 % = 3.66	**ISFP** N = 60 % = 2.24	**INFP** N = 232 % = 8.66	**INTP** N = 278 % = 10.38	PERCEPTION / INTROVERSION
	ESTP N = 79 % = 2.95	**ESFP** N = 73 % = 2.73	**ENFP** N = 367 % = 13.70	**ENTP** N = 241 % = 9.00	PERCEPTION / EXTRAVERSION
	ESTJ N = 145 % = 5.41	**ESFJ** N = 89 % = 3.32	**ENFJ** N = 143 % = 5.34	**ENTJ** N = 188 % = 7.02	JUDGMENT / EXTRAVERSION

	N	%
E	1325	49.48
I	1353	50.52
S	825	30.81
N	1853	69.19
T	1487	55.53
F	1191	44.47
J	1250	46.68
P	1428	53.32
IJ	685	25.58
IP	668	24.94
EP	760	28.38
EJ	565	21.10
ST	506	18.89
SF	319	11.91
NF	872	32.56
NT	981	36.63
SJ	515	19.23
SP	310	11.58
NP	1118	41.75
NJ	735	27.45
TJ	791	29.54
TP	696	25.99
FP	732	27.33
FJ	459	17.14
IN	914	34.13
EN	939	35.06
IS	439	16.39
ES	386	14.41
ET	653	24.38
EF	672	25.09
IF	519	19.38
IT	834	31.14
Sdom	433	16.17
Ndom	1012	37.79
Tdom	709	26.47
Fdom	524	19.57

Note: ■ = One Percent. Data collected by Mary H. McCaulley from 1974 to1997.
The subjects were high school students recommended by their schools to attend summer programs for scientifically gifted students at the University of Florida.
Students were 46% female and 54% male; the modal age was 17.
Data used with permission.

Table 12.3

Hypotheses are first stated as null hypotheses. Instead of predicting a difference related to type, a null hypothesis predicts no difference. An alternative hypothesis is proposed that states a difference *does* exist due to type. Data are analyzed to disprove or reject the null hypothesis, thus providing evidence supporting, but not proving, the alternative hypothesis. Ultimately proof builds from the aggregation and replication of many studies showing support for the alternative hypothesis.

In order to reject a null hypothesis, a level of significance or risk level alpha must be set before statistical analyses are done. This terminology is just a technical way of saying that when we conduct an experiment the statistics may suggest we found something when in fact it was an accidental or chance finding. So we decide ahead of time what chance of detecting something that is not real we wish to accept. That chance is called the *level of significance* or *alpha risk* and is usually set at .05, .01, or .001, indicating what percentage of the time we will get a particular result by chance alone. For example, if a finding is significant at $p<.001$, then there is less than one chance in a thousand that the result occurred by chance.

We can get too concerned about alpha risk. If we do, we can make another mistake called beta risk. Beta risk is the chance we do not reach statistical significance when a real relationship does exist. If we always set our alpha risk at the lowest level, especially in smaller samples, we increase the beta risk.

Both of these kinds of risk are reduced greatly by collecting large samples. The bigger the sample the more we can chose a low risk of saying we found something when we did not (alpha risk) and still have a low chance of missing something when it is really there (beta risk). The reality is we can not always obtain large samples and so we should think carefully about what level of risk we should choose before we begin the research.

Research Design

Research design is important but does not have to be daunting. All research design means is that you have put some thought into what you are doing before you do it. Simple experiments have simple designs. While it is also true that simple experiments have more risk, both alpha and beta, it does not mean that we should never conduct them. Ultimately truth and knowledge come from the aggregation of many studies not just one. A collection of the simple and the complex build the foundation of knowledge. Our design process then helps us know what we can say and how far we can generalize about the findings from our study.

The research design flows from a literature review. A good research design has two basic characteristics. One, it accounts for the influence of other factors that may affect the issues we are examining. Two, it provides statistical approaches best suited for the questions we are trying to answer.

Accounting for the influence of other factors is done in one of two ways. One approach is to control for the influence of every factor by measuring the size of its influence. This means collecting enough data from enough people to look at each factor, type, and the issue we are examining in the study. If there are a lot of factors that means a large sample size is required. Since there are sixteen types, we already have to collect a larger sample than other researchers looking at systems with less diversity.

Another approach is to randomize the sample. This method takes all the factors that could affect the variable being examined and spreads them out randomly, thereby minimizing the accidental impact of those factors on the findings of the study. The advantage is that a sample will be easier and more manageable to collect. The disadvantage is that the researcher can not tell what the size of the effect these other factors have on the situation.

No approach is perfect; each has its tradeoffs. The alpha risks we discussed earlier should be in part selected by how comfortable we are that we have controlled for or randomized the effects of other factors. The more robust our design the more risk we can take. Conversely, if we are concerned there may be hidden factors at work in our study, a more conservative risk is probably warranted. Remember, the reason we set these levels of risk in the first place is to protect against making inappropriate conclusions.

The Nature of Type Variables

There is an important and fundamental difference between a *type* theory and a *trait* theory. A scale on a trait-measuring instrument usually starts out with low scores indicating *less* of the trait and high scores indicating *more* of the trait. In the middle, is a neutral zone where people are said to be *average* in that trait. Proceeding up or down these trait-measuring scales represents small, incremental changes in magnitude and quality.

In contrast, type theory holds that there is a *definite and clear difference* in the characteristics of people on either side of the midpoint, not a small incremental change. This difference is a sudden and dramatic qualitative change analogous to a phase change in chemistry. For example, an element may change from a gas to a liquid; once it crosses that line it has very different properties.

The sixteen types (ISTJ, ISFJ, etc.) and the indices (E–I, S–N, T–F, and J–P) are unique to a type system. They are classified as nominal variables because of the fact that they name groups or categories rather than values. These variables cannot be averaged or correlated, so we need to use appropriate methods to examine the relationships of nominal variables.

Unlike scores from a trait system, the numeric scores of the MBTI instrument were not designed to act like a yardstick and quantify the amount of the characteristic that is possessed. These scores tell us how clearly someone voted for the preference. There are differences between how the numeric parts of the scores are created on the revised version (Form M) and all previous versions of the MBTI. If you use the computer scoring services, these scores will be provided to you using the appropriate standard scoring conventions.

On Form M these scores are called *preference clarity indices* (pci), while on all previous forms they are called *preference scores.* These scores are comprised of the letter indicating the direction of preference coupled with the numeric value indicating the clarity. We would use these scores in research where we wish to examine the behavior of another variable that we hypothesize is related to how clearly individuals report their preferences.

These scores can be converted to mimic a continuous score. The MBTI continuous score, called *theta* on Form M, was created explicitly for the purpose of correlational research. The procedure for creating these scores takes otherwise discontinuous preference scores generated from a measure of dichotomous preferences and mathematically gives them continuous characteristics. These scores are used with certain procedures where we are examining which direction on the index another variable is related.

Again, these scores are provided when computer scoring the MBTI instrument. Researchers who choose to template score Form M will need to contact the CAPT Research Department for instructions for converting pci values into continuous scores via a process similar to that used for Form G.

Chi-square and Selection Ratio Type Table

While knowing a type distribution in a sample is of interest, how that sample differs from another provides additional information. One of the most common hypotheses in type research addresses whether certain types are found more frequently in a given sample than would be expected based on a reference population.

The analysis that is most appropriate for determining if a type is more or less prevalent than expected is a *two-by-two contingency table analysis*. It is a measure of association. Here the null hypothesis is: If type does not affect selection into the sample, then the proportion of any type observed in the sample will not differ from the proportion expected of that same type in a reference population.

Technically speaking, this analysis tests to see if the observed frequencies are the same or different than the expected frequencies. A *chi-square* statistic is calculated for the hypothesis test. If the probability of the calculated chi-square value is less than the alpha level we chose, then we can reject the null hypothesis. We can then conclude that type factors are significant in that particular sample.

While this more technical analysis underlies the process, a simpler mathematical relationship is the part we look at to see the meaning. We calculate a selection ratio obtained by dividing the observed frequency by the expected frequency. The selection ratio thus is equal to 1.00 when the observed and expected frequencies are the same, grows increasingly larger as the observed frequency becomes larger than the expected frequency (seeing more than we expected), and grows increasingly smaller than 1.00 as the observed frequency becomes smaller than the expected frequency (seeing less than we expected).

This approach is built into a computer software program called the Selection Ratio Type Table (SRTT) program, which was developed by and is distributed by CAPT as a tool for researchers. While this analysis can be calculated by other programs or standard statistical packages, the SRTT program allows for the convenient analysis of type data, and it produces output from fifty separate analyses on a one-page type table format.

An example of the SRTT analysis comes from the study by Macdaid, McCaulley, and Kainz (1982). The question of what types excel academically was raised as part of a follow-up study of college freshmen. In theory, the Introverted Intuitives would be expected to excel because of their orientation to ideas and theory. College graduates elected to the Phi Beta Kappa honor society were selected as examples of excellence in academic performance. Since the sample of all college graduates already had a high percentage of IN types, simply examining the frequency distribution of the Phi Beta Kappa sample for a majority of INs would not provide evidence for the hypothesis. So the Phi Beta Kappa sample was compared to the entire college graduate sample using the SRTT analysis. This allows us to see if the INs were found more frequently in the academically excellent group than in the general population of college graduates.

Table 12.4 shows the results of this SRTT comparison. The right-hand column, under the letter "I" Index, displays the selection ratios for the various combinations of types. Next to the selection ratio is a symbol denoting the level of significance reached. The lack of a symbol means that the selection ratio Index for that type combination failed to reach the lowest level of significance, indicating the sample probably does not differ from the base population. The selection ratio reported for the IN group is 1.96 and is significant at the .001 level.

Phi Beta Kappas

N = 75

SENSING THINKING	SENSING FEELING	INTUITION FEELING	INTUITION THINKING	
ISTJ N = 6 % = 8.00 I = 1.12	**ISFJ** N = 3 % = 4.00 I = 0.48	**INFJ** N = 8 % = 10.67 I = 2.20*	**INTJ** N = 10 % = 13.33 I = 3.43***	JUDGMENT / INTROVERSION
ISTP N = 2 % = 2.67 I = 1.04	**ISFP** N = 2 % = 2.67 I = 0.51	**INFP** N = 10 % = 13.33 I = 1.20	**INTP** N = 8 % = 10.67 I = 2.30*	PERCEPTION / INTROVERSION
ESTP N = 1 % = 1.33 I = 0.56	**ESFP** N = 2 % = 2.67 I = 0.53	**ENFP** N = 8 % = 10.67 I = 0.73	**ENTP** N = 2 % = 2.67 I = 0.61	PERCEPTION / EXTRAVERSION
ESTJ N = 1 % = 1.33 I = 0.19	**ESFJ** N = 1 % = 1.33 I = 0.15	**ENFJ** N = 5 % = 6.67 I = 1.10	**ENTJ** N = 6 % = 8.00 I = 2.09	JUDGMENT / EXTRAVERSION

	N	%	I
E	26	34.67	0.66
I	49	65.33	1.37
S	18	24.00	0.52
N	57	76.00	1.42
T	36	48.00	1.33
F	39	52.00	0.81
J	40	53.33	1.07
P	35	46.67	0.93
IJ	27	36.00	1.49
IP	22	29.33	1.25
EP	13	17.33	0.65
EJ	13	17.33	0.67
ST	10	13.33	0.69
SF	8	10.67	0.39
NF	31	41.33	1.13
NT	26	34.67	2.07
SJ	11	14.67	0.47
SP	7	9.33	0.61
NP	28	37.33	1.07
NJ	29	38.67	2.07
TJ	23	30.67	1.39
TP	13	17.33	1.24
FP	22	29.33	0.81
FJ	17	22.67	0.81
IN	36	48.00	1.96
EN	21	28.00	0.97
IS	13	17.33	0.75
ES	5	6.67	0.29
ET	10	13.33	0.75
EF	16	21.33	0.62
IF	23	30.67	1.04
IT	26	34.67	1.90
Sdom	12	16.00	0.70
Ndom	28	37.33	1.35
Tdom	17	22.67	1.24
Fdom	18	24.00	0.77

I = self selection index
* = p > .05
** = p > .01
*** = p > .001

Note: ■ = One Percent; Base Population = 1972 Freshmen who graduated from University of Florida, N=1878. Sample and base are dependent.Subjects were graduates nominated to the Phi Beta Kappa honor society (56% female, 44% male).

Source: Macdaid, McCaulley & Kainz, 1982. The University of Florida Freshmen Study: Ten Year Follow-Up.

Table 12.4

This finding shows that when we look at all INs they are over-represented but we need to make sure it is also true for all four of the IN types. We check this by examining the selection ratio for each of the four IN types separately. All these ratios need to also be above 1.0, although all four do not need to be significant separately since they are significant in aggregate. As we can see they do indeed all have ratios over one. This is evidence to reject the null hypothesis that type is not related to academic excellence.

Since the SRTT analysis performs fifty independent contingency table analyses, there is a risk that some results may be significant just by chance. For example, if we pick an alpha risk level of $p<.05$, we are saying that any result that exceeds that threshold could be significant by chance five times in one hundred. That means two out of the fifty tests on the SRTT could be significant by chance. The effect of this problem is reduced by making explicit hypotheses ahead of time. This reduces the actual number of tests to be interpreted, which reduces the influence chance has on the results.

In a study where multiple questions are being examined, presenting multiple SRTT tables is not always the most efficient way to present the data. In these situations it is often helpful to extract the findings and present them in a summary form on a type. Tables 12.5a and 12.5b show the results from one such study where people were asked to report their favorite subjects in school. School subjects were reported for each type when the selection ratio was greater than 1.20 and significant at the $p<.05$ level.

Favorite Subject—Males			
ISTJ Business History Industrial Arts	**ISFJ** Geography Sports	**INFJ** None	**INTJ** Geography Physical Sciences Social Sciences
ISTP Math None	**ISFP** Sports	**INFP** Art Music Reading Social Sciences Theatre	**INTP** Art Physical Science
ESTP Sports	**ESFP** Sports	**ENFP** English Music Social Sciences	**ENTP**
ESTJ Business Math Sports	**ESFJ**	**ENFJ** Music Social Sciences	**ENTJ** Business Reading Physical Sciences

Table 12.5a *CAPT Data Bank, Forms F and G, 1994–1995.*
Source: Macdaid, 2000. Educational Information from the CAPT Data Bank.

Favorite Subject—Females			
ISTJ Business Geography Economics Math Other	**ISFJ** Economics Reading None	**INFJ** Art English Languages History Reading Theatre	**INTJ** History
ISTP	**ISFP** Languages Music Reading	**INFP** Art English Economics Music Reading Theatre	**INTP** Art None
ESTP Math	**ESFP** Sports	**ENFP** Art English Social Sciences	**ENTP** Social Sciences
ESTJ Business Math Physical Sciences	**ESFJ** Economics Music Sports	**ENFJ** Art Music Theatre	**ENTJ**

Table 12.5b *CAPT Data Bank, Forms F and G, 1994–1995.*
Source: Macdaid, 2000. Educational Information from the CAPT Data Bank.

Choosing a Proper Reference Sample for the SRTT

The validity of the SRTT depends on the selection of an appropriate reference population. The reference population chosen should be directly related to the hypothesis being tested. For example, suppose we wished to discover if the types of residents in a specialized residence hall program would not differ significantly from the type distribution of our entire residence hall program. The most valid reference population in this case would be the entire population of residence hall students from which the sample was drawn.

Sometimes this reference population is not available or obtainable. Choosing the next best reference population is a process that requires careful judgment, since the results of the SRTT comparison can be rendered meaningless by an inappropriate comparison. The base or reference population should have as many characteristics in common with the sample as possible. The more differences between the chosen base and the sample, the less the results of the SRTT procedure apply.

In the example above, the next best reference population would be a random sample drawn from the entire resident population. If this comparison population is not available, then finding another estimate of the entire resident population would be advisable. However, when estimated populations are used researchers must account for all identifiable demographic features in order to avoid an inappropriate comparison. In this case, some reasonable approaches to selecting a reference population are choosing a resident sample from another college similar in nature to your institution; selecting an aggregate of many colleges' residential students to average out potential biases of differences in colleges; using the next most similar population of students at your college; or using other representative samples of college students in general. Comparing the sample of special residents to a population of high school students, resident advisors, or roommates who have taken the MBTI for conflict resolution only shows how the students in the special residential program differ from these very specific populations. Comparison with any of these groups would not answer the original question of how these students differ in type from the residential students in general.

Correlations

A correlational analysis is another approach to discovering how other variables relate to type. Correlation is a measure of association, permitting examination of the relationship between the individual preference indices of the Indicator and the values of another variable.

The afore-mentioned continuous scores are artificial transformations that allow the researcher to use the four MBTI indices in correlational comparisons with other scales or numeric variables. For most studies of this nature, the Pearson correlation coefficient (r) will be the statistic of choice. Carlyn (1977) discusses the merits of the Pearson correlation coefficient and calls it "a good statistic to use with MBTI continuous scores because differences in the shapes of the two distributions being compared tend to have little effect on r in most cases" (p. 6). She warns that a sample size of at least thirty is recommended by most statisticians. She also notes that the Pearson Correlation usually understates the magnitude of the relationship. This correlation coefficient can only be used with MBTI continuous scores, not with the sixteen types.

The values of a correlation coefficient range from -1.00 to 1.00. A correlation of 1.00 indicates a perfect positive relationship. In other words, a high score on one variable is associated with a high score on the other variable. A negative correlation shows that a high score on one variable is associated with a low score on the other variable. A correlation of zero shows no relationship; as the numeric value of the correlation moves away from zero in either direction it indicates increasing covariance. Correlations do not indicate a causal relationship, but only indicate an association between variables.

When reading correlations of type with other variables, the underlying dichotomy must not be forgotten even when using continuous scores. The sign of the correlation indicates which half of the dichotomy the variable is related to. The conversion to continuous scores is designed so that positive correlations are related to I, N, F, or P and negative correlations are related to E, S, T, or J. The correlations in Table 12.6 are an example of results from correlational research and demonstrate how different measures of value orientation are associated with type preferences. These correlations can only be interpreted to examine the direction of association with the type index.

Sometimes correlations are computed with the preference clarity indices or preference scores instead of continuous scores. In this case eight correlations would be calculated. This approach is used when the hypothesis holds that scores on the other measure are expected to change as the clarity of preference changes in either direction.

Care must be taken when using this approach as one may inadvertently misinterpret the results. An example is found in data analyzed by Myers in the original MBTI manual (Myers, 1962). For a sample of 249, correlations were calculated for each preference score, the results were -0.21 for Introversion and 0.05 for Extraversion. It would be incorrect to interpret this result to say there is no relationship between gregariousness and Extraversion. The appropriate interpretation is that there is no relationship between the clarity with which people reported their preferences and their rated gregariousness.

To answer the question of whether there is a relationship between Extraversion–Introversion and student gregariousness as rated by faculty, a correlation using continuous scores on the E–I index is

Correlation of MBTI Continuous Scores with Values

Source	N	Sex	EI	SN	TF	JP	Relation
(5) Theoretical	1,351	M	11**	26**	–37**	–05*	-NT–
(5)	236	M	14*	20**	–36**	–03	-NT–
(5)	238	M	09	22**	–35**	–02	-NT–
(9)	65	M,F	09	–16	–42***	–13	—T–
(5)	877	M	10**	28**	–38**	–07*	-NT–
(5) Economic	1,351	M	–11**	–46**	–16**	–12**	-S—
(5)	236	M	01	–52**	–24**	–14*	-ST–
(5)	238	M	–22**	–55**	–07	–06	ES—
(9)	65	M,F	08	–58***	–39**	–54***	-STJ
(5)	877	M	–11**	–41**	–16**	–13**	-S—
(5) Aesthetic	1,351	M	20**	34**	–01	16**	IN—
(5)	236	M	17**	40**	05	22**	-N–P
(5)	238	M	25**	44**	06	25**	IN–P
(9)	65	M,F	–13	50***	10	45***	-N–P
(5)	877	M	20**	30**	–05	12**	IN—
(5) Social	1,351	M	–05	–06*	34**	01	—F–
(5)	236	M	–11	00	38**	02	—F–
(5)	238	M	02	03	30**	–05	—F–
(9)	65	M,F	00	23	33**	26*	—F–
(5)	877	M	–05	–11**	34**	02	—F–
(5) Political	1,351	M	–20**	–21**	–16**	03	ES—
(5)	236	M	–12	–26**	–18**	–03	-S—
(5)	238	M	–26**	–29**	–18**	04	ES—
(9)	65	M,F	–04	–30	–19	–06	——
(5)	877	M	–20**	–17**	–14**	05	E——
(5) Religious	1,351	M	00	08**	29**	–04	—F–
(5)	236	M	–15	* 04	32**	–11	—F–
(5)	238	M	08	13*	20**	–16*	—F–
(9)	65	M,F	02	15	38**	–02	—F–
(5)	877	M	01	07*	31**	01	—F–

Table 12.6 *From* Manual: A guide to the development and use of the Myers-Briggs Type Indicator, *(p. 187) by I. B. Myers and M. H. McCaulley, 1985, Palo Alto, CA: Consulting Psychologists Press. ©1985 by Peter B. Myers and Katharine D. Myers. Reprinted by permission.*

required. Here she found a correlation of 0.42. Myers' interpretation of this was that ". . . to the faculty eye, gregariousness is a general characteristic of extravert students, not perceptibly related to the clarity of preference for extraversion" (p. 100).

Differences among Types

Any variable that produces continuous values can be examined for differences across type. If the theory predicts that types will vary in tasks, developmental measures, academic achievement, etc., then the mean scores for the types should reflect the disparity. To statistically test to see if these differences are not likely to have been caused by chance, the *t* and *F* test statistics are employed.

The *t* statistic is used to test the likelihood that two means are significantly different. For example, you might test for difference in mean achievement levels between Sensing or Intuitive types. A one-way analysis of variance (ANOVA) employing the *F* statistic must be used to examine differences in performance for type groupings of more than two groups. Examples of groupings that would be tested in this way are IN, EN, IS and ES, or the sixteen types.

An example of this analysis is a study by McCaulley (1973). The hypothesis being tested was that grade-point averages would be higher for the Introverted and Intuitive group. The outer right-hand column in Table 12.7 shows the test statistic used (either t or F) and its significance level. For this hypothesis, the *F*-statistic (17.4) indicates a significant difference among the four groups. The IN group has the highest average GPA of any grouping and the *F*-test for the differences in variances is significant at the .001 level. Furthermore, the four IN types' GPAs are ranked 1, 2, 3, and 5.

University of Florida Students Cumulative Grade-Point Average

N = 2794

SENSING: THINKING	SENSING: FEELING	INTUITION: FEELING	INTUITION: THINKING	
ISTJ N = 193 % = 6.91 Mean 2.78 S.D. .60 6	**ISFJ** N = 232 % = 8.30 Mean 2.84 S.D. .59 4	**INFJ** N = 131 % = 4.69 Mean 2.95 S.D. .59 2	**INTJ** N = 116 % = 4.15 Mean 3.00 S.D. .55 1	INTROVERSION: JUDGMENT
ISTP N = 81 % = 2.90 Mean 2.64 S.D. .57 13	**ISFP** N = 152 % = 5.44 Mean 2.63 S.D. .61 14	**INFP** N = 294 % = 10.52 Mean 2.83 S.D. .58 5	**INTP** N = 138 % = 4.94 Mean 2.88 S.D. .59 3	INTROVERSION: PERCEPTION
ESTP N = 75 % = 2.68 Mean 2.59 S.D. .55 15	**ESFP** N = 139 % = 4.97 Mean 2.54 S.D. .57 16	**ENFP** N = 383 % = 13.71 Mean 2.76 S.D. .57 9	**ENTP** N = 126 % = 4.51 Mean 2.66 S.D. .60 12	EXTRAVERSION: PERCEPTION
ESTJ N = 176 % = 6.30 Mean 2.65 S.D. .57 11	**ESFJ** N = 259 % = 9.27 Mean 2.75 S.D. .55 10	**ENFJ** N = 186 % = 6.66 Mean 2.77 S.D. .61 7	**ENTJ** N = 113 % = 4.04 Mean 2.77 S.D. .66 8	EXTRAVERSION: JUDGMENT

Study conducted by M. H. McCaulley & R. I. Kainz as a follow-up of University of Florida entering students 1-2 years after admission in 1972. Total Mean = 2.76, S.D. = 0.58

	N	Mean	S.D.	F/t
E	1457	2.71	.58	24.8***
I	1337	2.82	.59	
S	1307	2.71	.58	22.8***
N	1487	2.81	.59	
T	1018	2.76	.60	0.2
F	1776	2.77	.58	
J	1406	2.80	.59	11.8***
P	1388	2.72	.58	
IJ	672	2.87	.59	
IP	665	2.77	.59	12.6***
EP	723	2.68	.57	
EJ	734	2.74	.59	
ST	525	2.69	.58	
SF	782	2.72	.58	
NF	994	2.81	.59	7.9***
NT	493	2.82	.61	
SJ	860	2.76	.58	
SP	447	2.60	.57	
NP	941	2.78	.58	17.5***
NJ	546	2.86	.61	
TJ	598	2.79	.60	
TP	420	2.71	.59	
FP	968	2.73	.58	4.2**
FJ	808	2.81	.59	
IN	679	2.89	.58	
EN	808	2.75	.60	
IS	658	2.75	.60	17.4***
ES	649	2.66	.56	

* > .05, ** > .01, *** > .001

Table 12.7

Case Studies

Another method for practitioners to capture and report data is by case studies. Often in teaching, counseling, or supervision, one has the opportunity to gather deeper insights about how type preferences manifest themselves in an individual's functioning. Since many practitioners have one-to-one contact with students, case study data are appropriate to collect. The case study allows documenting and reporting of observations of characteristics, behaviors, and phenomena that are often too complex to capture or observe in large sample studies.

Case studies also provide a chance to verify theoretical premises about type dynamics and uncover more complex patterns of type-related behavior. For example, from theory one could make a prediction about the probable process an ESTP might utilize to make decisions. Using case study approach, one could examine each step an ESTP might use during a decision-making process. Obviously with this approach, one can compile more detailed observations about what transpires. The richness of the observations helps give more depth to our theoretical predictions, and subtleties that are discovered by this approach then become new hypotheses to be tested with larger samples. The hypothesized behavior is examined to see if it is common to all of this type and not prevalent in other types.

Good examples of the case study can be found in *A Casebook: Applications of the Myers-Briggs Type Indicator in Counseling* by Judith A. Provost (1993). In this book, Provost presents vivid descriptions of how she integrates type theory into the counseling process, giving examples of the behavior of clients and tying it to type theory predictions.

The case study approach can also produce quantitative data. If the researcher can precisely label and define the nature of the behavior being observed, the occurrences of the behavior can be counted and compared using methods already described. For example, in theory we might expect Introverts to feel more uncomfortable getting to know new people. Furthermore, specific behaviors might be good indicators of discomfort. If the researcher counted the number of occurrences from logs of initial interviews or counseling sessions, then an analyzable database is created. These data could be analyzed using the SRTT procedure comparing high and low occurrences, a correlation of the occurrences and MBTI score, or means could be compared using the t or F statistic.

Collaboration

Collaboration with others can facilitate research. Networking with other professionals can be stimulating and rewarding and can also utilize the mutual usefulness of opposites as effective research teams can be built balancing strengths and weaknesses. Three avenues are available for networking. One avenue is the research interest group in the Association for Psychological Type, composed of professionals who are interested in type research. It is often possible to find someone with whom to collaborate or consult. A second avenue is to search your own institution to find other professionals or graduate students interested in research. A final avenue to consider is the possibility of contracting the research work. In a contract arrangement, an outside person is hired to perform all or part of the data analysis. CAPT's Research Services department can refer you to consultants to consider for this service or to others involved in similar research.

Conclusion

For the more experienced researcher, there are many other methodological approaches that can be considered. The appropriate choice always rests on the nature of the hypothesis in question, the nature of the data in hand, and of the sampling methods used. Complex multivariate statistics are getting easier to use with the advent of computer statistical packages. An important point to remember is the dichotomous, noncontinuous nature of type data. Knowing this fact will help avoid any grievous traps.

This introduction to MBTI research approaches in student development is intended to help demystify research, give the practitioner some simple yet useful tools, and generate more interest in doing research. The field of student development and the use of the MBTI instrument as a tool in that field are young and open to new research. Now is an exciting time to be contributing. It is possible to be a cutting-edge contributor since there are so many new horizons to explore and so few explorers. Take a good look at the work you are doing. What do you have to contribute?

Next Steps

Once you have your data collected, take the next step of sharing it with others who would be interested in your findings. You can contribute it to CAPT, publish it in JPT, and present it at APT conferences and meetings.

Center for Applications of Psychological Type

Donating Type Tables to CAPT

The Center for Applications of Psychological type (CAPT) collects type table data which may be published, with the contributors' permission, in books such as the Atlas of Type Tables or this book. A form for this is available from CAPT (800.777.2278).

The information requested includes:

- Name(s) and contact information of contributor(s); the title of the type table data (project or group title, e.g., 1972 Freshman, University of Florida); which form of the MBTI® instrument was used to collect the data; when and where collected.
- Were these cases previously scored by CAPT's computer scoring service?
- If these data were published, directly or indirectly, please cite the reference.
- Please describe your sample as specifically as you can (e.g., age, gender, education level, grade, major, occupation, specialty, ethnicity, religious group, counseling clients, medical patients, athletic team, retirees, families, etc.)
- For each type, supply the total number and also, if available, the numbers for males and for females.

Archiving Answer Sheets at CAPT

If you have MBTI® answer sheets you no longer need, you are invited to donate them to CAPT for archiving in the Data Bank. CAPT archives primarily Form F and Form G answer sheets, but also accepts Forms J, K, M, and Q. The answer sheets are scanned and the data becomes part of the CAPT Data Bank. CAPT protects the confidentiality of the answer sheets and uses them only for research on groups of records, maintaining complete anonymity of the individuals. A form to send with your answer sheets is available from CAPT (800.777.2278).

The information requested includes:

- Name(s) and contact information of contributor(s); the title of the project or group, e.g., Cardiologists, Mayo Clinic,

1995–2000); when and where collected.

- Were these cases previously scored by CAPT's computer scoring service?
- IIf these data were published, directly or indirectly, please cite the reference.
- Please add any information to describe your data (e.g., occupational field, specialty, ethnicity, etc.) which is not include on the answer sheets.

In preparing your answer sheets, please:

- Group your answer sheets and label groups and subgroups (e.g., main group Lawyers; subgroups Trial Lawyers, Corporate Lawyers, Public Defenders).
- Check over your answer sheets (add missing information such as male/female).

You may request forms for donating type tables or archiving answer sheets from

CAPT Research Services
2815 NW 13th Street, Suite 401
Gainesville, FL 32609
Phone: 3532.375.0160
www.capt.org

Journal of Psychological Type

The Journal of Psychological Type publishes original articles relating to the Myers-Briggs Type Indicator® instrument and theories of psychological type as described by Carl Jung, Isabel Myers, and others. Single research studies, integrative research reviews, theoretical papers, "action research," and descriptions of practical applications of type are welcome in all areas.

Authors may call the Editor and discuss their research or articles at any stage of development. Such contacts are best made by telephone or e-mail, as this allows two-way communication and results in the most efficient use of time. Our email address is recommended for international queries. All articles are subject to review and to editorial revision. Articles are normally reviewed by one member of the Journal of Psychological Type's Editorial Board and by one member of the Association for Psychological Type's Review Board, as well as by the Executive Editor and by the Editor. Articles should be submitted to:

Thomas G. Carskadon, Ph.D.
Editor/Publisher,
Journal of Psychological Type
Mississippi State University
Psychology Department, Box 6161
Mississippi State 39762
Telephone: 662.325.7655
Email: tomcar@ra.msstate.edu

Association for Psychological Type

The Association for Psychological Type (APT) provides several opportunities to present research findings. In the USA there are national and regional APT conferences, and also chapter meetings and workshops. In addition, there are APT organizations in other countries which hold conferences. To find out about these opportunities, contact APT:

Association for Psychological Type
4700 W. Lake Avenue
Glenview, IL 60025
Phone: 847.375.4717
www.aptcentral.org

References

Carlyn, M. (1977 November). Current research practices involving the MBTI: Design and methodology. Paper presented at MBTI-II, the Second Biennial National Conference on the Use of the Myers-Briggs Type Indicator, East Lansing, MI.

Carskadon, T. G., G. D. Lawrence, and M. H. McCaulley. (1983, May). Every MBTI user is a researcher. Symposium presented at APT-V, the Fifth Biennial International Conference of the Association for Psychological Type, College Park, MD.

Chickering, A. W. (1969). *Education and identity.* San Francisco, Jossey-Bass.

Granade, J. G., and I. B. Myers. (1987). Selection ratio type table PC program [computer software]. Gainesville, FL: Center for Applications of Psychological Type.

Hammer, A. L., and G. P. Macdaid. (1992). *MBTI career report manual.* Palo Alto, CA: Consulting Psychologists Press.

Macdaid, G. P. (1998 March). Educational information from the CAPT Data Bank. Presented at the Third Biennial International Conference on Education of the Center for Applications of Psychological Type, Orlando, FL.

Macdaid, G. P., M. H. McCaulley, and R. I. Kainz. (1982). The University of Florida freshman study: Ten year follow-up. Gainesville, FL: Center for Applications of Psychological Type.

Macdaid, G. P., M. H. McCaulley, and R. I Kainz. (1986). *Atlas of type tables.* Gainesville, FL: Center for Applications of Psychological Type.

Martin, C. R. (1995). *Looking at type and careers.* Gainesville, FL: Center for Applications of Psychological Type.

McCaulley, M. H. (1973). University of Florida counseling study (Report of Committee #13: Myers-Briggs Type Indicator applications, Parts I and II). Gainesville, FL: University of Florida, Department of Clinical Psychology.

McCaulley, M. H. (1985). The Selection Ratio Type Table (SRTT): A research strategy for comparing type distributions. *Journal of Psychological Type*, 10, 46-56.

McCaulley, M. H. and R. I. Kainz. (1974). The University of Florida longitudinal study: First follow-up. Unpublished paper. Gainesville, FL: University of Florida.

Myers, I. B. (1962). *Manual: The Myers-Briggs Type Indicator.* Princeton, NJ: Educational Testing Service.

Myers, I. B., and M. H McCaulley. (1985). *Manual: A guide to the development and use of the Myers-Briggs Type Indicator* (2nd ed.). Palo Alto, CA: Consulting Psychologists Press.

Myers, I. B., M. H. McCaulley, N. L. Quenk, and A. L. Hammer. (1998). *MBTI Manual: A guide to the development and use of the Myers-Briggs Type Indicator* (3rd ed.). Palo Alto, CA: Consulting Psychologists Press.

Provost, J. A. (1993). *Applications of the Myers-Briggs Type Indicator in counseling: A casebook* (2nd ed.). Gainesville, FL: Center for Applications of Psychological Type.

Todd, H. N. and A. D. Rickmers. (1967). *Statistics: An introduction.* New York, NY: McGraw Hill.

Zeisset, R. M. (2000). *Statistics and measurement: An introduction for MBTI users* (3rd ed.). Gainesville, FL: Center for Applications of Psychological Type.

1 Quote by John Tyndall on a plaque in the Space Sciences Research Building, University of Florida, Gainesville.

Appendix

This Appendix is a compilation of information from a variety of researchers and practitioners throughout the United States; each contribution has been carefully acknowledged. The editors wish to thank these contributors for their efforts in sharing type data.

The editors also wish to thank Jamelyn Johnson, coordinator of Research Services at the Center for Applications of Psychological Type (CAPT), for her work on the type tables in this book. She was able to enlist contributions for several new tables for the appendix. Jerry Macdaid, author of chapter 12, and Peter Ceballo, the scoring manager at CAPT, were generous with their time in assisting her in gathering data and making contacts with contributors. Glenn Granade, senior software developer at CAPT, created the program for generating the type tables in this edition and produced them for publication.

The type tables in this appendix illustrate the similarities and differences among samples within higher education. Type theory suggests that people will move into environments, roles, and situations that reinforce their types.

Readers are encouraged to contribute type tables that might be useful in the ongoing study and research of the Myers-Briggs Type Indicator® instrument and its applications. Please send your data to Research Services, Center for Applications of Psychological Type, 2815 NW 13th Street, Suite 401, Gainesville, FL 32609.

Ranking of Colleges by MBTI Preference

Extraversion–Introversion	Percent
St. Louis University	62% E
University of Wisconsin at Stevens Point	61% E
University of Maine at Orono	59% E
Mercer University	59% E
Nicholls State University	58% E
Auburn University	57% E
Adrian College	57% E
University of North Carolina at Greensboro	55% E
Rollins College	54% E
St. Clair College	54% E
University of Florida	54% E
Hope College	53% E
Franklin and Marshall College	50% E
Parks College	50% I
Berkshire Christian College	53% I
Concordia College	54% I

Sensing–Intuition	Percent
Nicholls State University	72% S
St. Clair College	68% S
Berkshire Christian College	67% S
Adrian College	64% S
Parks College	59% S
Mercer University	59% S
Auburn University	57% S
University of North Carolina at Greensboro	57% S
University of Wisconsin at Stevens Point	56% S
University of Maine of Orono	55% S
Concordia College	54% S
Franklin and Marshall College	50% S
Rollins College	52% N
St. Louis University	52% N
Hope College	53% N
University of Florida	55% N

Table 1 *From* Manual: A guide to the development and use of the Myers-Briggs Type Indicator, *(p. 137) by I. B. Myers and M. H. McCaulley, 1985, Palo Alto, CA; Consulting Psychologists Press. ©1985 by Peter B. Myers and Katherine D. Myers. Reprinted by permission.*

Rankings of Colleges by MBTI Preferences (cont'd)

Thinking–Feeling	Percent
Parks College	59% T
Franklin and Marshall College	54% F
Nicholls State University	57% F
University of Wisconsin at Stevens Point	60% F
University of North Carolina at Greensboro	61% F
St. Clair College	62% F
Mercer University	62% F
University of Florida	62% F
St. Louis University	63% F
Rollins College	63% F
University of Maine at Orono	67% F
Auburn University	69% F
Hope College	74% F
Concordia College	77% F
Adrian College	80% F
Berkshire Christian College	86% F

Judgment–Perception	Percent
University of North Carolina at Greensboro	60% J
Nicholls State University	54% J
Mercer University	54% J
Adrian College	53% J
Parks College	53% J
Berkshire Christian College	52% J
Franklin and Marshall College	51% J
Concordia College	51% J
University of Wisconsin at Stevens Point	51% P
St. Louis University	51% P
Rollins College	51% P
University of Florida	52% P
Hope College	53% P
Auburn University	54% P
St. Clair College	55% P
University of Maine at Orono	60% P

Table 1 *From* Manual: A guide to the development and use of the Myers-Briggs Type Indicator, *(p. 137) by I. B. Myers and M. H. McCaulley, 1985, Palo Alto, CA; Consulting Psychologists Press.*

High School and College Graduates

%	ISTJ	ISFJ	INFJ	INTJ
High School Graduates - Female	11.59	18.62	3.43	2.24
High School Graduates - Male	22.79	7.56	1.08	2.70
College Graduates - Female	10.75	10.93	7.07	6.11
College Graduates - Male	17.76	4.30	3.49	9.85

%	ISTP	ISFP	INFP	INTP
High School Graduates - Female	3.07	7.91	4.92	1.54
High School Graduates - Male	6.91	3.02	1.08	3.89
College Graduates - Female	1.61	2.69	7.65	3.71
College Graduates - Male	3.18	1.69	4.95	6.13

%	ESTP	ESFP	ENFP	ENTP
High School Graduates - Female	2.55	7.07	5.84	1.84
High School Graduates - Male	5.29	2.38	2.16	3.02
College Graduates - Female	1.06	2.62	9.17	3.96
College Graduates - Male	2.69	1.45	5.74	5.24

%	ESTJ	ESFJ	ENFJ	ENTJ
High School Graduates - Female	10.32	12.87	3.43	2.77
High School Graduates - Male	27.86	5.51	1.08	3.67
College Graduates - Female	8.56	8.58	8.35	7.19
College Graduates - Male	15.04	3.51	3.99	10.99

Note: High school female N = 2277, male N = 926. College female = 7952, male N = 6814.

Source: Atlas of Type Tables (pp. 53, 56, 60, 63) by Gerald P. Macdaid, Mary H. McCaulley, and Richard I. Kainz. Gainesville, FL: Center for Applications of Psychological Type, 1986. Used by permission.

Table 2

Percentage of Teachers in Each Type in Different Levels of Education

	ISTJ %	ISFJ %	INFJ %	INTJ %
Preschool	3.00	20.00	7.00	4.00
Elementary	10.70	17.91	5.10	2.11
Middle & Junior	11.17	12.23	4.96	4.52
High School	11.88	10.49	7.72	5.40
Adult	10.09	11.40	3.07	2.63
Junior College	12.12	8.20	4.99	6.95
University	12.84	6.09	7.54	10.87

	ISTP %	ISFP %	INFP %	INTP %
Preschool	0.001	4.00	8.00	2.00
Elementary	1.74	4.73	4.60	1.49
Middle & Junior	2.30	3.19	5.94	2.39
High School	1.54	2.47	6.33	2.93
Adult	4.39	4.82	6.14	1.75
Junior College	0.71	2.14	8.02	4.63
University	1.67	1.71	8.11	5.39

	ESTP %	ESFP %	ENFP %	ENTP %
Preschool	0.001	8.00	12.00	1.00
Elementary	0.87	5.72	10.20	1.49
Middle & Junior	1.77	3.81	10.99	3.90
High School	1.08	2.31	11.42	3.55
Adult	3.95	5.26	8.33	3.51
Junior College	1.43	2.85	13.55	4.99
University	1.18	1.67	9.07	5.30

	ESTJ %	ESFJ %	ENFJ %	ENTJ %
Preschool	6.00	12.00	8.00	5.00
Elementary	8.46	12.44	7.21	5.22
Middle & Junior	9.13	11.52	7.80	4.34
High School	11.27	8.49	8.80	4.32
Adult	11.40	13.60	4.39	5.26
Junior College	6.77	8.20	7.84	6.60
University	6.49	4.43	8.02	9.64

Note: Data are taken from Form F and Form G databanks of cases scored between March 1978 and December 1982 at the Center for Applications of Psychological Type. Levels are based on coding for occupations given by respondents.

From Manual: A Guide to the Development and Use of the Myers-Briggs Type Indicator (p. 134) by Isabel Briggs Myers and Mary H. McCaulley, 1985, Palo Alto, CA: Consulting Psychologists Press.

Table 3

Freshman

	ISTJ %	ISFJ %	INFJ %	INTJ %
Bunker Hill Community College	15.79	9.24	2.88	4.87
Saddleback Community College	1.83	4.59	2.75	2.75
Lubbock Christian College	6.67	9.61	2.35	0.59
Rollins College	5.50	4.50	4.50	4.25
Wayne State College	7.87	7.07	2.53	0.93
OSU Agricultural Technical Institute	12.30	4.81	2.14	2.14
Worcester Polytechnic Institute	12.09	3.68	3.10	7.52
Bucknell University	6.79	3.50	3.24	4.88
Hawaii Pacific University	7.01	5.77	2.47	2.27
Nicholls State University	9.48	8.85	1.86	1.53
University of Nebraska	7.55	6.87	1.95	1.63
University of Wisconsin	7.87	4.97	3.18	1.66

	ISTP %	ISFP %	INFP %	INTP %
Bunker Hill Community College	6.36	4.77	5.16	3.38
Saddleback Community College	9.17	2.75	7.34	6.42
Lubbock Christian College	5.88	7.65	5.88	1.96
Rollins College	6.25	2.50	8.75	3.75
Wayne State College	6.67	7.07	4.80	3.60
OSU Agricultural Technical Institute	9.63	4.81	1.07	3.21
Worcester Polytechnic Institute	7.89	2.73	7.73	14.18
Bucknell University	5.04	2.42	6.53	6.27
Hawaii Pacific University	4.74	4.12	5.98	5.36
Nicholls State University	5.57	5.26	4.24	3.15
University of Nebraska	5.28	4.45	4.88	2.96
University of Wisconsin	5.87	4.70	6.91	3.38

	ESTP %	ESFP %	ENFP %	ENTP %
Bunker Hill Community College	5.36	4.17	7.45	4.17
Saddleback Community College	12.84	5.50	11.93	9.17
Lubbock Christian College	5.88	10.00	11.18	2.35
Rollins College	3.75	5.00	19.00	6.50
Wayne State College	8.93	11.20	12.13	5.73
OSU Agricultural Technical Institute	20.32+	4.28	4.81	8.56
Worcester Polytechnic Institute	5.34	2.95	9.02	9.73
Bucknell University	6.48	3.60	12.85	10.08
Hawaii Pacific University	10.10	4.54	15.05	8.87
Nicholls State University	8.39	7.70	9.19	5.39
University of Nebraska	7.52	6.43	11.60	6.47
University of Wisconsin	7.46	10.22	15.19	5.87

	ESTJ %	ESFJ %	ENFJ %	ENTJ %
Bunker Hill Community College	13.70	7.15	2.38	3.18
Saddleback Community College	14.68	6.42	0.92	0.92
Lubbock Christian College	8.24	15.69	4.71	1.37
Rollins College	9.00	8.00	7.25	1.50
Wayne State College	4.80	10.27	4.00	2.40
OSU Agricultural Technical Institute	17.11	2.67	2.14	0.00
Worcester Polytechnic Institute	5.68	2.21	2.33	3.84
Bucknell University	9.97	5.60	7.25	5.50
Hawaii Pacific University	7.42	6.80	4.74	4.74
Nicholls State University	11.72	12.47	3.17	2.02
University of Nebraska	7.01	18.97	4.19	2.24
University of Wisconsin	6.49	8.98	4.14	3.11

Source of data (used by permission or from published sources):
Bunker Hill Community College: Mary Todd, 1987-1995, n=1007
Saddleback Community College: Jerilyn Chuman, 2000, n=109
Lubbock Christian University: Rickey Lyle Harman, 1979-1980, n=510
Rollins College: Shannon T. Andreas, 2000, n=400
Wayne State College: Dorothy Weber and Pearl Hansen, 1993-1996, n=750
Ohio State University Agricultural Technical Institute: Nancy A. Brooker, 2001, n=187
Worcester Polytechnic Institute: John M. Wilkes, 1997-2002, n=3262
Bucknell University: Charlotte Jacobsen Weddle, 1988-1990, n=1945
Hawaii Pacific University: Dale S. Burke, 2000, n=485
Nicholls State University: Michele E. Caruso, 2000-2002, n=4506
University of Nebraska: Robert C. Sorensen, 1986-1990, n=2494
University of Wisconsin: Fred Leafgren and Bob Renault, 1989, n=1448

Table 4

Non-Persisters in Higher Education

	ISTJ	ISFJ	INFJ	INTJ
	%	%	%	%
Salem College	0.001	9.02	6.56	1.64
Rollins College	5.76	2.62	5.24	5.24
	ISTP	**ISFP**	**INFP**	**INTP**
	%	%	%	%
Salem College	3.28	6.56	6.56	1.64
Rollins College	7.33	7.85	9.95	5.76
	ESTP	**ESFP**	**ENFP**	**ENTP**
	%	%	%	%
Salem College	3.28	11.48	18.03	7.38
Rollins College	5.24	4.71	14.66	3.66
	ESTJ	**ESFJ**	**ENFJ**	**ENTJ**
	%	%	%	%
Salem College	1.64	10.66	11.48	0.82
Rollins College	8.38	4.71	7.33	1.57

Note: Salem College N = 122, Rollins College N = 191.

Source: Salem College (1980-1983). (Students entering college between 1980 and 1983). Unpublished raw data collected by Roger Spearman, Winston-Salem, NC.
Rollins College (1984). (Class of 1984). Unpublished raw data collected by Judith Provost, Winter Park, FL.

Table 5

Persisters at Rollins College

	ISTJ	ISFJ	INFJ	INTJ
	%	%	%	%
Female Persisters	3.85	7.69	2.88	0.96
Male Persisters	7.06	5.88	1.18	5.88
Original Class	5.53	4.74	3.68	4.21
	ISTP	**ISFP**	**INFP**	**INTP**
	%	%	%	%
Female Persisters	0.00	5.77	9.62	3.85
Male Persisters	4.71	5.88	9.41	7.06
Original Class	4.74	6.84	9.74	5.53
	ESTP	**ESFP**	**ENFP**	**ENTP**
	%	%	%	%
Female Persisters	6.73	10.58	17.31	3.85
Male Persisters	8.24	4.71	8.24	4.71
Original Class	6.32	6.32	13.95	3.95
	ESTJ	**ESFJ**	**ENFJ**	**ENTJ**
	%	%	%	%
Female Persisters	4.81	10.58	7.69	3.85
Male Persisters	16.47	3.53	4.71	2.35
Original Class	9.21	6.05	6.84	2.37

Note: Female Persisters N = 104, Male Persisters N = 85, Original Class N = 380

Source: Rollins College (1984). (Class of 1984). Unpublished raw data by Judith Provost, Winter Park, FL.

Table 6

Resident Housing Assistants

	ISTJ	ISFJ	INFJ	INTJ
	%	%	%	%
CAPT Databank	2.82	6.78	4.52	2.82
University of Maine system	6.52	4.35	0.72	0.72
	ISTP	**ISFP**	**INFP**	**INTP**
	%	%	%	%
CAPT Databank	1.69	4.52	9.04	3.39
University of Maine system	0.72	5.80	6.52	0.72
	ESTP	**ESFP**	**ENFP**	**ENTP**
	%	%	%	%
CAPT Databank	2.82	2.26	17.51	3.95
University of Maine system	1.45	5.80	19.57	3.62
	ESTJ	**ESFJ**	**ENFJ**	**ENTJ**
	%	%	%	%
CAPT Databank	7.91	9.04	10.17	10.73
University of Maine system	8.70	20.29 +	7.97	6.52

Note: CAPT databank N=177, University of Maine System N = 138.

Sources: Center for Applications of Psychological Type databank (1985).
University of Maine system: Combined unpublished raw data from the University of Maine (1985), collected by Irene von Hoffman, Orono, Maine; and from the University of Southern Maine (1985), collected by Joe Austin, Gorham, Maine.

Table 7

Disciplinary Offenders Referred to University Conduct Officer from Residential Life Staff

N = 91

SENSING THINKING	SENSING FEELING	INTUITION FEELING	INTUITION THINKING	
ISTJ N = 7 % = 7.69 ■■■■■■■■	**ISFJ** N = 3 % = 3.30 ■■■	**INFJ** N = 2 % = 2.20 ■■	**INTJ** N = 4 % = 4.40 ■■■■	JUDGMENT / INTROVERSION
ISTP N = 8 % = 8.79 ■■■■■■■■■	**ISFP** N = 6 % = 6.59 ■■■■■■■	**INFP** N = 7 % = 7.69 ■■■■■■■■	**INTP** N = 5 % = 5.49 ■■■■■	INTROVERSION / PERCEPTION
ESTP N = 13 % = 14.29 ■■■■■■■■■■■■■■	**ESFP** N = 4 % = 4.40 ■■■■	**ENFP** N = 5 % = 5.49 ■■■■■	**ENTP** N = 12 % = 13.19 ■■■■■■■■■■■■■	PERCEPTION / EXTRAVERSION
ESTJ N = 5 % = 5.49 ■■■■■	**ESFJ** N = 3 % = 3.30 ■■■	**ENFJ** N = 4 % = 4.40 ■■■■	**ENTJ** N = 3 % = 3.30 ■■■	EXTRAVERSION / JUDGMENT

	N	%
E	49	53.85
I	42	46.15
S	49	53.85
N	42	46.15
T	57	62.64
F	34	37.36
J	31	34.07
P	60	65.93
IJ	16	17.58
IP	26	28.57
EP	34	37.36
EJ	15	16.48
ST	33	36.26
SF	16	17.58
NF	18	19.78
NT	24	26.37
SJ	18	19.78
SP	31	34.07
NP	29	31.87
NJ	13	14.29
TJ	19	20.88
TP	38	41.76
FP	22	24.18
FJ	12	13.19
IN	18	19.78
EN	24	26.37
IS	24	26.37
ES	25	27.47
ET	33	36.26
EF	16	17.58
IF	18	19.78
IT	24	26.37
Sdom	27	29.67
Ndom	23	25.27
Tdom	21	23.08
Fdom	20	21.98

Note: ■ = One Percent

Source: University of Maine (1985-1986), unpublished data collected by Scott Anchors, Orono, ME.

Table 8

Presidents of Greek Organizations

	ISTJ	ISFJ	INFJ	INTJ
	%	%	%	%
CAPT Databank	2.82	6.78	4.52	2.82
University of Maine system	6.52	4.35	0.72	0.72
	ISTP	**ISFP**	**INFP**	**INTP**
	%	%	%	%
CAPT Databank	1.69	4.52	9.04	3.39
University of Maine system	0.72	5.80	6.52	0.72
	ESTP	**ESFP**	**ENFP**	**ENTP**
	%	%	%	%
CAPT Databank	2.82	2.26	17.51	3.95
University of Maine system	1.45	5.80	19.57	3.62
	ESTJ	**ESFJ**	**ENFJ**	**ENTJ**
	%	%	%	%
CAPT Databank	7.91	9.04	10.17	10.73
University of Maine system	8.70	20.29	7.97	6.52

Note: CAPT databank N=177, University of Maine System N = 138.

Sources: Center for Applications of Psychological Type databank (1985).
University of Maine system: Combined unpublished raw data from the University of Maine (1985), collected by Irene von Hoffman, Orono, Maine; and from the University of Southern Maine (1985), collected by Joe Austin, Gorham, Maine.

Table 9

University of Nebraska Agricultural Undergraduate Majors Ranked by MBTI Preference

Extraversion–Introversion	n	Percent
agricultural education	110	61.82% E
animal science	260	52.31% E
agricultural economics	237	51.05% I
all agricultural majors	**1515**	**51.60% I**
agricultural honors	70	52.86% I
mechanized agriculture	70	52.86% I
pre-vet	60	53.33% I
natural resources	128	53.91% I
agronomy	85	56.47% I
general agriculture	111	58.56% I
[agricultural faculty]	126	64.30% I
agricultural engineering	44	70.45% I

Sensing–Intuition	n	Percent
mechanized agriculture	70	91.43% E
agronomy	85	85.88% E
agricultural economics	237	82.70% I
agricultural education	110	81.82% I
animal science	260	80.38% I
general agriculture	111	76.58% I
agricultural engineering	44	75.50% I
all agricultural majors	**1515**	**75.30% I**
natural resources	128	69.53% I
pre-vet	60	65.50% I
agricultural honors	70	55.71% I
[agricultural faculty]	126	51.60% I

Table 10 *University of Nebraska at Lincoln (1985). Unpublished raw data collected by Leverne Barrett, Lincoln, NE.*

University of Nebraska Agricultural Undergraduate Majors Ranked by MBTI Preference (cont'd)

Thinking–Feeling	***n***	**Percent**
mechanized agriculture	70	72.66% T
agricultural economics	237	68.35% T
agricultural education	110	66.36% T
[agricultural faculty]	126	65.10% T
agricultural engineering	44	63.64% T
agronomy	85	63.33% T
animal science	260	63.08% T
agricultural honors	70	62.86% T
all agricultural majors	**1515**	**62.80%** T
general agriculture	111	56.76% T
natural resources	128	53.13% T
pre-vet	60	51.67% T

Judgement–Perception	***n***	**Percent**
[agricultural faculty]	126	80.20% J
agricultural honors	70	62.86% J
agricultural education	110	55.45% J
agronomy	85	55.29% J
all agricultural majors	**1515**	**53.70% J**
animal science	260	53.46% J
pre-vet	60	53.33% J
agricultural economics	237	53.16% J
agricultural engineering	44	50.00% P
general agriculture	70	50.45% P
natural resources	128	57.81% P
mechanized agriculture	111	60.00% P

Table 10 *University of Nebraska at Lincoln (1985). Unpublished raw data collected by Leverne Barrett, Lincoln, NE.*

Post-Secondary Health Occupations Majors Ranked by MBTI Preference

Extraversion–Introversion	***n***	**Percent**
radiography	61	66.30% E
dental hygiene	58	65.91% E
dental assisting	63	63.64% E
radiological technician	51	61.45% E
respiratory therapy technician	44	61.11% E
physical therapy assisting	15	55.56% E
respiratory therapy	40	55.56% E
all post-secondary health occupation students	**659**	**55.52% E**
occupational therapy	23	54.76% E
surgical technician	18	54.55% E
medical records	28	52.83% E
medical assisting	96	52.46% E
physical therapy	36	51.43% E
med lab technician	53	46.49% I
med technology	82	53.59% I
radiography technician	4	66.67% I

Sensing–Intuition	***n***	**Percent**
medical records	43	81.13% S
surgical technician	26	78.79% S
physical therapy assisting	21	77.78% S
dental hygiene	67	76.14% S
medical records	137	74.86% S
physical therapy	50	71.43% S
radiography technician	58	69.88% S
dental assisting	68	68.69% S
radiography	63	68.48% S
all post-secondary health occupation students	**795**	**66.98% S**
radiological technician	4	66.67% S
respiratory therapy technical	42	58.33% S
med technology	89	58.17% S
med lab technician	64	56.14% S
respiratory therapy	40	55.56% S
occupational therapy	23	54.76% S

Table 11 *Indiana University (1985). Doctoral dissertation data collected by Karen Gables, Indianapolis, IN.*

Post-Secondary Health Occupations Majors Ranked by MBTI Preference (cont'd)

Thinking–Feeling	***n***	**Percent**
physical therapy assisting	5	18.52% T
dental hygiene	18	20.45% T
radiological technician	47	56.63% F
med lab technician	66	57.89% F
med technology	89	58.17% F
respiratory therapy	43	59.72% F
radiography	55	59.78% F
respiratory therapy technician	44	61.11% F
medical records	33	62.26% F
surgical technician	21	63.64% F
all post-secondary health occupation students	**781**	**65.80% F**
radiography technician	4	66.67% F
medical assisting	127	69.40% F
physical therapy	51	72.86% F
occupational therapy	32	76.19% F
dental assisting	77	77.78% F

Judgment–Perception	***n***	**Percent**
surgical technician	24	72.73% J
dental hygiene	61	69.32% J
med technology	104	67.97% J
radiological technician	4	66.67% J
medical records	35	66.04% J
physical therapy	44	62.86% J
physical therapy assisting	16	59.26% J
all post-secondary health occupation students	**700**	**58.97% J**
medical assisting	106	57.92% J
radiography	53	57.61% J
dental assisting	56	56.57% J
respiratory therapy technical	39	54.17% J
radiography technician	44	53.01% J
med lab technician	58	50.88% J
occupational therapy	21	50.00% P
respiratory therapy	37	51.39% P

Table 11 *Indiana University (1985). Doctoral dissertation data collected by Karen Gables, Indianapolis, IN.*

Saint Louis University Academic Majors Ranked by MBTI Preference

Extraversion–Introversion	***n***	**Percent**
nursing	178	72.47% E
allied health professionals	320	69.06% E
undecided majors	258	66.67% E
communication	79	65.82% E
psychology	103	65.05% E
business administration	547	63.25% E
total freshmen 1986	**386**	**62.18% E**
pre-medial students	369	58.81% E
political science	56	58.93% E
accounting	188	58.51% E
arts and science	1195	56.07% E
chemistry	83	53.01% E
biology	264	51.14% E
computer science	63	50.79% I
math	27	66.67% I

Sensing–Intuition	***n***	**Percent**
accounting	188	61.70% S
nursing	178	60.11% S
business administration	547	59.05% S
total freshmen 1986	**386**	**58.81% S**
allied health professionals	320	56.88% S
undecided majors	258	54.65% S
chemistry	83	54.22% S
computer science	63	53.97% S
pre-medical students	369	50.95% S
biology	264	50.76% S
political science	56	50.00% N
math	27	51.85% N
arts and science	1195	52.05% N
communication	79	55.70% N
psychology	103	65.05% N

Table 12 *St. Louis University (1982–1985). TRAILS project. Raw data collected by Dave Kalsbeek, Saint Louis, MO.*

Saint Louis University Academic Majors Ranked by MBTI Preference (cont'd)

Thinking–Feeling	***n***	**Percent**
computer science	63	58.73% I
political science	56	57.14% E
pre-medial students	369	56.10% E
chemistry	83	55.42% E
biology	264	52.65% E
total freshmen 1986	**386**	**55.18% E**
business administration	547	55.39% E
arts and science	1195	56.65% E
undecided majors	258	58.91% E
accounting	188	59.04% E
math	27	66.67% I
psychology	103	66.99% E
communication	79	68.35% E
nursing	178	75.28% E
allied health professionals	320	75.31% E

Judgment–Perception	***n***	**Percent**
biology	264	60.61% S
chemistry	83	60.24% S
pre-medical students	369	59.62% S
computer science	63	55.56% S
total freshmen 1986	**386**	**54.15% S**
accounting	188	52.13% S
nursing	178	51.69% S
psychology	103	50.49% N
arts and science	1195	50.21% N
political science	56	50.00% N
business administration	547	50.64% S
allied health professionals	320	50.94% S
math	27	51.85% N
undecided majors	258	55.43% S
communication	79	59.49% N

Table 12 *St. Louis University (1982–1985). TRAILS project. Raw data collected by Dave Kalsbeek, Saint Louis, MO.*

Students Attending Graduate School Immediately After Graduation

N = 45

	SENSING THINKING	SENSING FEELING	INTUITION FEELING	INTUITION THINKING	
	ISTJ N = 2 % = 4.44 ■■■■	**ISFJ** N = 1 % = 2.22 ■■	**INFJ** N = 1 % = 2.22 ■■	**INTJ** N = 5 % = 11.11 ■■■■■■■■■■■	JUDGMENT / INTROVERSION
	ISTP N = 2 % = 4.44 ■■■■	**ISFP** N = 0 % = 0.00	**INFP** N = 1 % = 2.22 ■■	**INTP** N = 7 % = 15.56 ■■■■■■■■■■■■■■■■	PERCEPTION / INTROVERSION
	ESTP N = 4 % = 8.89 ■■■■■■■■■	**ESFP** N = 1 % = 2.22 ■■	**ENFP** N = 8 % = 17.78 ■■■■■■■■■■■■■■■■■■	**ENTP** N = 4 % = 8.89 ■■■■■■■■■	PERCEPTION / EXTRAVERSION
	ESTJ N = 5 % = 11.11 ■■■■■■■■■■■	**ESFJ** N = 1 % = 2.22 ■■	**ENFJ** N = 1 % = 2.22 ■■	**ENTJ** N = 2 % = 4.44 ■■■■	JUDGMENT / EXTRAVERSION

	N	%
E	26	57.78
I	19	42.22
S	16	35.56
N	29	64.44
T	31	68.89
F	14	31.11
J	18	40.00
P	27	60.00
IJ	9	20.00
IP	10	22.22
EP	17	37.78
EJ	9	20.00
ST	13	28.89
SF	3	6.67
NF	11	24.44
NT	18	40.00
SJ	9	20.00
SP	7	15.56
NP	20	44.44
NJ	9	20.00
TJ	14	31.11
TP	17	37.78
FP	10	22.22
FJ	4	8.89
IN	14	31.11
EN	15	33.33
IS	5	11.11
ES	11	24.44
ET	15	33.33
EF	11	24.44
IF	3	6.67
IT	16	35.56
Sdom	8	17.78
Ndom	18	40.00
Tdom	16	35.56
Fdom	3	6.67

Note: ■ = One Percent.

Source: Rollins College (1984). Unpublished raw data collected by Melinda McDonald, Winter Park, FL.

Table 13

Placement Data, Summer Following Graduation

ISTJ $n = 9$ .05% Admin.—Insurance Admin.—Real estate MBA Medicine Sales—Investments (2) Sports Professional Unknown (2)	**ISFJ** $n = 5$ .03% Accounting (2) Grad.—Political Science Teaching—Elementary Unknown	**INFJ** $n = 5$ .03% Admin.—Government Grad.—Arts/Graphics Reporter Sales—Business products Waiter/Waitress	**INTJ** $n = 10$ .06% Admin.—Government Computer operation Grad.—English (2) Grad.—Psychology (2) MBA Medicine Management—Retail Teaching
ISTP $n = 4$ .02% Chiropractor Computer operation Grad.—Engineering Sales—Printing	**ISFP** $n = 7$ .04% Athletic coach Mgmt.—Retail Sales—Business products Sales—Insurance Sports professional Teaching—Elementary Unknown	**INFP** $n = 19$ .11% Admin.—mgmt. company (2) Advertising Grad.—Computer science Investor (self-employed) Mgmt.—Banking Sales—Insurance Sales—Investments (2) Sales—Retail Teaching—Special education Unknown (6)	**INTP** $n = 11$ .06% Admin.—Steel industry Grad.—Urban planing Law school (4) MBA (2) Teaching Unknown (2)

Table 14 *Note: N = 45.*
Rollins College (1984). Unpublished raw data collected by Melinda McDonald, Winter, Park, FL.

(continued)

Placement Data, Summer Following Graduation (cont'd)

ESTP	ESFP	ENFP	ENTP
n = 10 .06%	*n* = 11 .06%	*n* = 29 .16%	*n* = 11 .06%
Financial analyst Grad.—English Law school (2) MBA Mgmt.—Manufacturing Mgmt.—Retail (2) News assistant Sales—Travel industry	Computer programming Coordinator—Chamber of Commerce Counseling—Admissions Grad.—Deaf ed. Interior design Mgmt.—Banking Mgmt.—Office Mgmt.—Retail Sales—Bus. products Stockperson	Accounting Admin.—Publishing Air Force Athletics (2) Computer operation Grad.—Counseling; Env. Mgmt.; MSW; Planning; Technology Law school (2) MBA Mgmt.—Banking; Food/Bev. Performer Sales—Food/Bev.; Investments (2); Telephone systems Teaching Waiter/Waitress Unknown (2)	Admin.—Manufacturing Forensic Science Grad.—Mathematics MBA (2) Teaching Unknown (4)
ESTJ	**ESFJ**	**ENFJ**	**ENTJ**
n = 18 .10%	*n* = 16 .09%	*n* = 9 .05%	*n* = 6 .03%
Computer Programmer (2) Grad.—Music Grad.—Theatre marketing MBA Medicine Mgmt.—Banking (3) Mgmt.—Retail (4) Nursing Sales—Automobiles Sales—Real estate Waiter/Waitress	Advertising/PR (2) Counseling/Personnel Flight attendant Law school Mgmt.—Banking (2) Mgmt.—Hotel Mgmt.—Retail (3) Sales—Manufacturing Sales—Travel industry Stockperson Unknown (2)	Computer programming Grad.—Sociology Mgmt.—Banking Public Relations Sales—Investments Sales—Paper Travel consultant Waiter/Waitress Unknown	Admin.—Government Law school Medicine Sales—Business products Sales—Telephone Unknown

Table 14 *Note: N = 45.*
Rollins College (1984). Unpublished raw data collected by Melinda McDonald, Winter, Park, FL.

Honors Program Students

	ISTJ %	ISFJ %	INFJ %	INTJ %
Tennessee Technological University	12.63	5.29	5.12	8.19
University of Cincinnati	10.63	5.27	4.02	6.61
University of North Florida	7.88	4.95	4.58	4.76

	ISTP %	ISFP %	INFP %	INTP %
Tennessee Technological University	4.61	3.24	8.53	11.09
University of Cincinnati	3.54	2.01	8.72	11.11
University of North Florida	2.75	3.11	8.61	9.71

	ESTP %	ESFP %	ENFP %	ENTP %
Tennessee Technological University	2.22	3.07	11.26	5.63
University of Cincinnati	4.12	2.97	12.45	6.80
University of North Florida	4.76	3.30	13.00	8.61

	ESTJ %	ESFJ %	ENFJ %	ENTJ %
Tennessee Technological University	5.80	4.44	4.61	4.27
University of Cincinnati	7.66	4.50	4.79	4.79
University of North Florida	8.06	4.95	6.78	4.21

Source of data:

TTU: Connie K. Hood, Honors Program, Tennessee Technological University, 1999-2002 (n=587)

UC: Philip K. Way, Honors Scholars Program, University of Cincinnati, 2000-2002 (n=1044)

UNF: Michael J. Malec, Honors Program, University of North Florida, 2000-2001 (n=546)

Data used with permission.

Table 15

United States Naval Academy

N = 2334

	SENSING		INTUITION		
	THINKING	FEELING	FEELING	THINKING	
INTROVERSION	**ISTJ** N = 288 % = 12.34	**ISFJ** N = 54 % = 2.31	**INFJ** N = 46 % = 1.97	**INTJ** N = 152 % = 6.51	JUDGMENT
INTROVERSION	**ISTP** N = 148 % = 6.34	**ISFP** N = 37 % = 1.59	**INFP** N = 94 % = 4.03	**INTP** N = 161 % = 6.90	PERCEPTION
EXTRAVERSION	**ESTP** N = 172 % = 7.37	**ESFP** N = 56 % = 2.40	**ENFP** N = 149 % = 6.38	**ENTP** N = 280 % = 12.00	PERCEPTION
EXTRAVERSION	**ESTJ** N = 365 % = 15.64	**ESFJ** N = 61 % = 2.61	**ENFJ** N = 65 % = 2.78	**ENTJ** N = 206 % = 8.83	JUDGMENT

	N	%
E	1354	58.01
I	980	41.99
S	1181	50.60
N	1153	49.40
T	1772	75.92
F	562	24.08
J	1237	53.00
P	1097	47.00
IJ	540	23.14
IP	440	18.85
EP	657	28.15
EJ	697	29.86
ST	973	41.69
SF	208	8.91
NF	354	15.17
NT	799	34.23
SJ	768	32.90
SP	413	17.69
NP	684	29.31
NJ	469	20.09
TJ	1011	43.32
TP	761	32.60
FP	336	14.40
FJ	226	9.68
IN	453	19.41
EN	700	29.99
IS	527	22.58
ES	654	28.02
ET	1023	43.83
EF	331	14.18
IF	231	9.90
IT	749	32.09
Sdom	570	24.42
Ndom	627	26.86
Tdom	880	37.70
Fdom	257	11.01

Note: ■ = One Percent

Data collected by Paul E. Roush from classes of 1992 and 1994.
89.7% male, 10.3% female. Data collected in 1992 using Form G.

Table 16

Sorority Women

N = 606

	SENSING THINKING	SENSING FEELING	INTUITION FEELING	INTUITION THINKING	
	ISTJ N = 24 % = 3.96	**ISFJ** N = 27 % = 4.46	**INFJ** N = 18 % = 2.97	**INTJ** N = 4 % = 0.66	INTROVERSION JUDGMENT
	ISTP N = 6 % = 0.99	**ISFP** N = 9 % = 1.49	**INFP** N = 16 % = 2.64	**INTP** N = 7 % = 1.16	INTROVERSION PERCEPTION
	ESTP N = 27 % = 4.46	**ESFP** N = 49 % = 8.09	**ENFP** N = 126 % = 20.79	**ENTP** N = 30 % = 4.95	EXTRAVERSION PERCEPTION
	ESTJ N = 72 % = 11.88	**ESFJ** N = 104 % = 17.16	**ENFJ** N = 63 % = 10.40	**ENTJ** N = 24 % = 3.96	EXTRAVERSION JUDGMENT

	N	%
E	495	81.68
I	111	18.32
S	318	52.48
N	288	47.52
T	194	32.01
F	412	67.99
J	336	55.45
P	270	44.55
IJ	73	12.05
IP	38	6.27
EP	232	38.28
EJ	263	43.40
ST	129	21.29
SF	189	31.19
NF	223	36.80
NT	65	10.73
SJ	227	37.46
SP	91	15.02
NP	179	29.54
NJ	109	17.99
TJ	124	20.46
TP	70	11.55
FP	200	33.00
FJ	212	34.98
IN	45	7.43
EN	243	40.10
IS	66	10.89
ES	252	41.58
ET	153	25.25
EF	342	56.44
IF	70	11.55
IT	41	6.77
Sdom	127	20.96
Ndom	178	29.37
Tdom	109	17.99
Fdom	192	31.68

Note: ■ = One Percent

Unpublished data from study by Jonathan C. Ziegert and Benjamin Schneider, Department of Psychology, University of Maryland.
Data collected in 2000 using Form G. Used by permission.

Table 17

College Marching Bands

N = 116

SENSING THINKING	SENSING FEELING	INTUITION FEELING	INTUITION THINKING	
ISTJ N = 22 % = 18.97	**ISFJ** N = 4 % = 3.45	**INFJ** N = 2 % = 1.72	**INTJ** N = 3 % = 2.59	JUDGMENT / INTROVERSION
ISTP N = 9 % = 7.76	**ISFP** N = 3 % = 2.59	**INFP** N = 2 % = 1.72	**INTP** N = 5 % = 4.31	PERCEPTION / INTROVERSION
ESTP N = 5 % = 4.31	**ESFP** N = 5 % = 4.31	**ENFP** N = 10 % = 8.62	**ENTP** N = 6 % = 5.17	PERCEPTION / EXTRAVERSION
ESTJ N = 17 % = 14.66	**ESFJ** N = 12 % = 10.34	**ENFJ** N = 4 % = 3.45	**ENTJ** N = 7 % = 6.03	JUDGMENT / EXTRAVERSION

	N	%
E	66	56.90
I	50	43.10
S	77	66.38
N	39	33.62
T	74	63.79
F	42	36.21
J	71	61.21
P	45	38.79
IJ	31	26.72
IP	19	16.38
EP	26	22.41
EJ	40	34.48
ST	53	45.69
SF	24	20.69
NF	18	15.52
NT	21	18.10
SJ	55	47.41
SP	22	18.97
NP	23	19.83
NJ	16	13.79
TJ	49	42.24
TP	25	21.55
FP	20	17.24
FJ	22	18.97
IN	12	10.34
EN	27	23.28
IS	38	32.76
ES	39	33.62
ET	35	30.17
EF	31	26.72
IF	11	9.48
IT	39	33.62
Sdom	36	31.03
Ndom	21	18.10
Tdom	38	32.76
Fdom	21	18.10

Note: ■ = One Percent

Nonmusic majors who persist in selected college marching bands.
Doctoral dissertation data collected by Sylvester Young from
Florida A&M University, Hampton University, and Ohio State University.
59.6% male, 40.4% female. Data collected in 1999-2000 using Form G.

Table 18

Football Players

N = 263

SENSING THINKING	SENSING FEELING	INTUITION FEELING	INTUITION THINKING	
ISTJ N = 34 % = 12.93 ▪▪▪▪▪▪▪▪▪▪▪▪▪	**ISFJ** N = 12 % = 4.56 ▪▪▪▪	**INFJ** N = 8 % = 3.04 ▪▪▪	**INTJ** N = 6 % = 2.28 ▪▪	JUDGMENT INTROVERSION
ISTP N = 20 % = 7.60 ▪▪▪▪▪▪▪	**ISFP** N = 7 % = 2.66 ▪▪	**INFP** N = 10 % = 3.80 ▪▪▪	**INTP** N = 8 % = 3.04 ▪▪▪	PERCEPTION INTROVERSION
ESTP N = 27 % = 10.27 ▪▪▪▪▪▪▪▪▪▪	**ESFP** N = 18 % = 6.84 ▪▪▪▪▪▪	**ENFP** N = 18 % = 6.84 ▪▪▪▪▪▪	**ENTP** N = 17 % = 6.46 ▪▪▪▪▪▪	PERCEPTION EXTRAVERSION
ESTJ N = 45 % = 17.11 ▪▪▪▪▪▪▪▪▪▪▪▪▪▪▪▪▪	**ESFJ** N = 14 % = 5.32 ▪▪▪▪▪	**ENFJ** N = 6 % = 2.28 ▪▪	**ENTJ** N = 13 % = 4.94 ▪▪▪▪	JUDGMENT EXTRAVERSION

	N	%
E	158	60.08
I	105	39.92
S	177	67.30
N	86	32.70
T	170	64.64
F	93	35.36
J	138	52.47
P	125	47.53
IJ	60	22.81
IP	45	17.11
EP	80	30.42
EJ	78	29.66
ST	126	47.91
SF	51	19.39
NF	42	15.97
NT	44	16.73
SJ	105	39.92
SP	72	27.38
NP	53	20.15
NJ	33	12.55
TJ	98	37.26
TP	72	27.38
FP	53	20.15
FJ	40	15.21
IN	32	12.17
EN	54	20.53
IS	73	27.76
ES	104	39.54
ET	102	38.78
EF	56	21.29
IF	37	14.07
IT	68	25.86
Sdom	91	34.60
Ndom	49	18.63
Tdom	86	32.70
Fdom	37	14.07

Note: ▪ = One Percent

Varsity football players at Ball State University, Muncie, Indiana.
Data collected by K. Terry Schurr, Mike Mahan, and Virgil Ruble.
Data collected in 1980-1989 using Form G.

Scholarship Athletes

N = 70

SENSING THINKING	SENSING FEELING	INTUITION FEELING	INTUITION THINKING	
ISTJ N = 8 % = 11.43 ■■■■■■■■■■■	**ISFJ** N = 1 % = 1.43 ■	**INFJ** N = 0 % = 0.00	**INTJ** N = 2 % = 2.86 ■■	INTROVERSION JUDGMENT
ISTP N = 17 % = 24.29 ■■■■■■■■■■■■■■■■■■■■■■■■	**ISFP** N = 3 % = 4.29 ■■■■	**INFP** N = 0 % = 0.00	**INTP** N = 5 % = 7.14 ■■■■■■■	INTROVERSION PERCEPTION
ESTP N = 7 % = 10.00 ■■■■■■■■■■	**ESFP** N = 2 % = 2.86 ■■	**ENFP** N = 1 % = 1.43 ■	**ENTP** N = 8 % = 11.43 ■■■■■■■■■■■	EXTRAVERSION PERCEPTION
ESTJ N = 12 % = 17.14 ■■■■■■■■■■■■■■■■■	**ESFJ** N = 1 % = 1.43 ■	**ENFJ** N = 2 % = 2.86 ■■	**ENTJ** N = 1 % = 1.43 ■	EXTRAVERSION JUDGMENT

	N	%
E	34	48.57
I	36	51.43
S	51	72.86
N	19	27.14
T	60	85.71
F	10	14.29
J	27	38.57
P	43	61.43
IJ	11	15.71
IP	25	35.71
EP	18	25.71
EJ	16	22.86
ST	44	62.86
SF	7	10.00
NF	3	4.29
NT	16	22.86
SJ	22	31.43
SP	29	41.43
NP	14	20.00
NJ	5	7.14
TJ	23	32.86
TP	37	52.86
FP	6	8.57
FJ	4	5.71
IN	7	10.00
EN	12	17.14
IS	29	41.43
ES	22	31.43
ET	28	40.00
EF	6	8.57
IF	4	5.71
IT	32	45.71
Sdom	18	25.71
Ndom	11	15.71
Tdom	35	50.00
Fdom	6	8.57

Note: ■ = One Percent

Male football and basketball athletes receiving scholarships at University Florida, Gainesville. Doctoral dissertation data collected by Sandra R. Chesborough in 1992 using Form F.

Table 20

Contributors

Scott Anchors, Ph.D., (ISFJ) is currently director of advancement, and a cooperating professor in the College of Education and Human Development at the University of Maine in Orono. Prior to this position, he worked for five years as executive assistant to the president of the University of Maine and served over two decades in various Student Affairs positions at the University of Maine, Mercer University, Auburn University, University of South Florida, and Iowa State University.

His work with the Myers-Briggs Type Indicator® instrument began in the late 1970s, and has resulted in his co-authoring with Judy Provost *Applications of the Myers-Briggs Type Indicator in Higher Education*, as well as a variety of published articles including those on student retention, roommate relationships, and academic success. He is also co-editor with Roger Winston of *Student Housing and Residential Life* and also wrote (with Schroeder and Smith), *Making Yourself a Home: A Guide to personalizing your Residential Hall Environment.*

Dr. Anchors is a long standing member of the Association of Psychological Type, does training for the Center for the Application of Psychological Type, and serves on the editorial board for the *Journal of Psychological Type.*

A passionate whitewater kayaker, he is also a Registered Maine

Guide, an American Canoe Association Certified Sea-Kayaking Instructor and enjoys leading trips in Maine's rivers and coastal waters. He has collaborated with a variety of outdoor educators in Maine to form an organization called TRUE COURSE. This consortium offers corporate and institutional teams the opportunity to integrate team-building experiences through sea kayaking and MBTI instruction in beautiful coastal Maine settings.

Barbara H. Carson, Ph.D., (ENFJ) is the Theodore Bruce and Barbara Lawrence Alfond Professor of English at Rollins College. She received her B.A. from Florida State University and her M.A. and Ph.D. from John Hopkins University, after which she taught at Towson State College in Baltimore and at the University of Massachusetts in Amherst.

Her teaching has been recognized both nationally and in her own college, most notably in her selection as a finalist in the CASE Professor of the Year program and in being twice named an Arthur Vining Davis Fellow at Rollins.

Dr. Carson's journal publications reflect her interests in both pedagogy and American literature. She is the author of the critical study, *Eudora Welty: Two Pictures at Once in Her Frame* and is now writing a study of the idea of "the good life" as reflected in American literature.

Faith Gabelnick, Ph.D., (INTJ) is president of Pacific University in Forest Grove, Oregon. Pacific University is a private institution (2,000 students) with undergraduate programs in the arts and sciences; and professional degree programs in education, occupational therapy, optometry, physical therapy, physician assistant studies, and professional psychology.

Before coming to Pacific University in 1995, Dr. Gabelnick held teaching positions at The American University and the University of Maryland. She also served as associate director of the General Honors Program, and at Western Michigan University in Kalamazoo she was named Dean of the Carl Winifred Lee Honors College. In 1992, she accepted the posts of provost and dean of faculty and Cyrus B. Mills Professor at Mills College in Oakland.

Dr. Gabelnick attended Simmons College in Boston where she received her B.A. degree with General Honors (1964), and Honors in English from Douglas College of Rutgers University. She is a member of Phi Beta Kappa. She went on to earn a M.A. degree in Literature form the University of Massachusetts (1969), and a Ph.D. in Literary Studies from the American University in Washington D.C. (1974).

She is the author and editor of several books and many articles and a frequent consultant and speaker on higher education topics such as women and leadership, learning communities, curriculum development, assessment, and transformational leadership. Dr. Gabelnick has used extensively the Myers-Briggs Type Indicator to assist university personnel to understand their natural strengths and stressors in relation to leadership. Her recent publications include *Learning Communities: Creating Connections Among Students, Faculty, and Disciplines* (Jossey-Bass, 1990), *The Psychodynamics of Leadership* (Psychosocial Press, 1998), and *Dynamic Consultation in a Changing Workplace* (Psychosocial Press, 2000).

Judith Grutter, M.S., (INTJ) has incorporated MBTI theory and applications in her career development program consulting, teaching, training and writing for more than thirty years. A National Certified Counselor and Master Career Counselor, she developed, and for several years coordinated, the graduate programs in career counseling at California State University, Northridge. Dr. Grutter is currently a principal with G/S CONSULTANTS in South Lake Tahoe, California, and a member of the APT MBTI® Qualifying Program faculty. She continues on the adjunct faculty of California State at Northridge and teaches in the John F. Kennedy University School of Management.

A recognized authority on the uses of assessment in career counseling and consulting, Judi is co-author of the *Strong and MBTI Career Report*, and a facilitator's guide and series of workbooks entitled *Making It In Today's Organizations Using the Strong and MBTI.*

A past president of the California Career Development Association, Ms. Grutter is a recipient of the National Career Development Association's Practitioner of the Year Award, and the California Career Development Association's first Judith Grutter *Practitioner of the Year Award*, awarded in 1996 and named in her honor.

Dr. Grutter received her M.S. in Counseling from California State University, Los Angeles, and has completed the coursework for her Ph.D. in Higher Education, Work and Adult Development at UCLA.

Smith Jackson, Ed.D., (INTP) is vice president for Student life at Elon University in North Carolina. He previously held the positions of director of Magnolia Dormitories at Auburn University in Alabama, assistant dean of students at Muskingum College in Ohio, director of housing at Saint Louis University, and dean of students at Huntingdon College in Alabama. He was first introduced to type at Auburn University in the mid-70s where he completed his Ed.D. His dissertation investigated the inter-relationships among roommate congruence on the MBTI, roommate satisfaction, personality development and academic achievement. He has applied psychological type concepts for 25 years in the areas of student space utilization and room decorations, room and hall assignments, student organization, and leadership development.

George H. Jensen, Ph.D., (INTJ) is an assistant professor with the Division of Developmental Studies at Georgia State University. He earned a Ph.D. in English from the University of South Carolina in 1977 and has used the MBTI instrument to teach composition, reading and study skills in a variety of settings. He has published articles in *Proof, MBTI News, College Composition and Communication*, and the *Journal of Basic Writing*. With John K. DiTiberio, he recently completed the manuscript of *Personality Type and the Teaching of Composition* currently in submission.

David H. Kalsbeek, Ph.D., currently serves as a vice president for Enrollment Management at DePaul University in Chicago, Illinois. In that capacity he leads the marketing and enrollment development strategies for the nation's largest and fastest-growing Catholic university, which has 20,000 students, enrolled in eight colleges and seven campuses throughout the greater Chicago region. His responsibilities at DePaul encompass enrollment, management, alumni relations and annual giving, career center and employer relations, university and media relations, and marketing communications.

Prior to joining DePaul in 1997, Dr. Kalsbeek served as senior enrollment management administrator at Xavier University at Cincinnati, in Ohio and before that at Saint Louis University in St. Louis, Missouri.

Dr. Kalsbeek is a frequent speaker on issues related to strategic enrollment management and marketing, net revenue planning, assessment and learning organizations. He has been a plenary speaker or presenter at nine of AACRAO's (Association of Collegiate Registrars and Admissions Officers) ten Strategic Enrollment Management conferences, as well as NASPA (National Association of Student Personnel Administrators), AAHE (American Association for Higher

Education), AIR (Association of Institutional Research), AACSB (Association to Advance Collegiate Schools of Business), and AMA (American Marketing Association) conferences. He currently serves on the editorial board of the *Journal of College Student Retention* and previously served as feature editor for *About Campus* magazine. He has been a consultant to more than twenty-five colleges, universities and associations on issues related to strategic enrollment management.

He received his Ph.D. in Public Policy Analysis from Saint Louis University. He earned his M.A. in higher education administration at Ohio State University and a B.A. from Muskingum College in New Concord, Ohio, where he graduated summa cum laude with a major in Philosophy.

Ann Q. Lynch, Ed.D., (INFP) professor of Counselor Education, Florida Atlantic University, Boca Raton, Florida, is a Licensed Mental Health Counselor and Marriage and Family Therapist. She is as also a licensed Counseling Psychologist in Tennessee and a National Certified Counselor. She received her Ph.D. from the University of Florida.

She was an associate professor in the Counseling and Personnel Services Department and in the Center for the Study of Higher Education at Memphis State University where she served as executive director of the Higher Education for Adult Mental Health, NIMH (National Institute of Mental Health) Project. While working as a University Counseling Psychologist at the University of Florida, in 1970 she was introduced to the MBTI instrument by Isabel Briggs Myers when Myers consulted with Mary McCaulley, Ph.D., in establishing the Topology Laboratory (later Center for Applications of Psychological Type). She has served as president of the southeast region of the Association of Psychological Type (APT), on the board of APT, and on the APT and CAPT faculties. She made a presentation at the first MBTI Conference in Gainesville in 1975, has presented at many APT Conferences, and was coauthor with Schlossberg and Chickering of *Improving Higher Education Environments for Adults.* She has used the MBTI instrument extensively in counseling university students, couples, and families; in working with administrators, faculty, and student services professionals; and in teaching counseling courses in higher education.

Gerald P. Macdaid, (ENFP) is an independent trainer and consultant. Previously, he worked at the Center for Applications of Psychological Type (CAPT), serving as chief executive officer, director of research, consultant and trainer during his tenure from 1981 to 1999. He is currently on the faculty and serves in various consulting capacities at CAPT.

He worked closely with Mary McCaulley, Ph.D., on the *Manual: A Guide to the Development and Use of the Myers-Briggs Type Indicator*, 2nd edition, running extensive databank analyses and compiling contributed studies. Other major projects at CAPT included the longitudinal Engineering Education Research Consortium, MBTI® Form AV analysis, validation studies for the Spanish and Korean translations of the MBTI instrument, and the University of Florida Freshmen Ten Year Follow-Up Study. Each year Jerry presents reports about his ongoing CAPT databank studies at regional and national conferences. He is a contributing author for *Applications of the Myers-Briggs Type Indicator in Higher Education* and co-authored *The MBTI Career Report Manual* and CAPT's Computer Scoring Career Reports. He is the senior author of the *CAPT Atlas of Type Tables*, which is a compendium of type data on careers. Jerry is extensively involved in suicide and crisis intervention for the Alachua County Crisis Center in Gainesville, Florida, where he has been a trainer, consultant, and crisis counselor since 1979. He is currently collecting data on the relationship between type and training crisis counselors.

Judith A. Provost, Ed.D., LMHC, NCC, (ENFP) professor of Graduate Studies in Counseling at Rollins College, is a psychotherapist, writer, and trainer who has incorporated MBTI concepts in her work for twenty-five years. Formerly director of the Counseling Center at Rollins College, she is on the faculties of the Center for Applications of Psychological Type and the Association for Psychological Type.

Her research interests in higher education have resulted in several journal articles and a dissertation, "Personality type and leisure satisfaction as factors in college attrition." Other publications include *A Casebook: Applications of the Myers-Briggs Type Indicator in Counseling; Work, Play, and Type; Procrastination;* and *Student Strategies for Success.* She has degrees from the University of Connecticut, the University of California at Los Angeles, and University of Florida, and extensive training with the Gestalt Institute of Florida.

Daniel C. Robinson, Ph.D., (ENFP) is a professor of Educational Leadership and Policy Studies and director of Graduate Education in the College of Education at Iowa State University. He is a member of the Association of Psychological Type and on the training faculty for the Center for Applications of Psychological Type. His research interests include multicultural, cross-cultural and international uses of the MBTI.

Charles C. Schroeder (ESTJ) received his B.A. and M.A. degrees from Austin College and his Ph.D. (1972) from Oregon State University. During the past twenty-three years, he has served as the Chief Student Affairs Officer at Mercer University, Saint Louis University, Georgia Institute of Technology and University of

Missouri-Columbia. In 2001, he accepted a new position, professor of Higher Education in the Educational Leadership and Policy Analysis Department at the University of Missouri-Columbia. He has assumed various leadership roles in the American College Personnel Association serving as president in 1986 and 1993 and as executive editor of *About Campus: Enriching the Student Learning Experience.* Dr. Schroeder has authored more than 50 articles and published a book in 1994 with Phyllis Mable entitled *Realizing the Educational Potential of Residence Halls.* He has utilized type concepts for more than thirty years in roommate assignments, organization and leadership development, and learning styles research.

Kay A. Taylor, Ph.D., (INTP) is a postdoctoral lecturer, Curriculum and Instruction in the College of Education at Iowa State University. She is a member of the American Educational Research Association, the History of Education Society, and the American Educational Studies Association. Her research interests are oral narrative biographical histories of African-American educators as they intersect with Critical Race Theory, Black Feminist Thought, and social justice; and learning styles of pre-service teachers as they impact teaching and learning for social justice.

Other Books of Interest

Applications of the Myers-Briggs Type Indicator® in Counseling: A Casebook by Judith A. Provost

Particularly suited to MBTI® practitioners working in university settings, this book demonstrates the use of the Indicator in counseling and examines type development in clients representing all sixteen personality types. Second edition. Paperback, 118 pages, $12.

Pathways to Integrity: Ethics and Psychological Type by Blake W. Burleson

A senior lecturer in Religion at Baylor University, Blake Burleson uses highly approachable examples to explore the ways in which psychological type affects habitual patterns of ethical choice making. Paperback, 111 pages, $14.95.

People Types & Tiger Stripes by Gordon D. Lawrence

A true classic, People Types & Tiger Stripes is considered to be the definitive text in the field of psychological type and education. This book is also an outstanding general reference on the use and application of the MBTI® instrument. Third edition. Paperback, 243 pages, $15.

Portraits of Self-Esteem: Sixteen Paths to Competency and Self-Worth by Bonnie J. Golden

Through her studies of community college students, author Bonnie Golden reveals how various psychological types express self-esteem, including how each type approaches the learning process. Paperback, 117 pages, $16.95.

To order, call **800.777.2278** or go to **www.capt.org**

Center for Applications of Psychological Type
2815 NW 13th Street, Suite 401, Gainesville FL 32605 USA